Petros Dragoumis

THE COMPLETE GUITAR BOOK

Volume 1

major
and
minor

ISBN-13 978-1-949880-01-4

Copyright © 2018 by Petros Dragoumis.
All Rights Reserved
Published 2018 by Odeion Books , Chicago, Illinois.

No part of this publication may be reproduced in any form or by any means
without the prior written permission of the Publisher

Contents

Forward	7
Intoduction	9
Study guide	11

1 guitar box studies 12
Guitar box studies	13

2 finger & pick studies 16
Finger & pick studies 1	17
Finger & pick studies 2	22
Finger & pick studies 3	24

3 triad studies 26
Triad inversions in 2 strings - shape 1	27
Triad inversions in 2 strings - shape 2	28
Triad inversions in 3 strings - shape 1	29
Triad inversions in 3 strings - shape 2	31
Triad inversions in 3 strings - shape 3	33

4 modes of the major scale 35

Ionian mode 38
Shape 1	39
Studies shape 1	40
Shape 2	44
Studies shape 2	45
Shape 3	49
Studies shape 3	50
In 2 octaves with shape 1+2	54
In 2 octaves with shape 1+3	56

Dorian mode 58

Shape 1	59
Studies shape 1	60
Shape 2	64
Studies shape 2	65
Shape 3	69
Studies shape 3	70
In 2 octaves with shape 1+2	74
In 2 octaves with shape 1+3	76

Phrygian mode 78

Shape 1	79
Studies shape 1	80
Shape 2	84
Studies shape 2	85
Shape 3	89
Studies shape 3	90
In 2 octaves with shape 1+2	94
In 2 octaves with shape 1+3	96

Lydian mode 98

Shape 1	99
Studies shape 1	100
Shape 2	104
Studies shape 2	105
Shape 3	109
Studies shape 3	110
In 2 octaves with shape 1+2	114
In 2 octaves with shape 1+3	116

Mixolydian mode 118

Shape 1	119
Studies shape 1	120
Shape 2	124
Studies shape 2	125
Shape 3	129
Studies shape 3	130
In 2 octaves with shape 1+2	134
In 2 octaves with shape 1+3	136

Aeolian mode 138

Shape 1	139
Studies shape 1	140
Shape 2	144
Studies shape 2	145
Shape 3	149
Studies shape 3	150
In 2 octaves with shape 1+2	154
In 2 octaves with shape 1+3	156

Locrian mode 158

Shape 1	159
Studies shape 1	160
Shape 2	164
Studies shape 2	165
Shape 3	169
Studies shape 3	170
In 2 octaves with shape 1+2	174
In 2 octaves with shape 1+3	176

5 key center horizontal studies 178

Horizontal mode studies in C major - shape 1	179
Horizontal mode studies in F major - shape 2	187
Horizontal mode studies in B♭ major - shape 3	195

6 vertical position studies 203

position 7-1 studies	205
position 2 studies	210
position 3-4 studies	215
position 5 studies	220
position 6 studies	225

7 chords & arpeggios in the 5 positions 230

position 7-1 arpeggio & chord studies in C major	231
position 2 arpeggio & chord studies in C major	238
position 3-4 arpeggio & chord studies in C major	245
position 5 arpeggio & chord studies in C major	252
position 6 arpeggio & chord studies in C major	259

8 all 12 major & minor key positions 266

All positions in C major key	267
All positions in G major key	268
All positions in D major key	269
All positions in A major key	270
All positions in E major key	271
All positions in B major key	272
All positions in F♯ major key	273
All positions in D♭ major key	274
All positions in A♭ major key	275
All positions in E♭ major key	276
All positions in B♭ major key	277
All positions in F major key	278

9 modes diagonal development 279

Ionian diagonal tetrachords	281
Dorian diagonal tetrachords	281
Phrygian diagonal tetrachords	282
Lydian diagonal tetrachords	282
Mixolydian diagonal tetrachords	283
Aeolian diagonal tetrachords	283
Locrian diagonal tetrachords	284

Forward

I consider myself a pretty harsh critic given the fact that I have been studying and teaching music for over 25 years, I continuously strive for excellence, and I always seek and appreciate any outstanding music educators and music books.

Not only have I read and studied Petros' books, but I have also used his guitar book and have applied his guitar learning system as a beginning guitar student. I started learning how to play the guitar for the first time, without any prior knowledge, only a couple of months ago under the tutelage and guidance of Petros accompanied by his guitar book and instructional method. I am so happy and excited to declare that in just two months I have learned more than I had ever imagined that even the most knowledgeable and experienced music student could learn in such a short period of time while exploring a new instrument from scratch. This amazing first-hand experience was an undoubtedly pleasant surprise both from a student's as well as an educator's perspective.

The book's approach is totally refreshing because it provides an understanding of the reasoning behind all learning material, and it clearly explains the learning process and how each learning step leads to the next. Every lesson leaves the student with a thorough understanding of any new concept, and a deep feeling of complete ownership of the material which results in a state of self-satisfaction. The book's approach and systematic methodology and the way it provides the deeper understanding explained above enhances the student's sense of self-confidence and stimulates the student's motivation to keep learning. **In my opinion, any teaching method that positively affects a student's self-confidence and motivation to learn, assuming that it also covers the required material, is a very successful method.** I am disappointed to say that such methods are rare to find, and at the same time very happy that I have found one that works so effectively.

The following words come to mind when thinking of descriptive characterizations for this book series:

- **Creative:** It makes you think outside of the box and differently from other such methods.
- **Grounded:** It stays within approachable concepts and material and it remains faithful to the traditional fundamentals of music theory that every music student should learn.
- **Fresh:** It offers your brain a "new window" of approaching and applying all concepts, and this "new window" works very effectively.
- **Thorough:** It does not leave anything unexplored or unexplained, and it provides a step further from knowledge, which is ownership.

- **Friendly:** It motivates you to keep going and to learn more because all steps you take are logical, they make sense, and the progression becomes effortless.

The ***Psychology of Teaching and Learning*** has always been a journey of exploration for me. It does not matter what you are teaching or what you are learning. The psychology behind it can make all the difference, and when a method, system, or approach offers a positive effect on a student's learning process and motivation, while at the same time providing the knowledge background that it is supposed to provide, then that is a true gem – a treasure!

I wholeheartedly give Petros and his book series my highest recommendation.

I can't wait till my first guitar performance! I feel so pumped – Thank you Petros!

Eftihia Papageorgiou
M.A. Music-Vocal Pedagogy, NEIU
B.A. Music–Vocal Performance & Psychology, NEIU
Adjunct Music Professor, Wilbur Wright College, Chicago, IL

Introduction

The series of books for learning guitar with the system of modes is based on the processing and the geometrical structure and coexistence of the modes in every key. The system begins with the mother scales, the principal scales that exist in the western musical system. Those are the major scale, the harmonic minor scale, and the melodic minor scale. We do not mention the natural minor scale as a mother scale because its construction is covered during the studies of the major scale in which we find the natural minor as its 6th mode, known as the Aeolian.

When we look at each mother scale, we find the modes that are built on each scale degree, and we study them through a specific shape pattern, harmonization, and most importantly specific fingering positions. The most essential point is that with this system we have to maintain a very specific fingering pattern for each mode, so that the movement becomes consistent and automatic through our fingers but also our brain, which leads to flexible and effortless playing. Since there is no symmetry among all the guitar strings, we create three shapes for each mode and chord that we come across, so that we can cover the whole range of the fingerboard.

We have **shape 1** for anything that is played among strings E, A, D, and A, D, G, and its tonic is found on the E or A string.

We have **shape 2** for anything that is played among strings D, G, B, and its tonic is found on the D string.

We have **shape 3** for anything that is played among strings G, B, E, and its tonic is found on the G string.

With every mode, we first learn its shape on one octave with specific fingerings, and by studying the exercises included in this book we are able to establish its geometrical pattern. In addition, through the continuous repetition that the exercises demand, we are able to own its melodic presence. We also find all the intervals that are formed on all the scale degrees of each mode which are based on the tonic note, and as a result we learn the character and the sound quality they create within the environment of each mode. Consequently, we harmonize each mode, which means that we find the triad and 7th chord that are created through the vertical building of the scale degrees, which is based on intervals of thirds. That is how we find the triad of the 1st, 3rd, and 5th scale degrees of each mode, as well as the seventh chord by adding the 7th degree of the mode.

This is how we complete the detailed research of each mode while building the basis for the further study of the entire system.

Once we have thoroughly learned each mode separately, in chapter 5 we find its placement as part of the key where it belongs, establishing its place (scale degree), and from there we study and learn the modes as scale degrees of the mother scale. We construct the modes horizontally, one scale degree after another, in order, as well as their diatonic chords and arpeggios, and that way we establish the entire key center on the fingerboard by learning it as a combined group of notes.

The next stage in chapter 6 is the vertical placement of the modes on the fingerboard, by finding each mode that is on top or below another mode, and by following the geometry of the instrument. This gives us the ability, by applying the fingering and geometry that we learned in the previous chapters, to comfortably construct the key center vertically. At this point we will also comprehend the meaning behind the **specific fingering** that the system required in the initial chapters, which will offer us the ability to easily and comfortably play the modes in a vertical manner. Based on the placement of all vertical ways of combinations of the modes, we find 5 vertical positions on our fingerboard through which we construct fully each key center while at the same time exploring every angle of our instrument.

Continuing, in chapter 7, through those vertical positions we study all the modes, chords, inversions, etc. that derive from the key center, and as a result, by combining all 5 positions we will be able to play both melodically and harmonically any key center on the entire length and width of our fingerboard.

In chapter 8 we find the complete structure of each key center through the 5 vertical positions. Those positions have a repeated pattern on the fingerboard, meaning that each key center begins with a specific position, and once we have played all of them following the order of the numbers, they start all over from the beginning in a circular manner, and they finish where the fingerboard ends.

Finally, in chapter 9, we figure out through the tetrachords of the modes how we can play each mode on the fingerboard diagonally in 3 octaves, by moving from one string to the next while following the progression of the tetrachords.

By the end of the book we get to the point where we can expand on every key center, horizontally, vertically, and diagonally, throughout the length and width of the fingerboard. Once we have completed the system, and through the automatic use of the various fingering positions and the geometrical correlation of the various chords, we are able to express ourselves both melodically and harmonically, and we are able to follow the progression of any musical piece, no matter how difficult it is, with comfort and ease.

The whole system covers the modes of all the mother scales, and due to the volume of the material, it is necessary to create a series of books with each one of them covering the study of a specific mother scale. With this in mind, Volume 1 covers major and natural minor modes, Volume 2 covers harmonic minor modes, Volume 3 covers melodic minor modes, and finally Volume 4 covers all the symmetrical and pentatonic scales.

Study guide

While studying this book, students need to follow precisely the structure of each exercise. The exercises are written based on the classical way of teaching, and through multiple repetitions they give the student the ability to overcome any difficult passages.

Once we understand the complete system, we will find that we do not need to learn each mode/scale with the different finger positions, because the geometrical shapes and patterns that exist among them allows us to play them spontaneously and without much thought. We will be surprised to find out what I like to call the "**secret**" scales, chords, and finger positions, and we will discover that if we follow the guidelines of the book, we have already learned them without separate effort for each one. The mode system includes all the necessary elements that are required for a strong, comprehensive, and complete program of studies for learning guitar, as well as all other string instruments, combined with the fundamentals of music theory.

When a student studies one key center, he or she also learns the structure of other key centers. This occurs because each mode of a specific key center can become the tonic, and the rest become its satellite scale degrees. For example, in the key of C, during the initial development of the key center, the C Ionian mode is the mother scale and the main scale degree of the key center. At the same time, we could replace the main scale degree with the A Aeolian mode, and a musical piece could similarly be based on the Aeolian mode. We could also have as the main scale degree the E Phrygian mode. All of the above are scale degrees of the major scale we have studied, and by using the same automatic fingering that we use with a major key center, we can play any other key center that derives from any of its modes with the same ease.

Due to the volume of the detailed structure of each exercise, it is not feasible to present them in all the key centers, which would require many more books. Therefore, the students have to transfer each exercise to different key centers on their own.

I wish you the best in your studies and application of your knowledge throughout your musical journey.

Petros Dragoumis

Chapter 1
box studies

In this chapter we will learn on the fingerboard all the positions of each of the twelve notes that we find within our tonal music system.

It is very important to know where each note is located so that we are able to find it quickly whenever we need to during each musical progression.

The meaning of the box has to do with the construction of an octave on the fingerboard of the guitar, which is developed for each note on alternate groups of three strings. This is how we identify the three different shapes for each octave since each note has a corresponding octave. Depending on the length of the fingerboard we can find on how many octaves we can play each note.

We use a basic melodic pattern which includes the first, the eighth, the minor seventh, and the fifth note of each octave.

It is very important that you follow precisely the order of each exercise. Later on, as we will be learning each mode and its chords, a very good exercise will be to use the same pattern that we use here for each mode and chord, keeping the order of each exercise consistent.

Guitar box studies

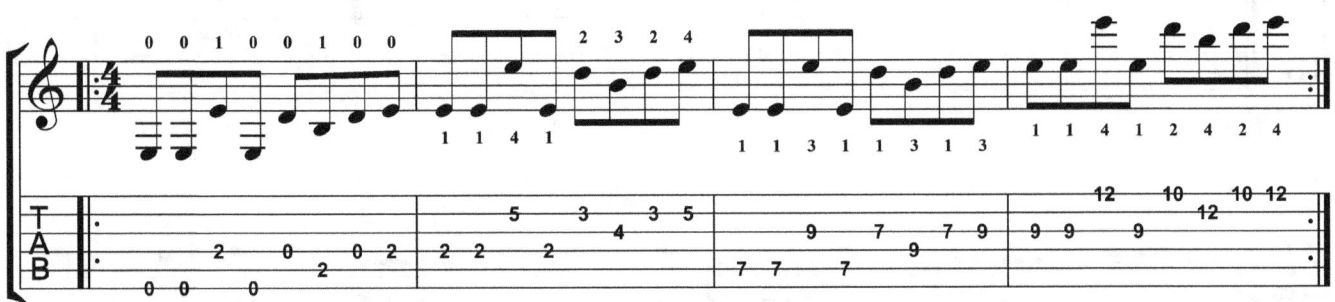

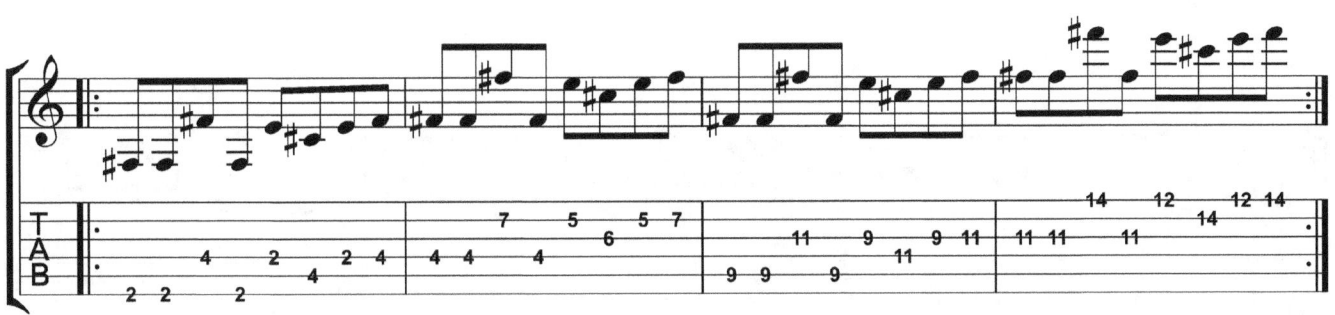

Chapter 1 box studies

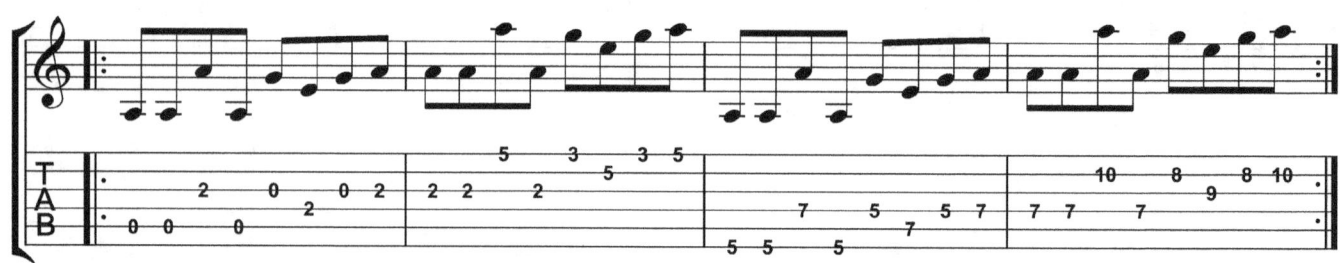
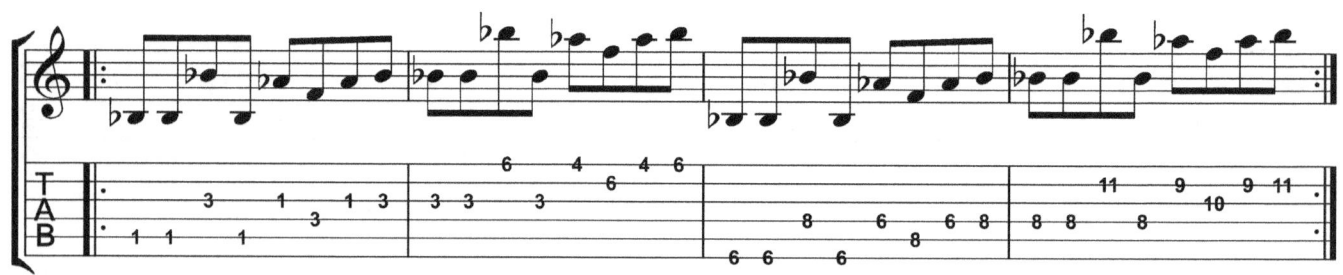

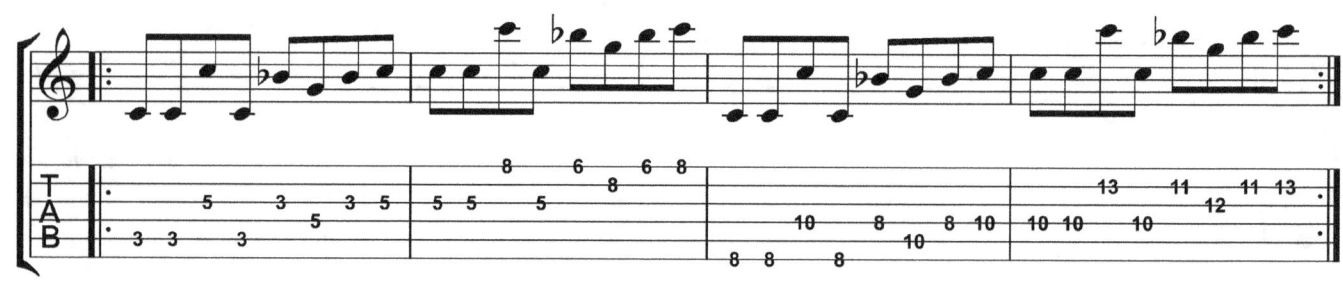

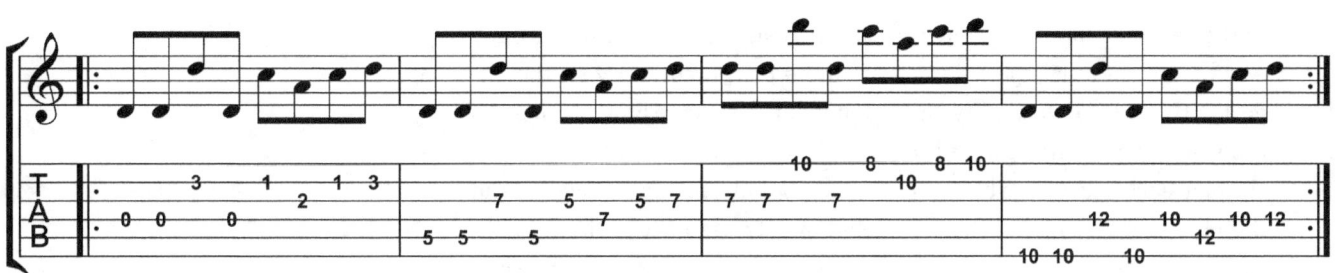

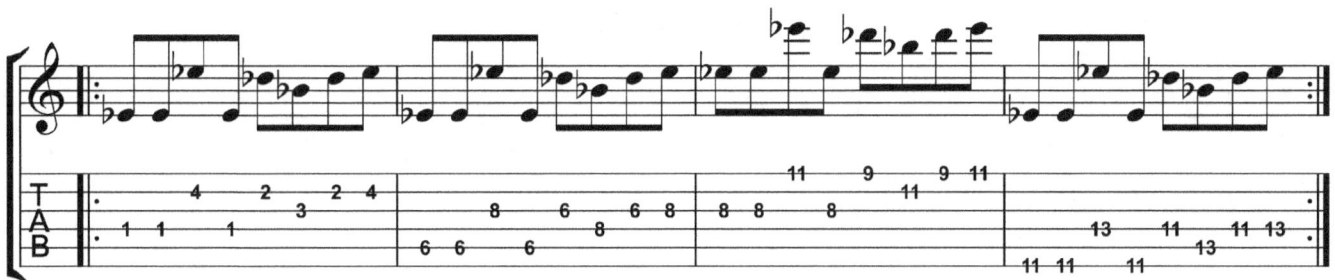

Chapter 1 box studies

15

Chapter 2
finger & pick studies

In the second chapter we find exercises that strengthen and balance the weaknesses of our fingers, help them to be placed correctly on the fingerboard, and gain flexibility and independence so as to move with great ease between the strings, creating melodies.

We play each exercise in all strings vertically and back up in reverse, and then we move chromatically with semitones to the next position by repeating the movement, and this way, a) we spread each exercise throughout the fingerboard, and b) most importantly , through this study routine we end up with a large number of repetitions for each exercise, and as a result we gain the ultimate benefits that this chapter can offer us.

Finger and Pick studies 1

ex. 1

ex. 2

ex. 3

ex. 4

Chapter 2   finger & pick studies

ex. 5

ex. 6

ex. 7

ex. 8

ex. 9

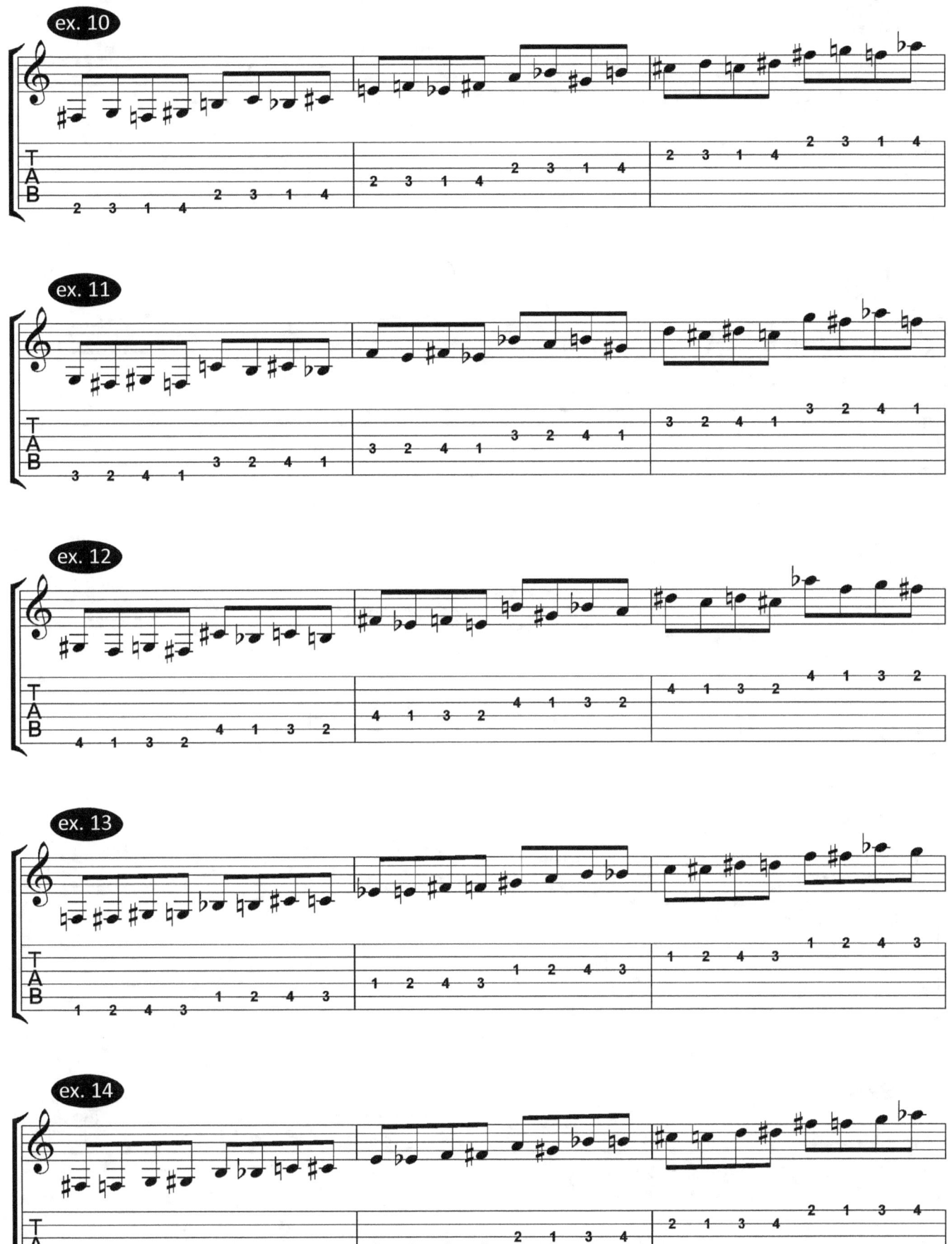

Chapter 2 finger & pick studies

ex. 15

ex. 16

ex. 17

ex. 18

ex. 19

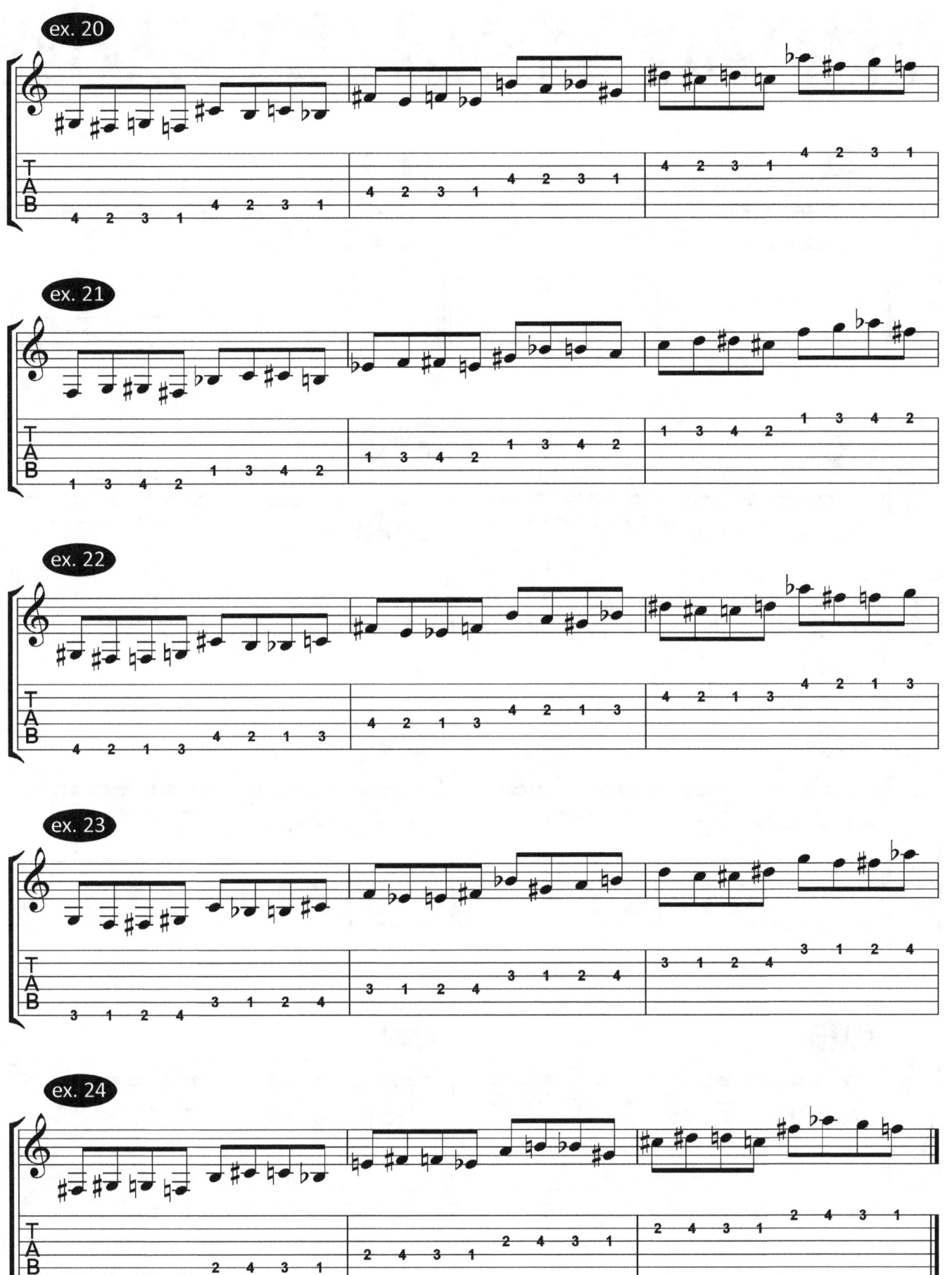

Chapter 2 finger & pick studies

Finger and Pick studies 2

Chapter 2 finger & pick studies

23

Finger and Pick studies 3

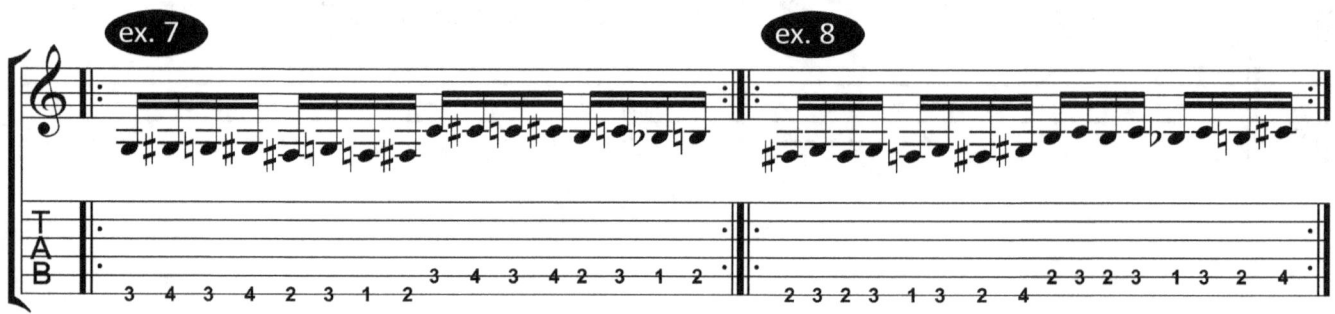

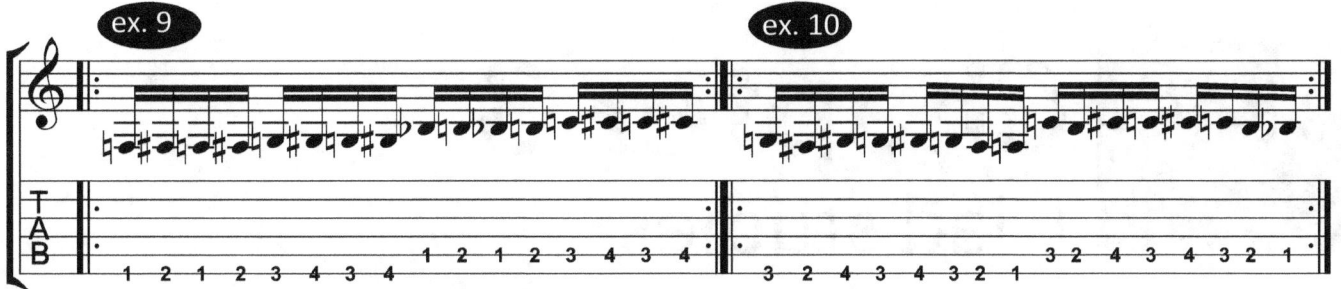

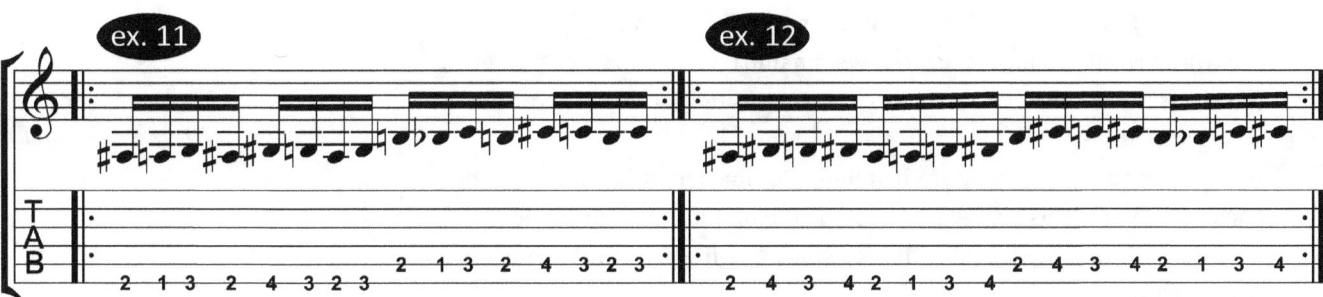

Chapter 2 finger & pick studies

Chapter 3
triad studies

In this chapter we will learn how we develop triads in their root position (1-3-5), in first inversion (3-5-1), and in second inversion (5-1-3).
We will learn all the finger positions we can find on two and three strings, as well as the corresponding shapes that are created through the various string structures.
Each repetition needs to be studied multiple times in order to establish each movement. This way, when we study the building of chords, we will be able to follow it without difficulty since our fingers will have been properly exercised.

Triad inversions on 2 strings - shape 1

Chapter 3 triad studies

Triad inversions on 2 strings - shape 2

Triad inversions on 3 strings - shape 1

Chapter 3 triad studies

diminished triad inversions

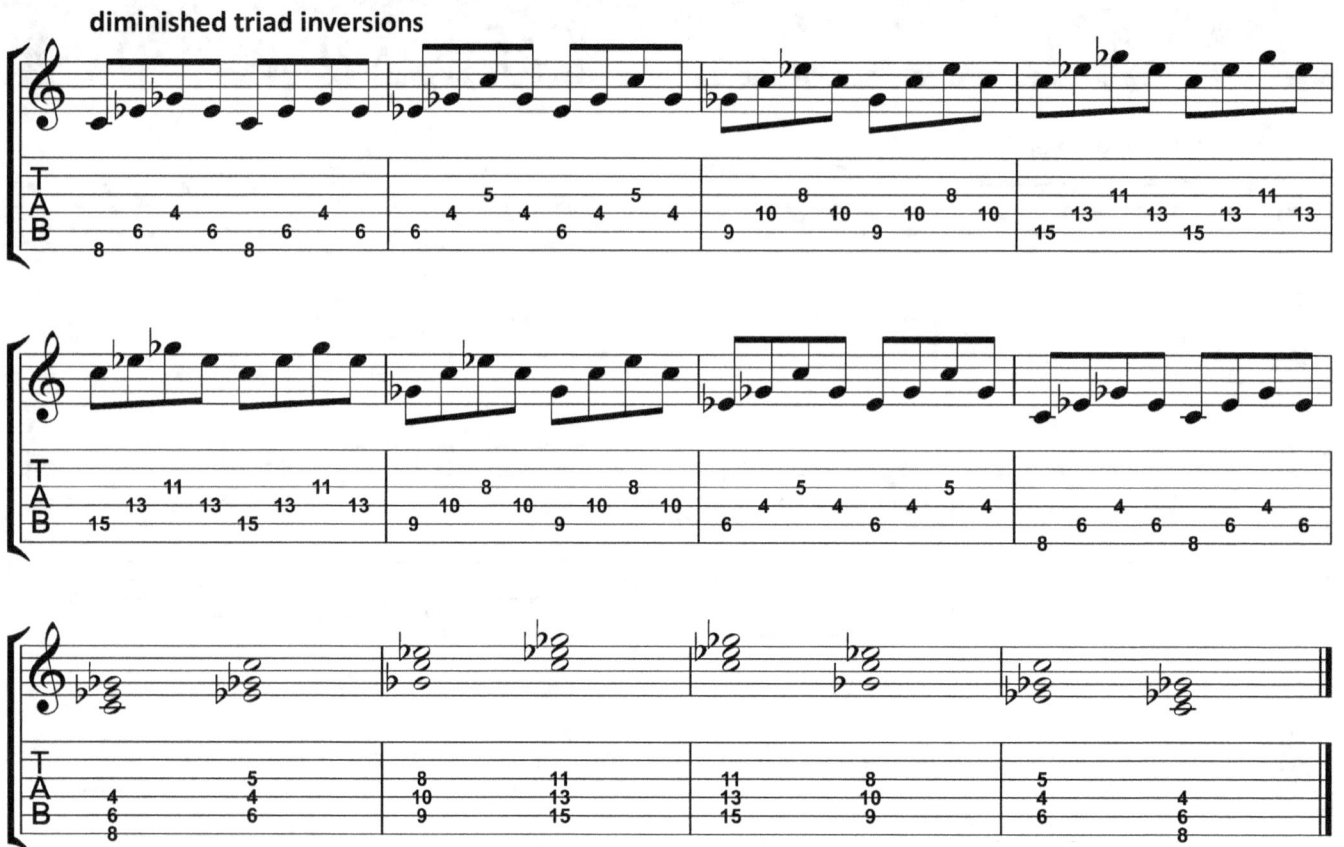

Triad inversions on 3 strings - shape 2

Chapter 3   triad studies

diminished triad inversions

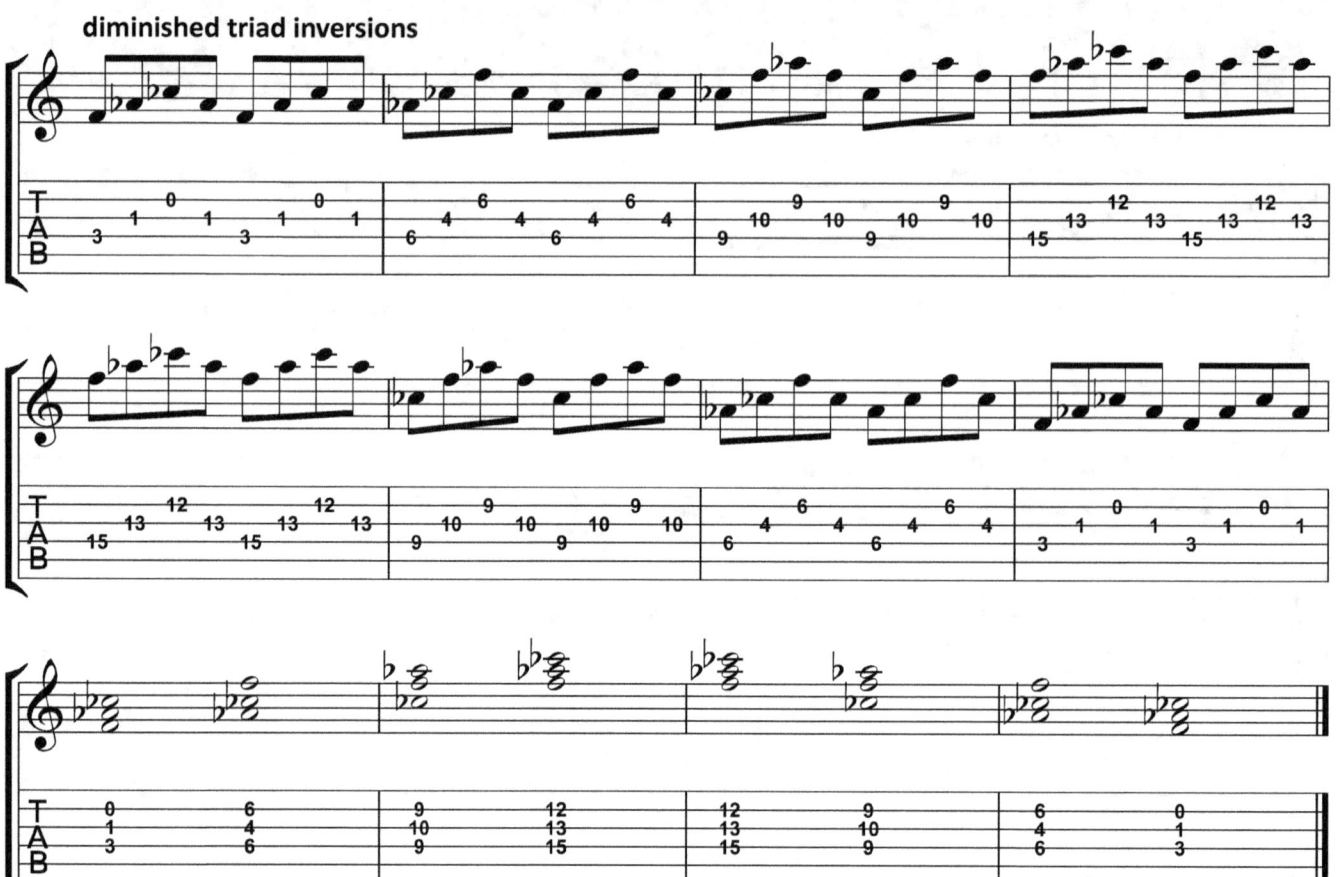

Triad inversions on 3 strings - shape 3

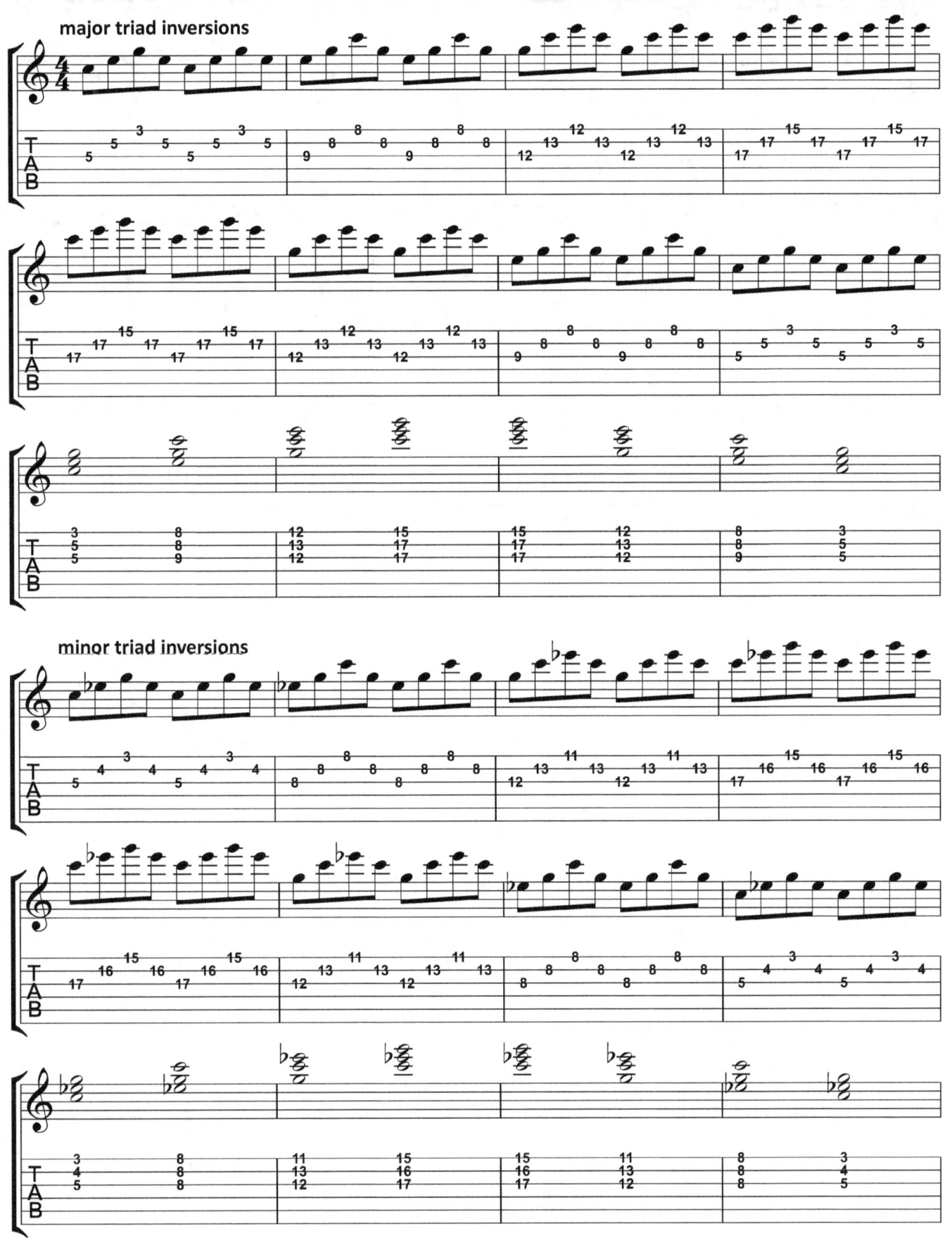

Chapter 3 triad studies

diminished triad inversions

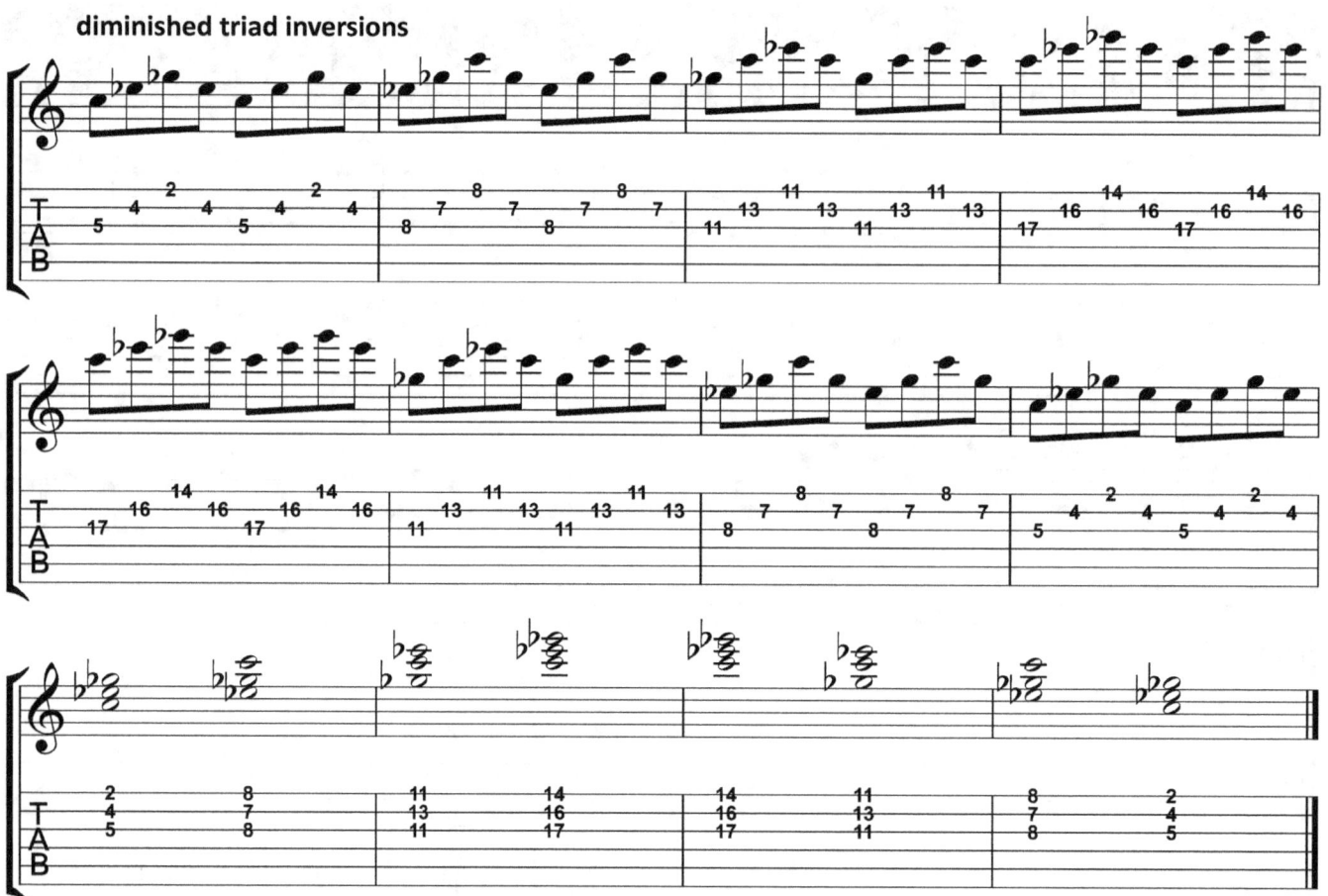

Chapter 4
the modes of the major scale

In this chapter we will examine and study the modes of the major scale.

Modal System

Modal System is called a group of rules that examines the creation of key centers related to specific scales of our music system. Each scale that we know can be inverted into new scales, as many as the number of notes of our original scale. This works the same way as it does with chord inversions by raising each time the tonic note an octave higher, the subsequent note of our previous scale becomes the next tonic, and this process repeats until the last note of our initial scale becomes the tonic. Therefore, we have as many inversions as the number of notes of our initial scale. Each note of a scale creates its own new scale, and that note becomes the tonic of the new scale. The scales that are created from the inverted scale degrees of a scale are called Modes, and we study this inversion and creation process in this chapter which is called "Modal System".

On the following chart we can see the inversion of the major scale into seven new scales, each of which begins on one of the scale degrees of the major scale. What all those scales have in common is that they use the notes of the major scale, which is also called Ionian, but each one uses the notes in a different order. Each one of those scales has its own tone color, its own musical environment, it creates its own chords, and, in general, it functions in an entirely autonomous way even though it ultimately belongs to the mother major scale. Each mode has its own pattern since the half and whole steps appear in a different order, and the result is a different sound, which is why we need to be able to recognize the modes by their sound quality. In addition, each mode builds its own chord from the 1st, 3rd, 5th, and 7th degrees. Therefore, we have seven chords that derive from the seven modes of the major scale. Those are called diatonic chords, which means that they all belong to the tonality of the mother scale. The modes of the major scale have been given names from the Ancient Greek language since they originated from the modes that the Ancient Greeks used, but with a different order.

Tetrachords

Before we move on to the study of the modes, we will examine how tetrachords are built, which are historically the foundation for building scales of all musical systems.

Tetrachords exist in the construction of music since ancient times on all the musical systems, in Ancient Greece in descending form, and in Rome in ascending form. In traditional Middle Eastern music we have the *makam* which are developed both in tetrachords and pantachords, and in traditional Indian music we have the *ragas*. As we already saw, each major scale involves two tetrachords. This is the case for all 7-note scales as well as their modes that we are going to come across in this book. Therefore, depending on its pattern of intervals, each tetrachord has a certain name which determines the sound quality that it represents. Let's look at the names of the tetrachords in order to be able to identify them in the development of the scales in subsequent chapters.

Major tetrachord, W-W-H: It is called *major* because it contains a major 3rd and it is the first tetrachord of the natural major scale.

Minor tetrachord, W-H-W: It is called *minor* because it contains a minor 3rd and it is the first tetrachord of the natural minor scale.

Phrygian tetrachord, H-W-W: It is called *Phrygian* because it contains a minor 2nd and a minor 3rd and it is the first tetrachord of the Phrygian mode.

Lydian tetrachord, W-W-W: It is called *Lydian* because it contains an augmented 4th which we find in the first tetrachord of the Lydian mode.

Content of exercises

- With each mode that we examine, we will first look at its basic construction on the fingerboard of the guitar and its specific position depending on the *shape* it requires. That way we will find each mode in 3 different shapes depending on which strings we build it.
- We will find the tetrachords that each mode contains.
- We will find the intervals between the tonic and each scale degree of every mode.
- We will construct the triad and the 7th chord that are formed from each scale degree of every mode by using the 1st, 3rd, 5th, and 7th note of the mode.

Tips for studying

- During the first 6 exercises of each mode and for space efficiency, we show only the beginning and the direction of each exercise.
- On each of those exercises we move chromatically on our fingerboard starting on the lowest possible position for forming each mode and its chord, and ending on the highest possible position. This means that we will first play each mode exactly how it appears on the exercise, and then we will move it over by a half step, and we will keep repeating that until we run out of room on our fingerboard.
- When we get to the highest position where we can play each exercise, we start to move in reverse by moving the exercise half a step back each time, and we repeat that until we run out of room on our fingerboard.
- Each time that we move chromatically to a new position, we name the first note of the exercise, which is our new tonic. When we ascend on our fingerboard towards the higher area, we indicate any accidentals with sharps, while when we are descending we indicate them with flats.

Following the above, we have a segment with 9 different melodic exercises which will help us learn how to use each mode in a melodic way. We need to apply each of those exercises to all 12 tonalities of our system.

Afterwards, we move on to the block of exercises for triads and 7th chords, with all the possible combinations among all scale degrees. We still need to transfer each exercise to all tonalities.

Finally, we learn all the intervals that are formed between the tonic and each scale degree, as well as the chords that derive from each mode.

As we already mentioned, each exercise should be played on all 12 tonalities using the circle of fifths by moving in perfect fourths each time we go to the next tonality. After we have played them all, we move on to the next exercise. We will not gain much if we only play each exercise once and then rush on to the next because we will not accomplish the knowledge that this book has to offer.

Ionian
1st mode of the Major scale

General formula: W-W-H-W-W-W-H

Scale: Major with a major seventh

Tetrachords: major – major

Characteristic note of the mode: the major 7

The intervals that are formed between the tonic and each scale degree: I-II = 2, I-III = 3, I-IV = 4, I- V = 5, I-VI = 6, I-VII = 7

The diatonic half steps are found on the scale degrees III-IV and VII-I

Triad: Major I

Seventh chord: Major seventh Imaj7, IΔ7, I Δ, I(maj7)

Extensions: 9, 13

Generally: The Ionian mode is the natural major scale and from its notes we form the remaining 7 modes of the key center. It is therefore a mother scale. It is a seven-tone scale with a balanced sound. The 4th degree is used melodically only on weak beats as a passing tone because an extended sound could ruin the stability of the sound of the tonic scale.

Ionian shape 1

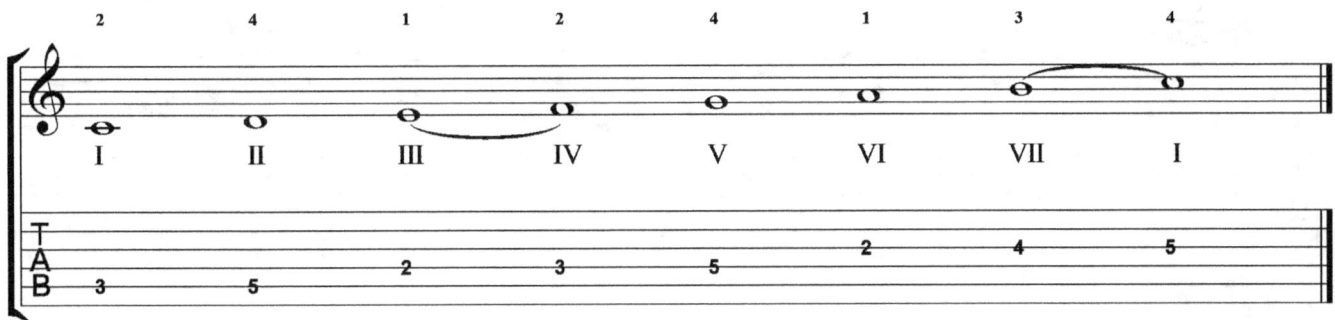

Tetrachords

Intervals

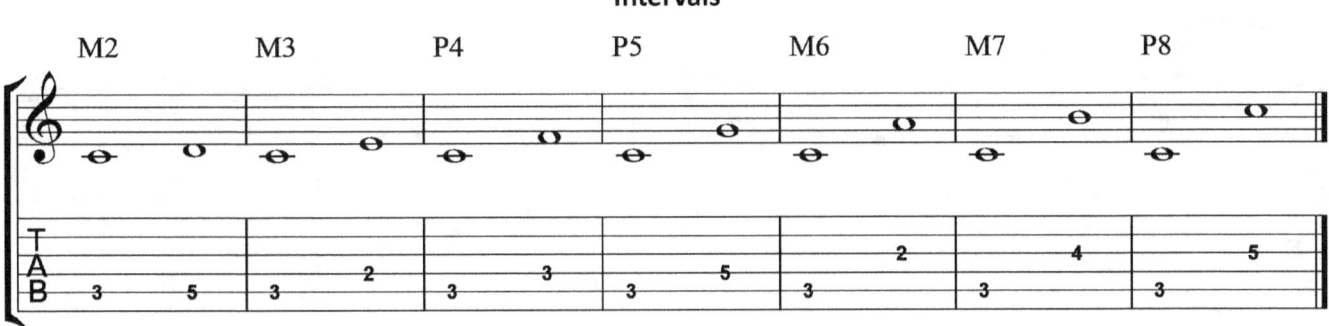

triad: major   7th chord: Imaj7

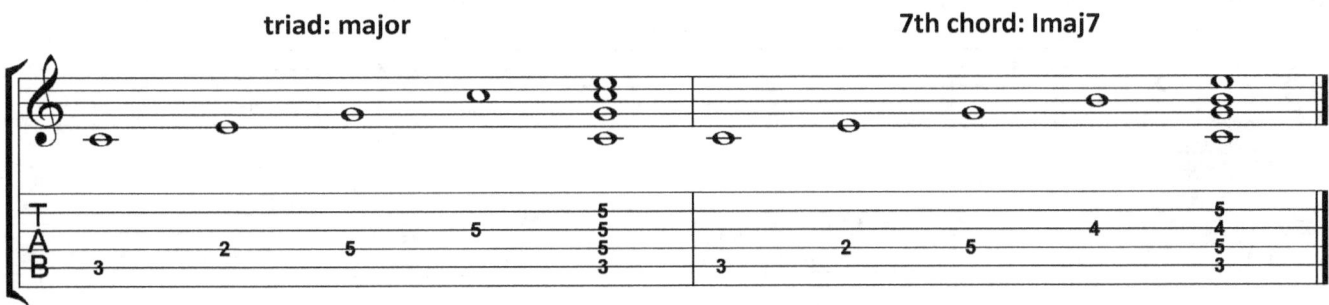

Chapter 4 the modes of the major scale - ionian

Ionian mode studies - shape 1

Mode exercises

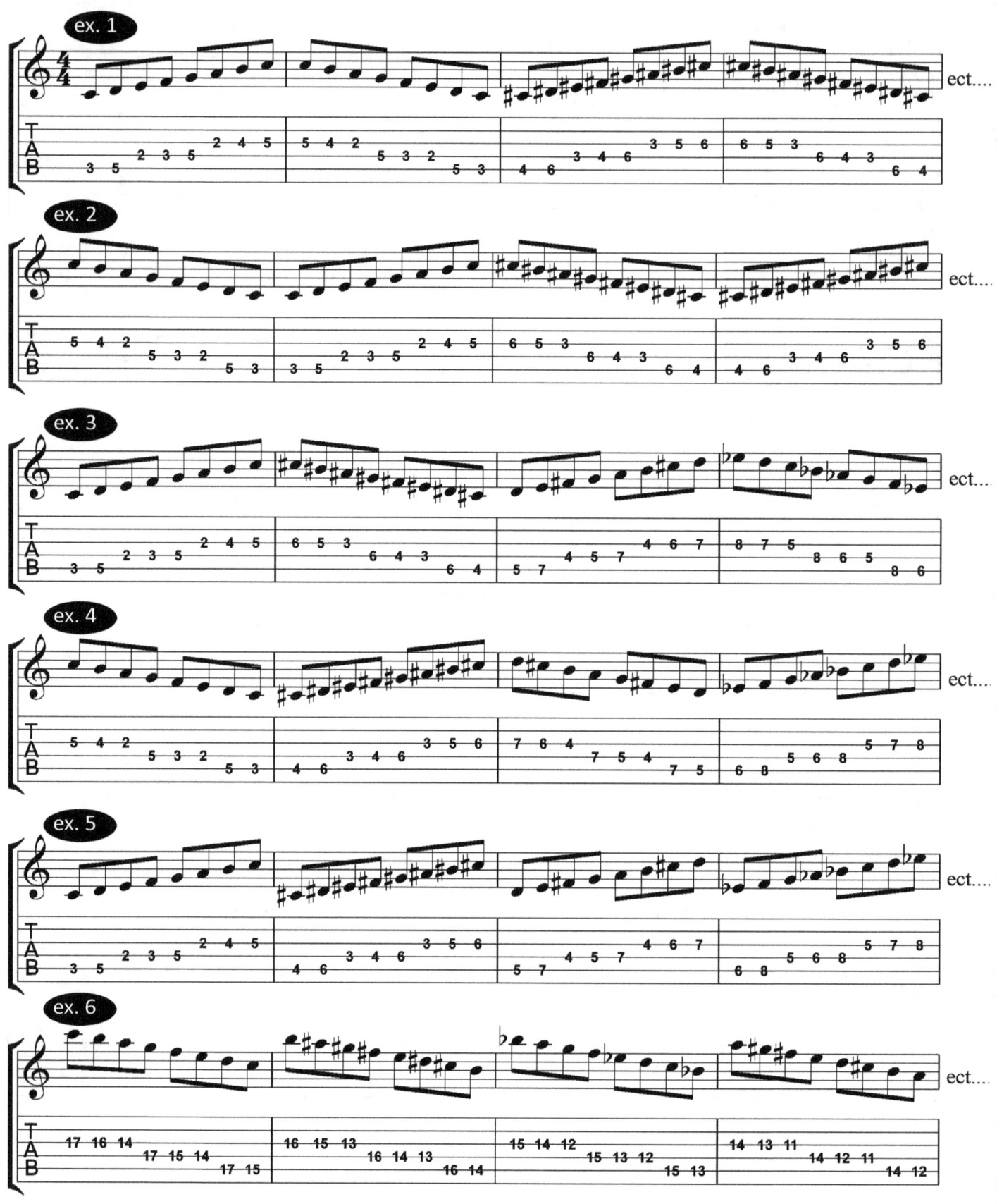

Melodic exercises

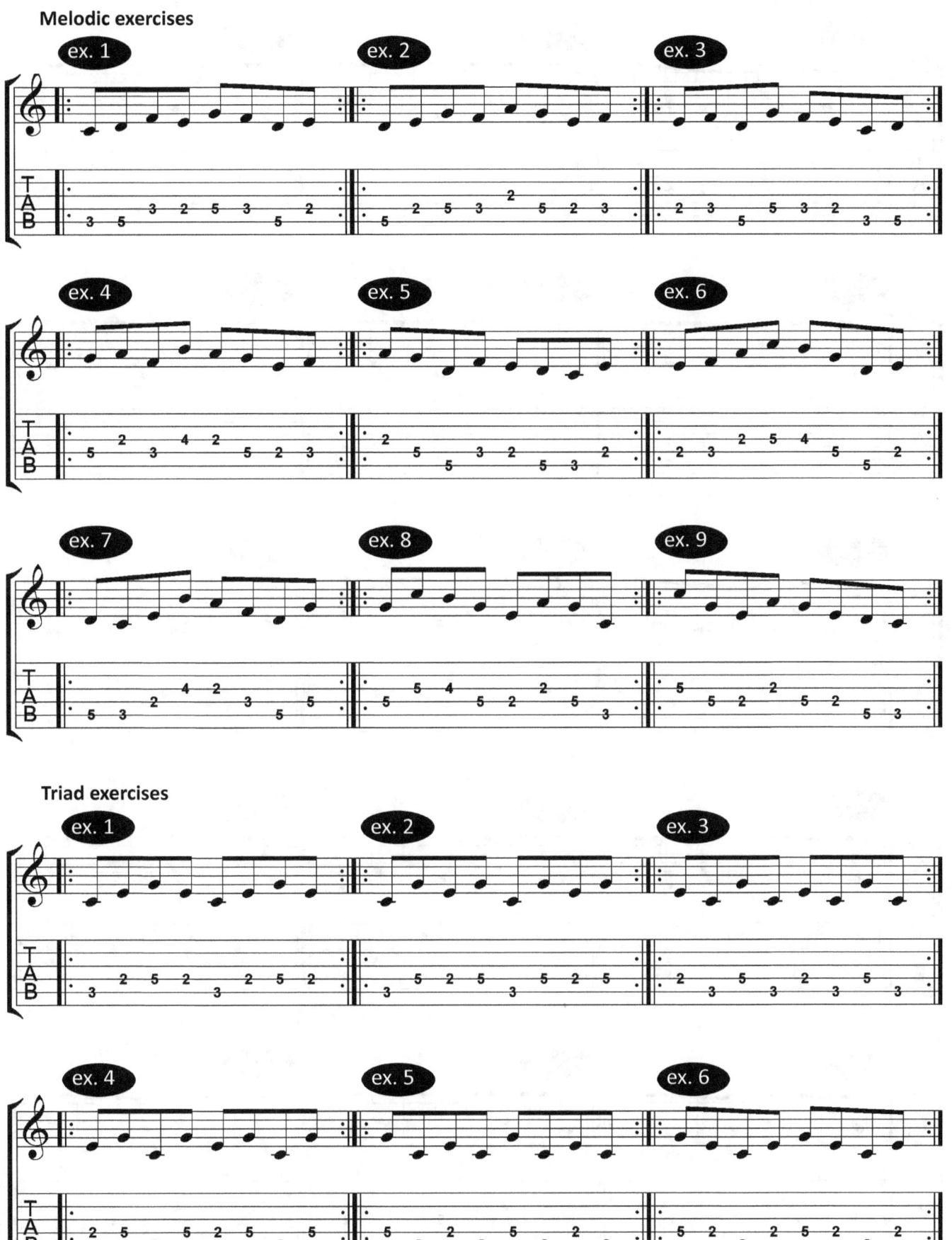

Triad exercises

Chapter 4   the modes of the major scale - ionian

7th chord exercises

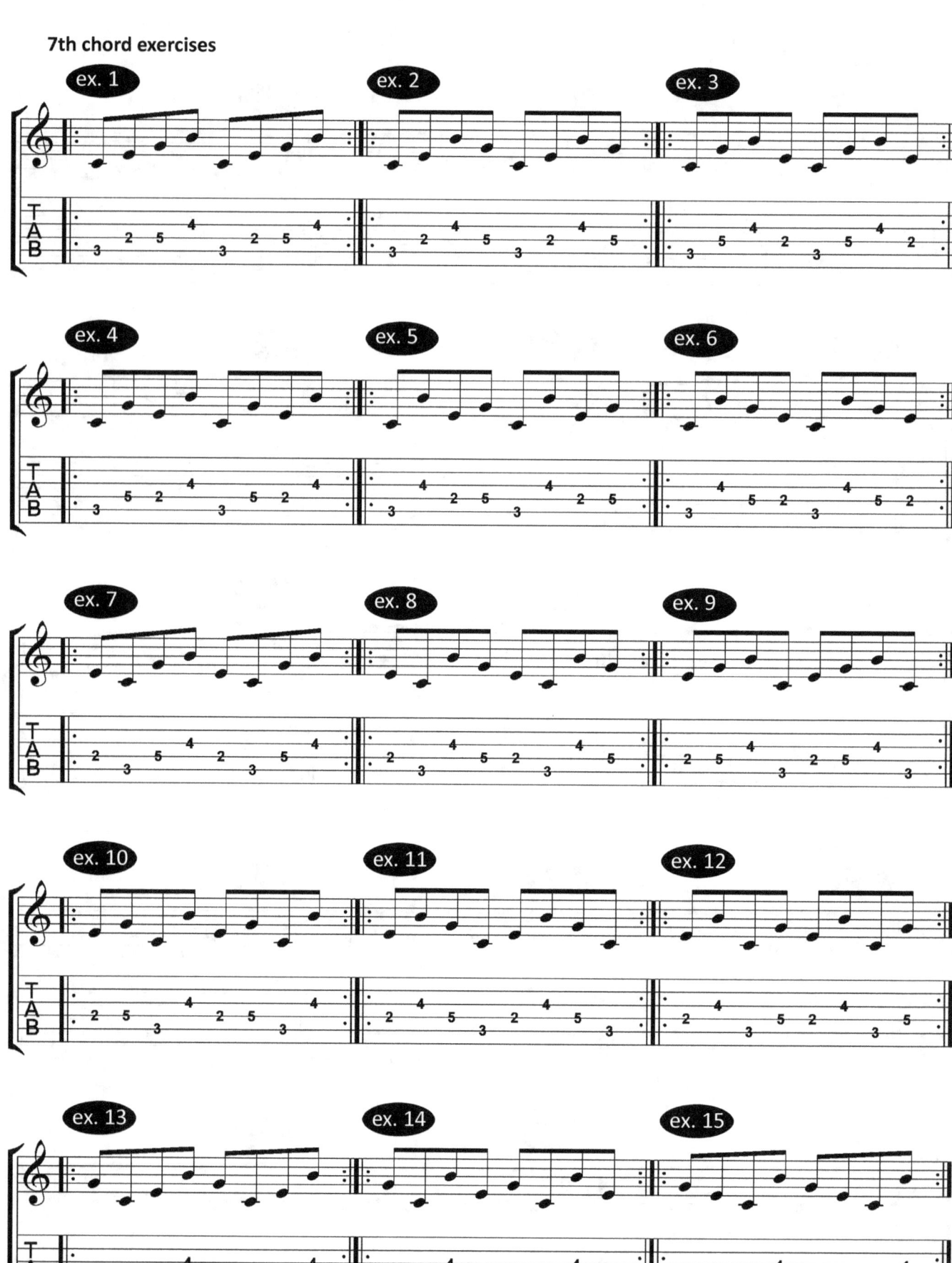

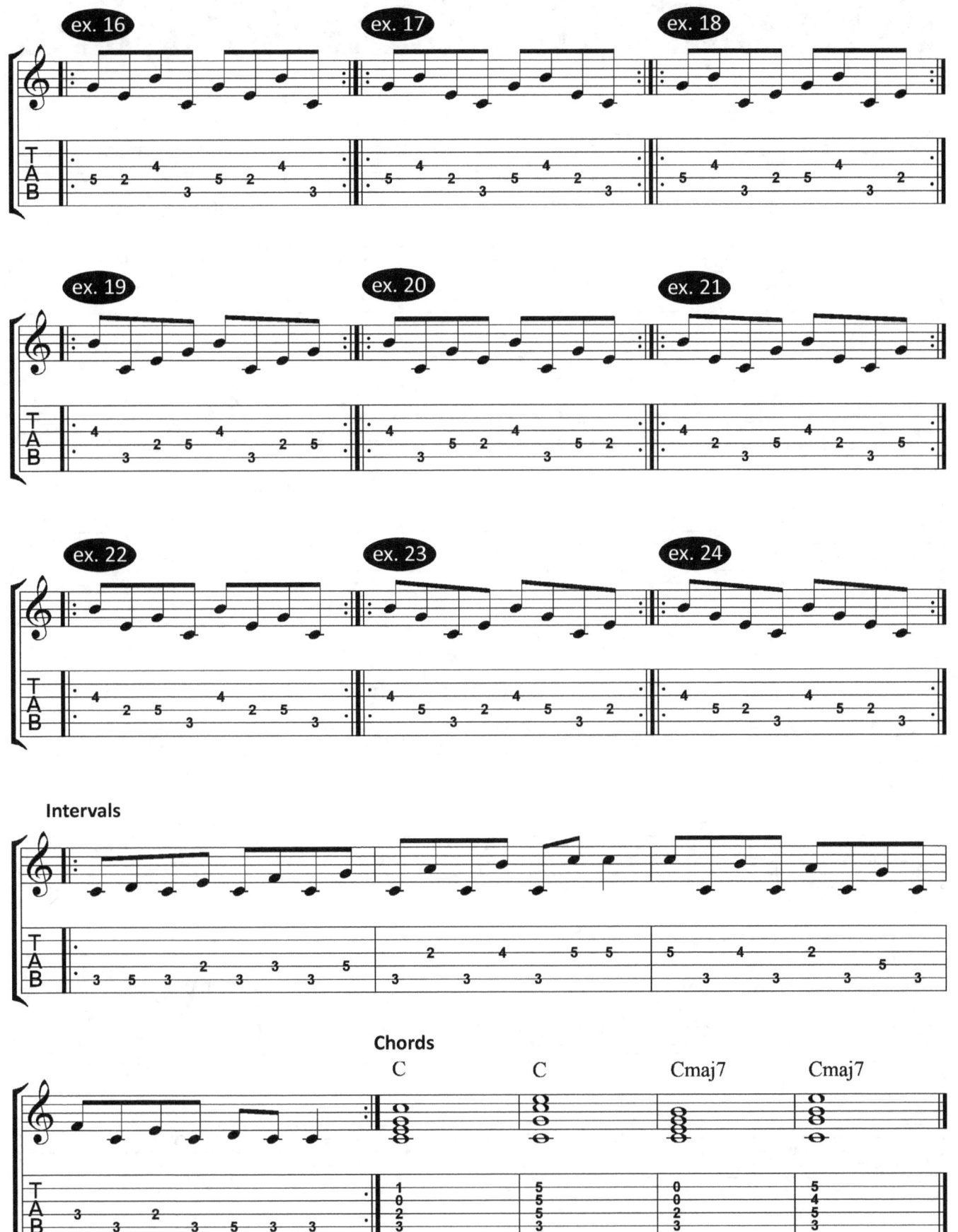

Chapter 4 the modes of the major scale - ionian

Ionian shape 2

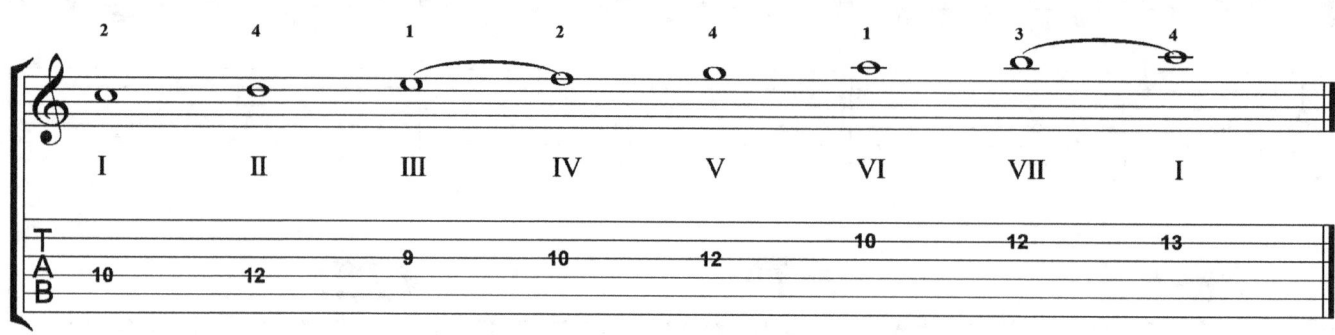

Tetrachords

Intervals

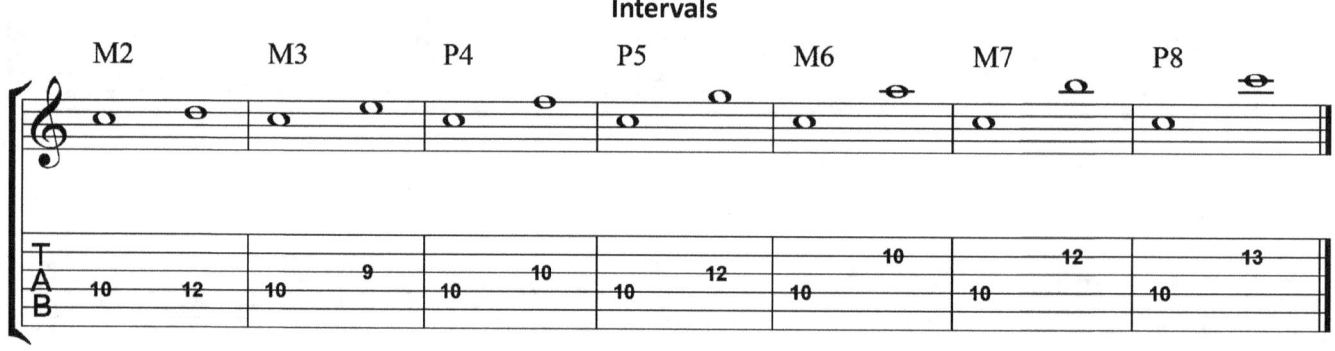

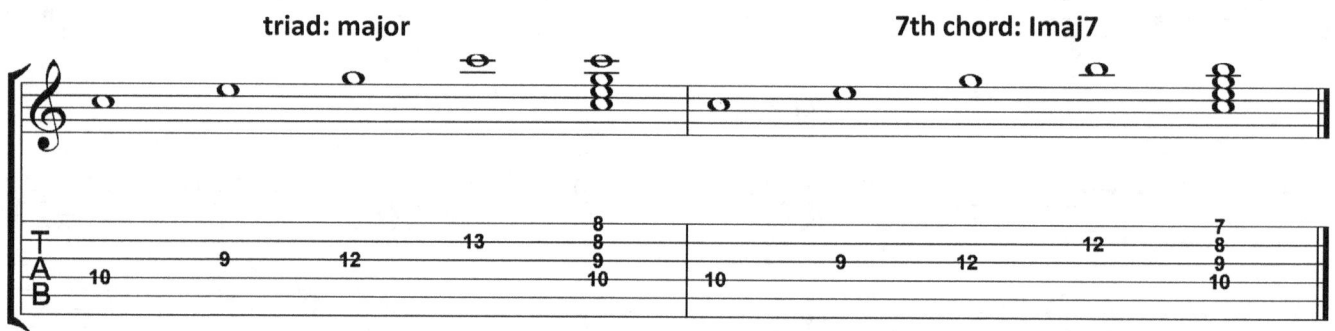

Ionian mode studies - shape 2

Mode exercises

Chapter 4   the modes of the major scale - ionian

Melodic exercises

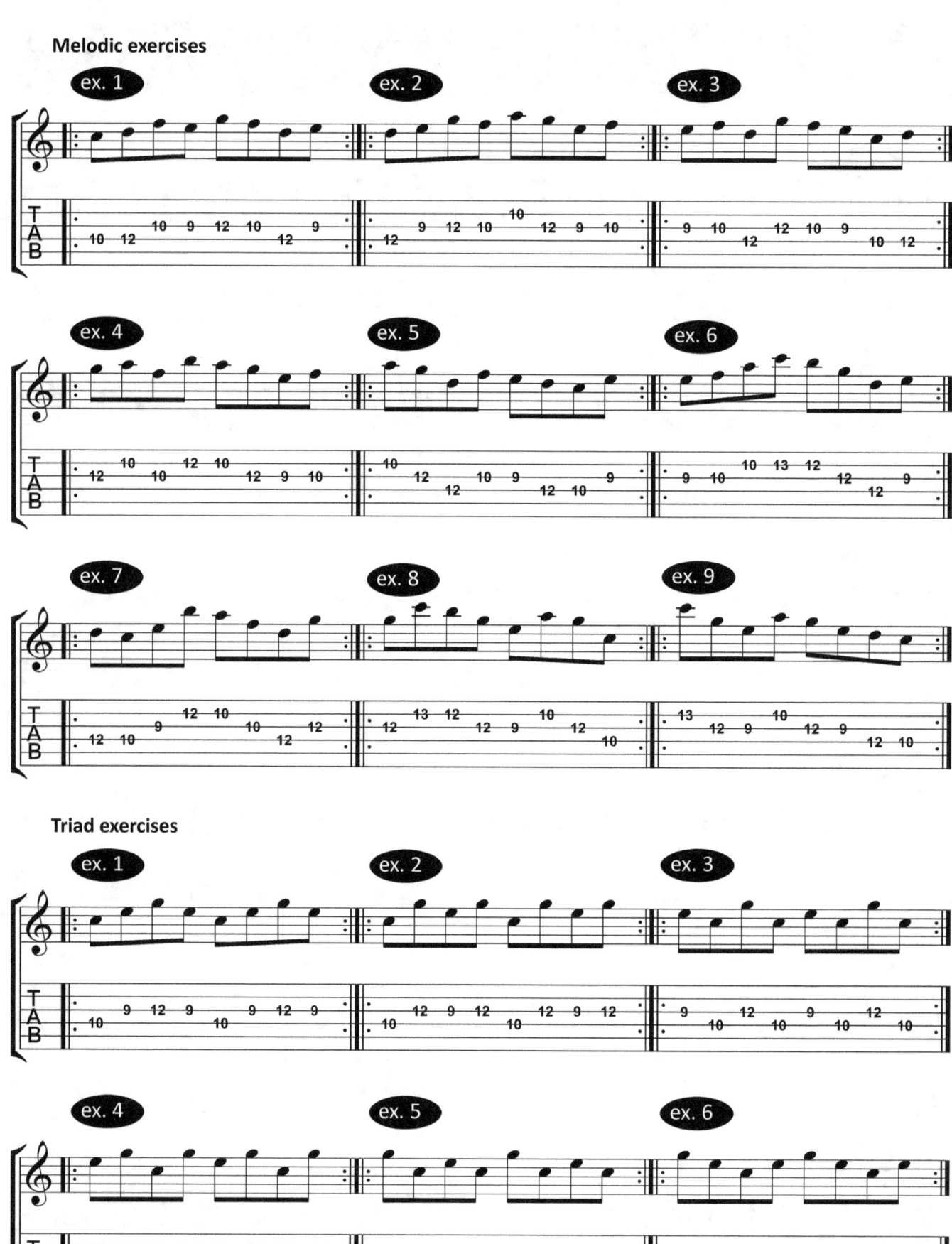

Triad exercises

7th chord exercises

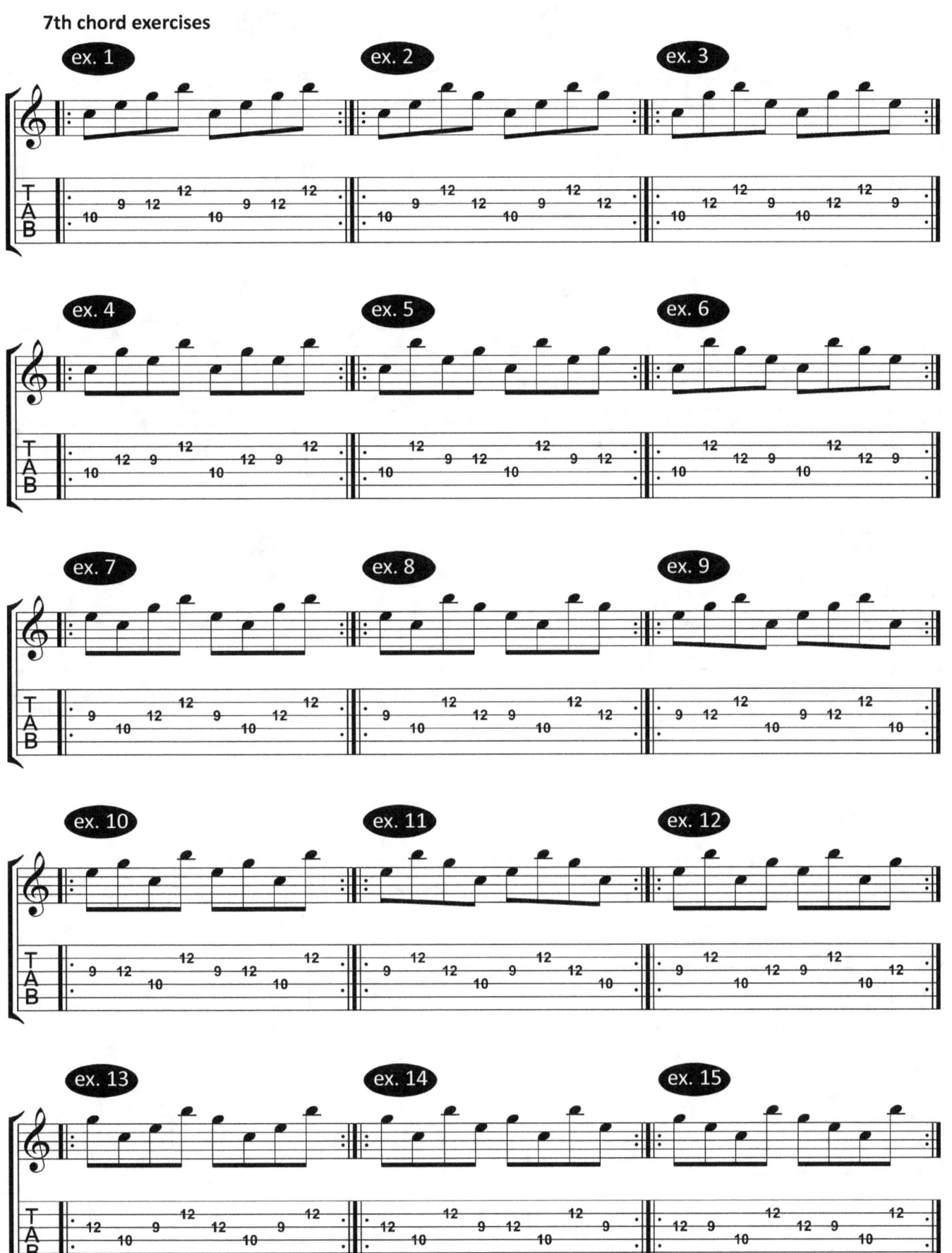

Chapter 4   the modes of the major scale - ionian

47

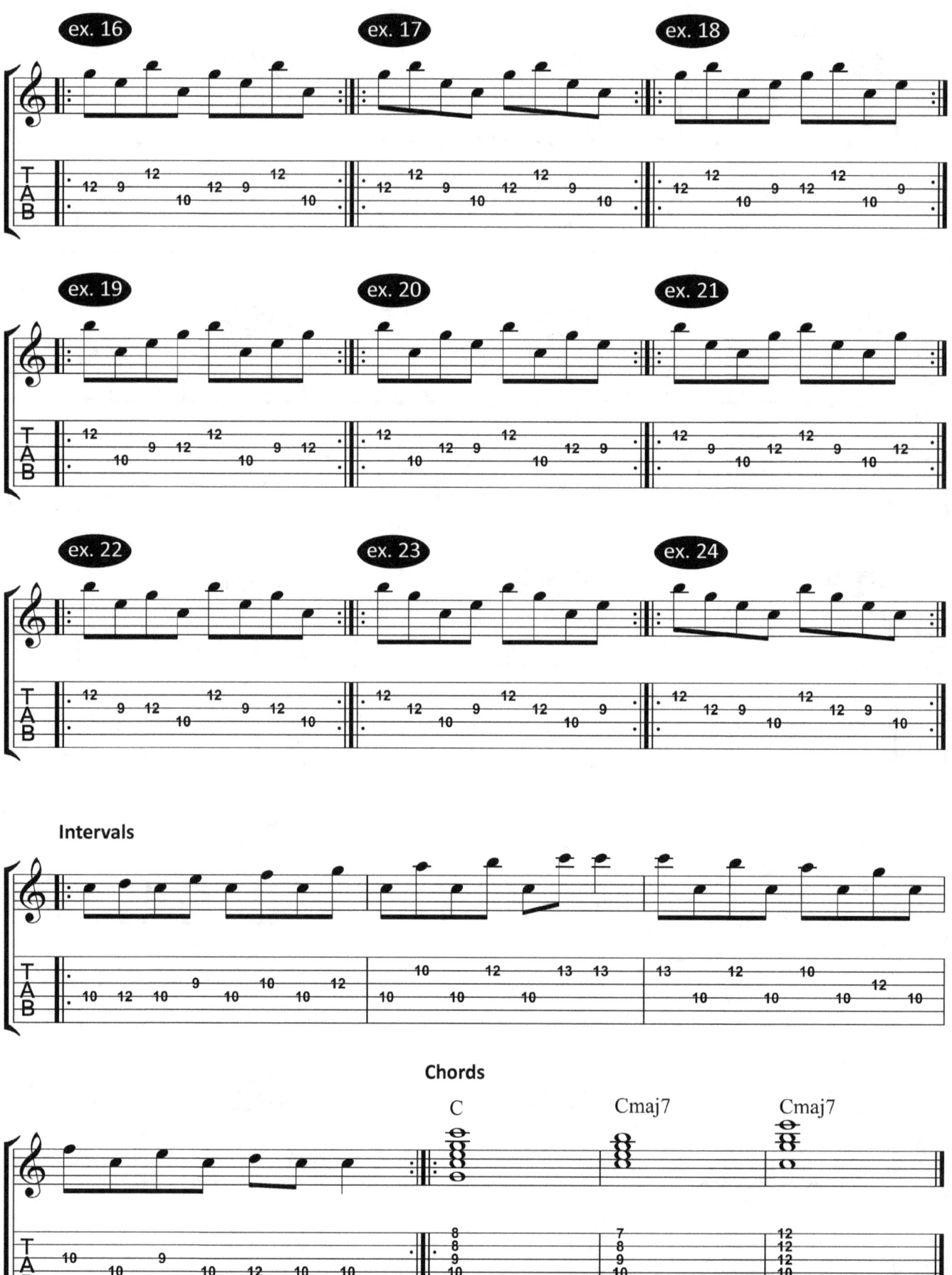

Ionian shape 3

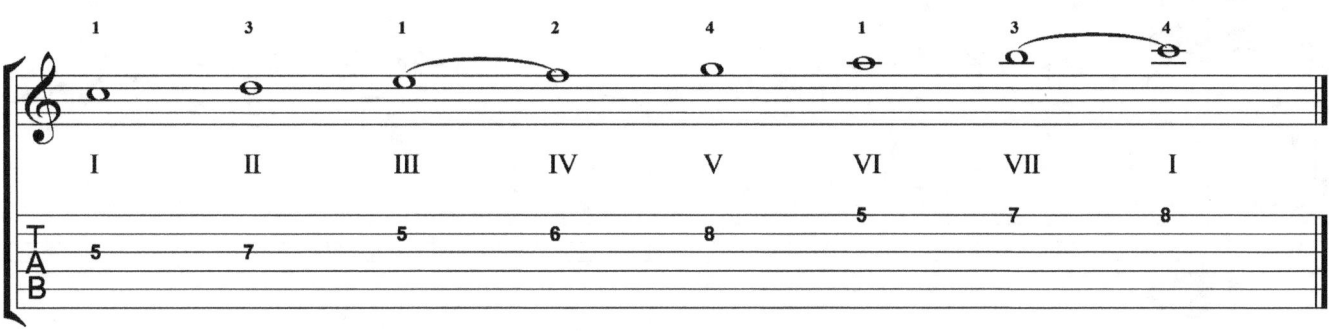

Tetrachords

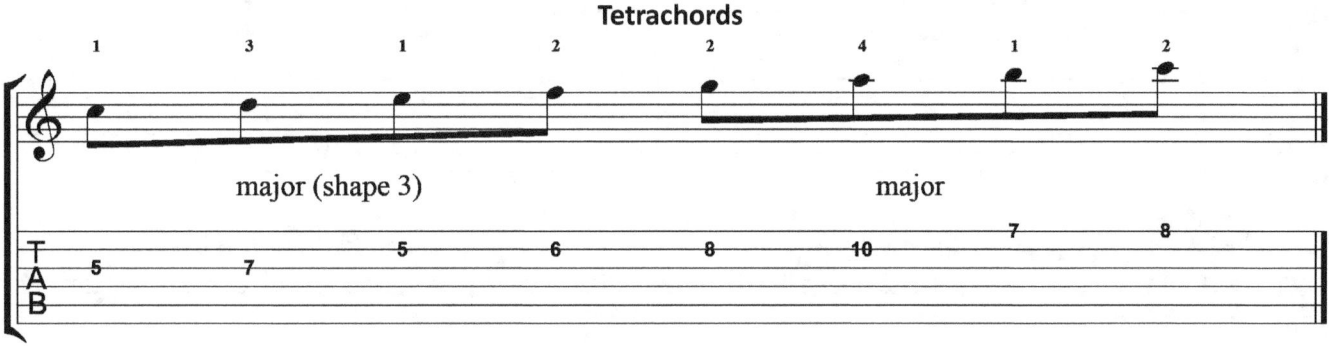

Intervals

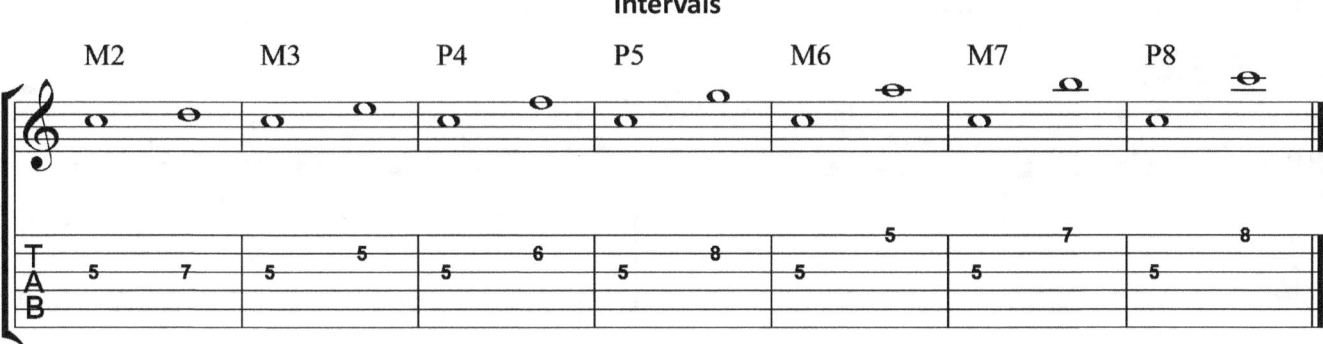

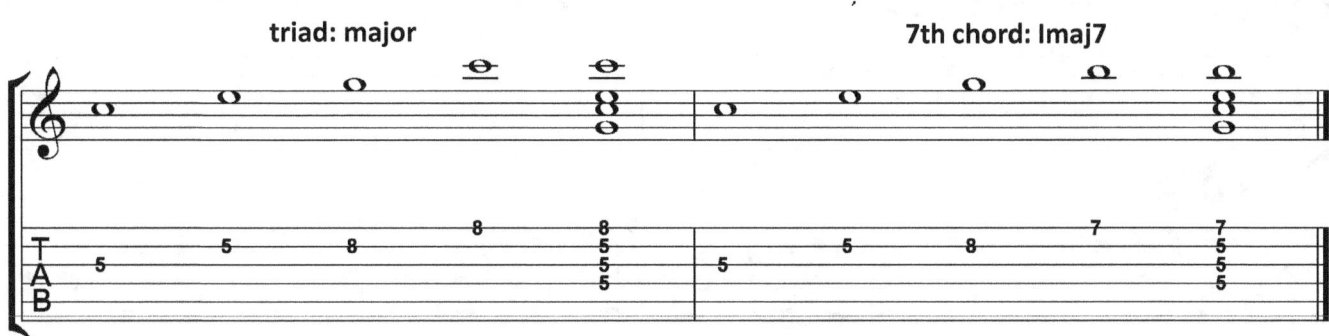

Chapter 4 the modes of the major scale - ionian

Ionian mode studies - shape 3

Mode exercises

Melodic exercises

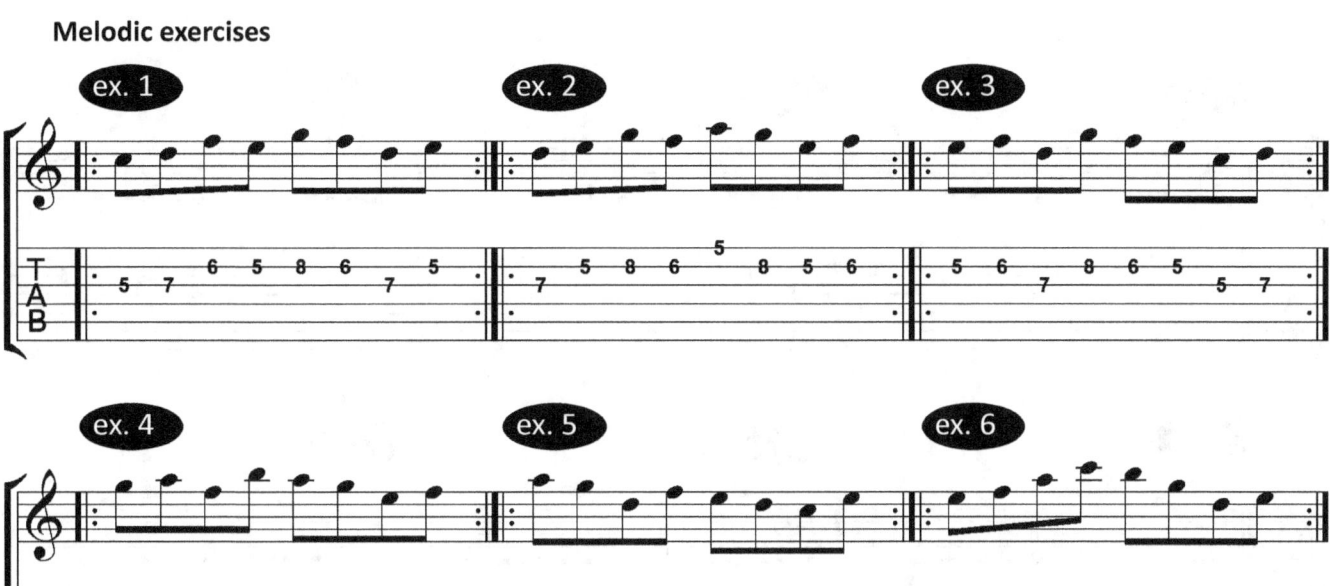

Triad exercises

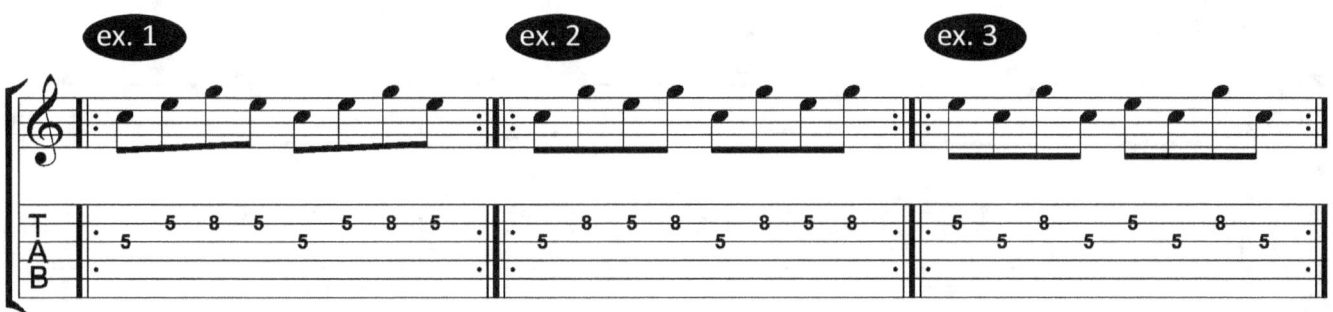

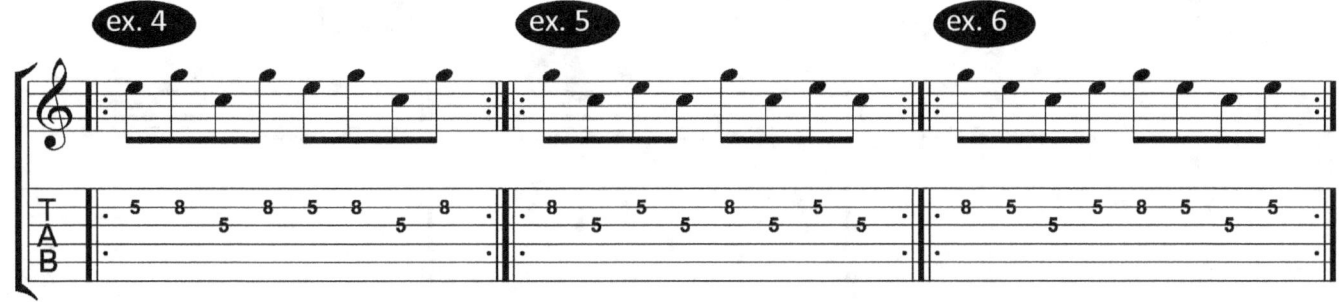

Chapter 4   the modes of the major scale - ionian

7th chord exercises

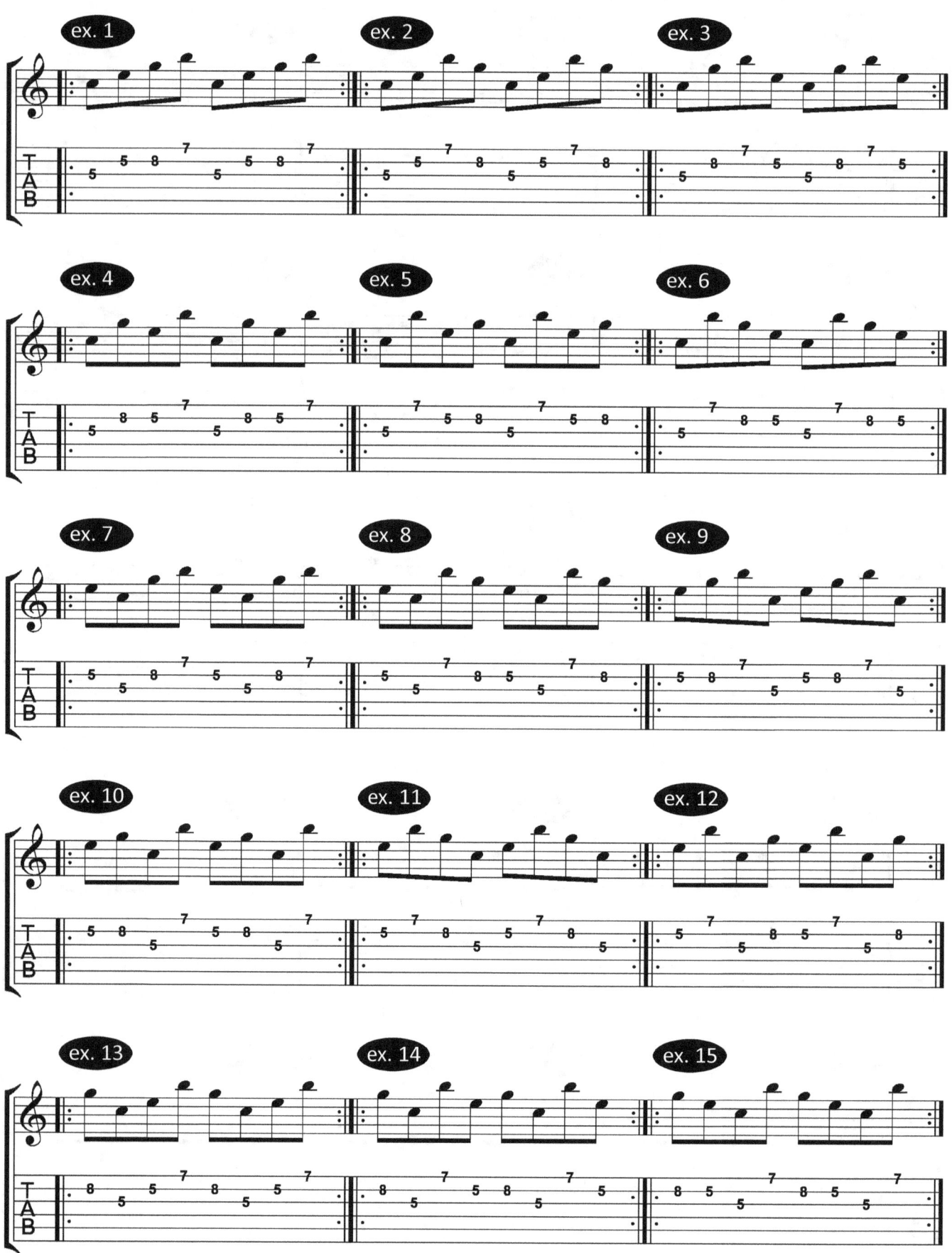

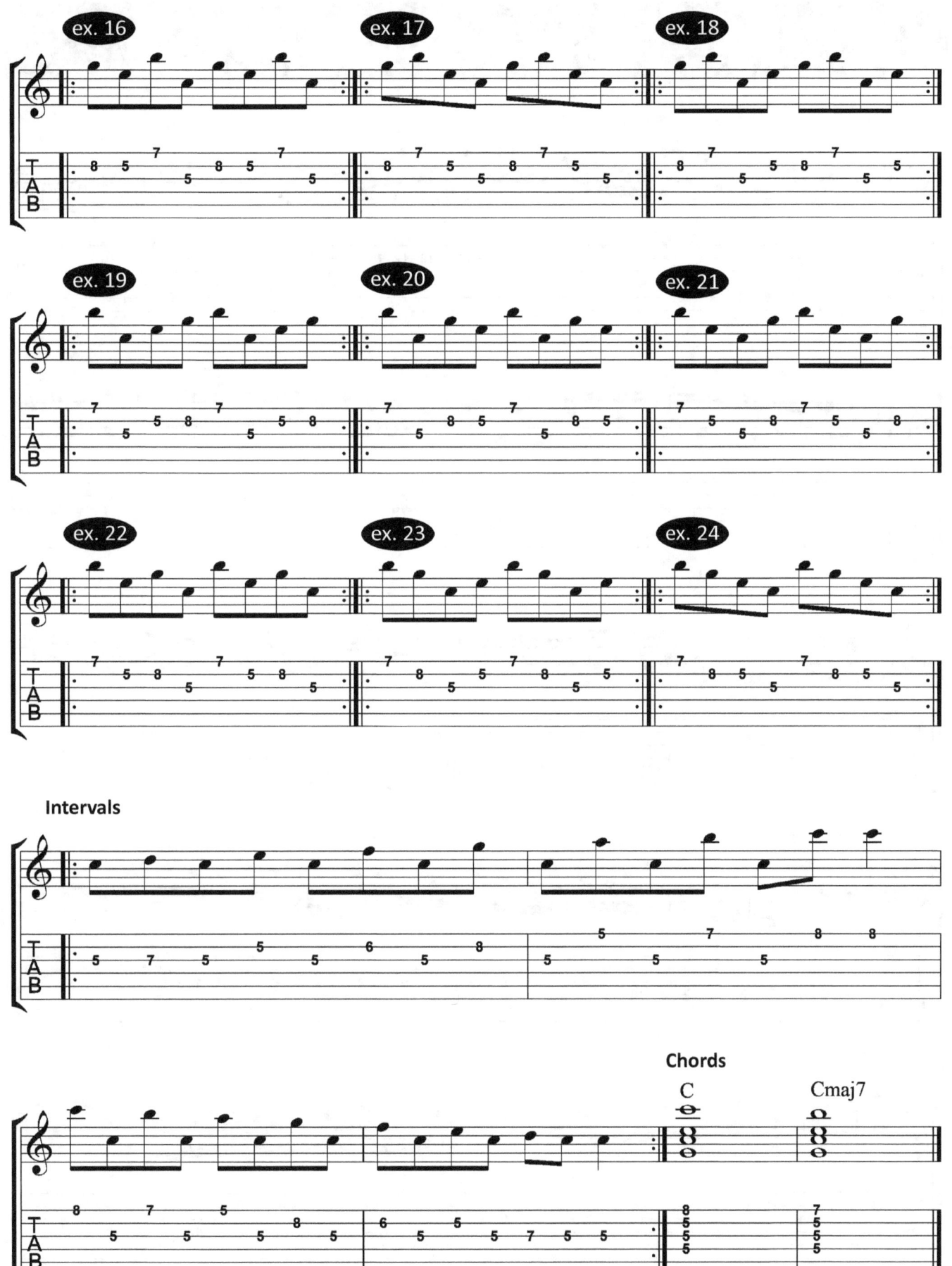

Chapter 4 the modes of the major scale - ionian

Ionian in 2 octaves with shapes 1 + 2

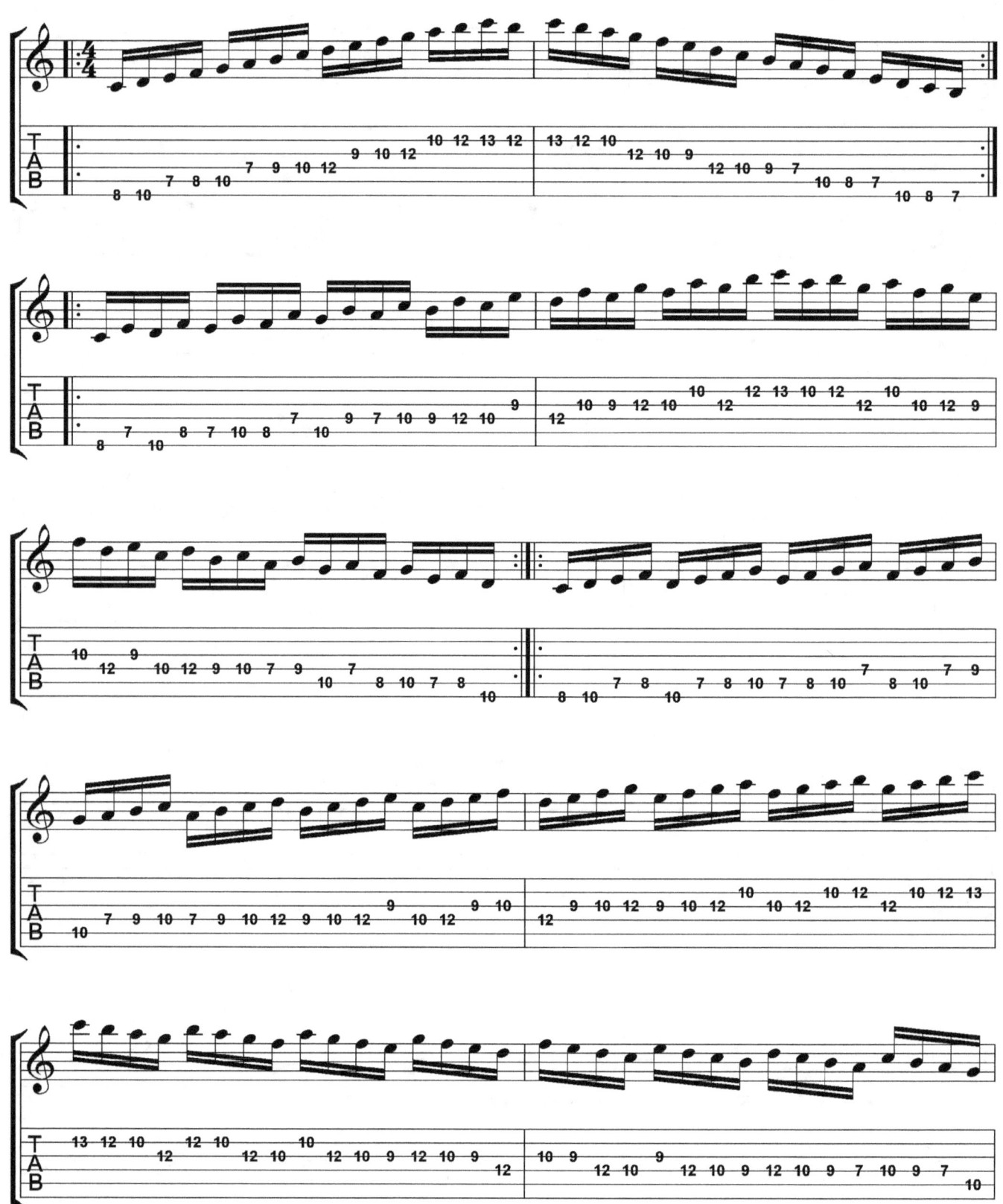

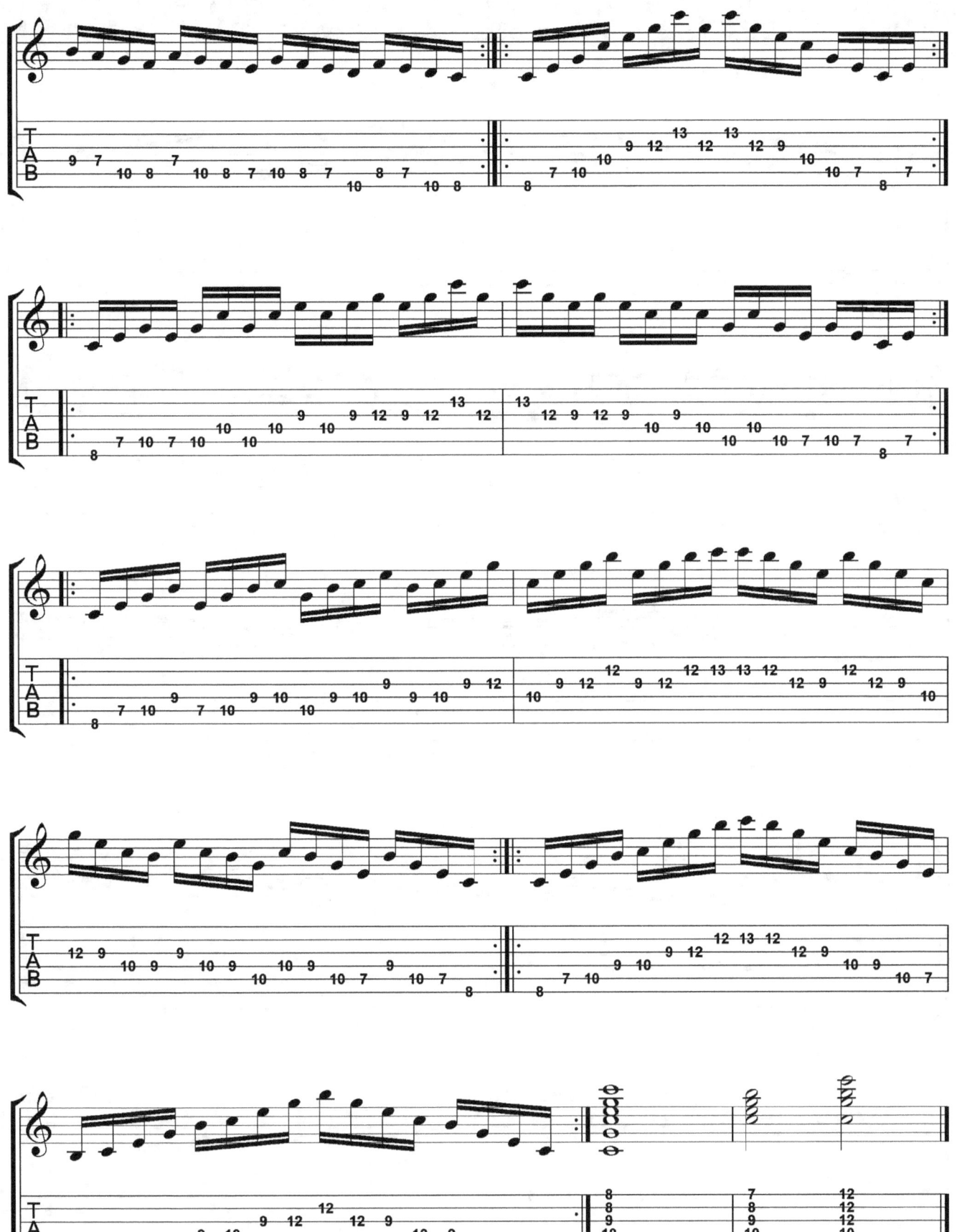

Chapter 4 the modes of the major scale - ionian

Ionian in 2 octaves with shapes 1 + 3

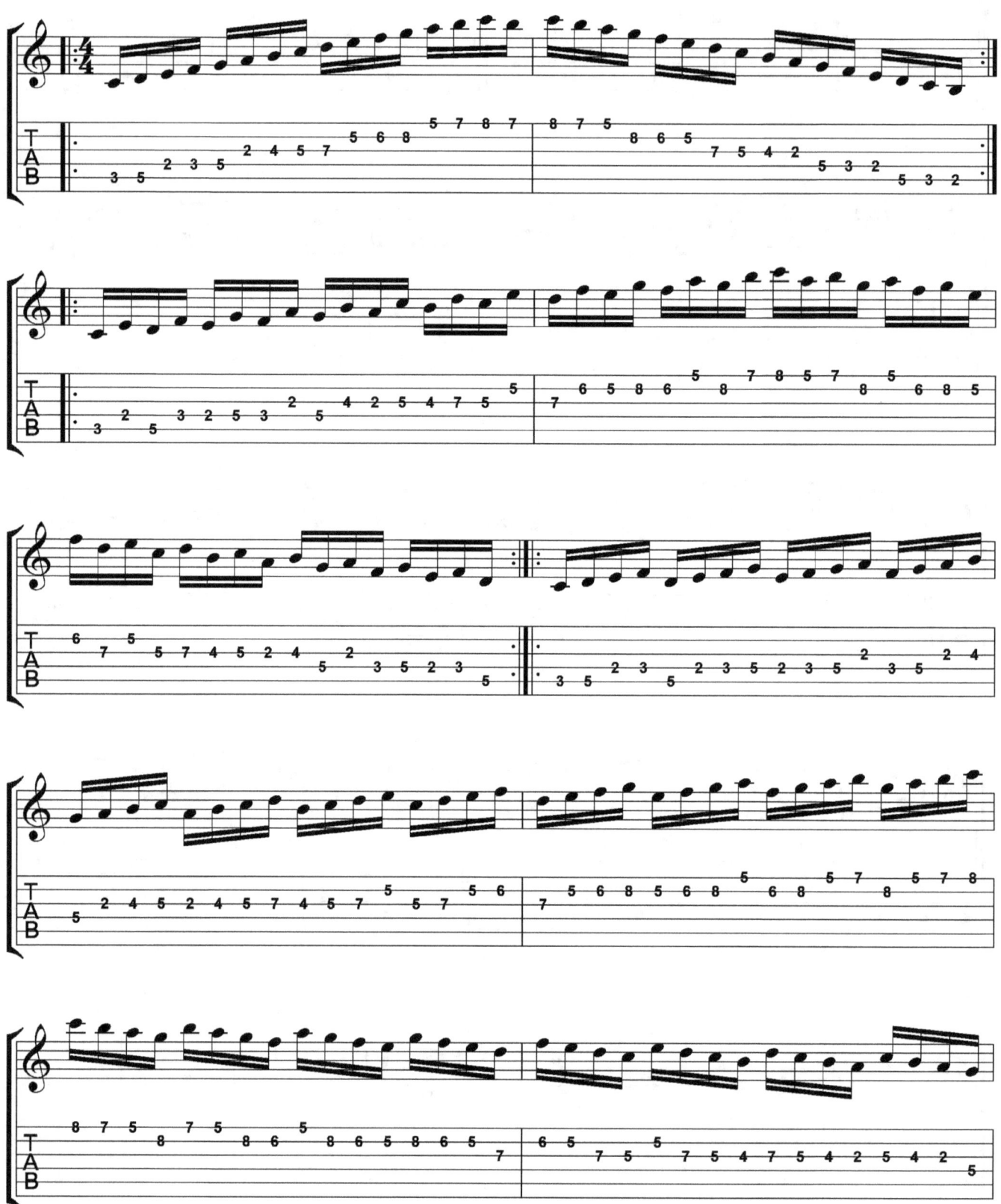

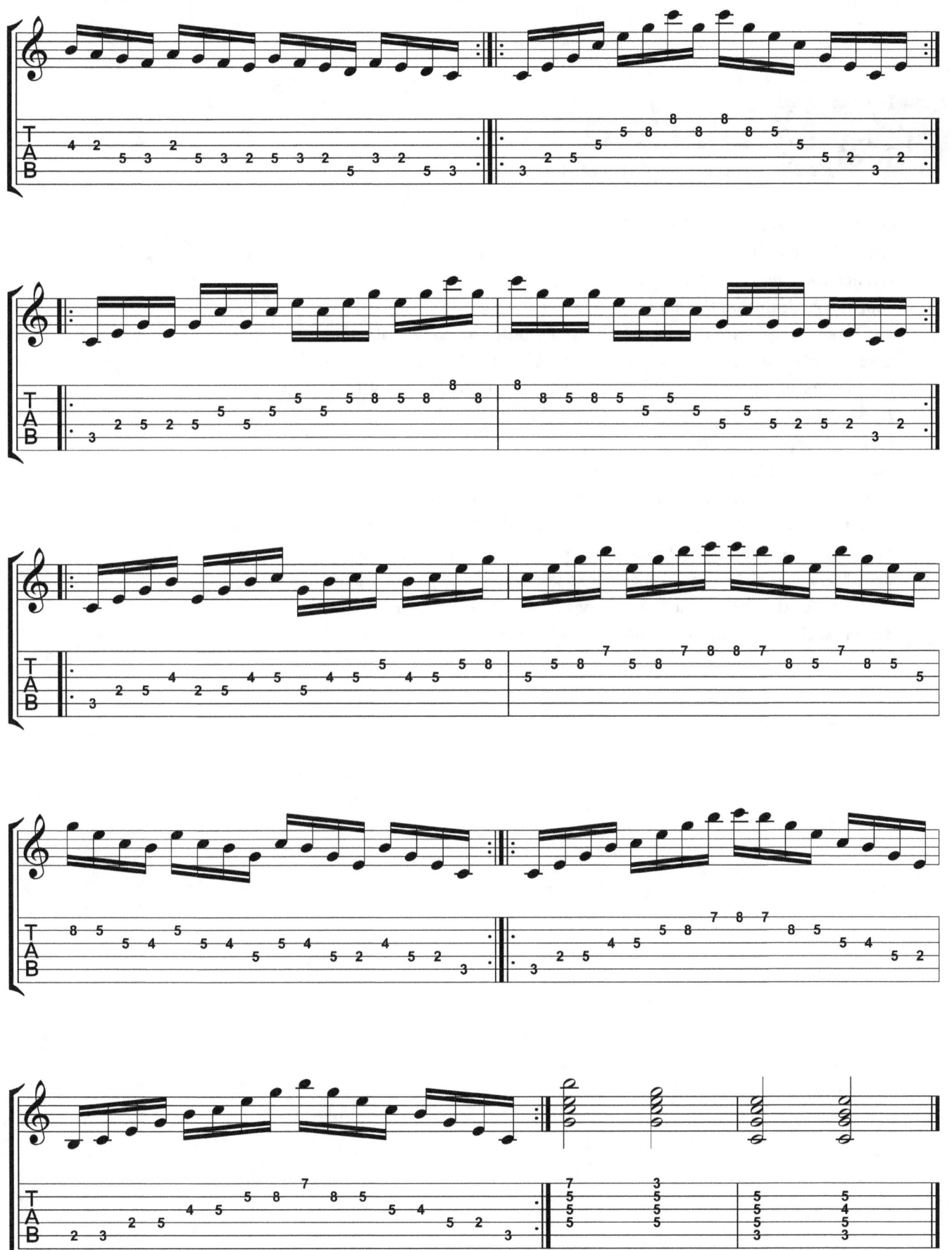

Chapter 4 the modes of the major scale - ionian

Dorian
2nd mode of the Major scale

General formula: W-H-W-W-W-H-W
Scale: Minor with a major sixth
Tetrachords: minor - minor
Characteristic note of the mode: the major 6
The intervals that are formed between the tonic and each scale degree: I-II = 2, I-III = ♭3, I-IV = 4, I-V = 5, I-VI = 6, I-VII = ♭7
The diatonic half steps are found on the scale degrees II-III and VI-VII
Triad: Minor ii-
Seventh chord: Minor 7th ii-7
Extensions: 9, 11, 13
Generally: The Dorian mode is the second degree of the mother major. It is a minor scale because it has a minor third in its structure, but it has a major sixth as opposed to the minor scales which usually have a minor sixth. The major sixth gives it an edgier sound similar to the major tone color, and for that reason the Dorian mode is often called *jazzminor* and is the first choice to play over min6 and min7 chords.

Dorian shape 1

Tetrachords

Intervals

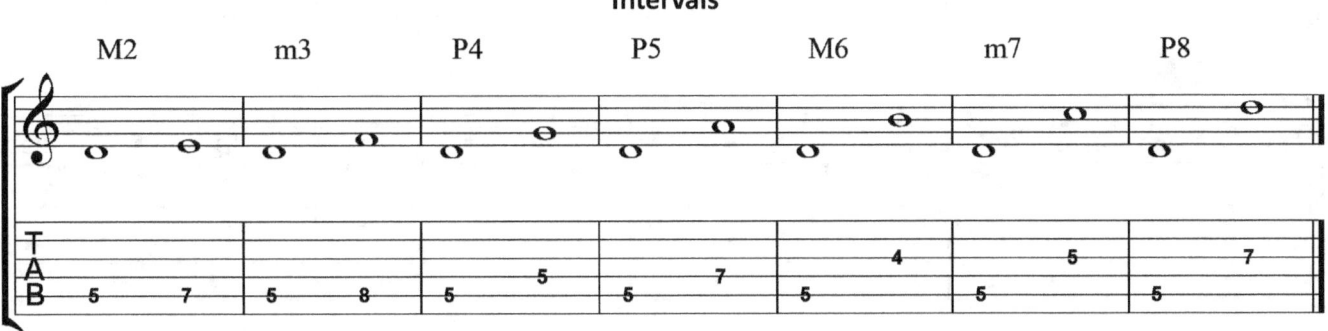

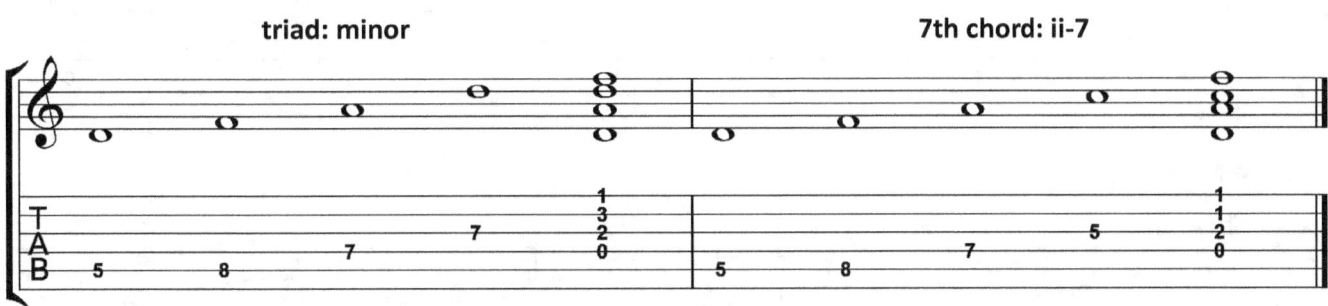

Chapter 4 the modes of the major scale - dorian

Dorian mode studies - shape 1

Mode exercises

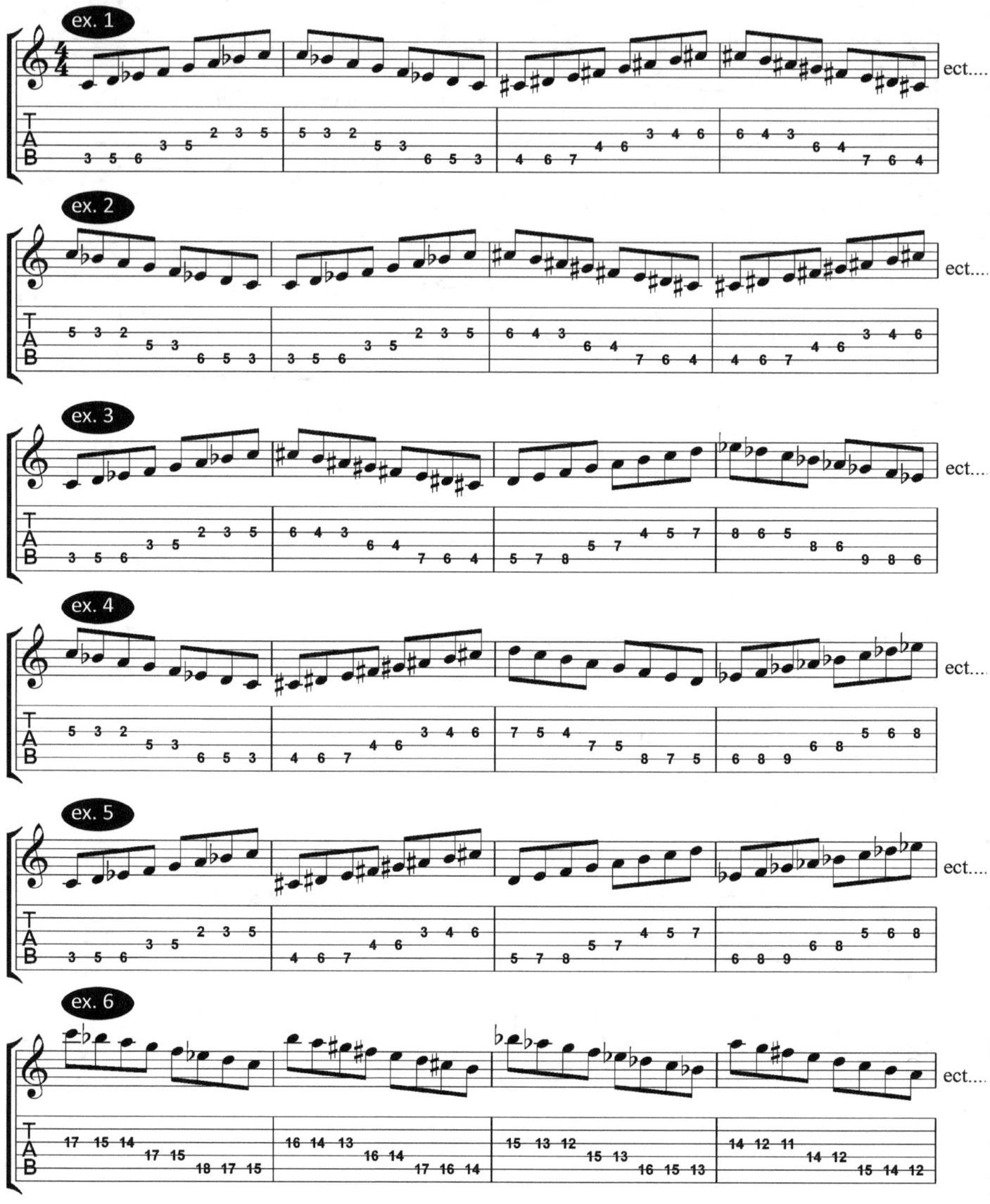

Melodic exercises

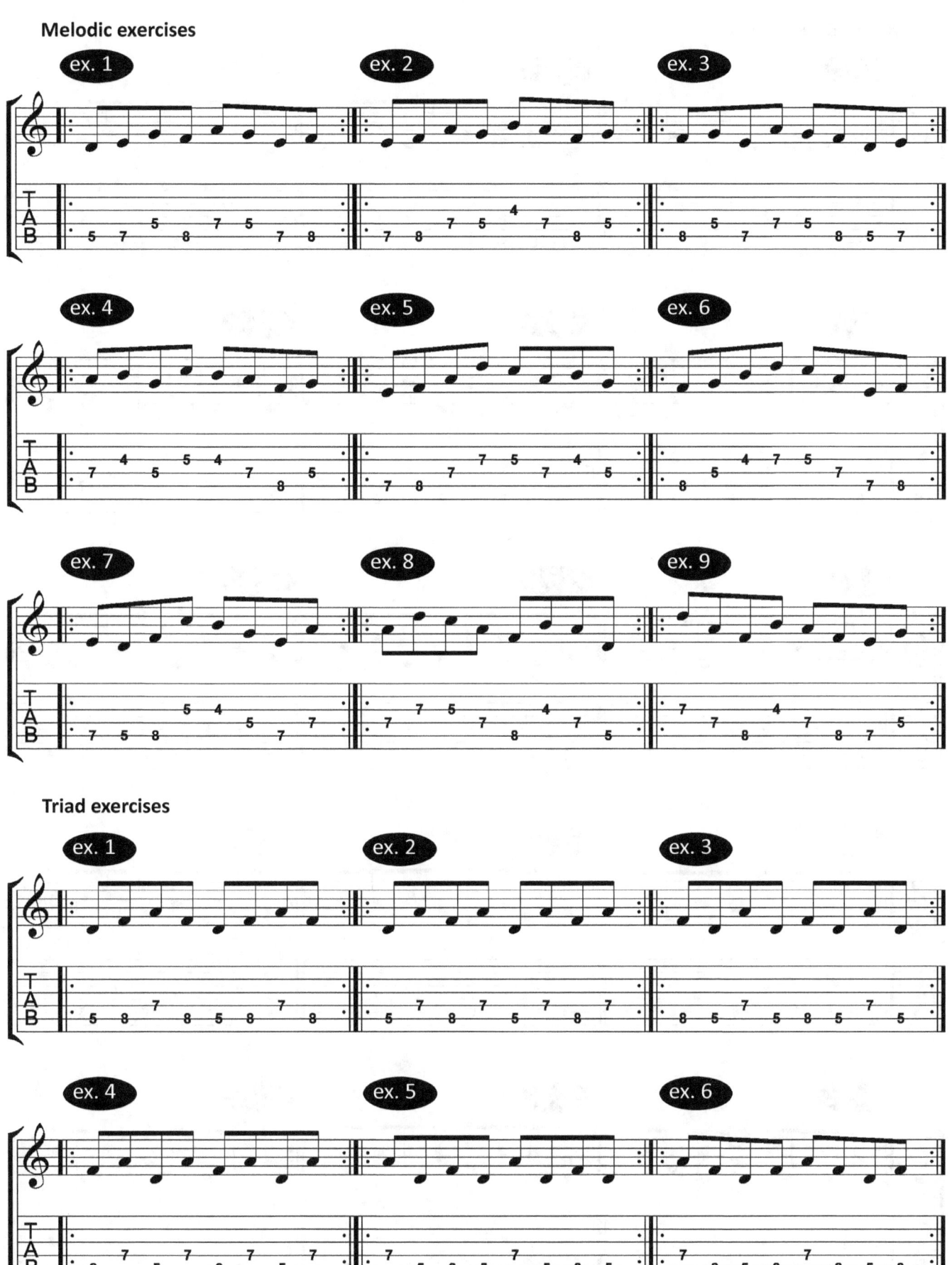

Triad exercises

Chapter 4   the modes of the major scale - dorian

7th chord exercises

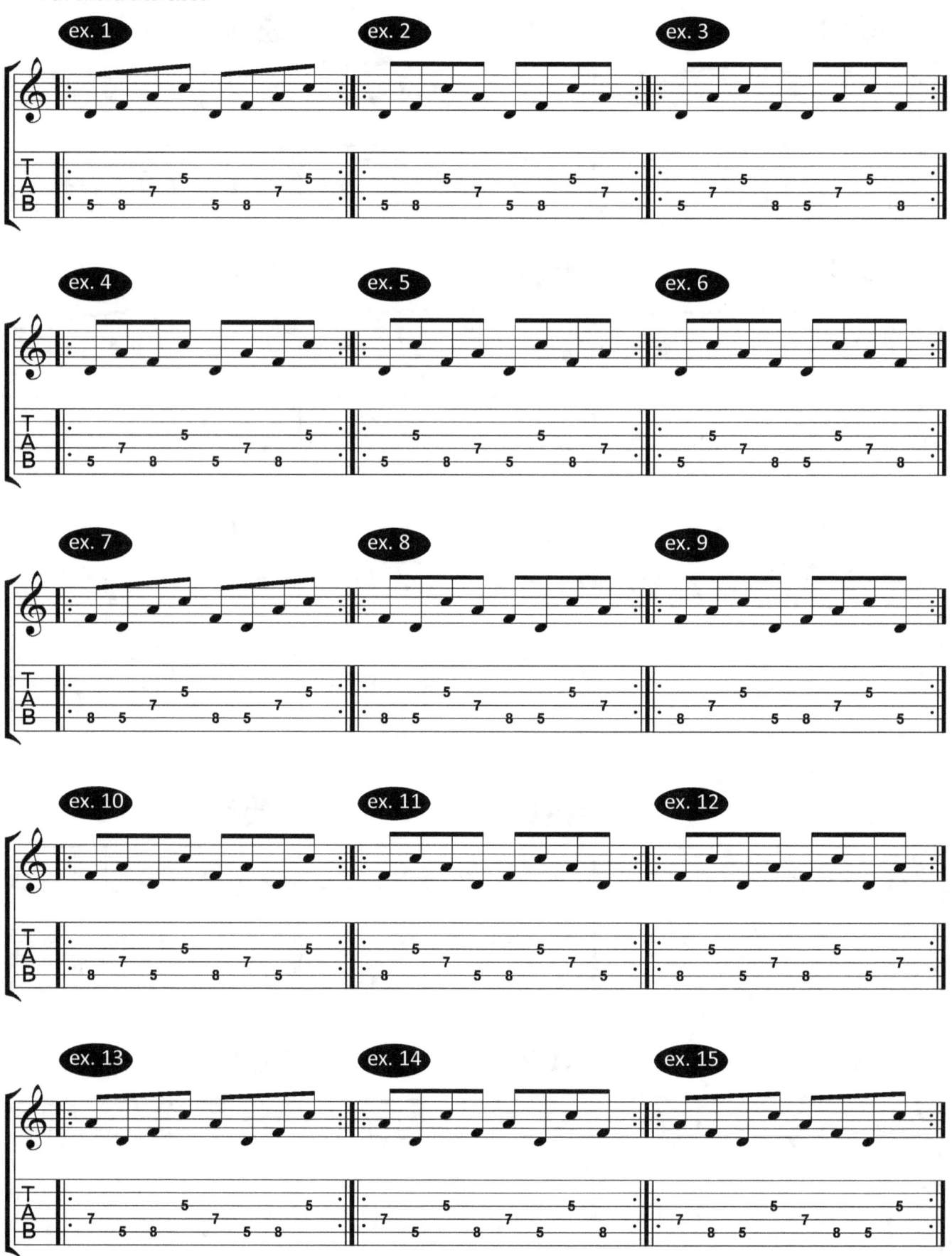

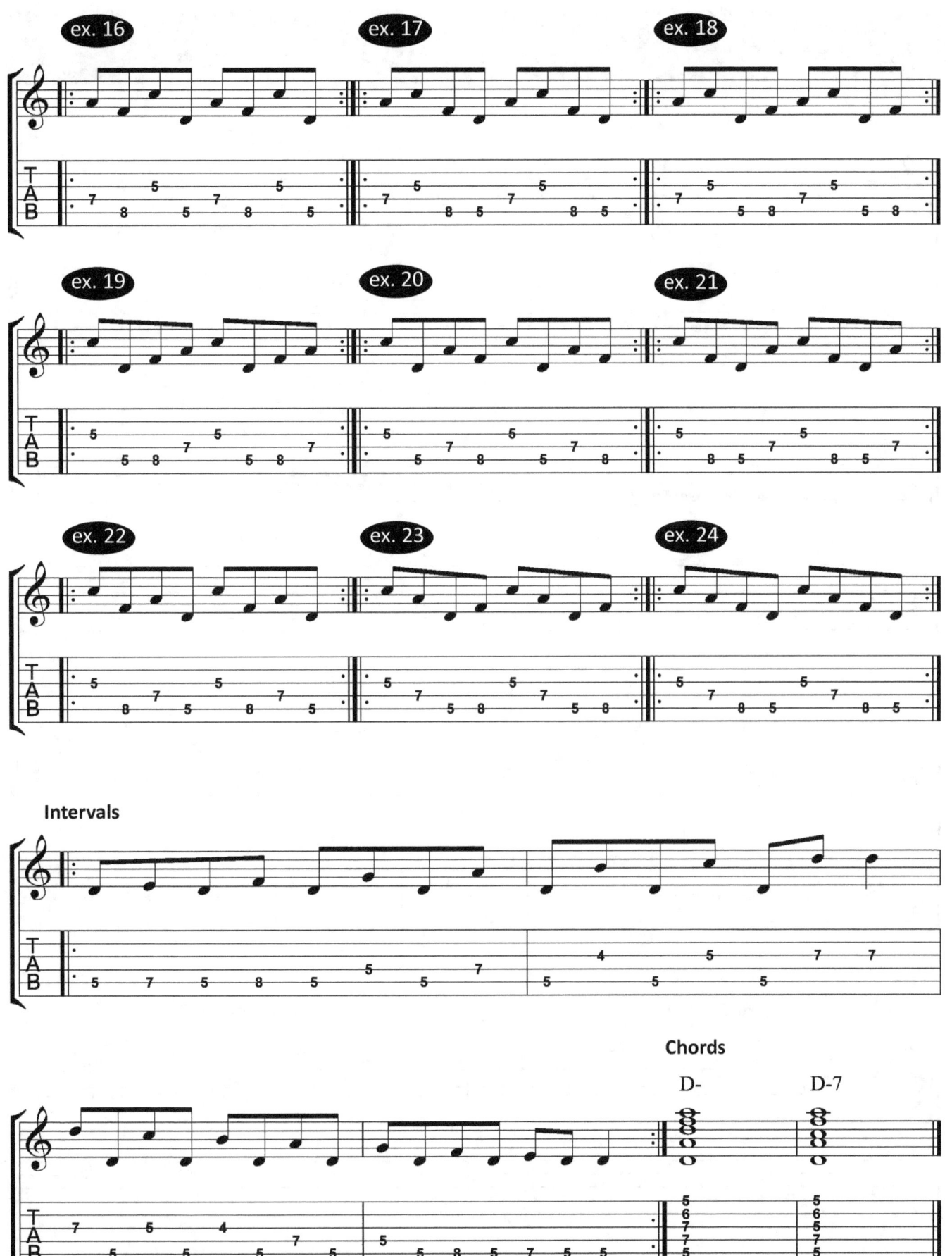

Chapter 4 the modes of the major scale - dorian

Dorian shape 2

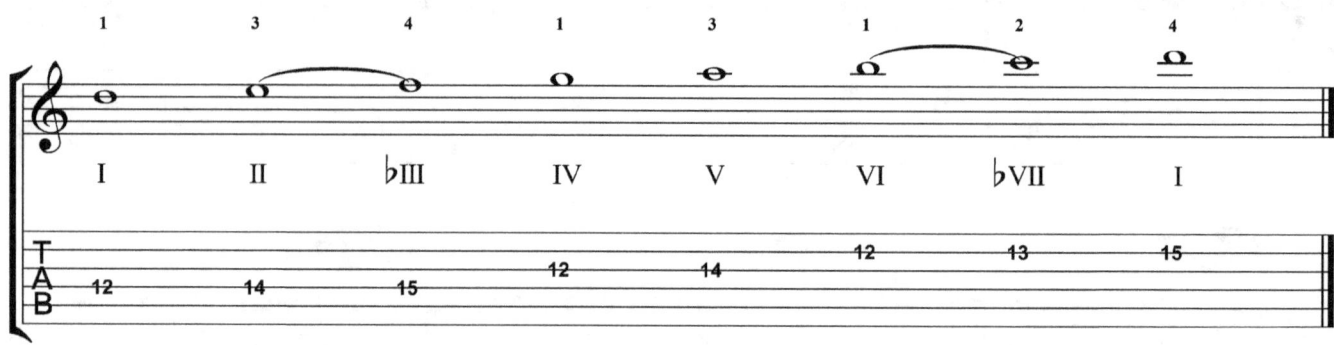

Tetrachords

Intervals

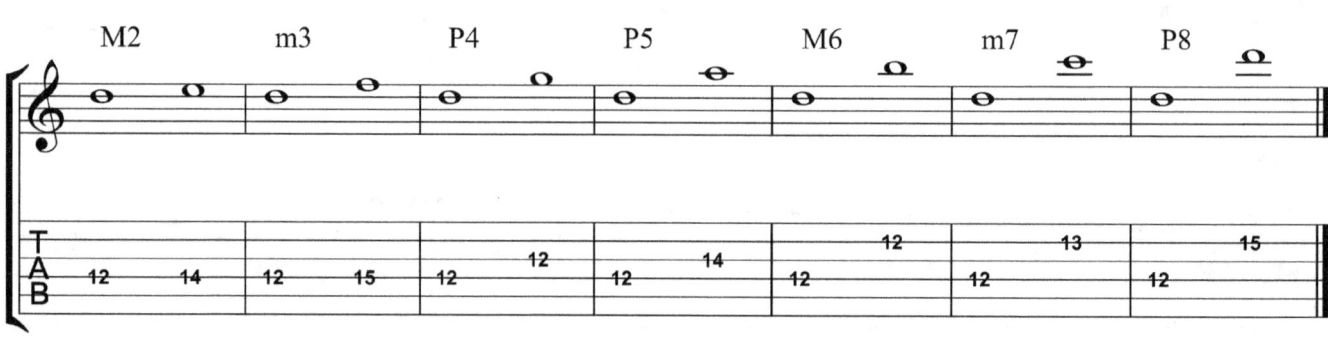

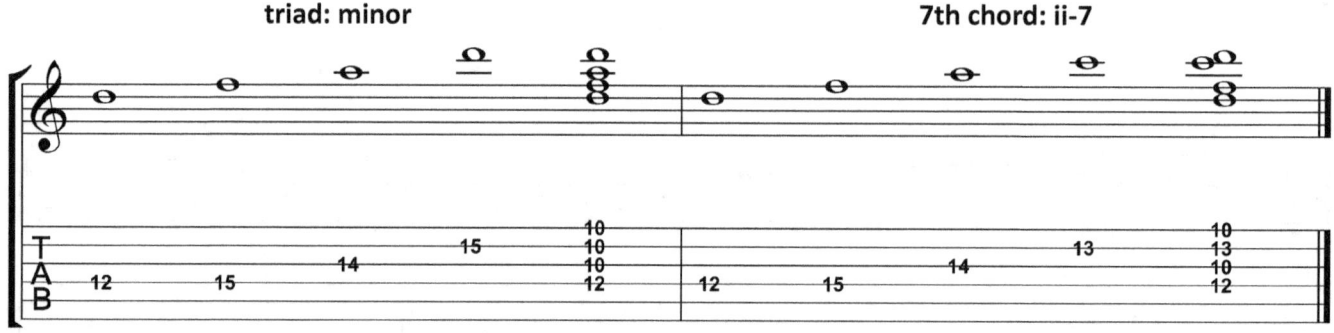

Dorian mode studies - shape 2

Mode exercises

ex. 1

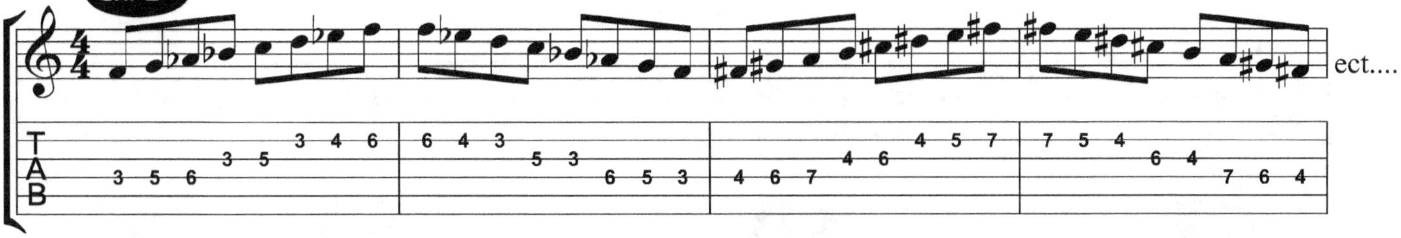

ex. 2

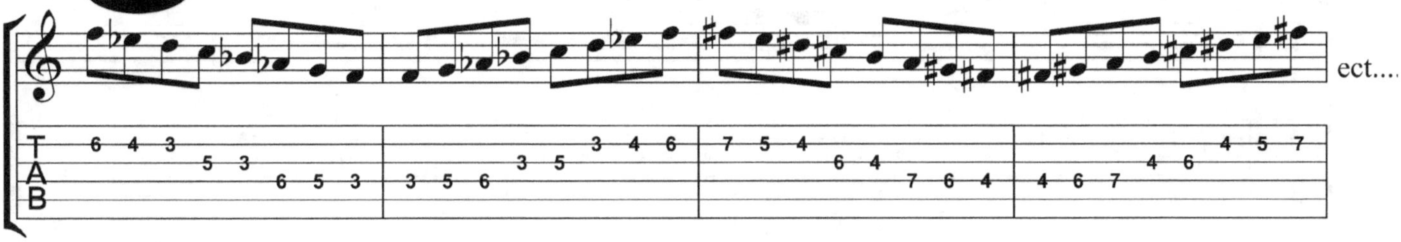

ex. 3

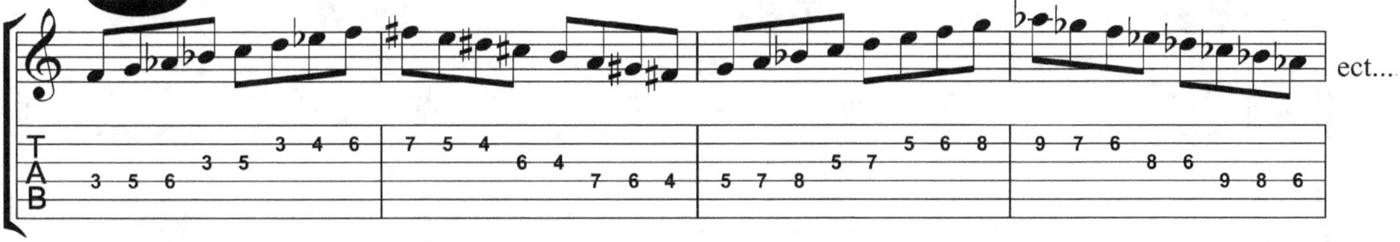

ex. 4

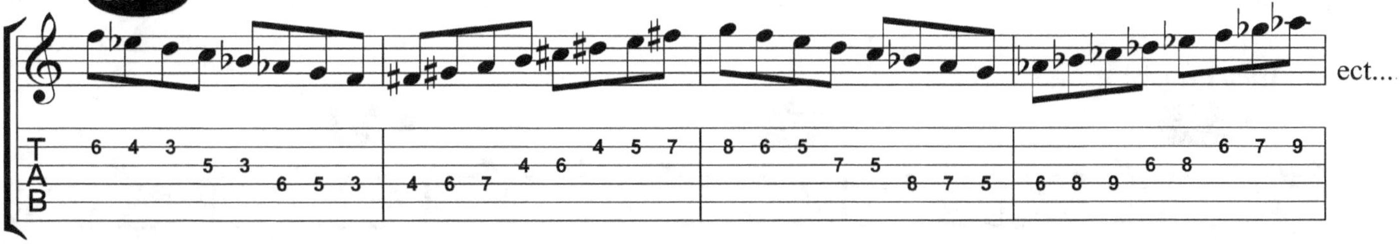

ex. 5

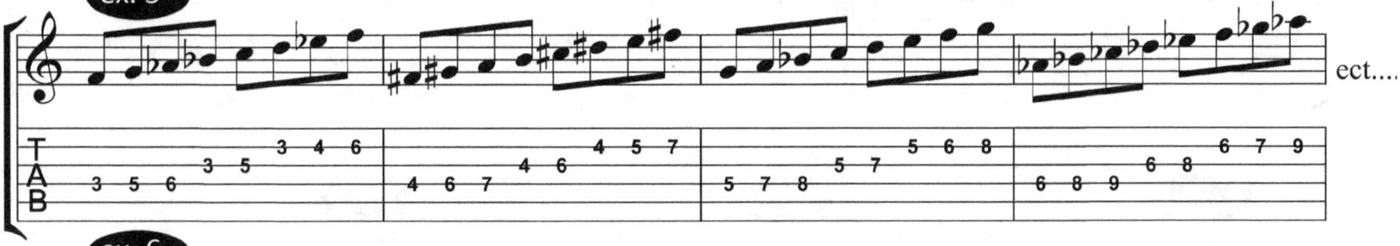

ex. 6

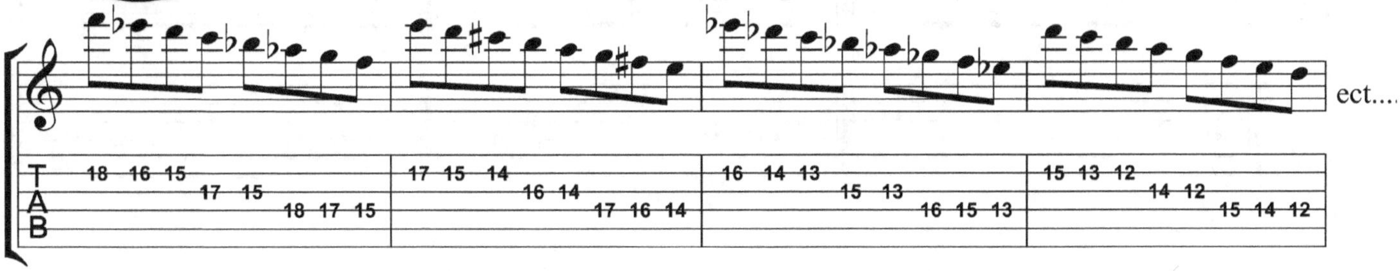

Melodic exercises

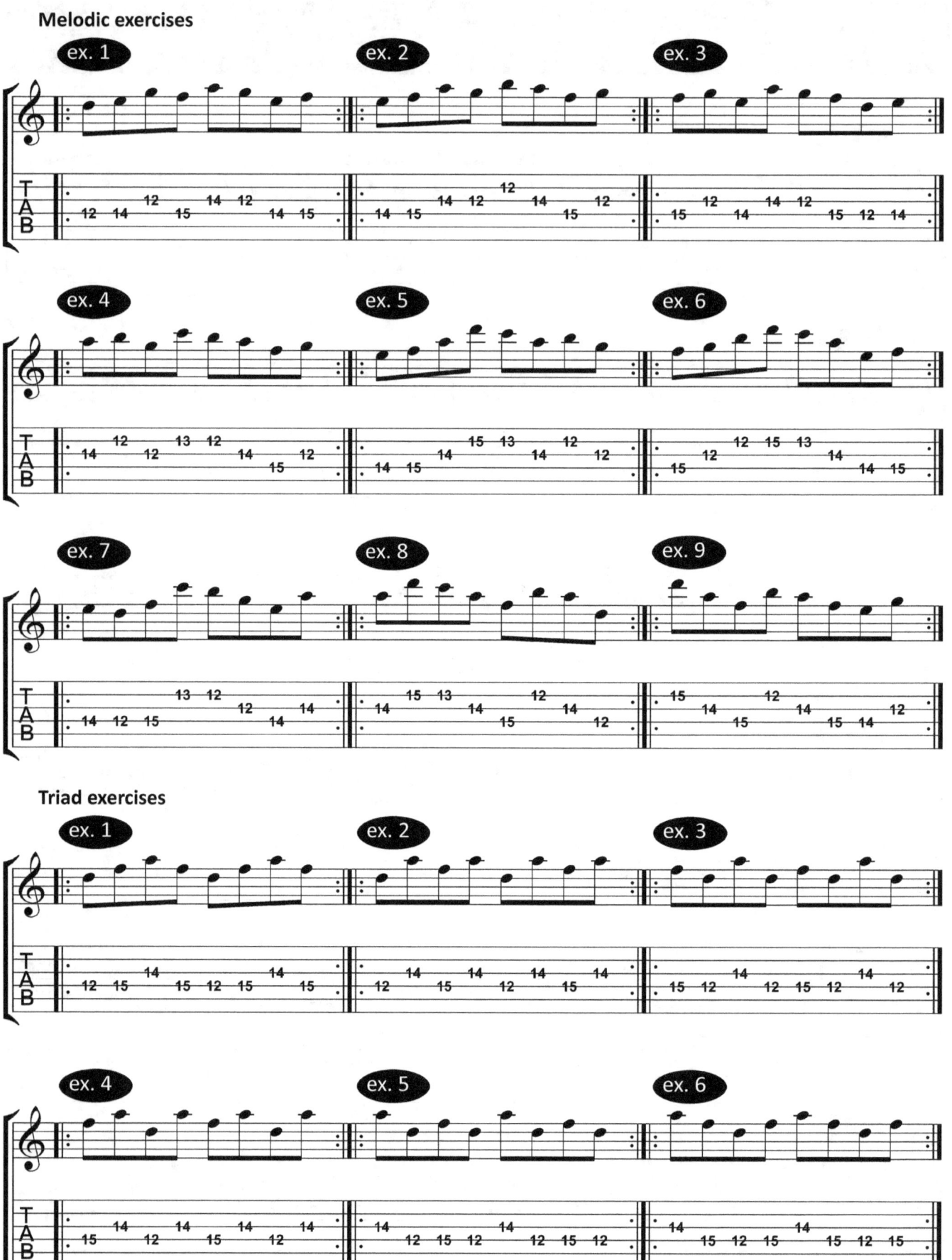

Triad exercises

7th chord exercises

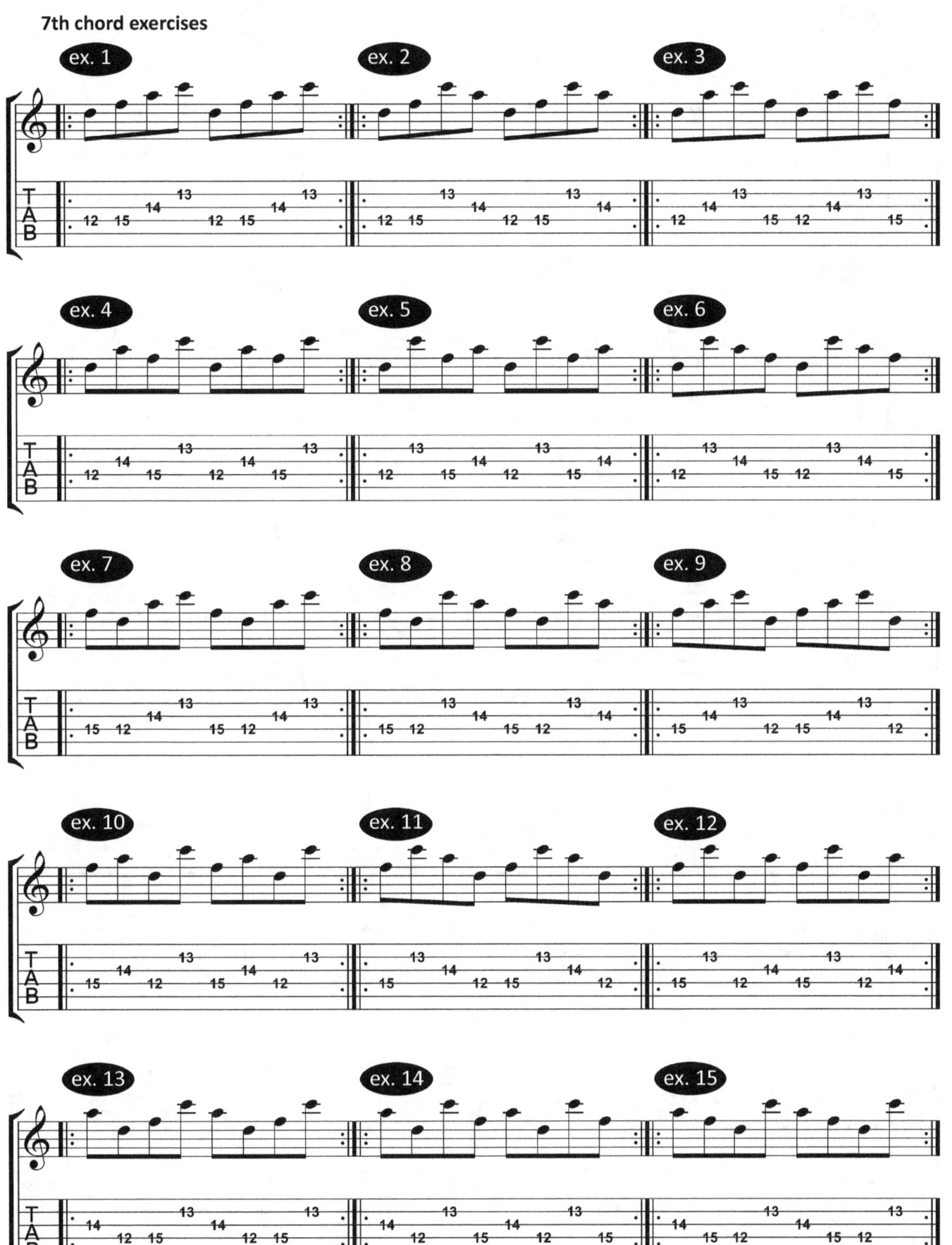

Chapter 4   the modes of the major scale - dorian

67

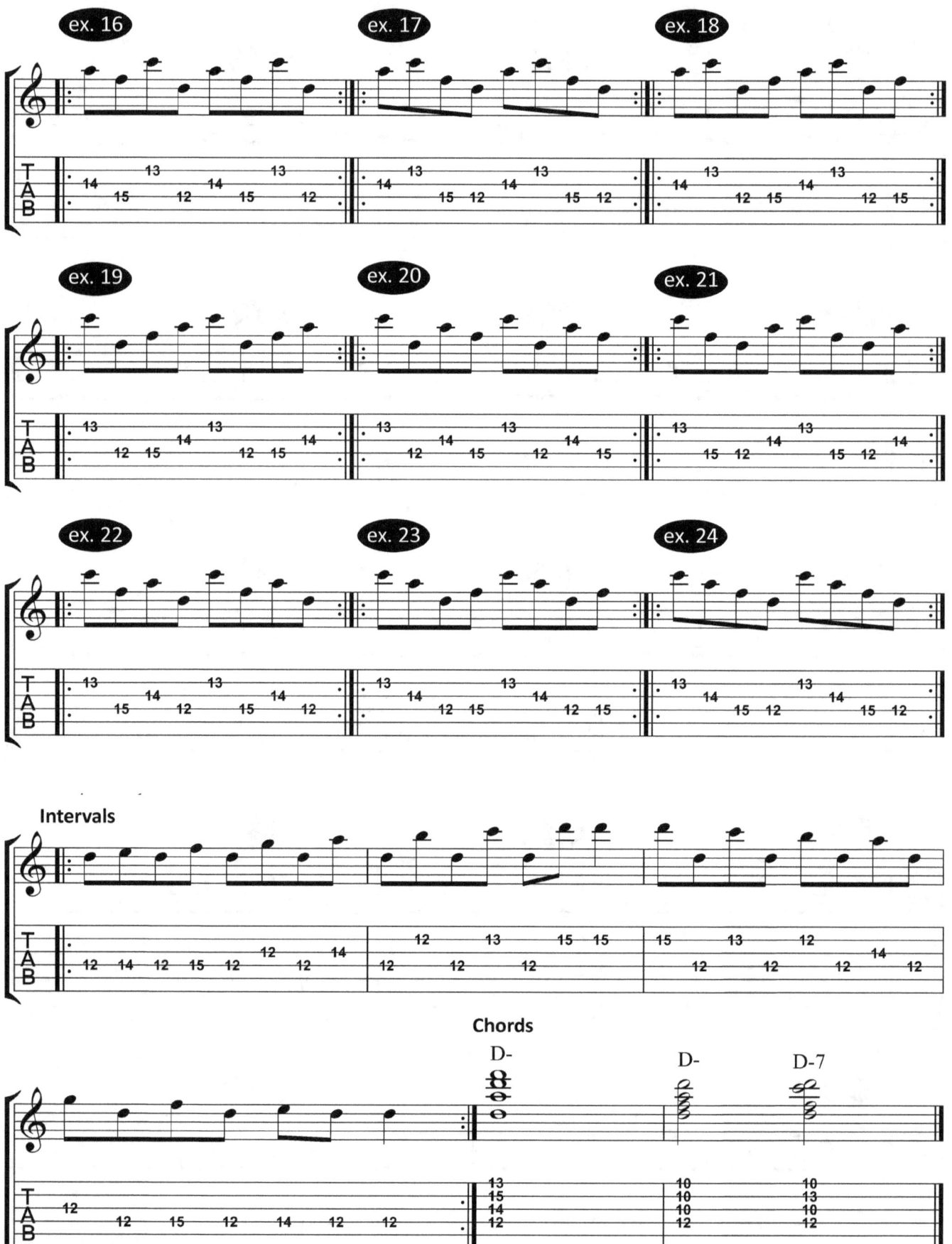

Dorian shape 3

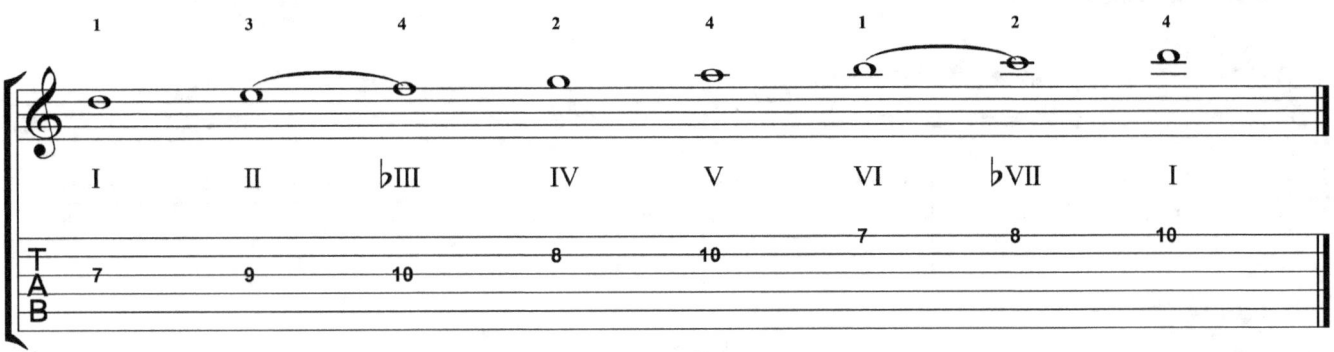

Tetrachords

minor (shape 3)   minor

Intervals

triad: major   7th chord: Imaj7

Chapter 4   the modes of the major scale - dorian

Dorian mode studies - shape 3

Mode exercises

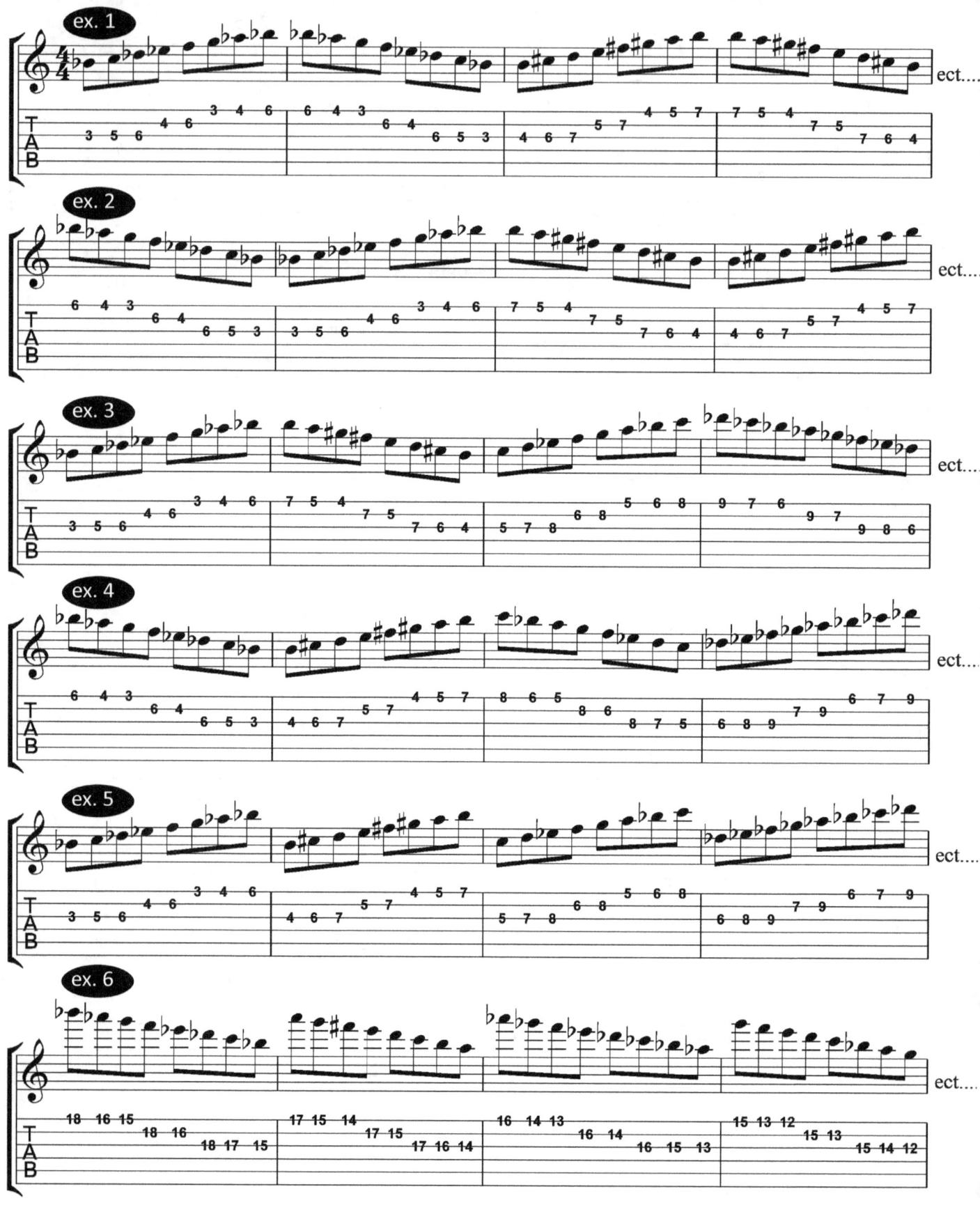

Melodic exercises

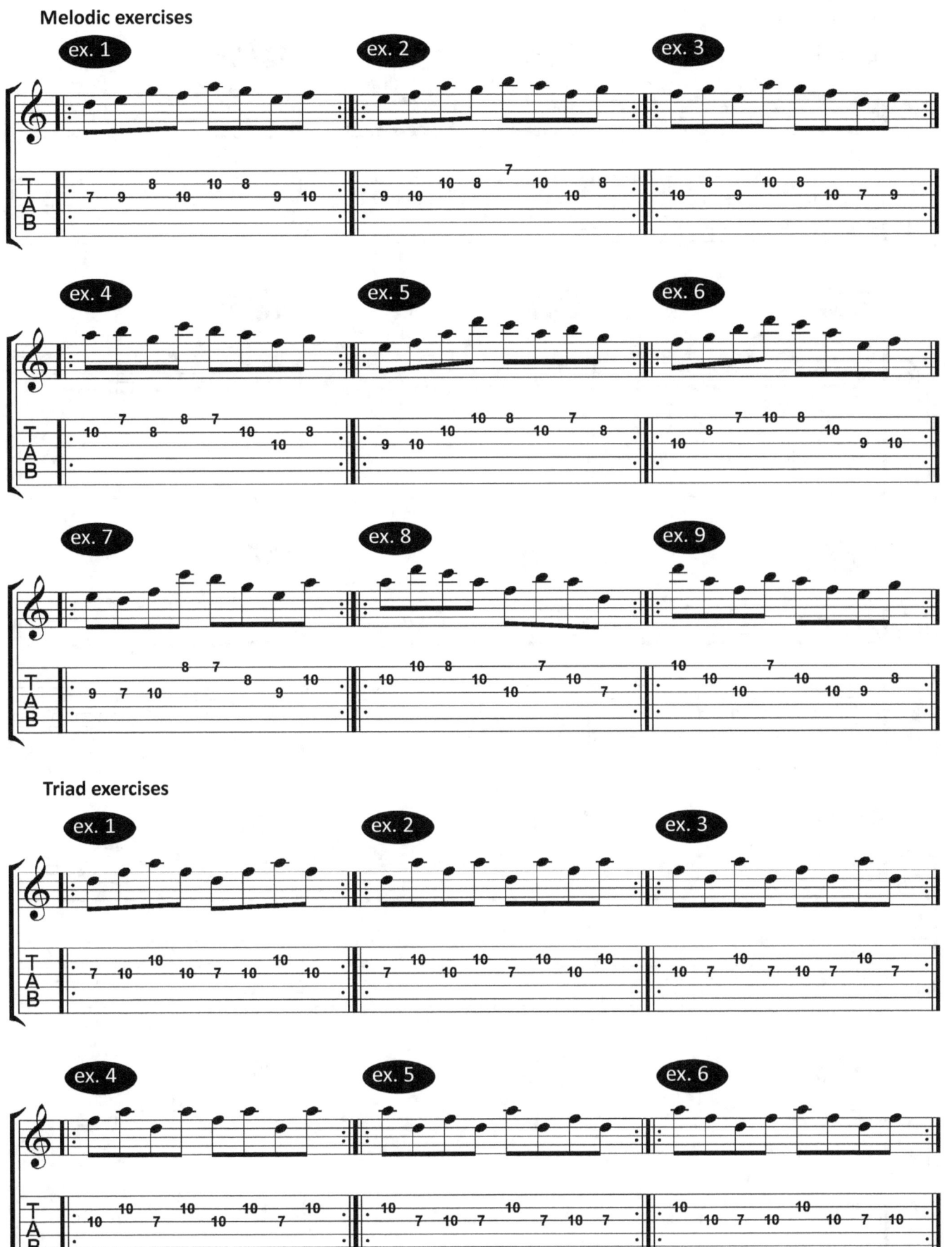

Triad exercises

Chapter 4   the modes of the major scale - dorian

7th chord exercises

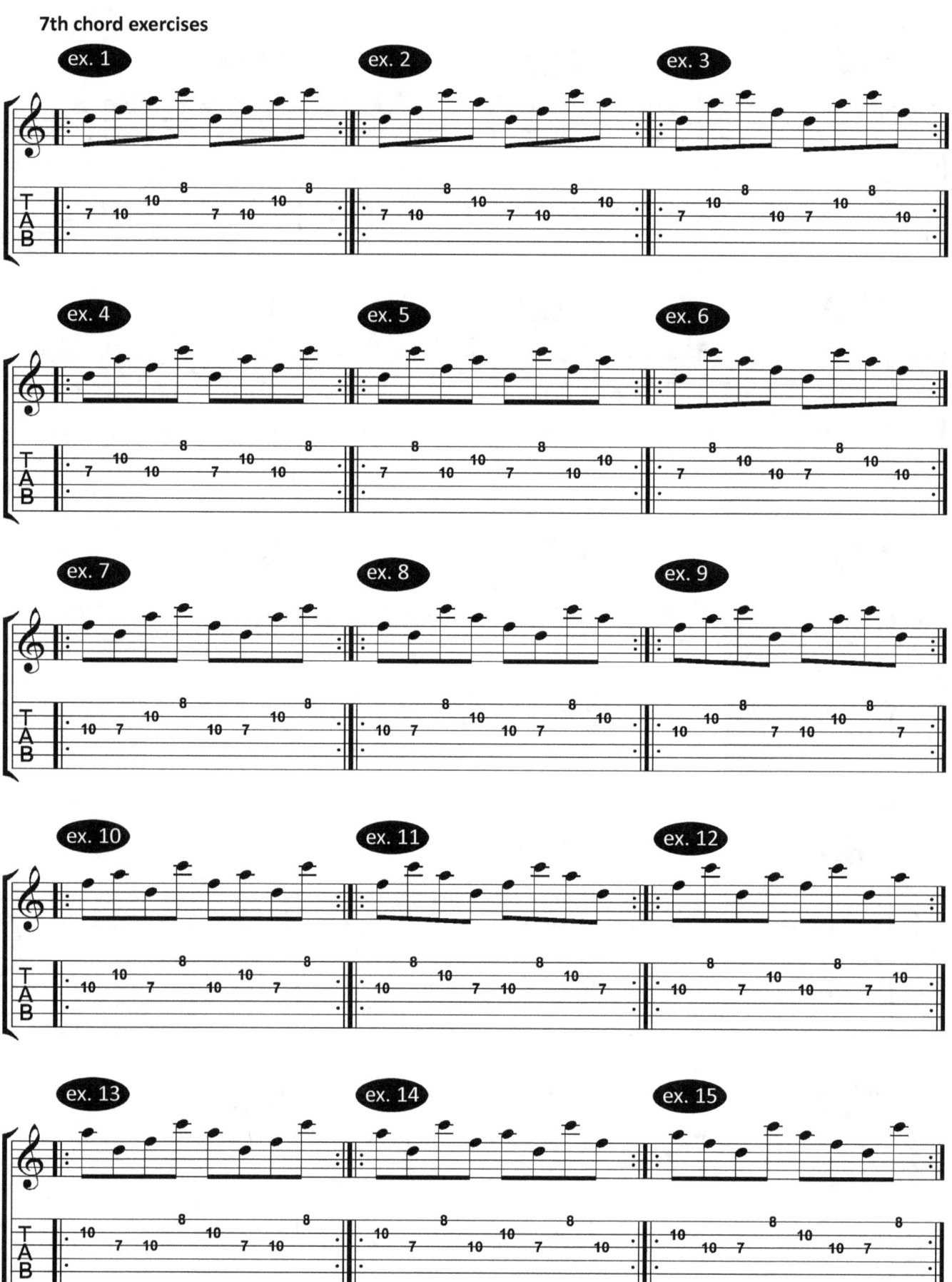

72   The complete guitar book 1

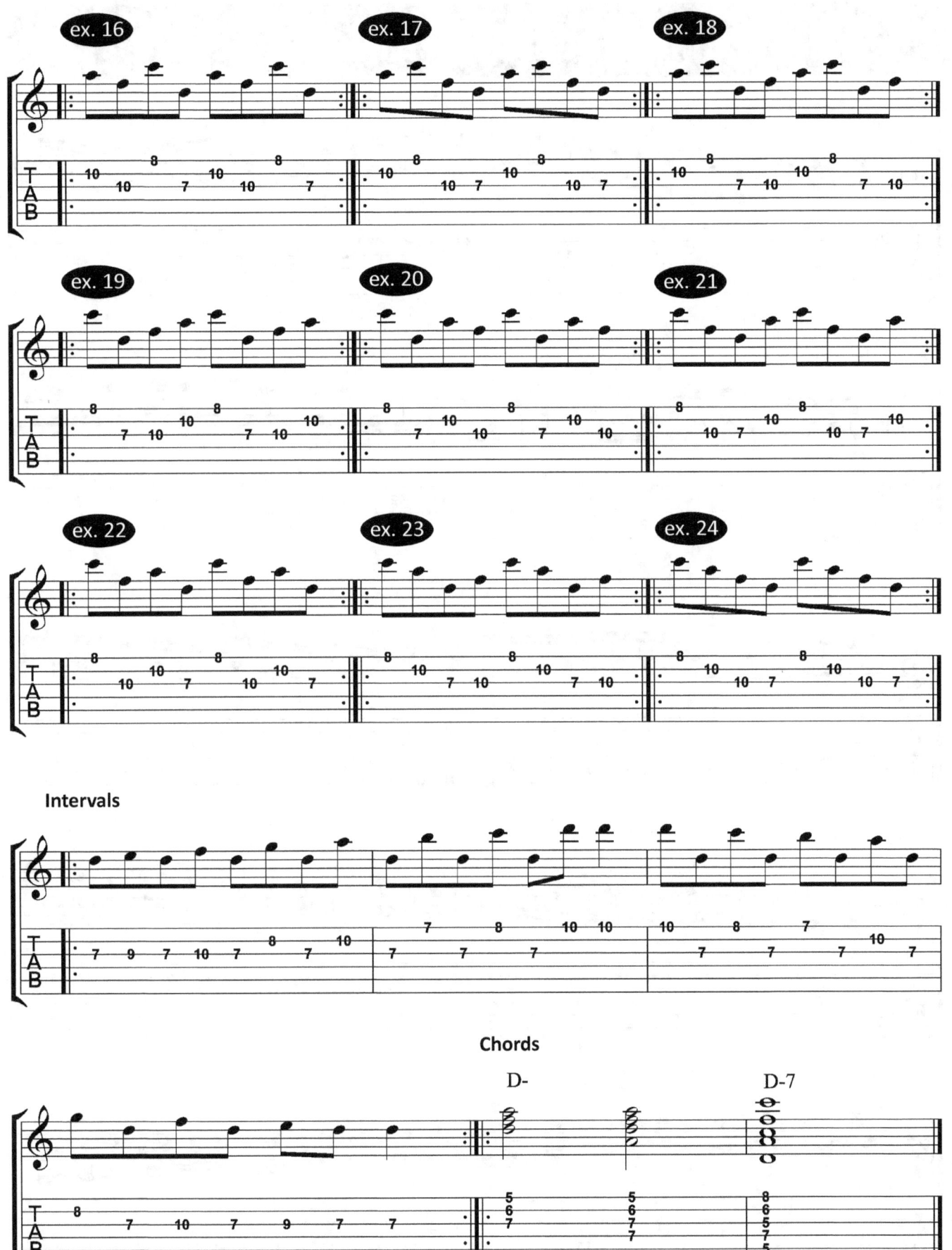

Chapter 4   the modes of the major scale - dorian

Dorian in 2 octaves with shapes 1 + 2

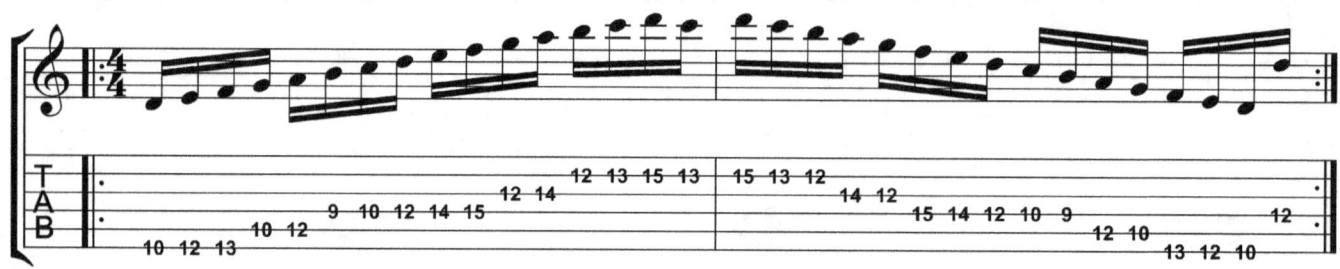

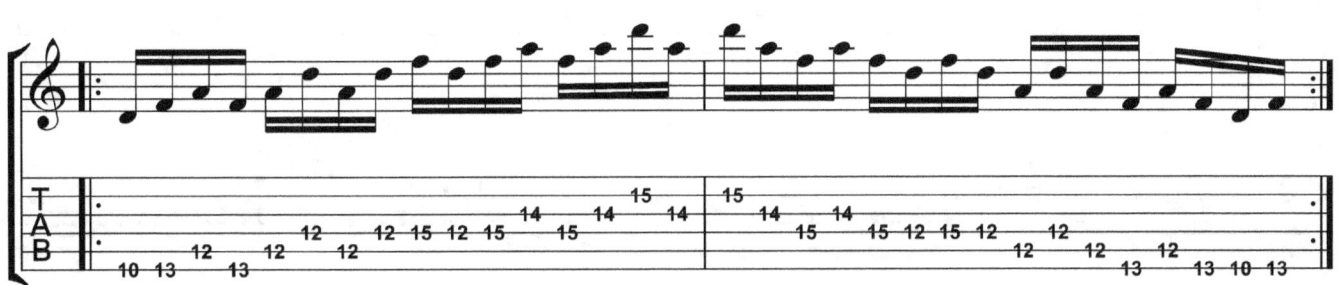
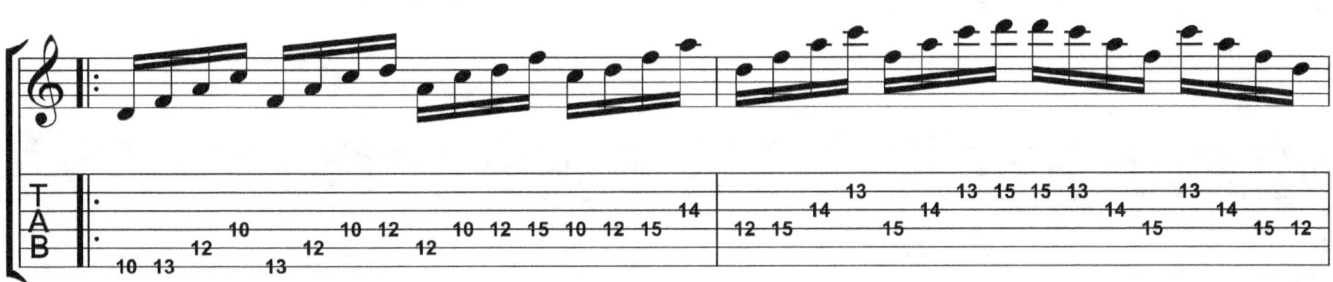

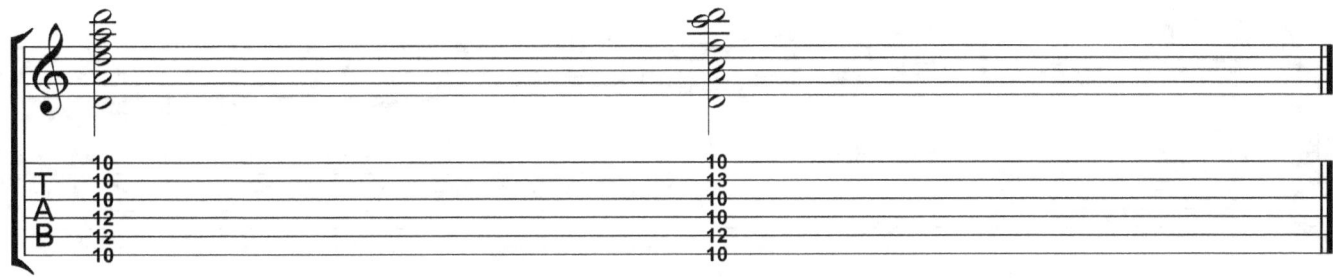

Chapter 4 the modes of the major scale - dorian

Dorian in 2 octaves with shapes 1 + 3

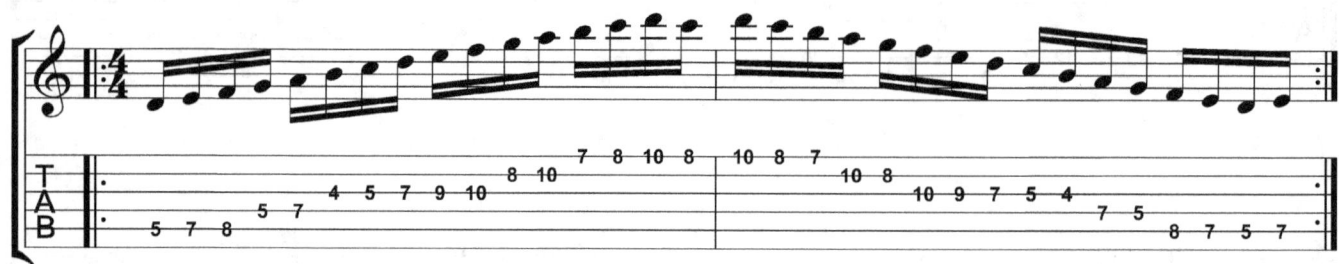

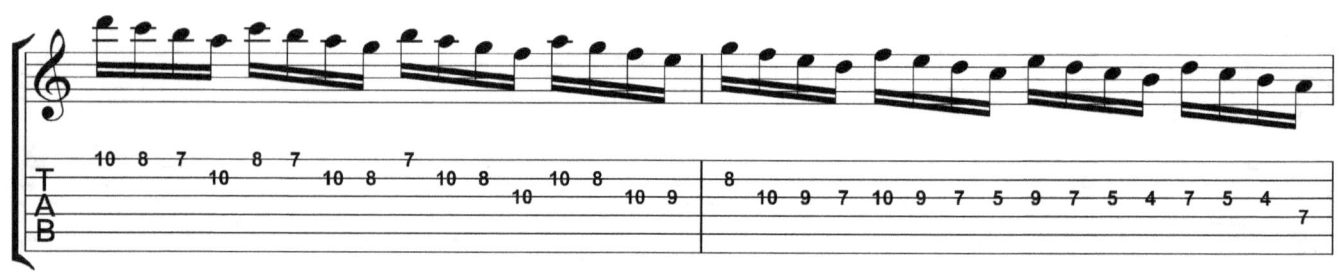

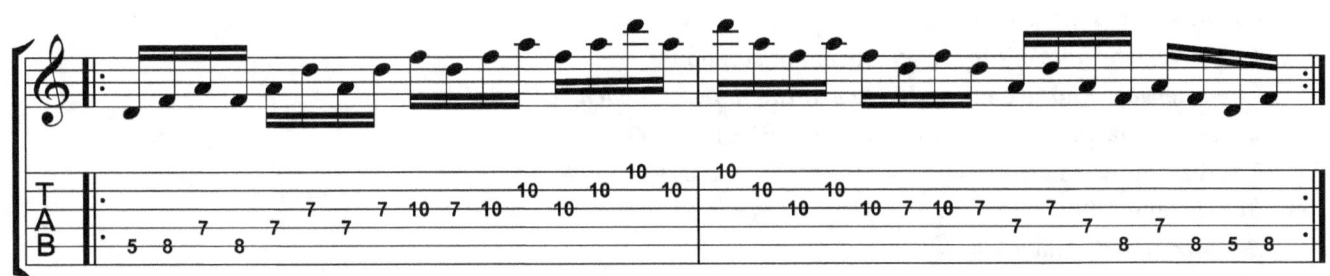
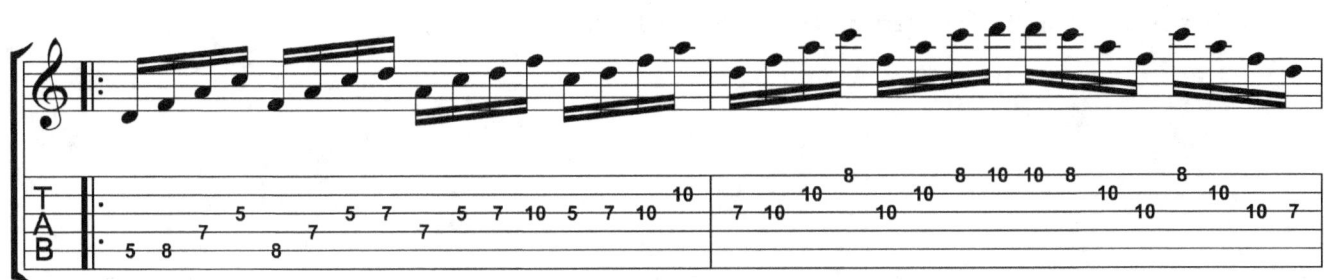

Chapter 4 the modes of the major scale - dorian

Phrygian
3rd mode of the Major scale

General formula: H-W-W-W-H-W-W

Scale: Minor seventh with a minor second

Tetrachords: Phrygian - Phrygian

Characteristic note of the mode: the minor second ♭2

The intervals that are formed between the tonic and each scale degree: I-II = ♭2, I-III = ♭3, I-IV = 4, I-V = 5, I-VI = ♭6, I-VII = ♭7

The diatonic half steps are found on the scale degrees I-II and V-VII

Triad: Minor iii-

Seventh chord: Minor 7th iii-7

Extensions: 11

Generally: The Phrygian mode is also a minor scale because it contains a minor third, but the note that distinguishes it is its minor second. This scale is used a lot in Middle Eastern music as well as in Greek music.

Phrygian shape 1

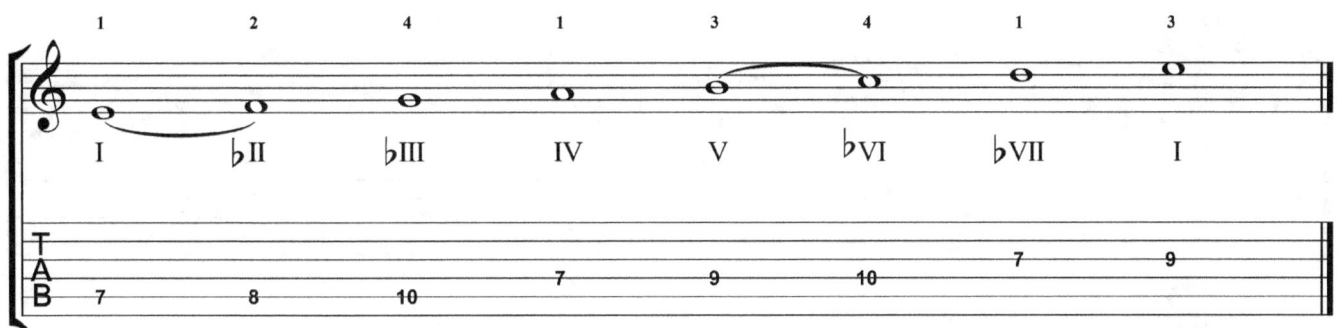

Tetrachords

Intervals

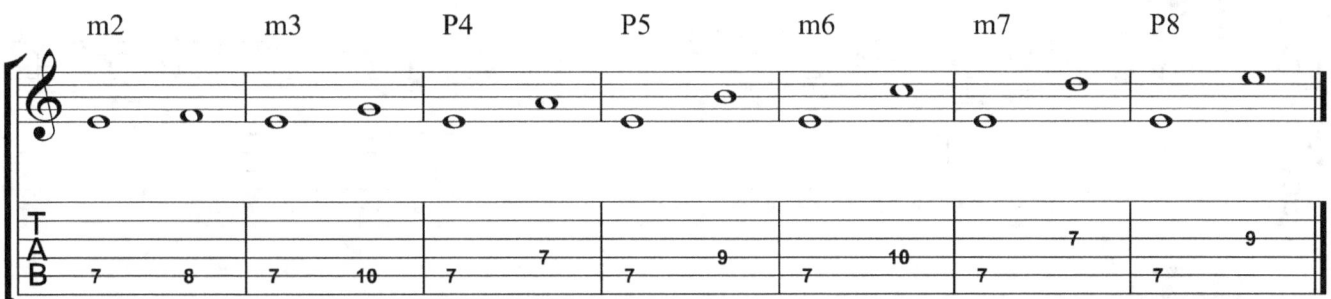

triad: minor **7th chord: iii-7**

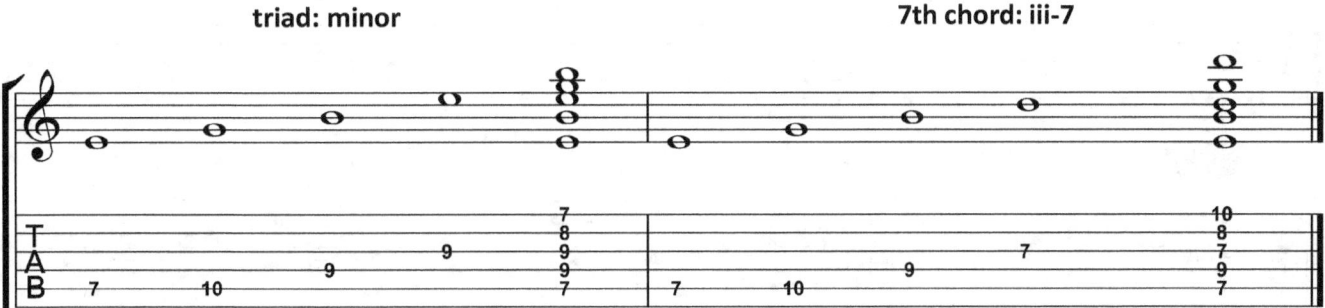

Chapter 4 the modes of the major scale - phrygian

Phrygian mode studies - shape 1

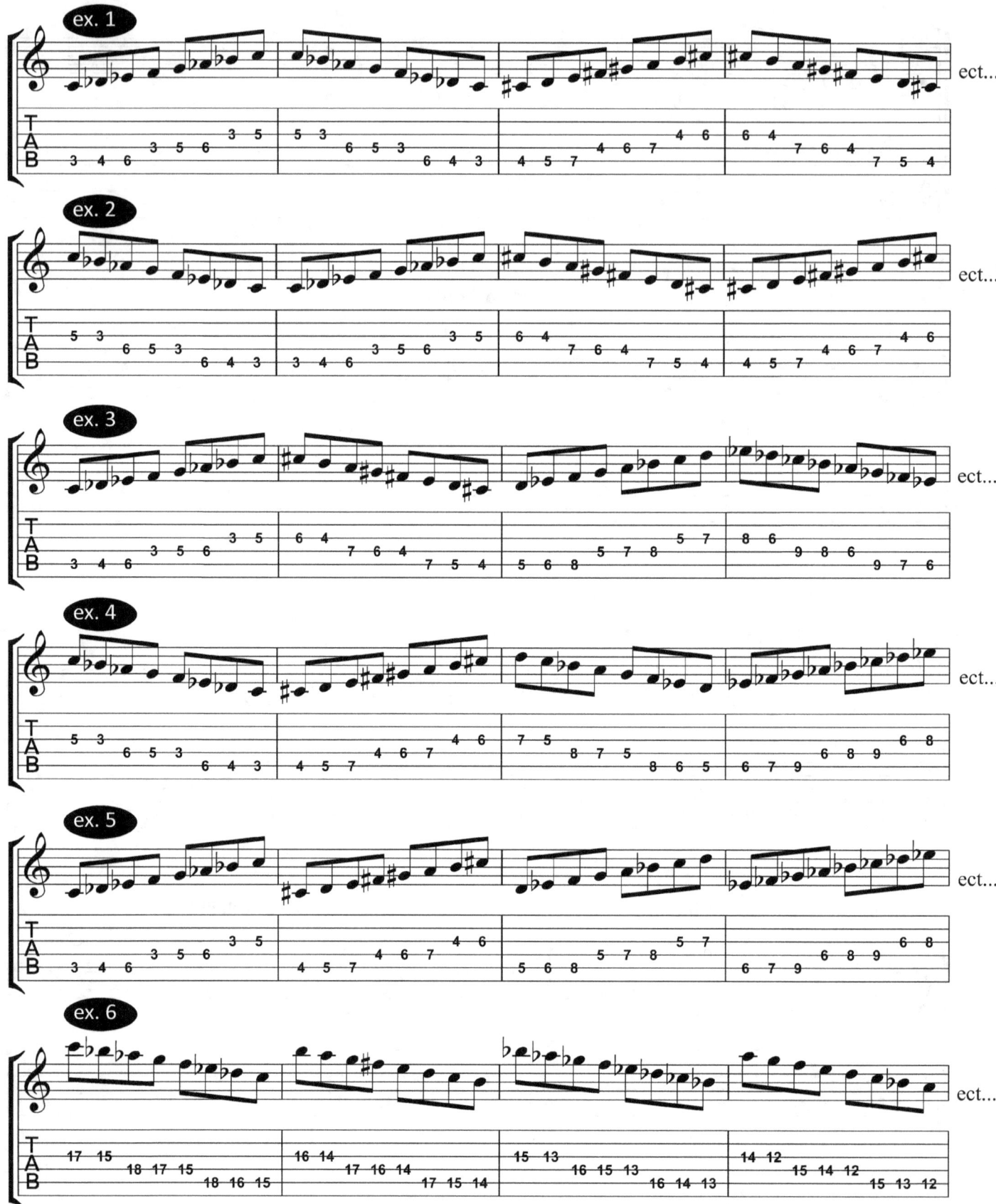

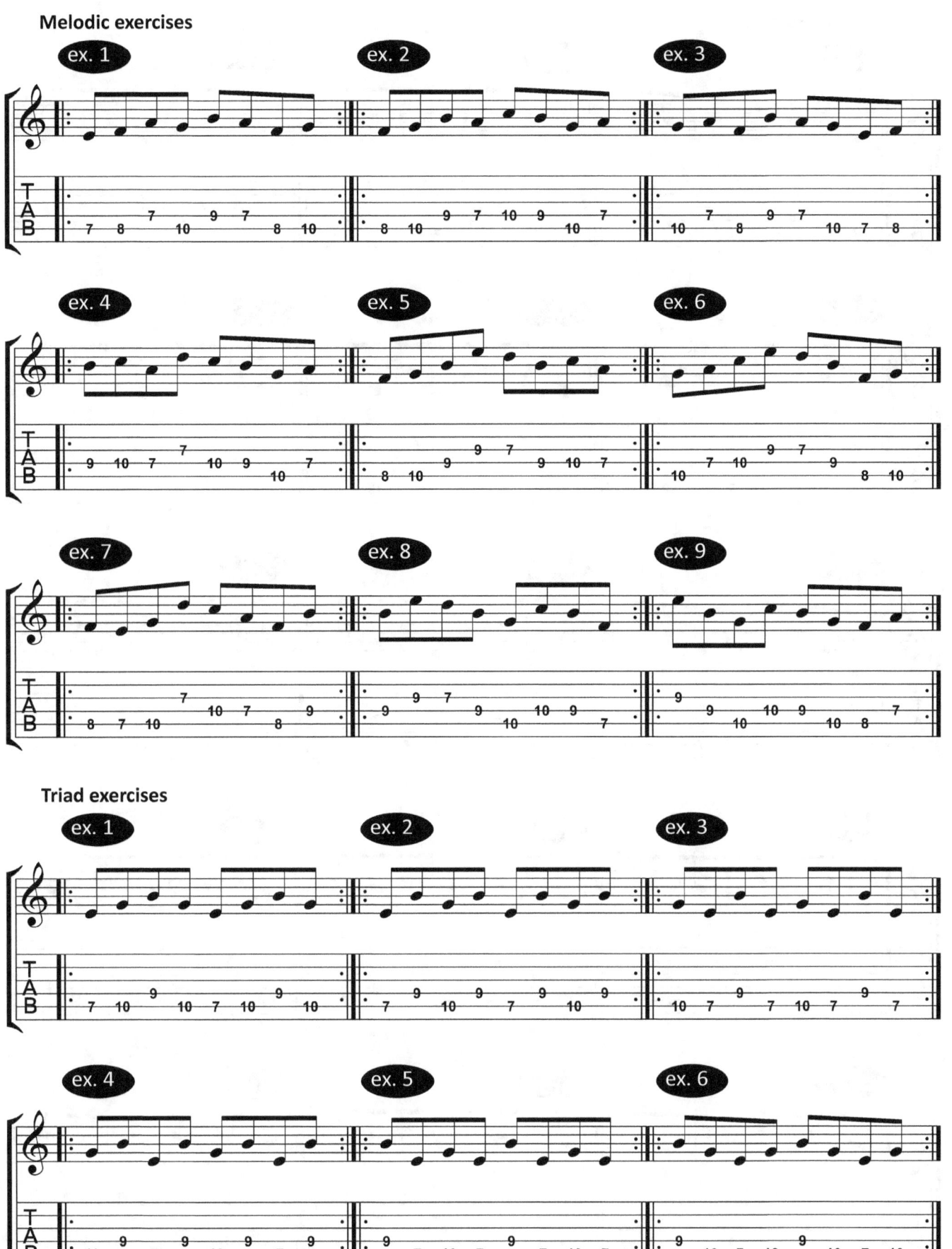

Chapter 4 the modes of the major scale - phrygian

7th chord exercises

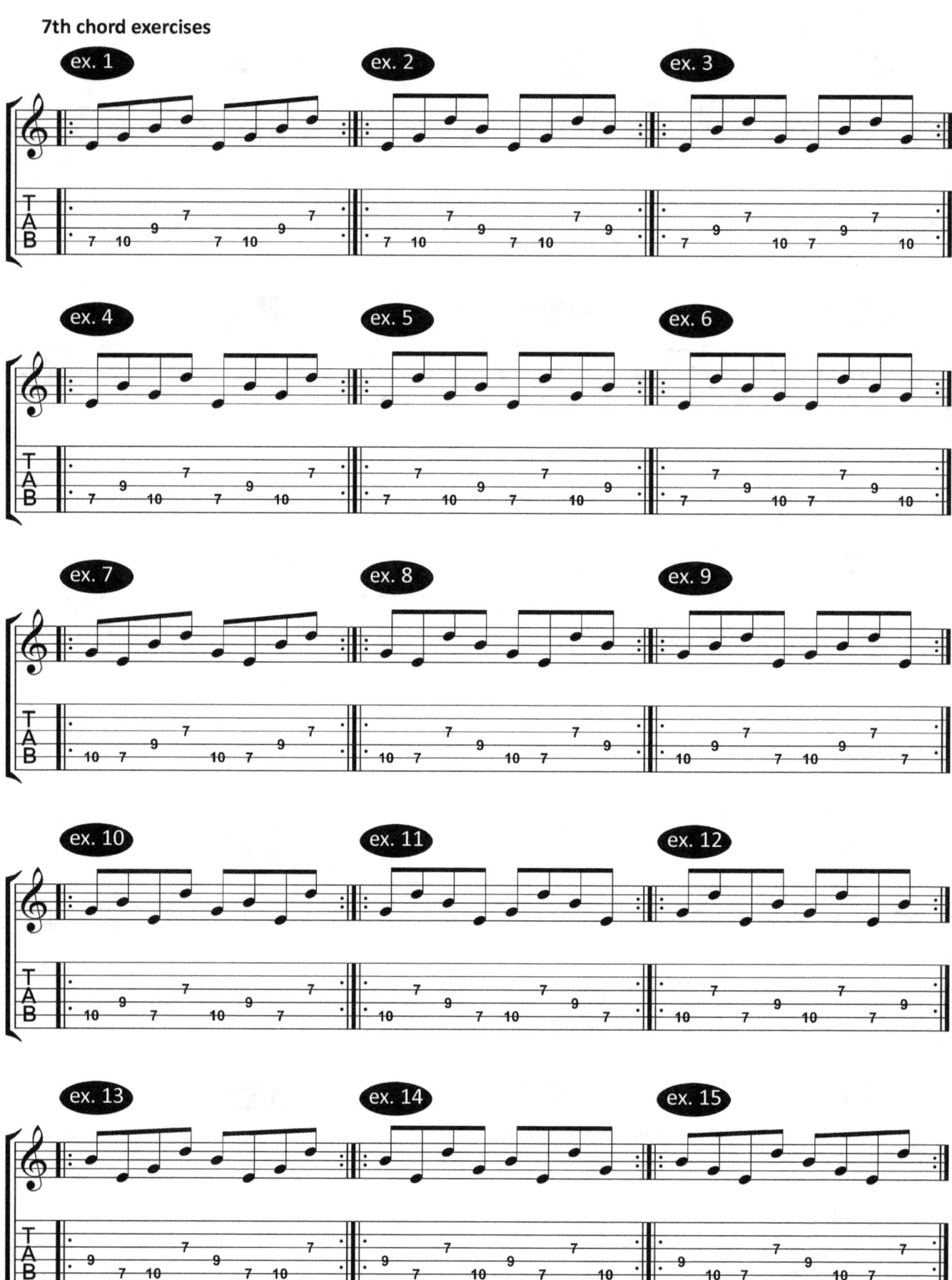

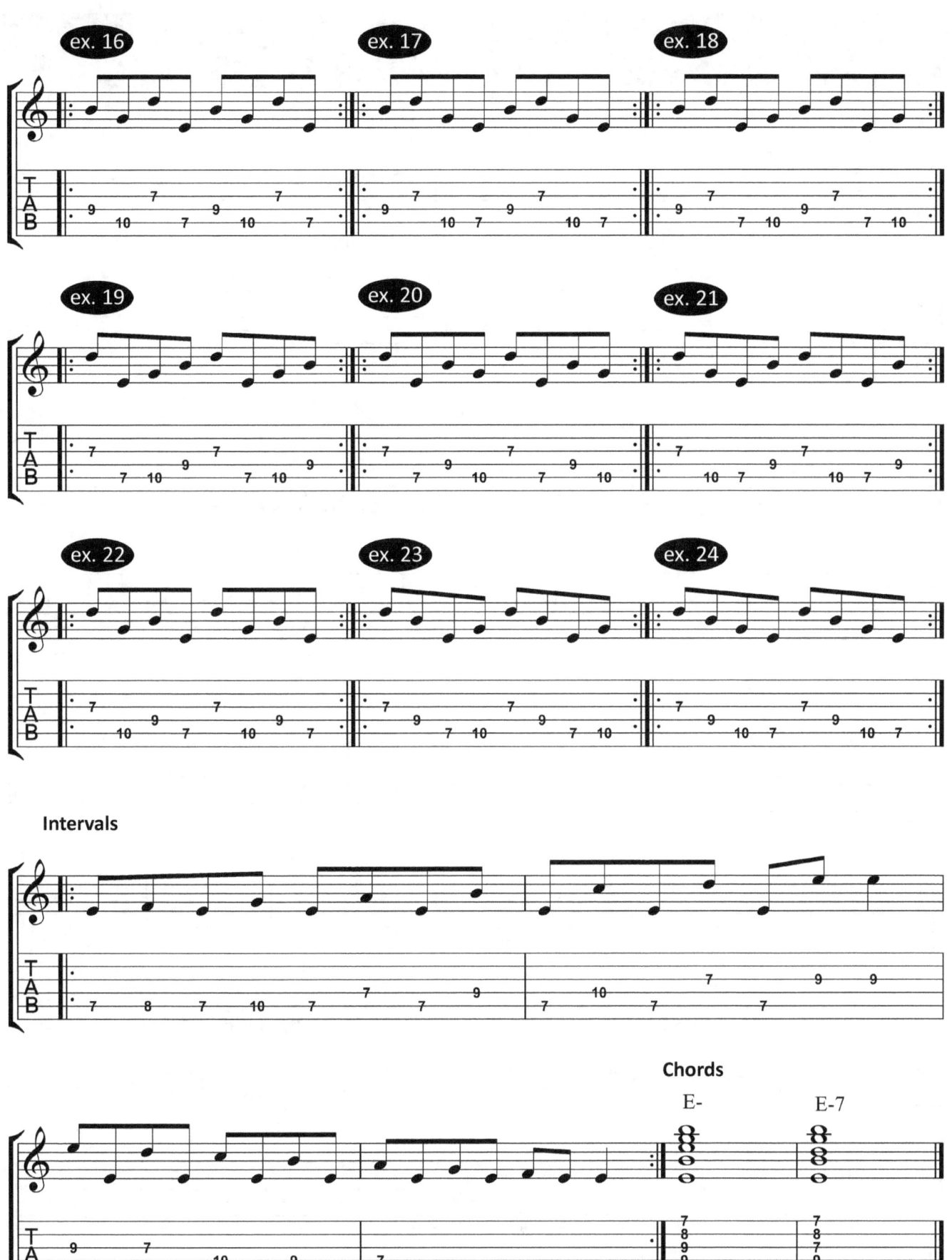

Chapter 4 the modes of the major scale - phrygian

Phrygian shape 2

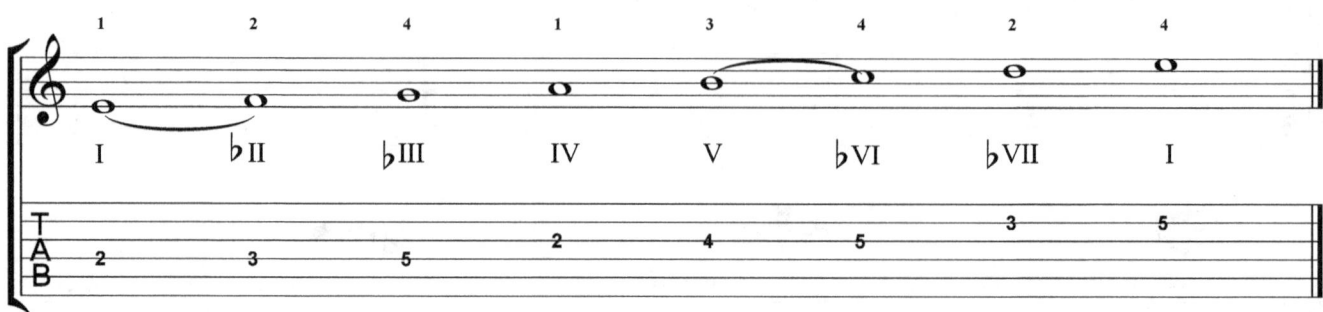

Tetrachords

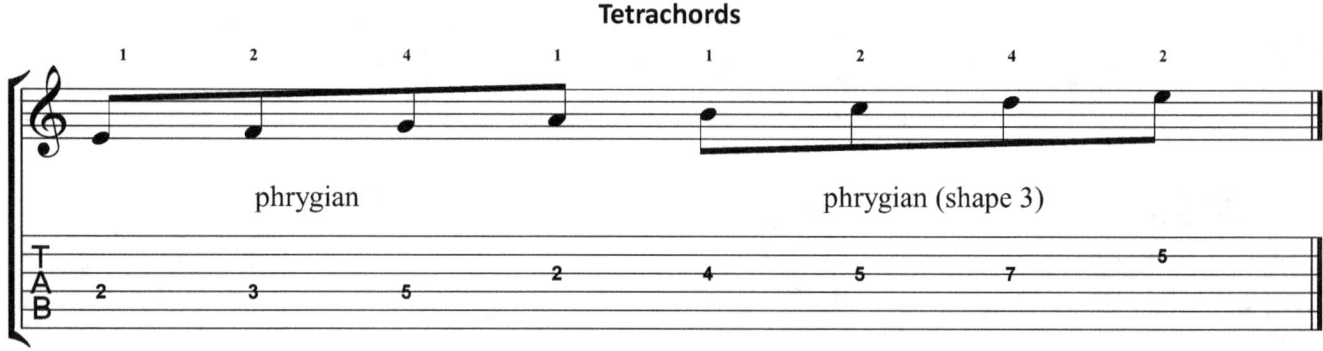

Intervals

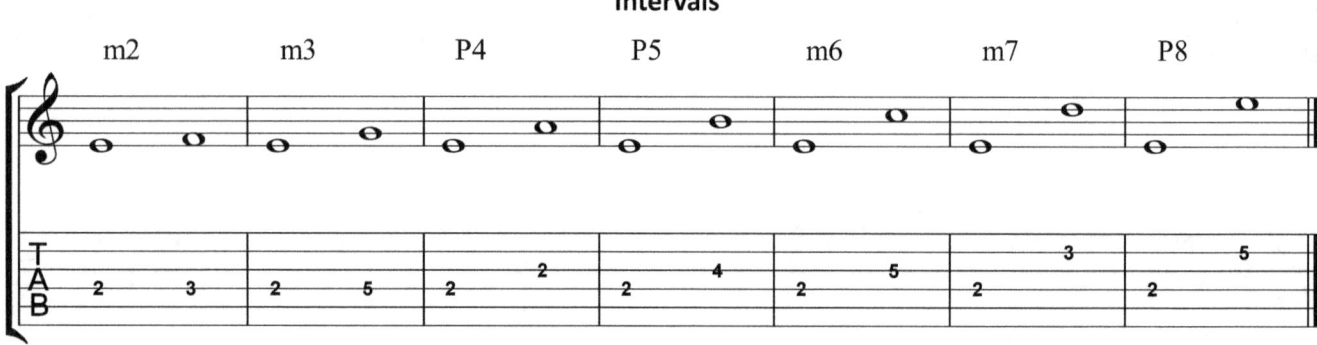

triad: minor   **7th chord: iii-7**

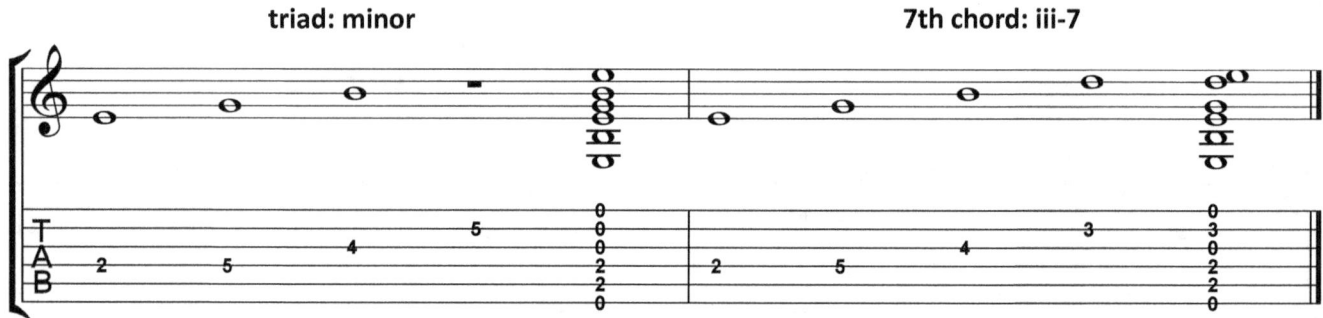

Phrygian mode studies - shape 2

Mode exercises

ex. 1

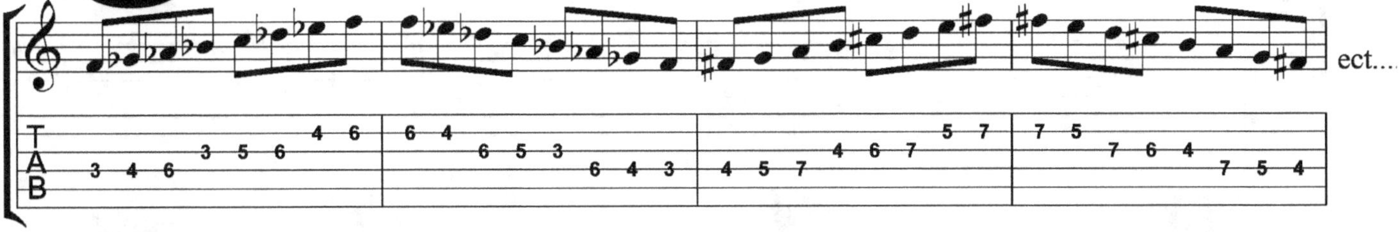

ex. 2

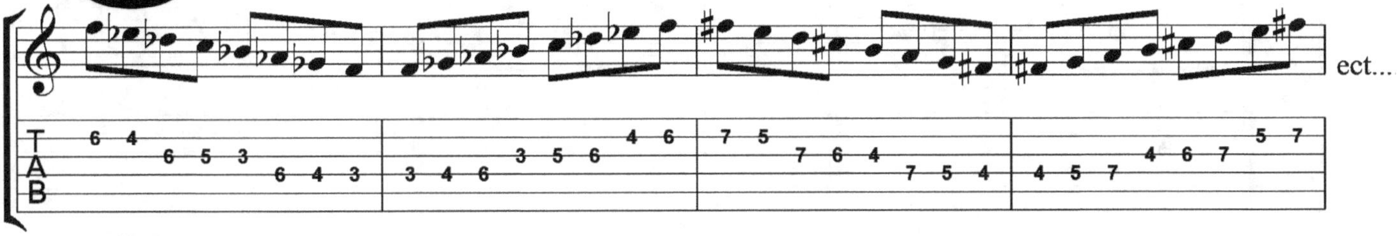

ex. 3

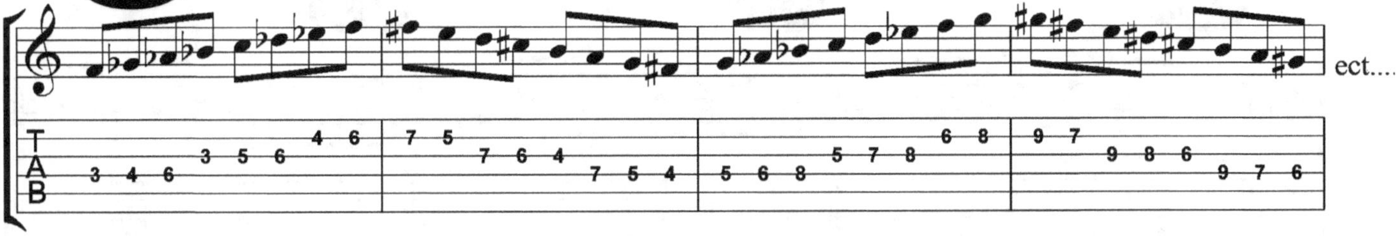

ex. 4

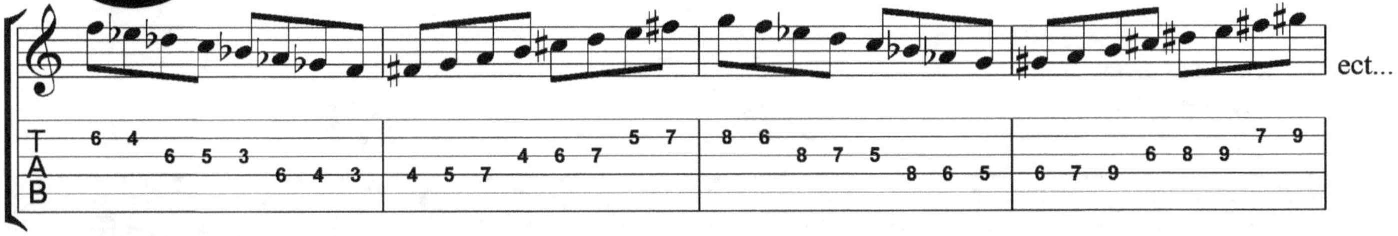

ex. 5

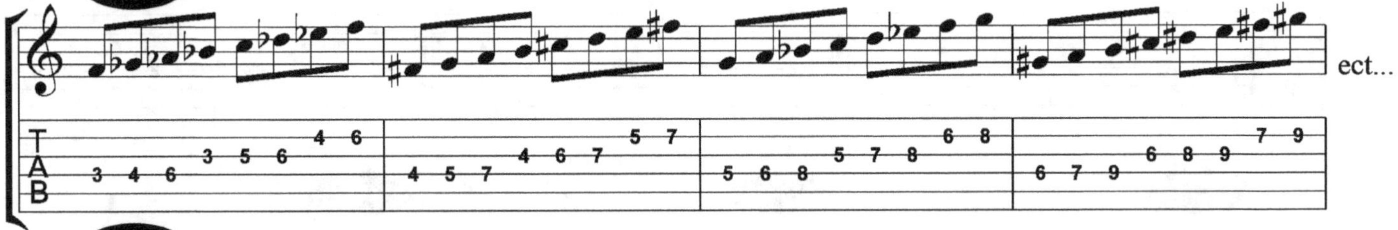

ex. 6

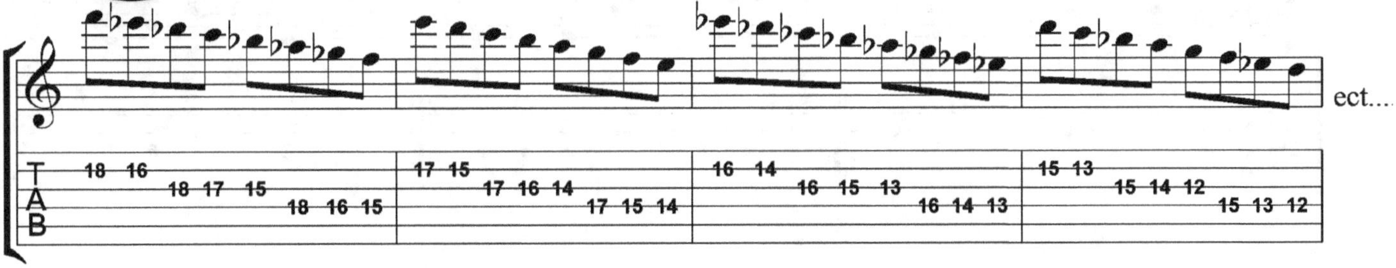

Melodic exercises

Triad exercises

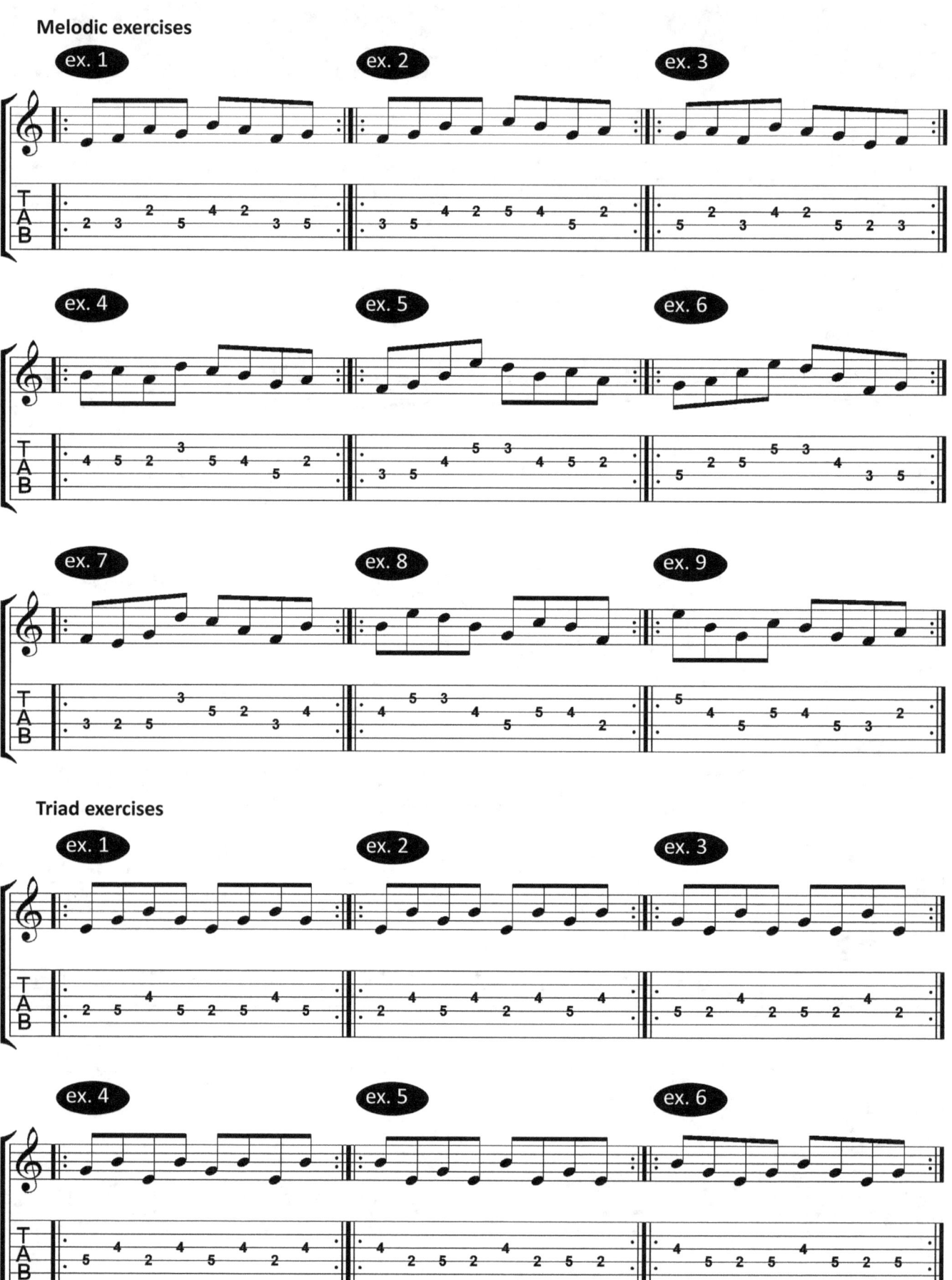

7th chord exercises

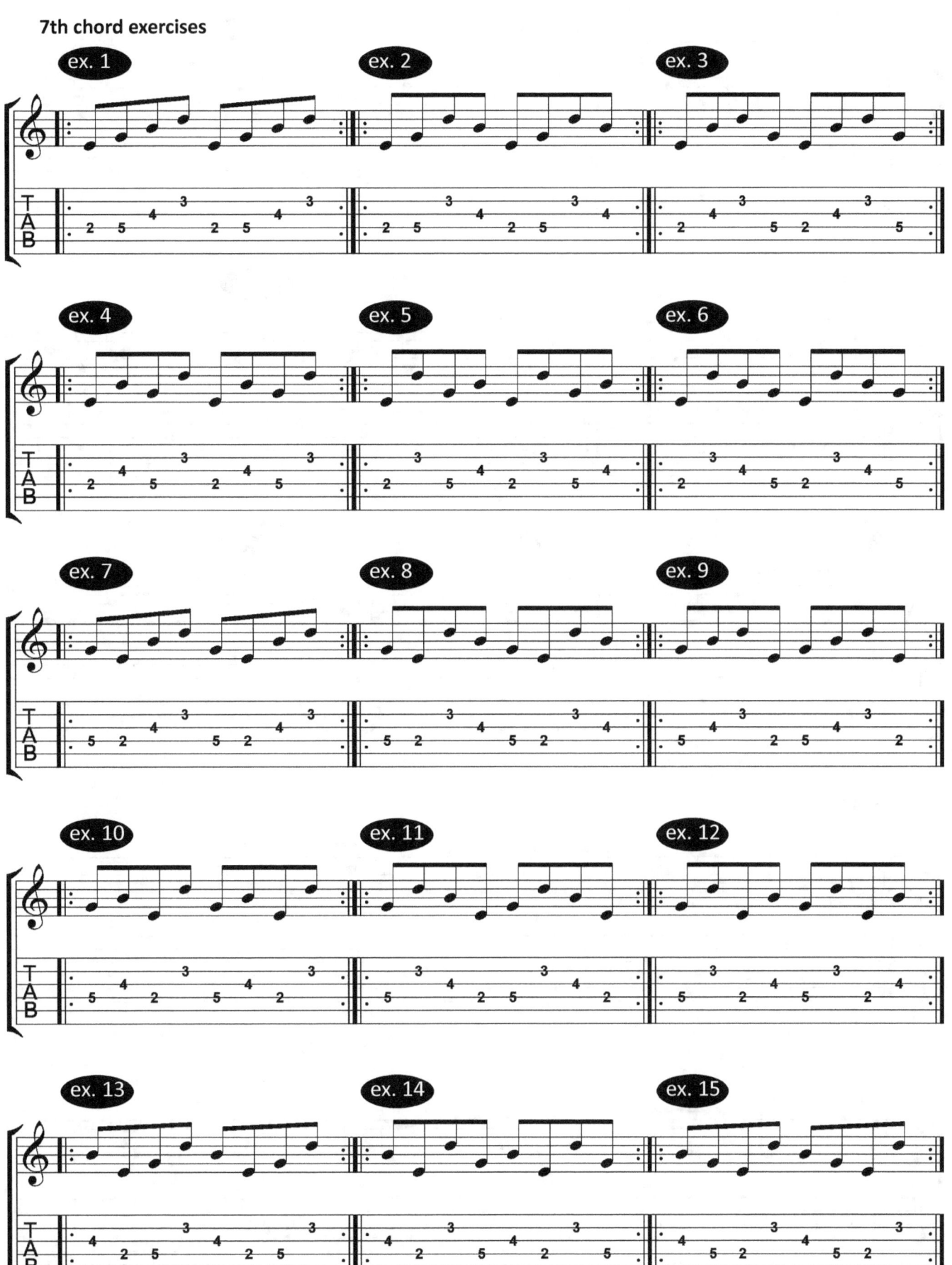

Chapter 4 the modes of the major scale - phrygian

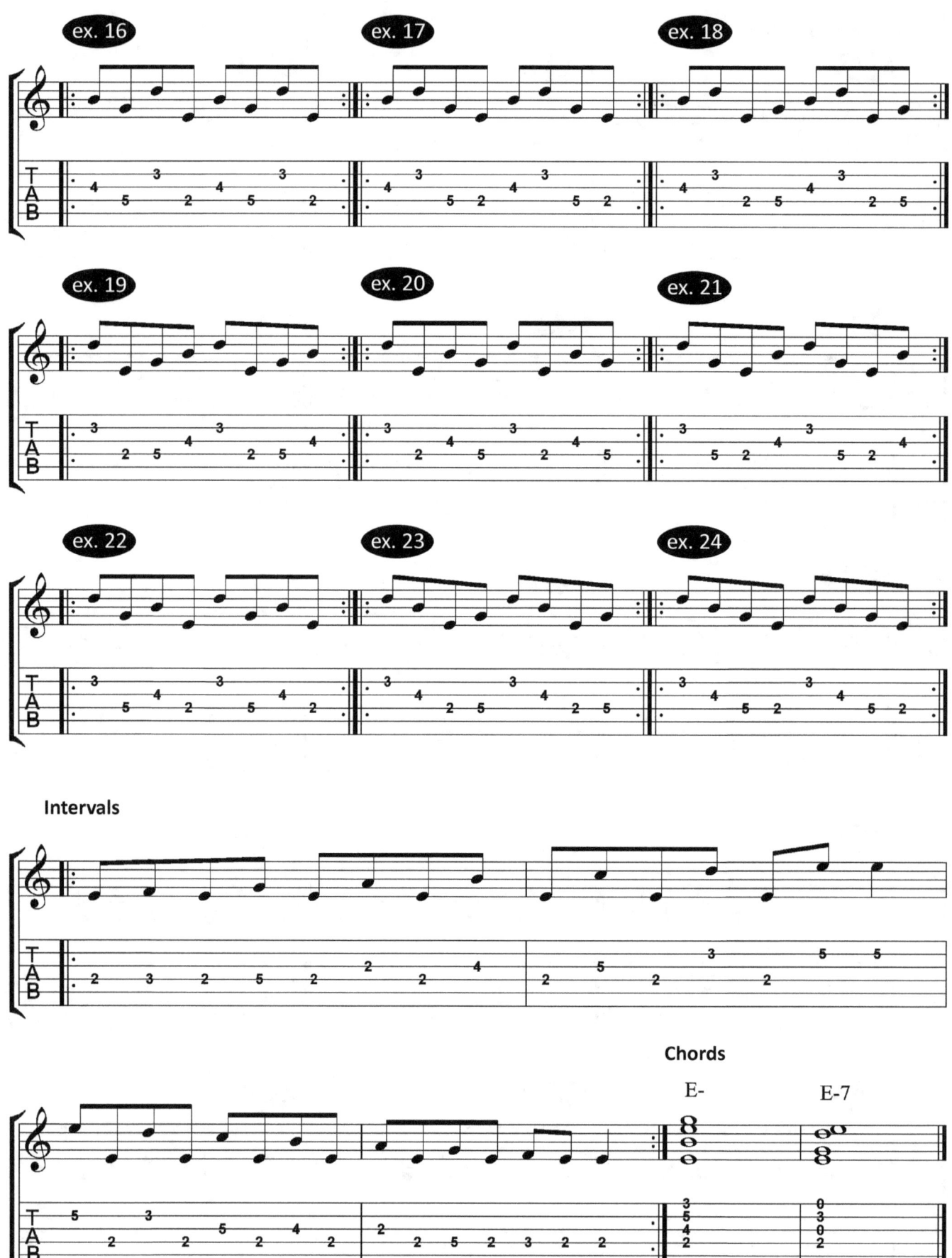

Phrygian shape 3

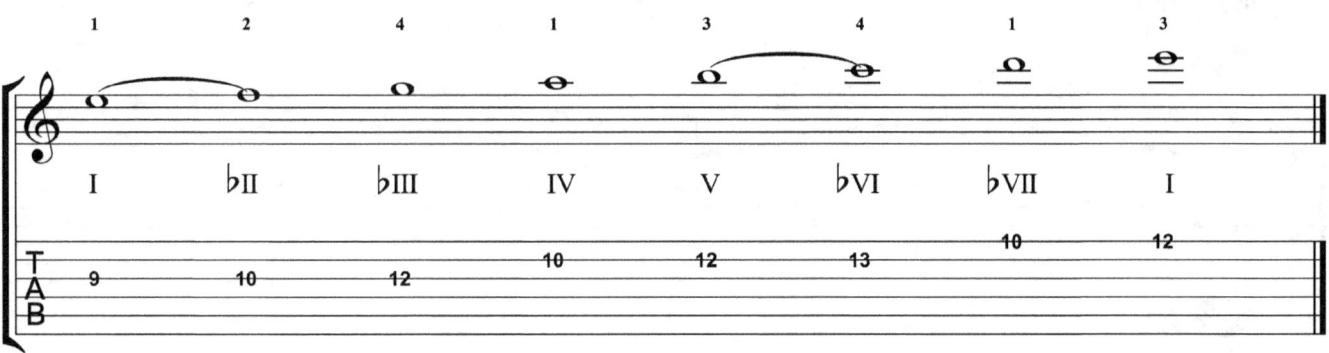

Tetrachords

Intervals

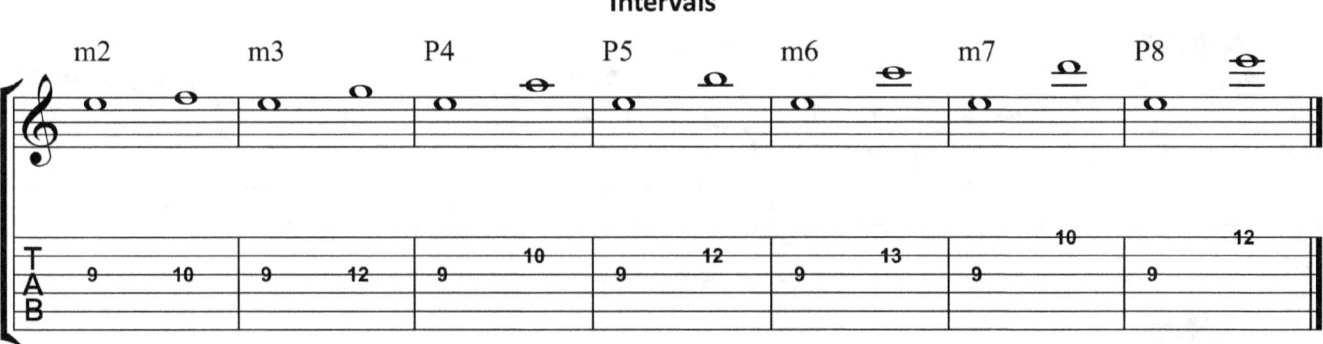

triad: minor **7th chord: iii-7**

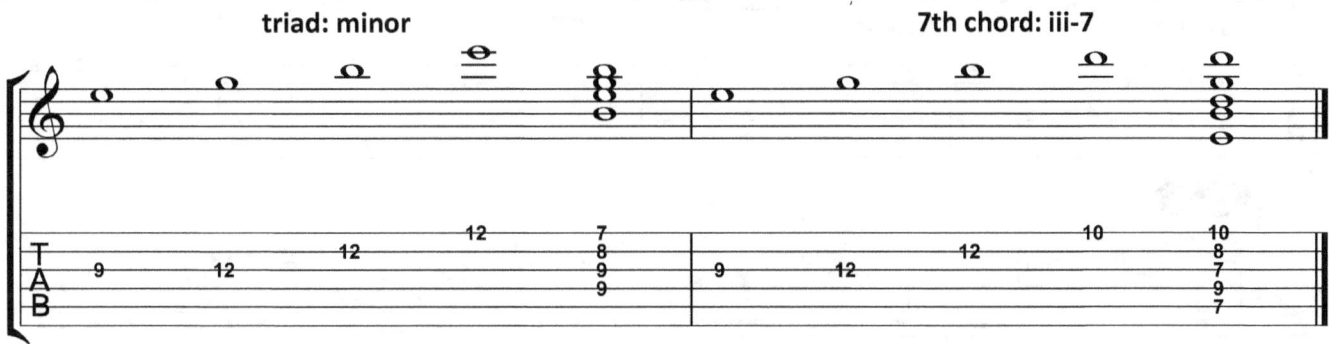

Phrygian mode studies - shape 3

Mode exercises

ex. 1

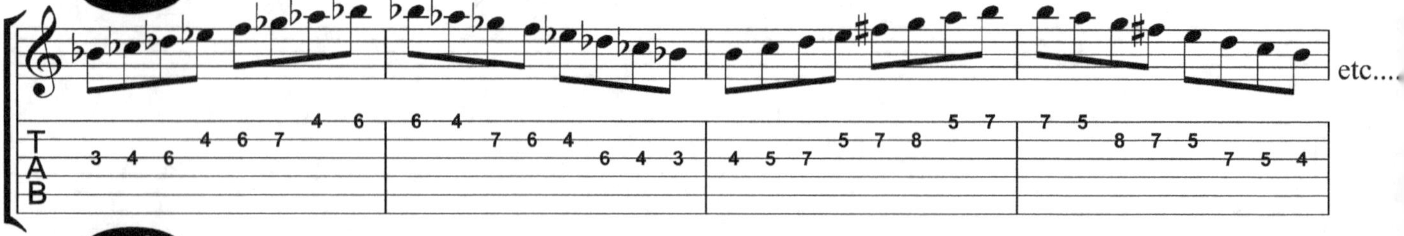

ex. 2

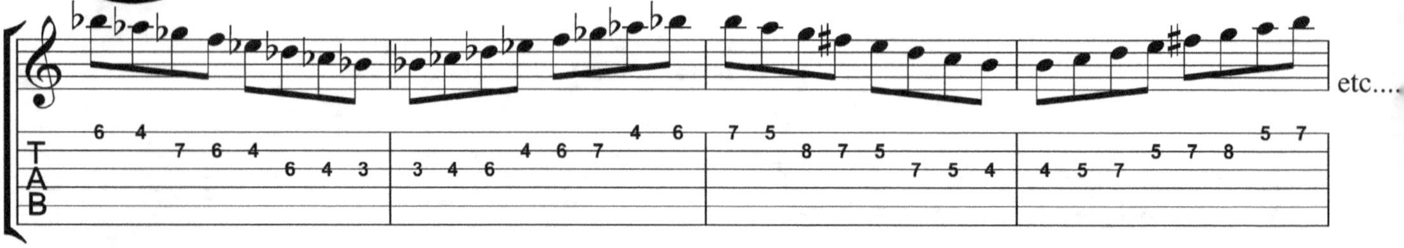

ex. 3

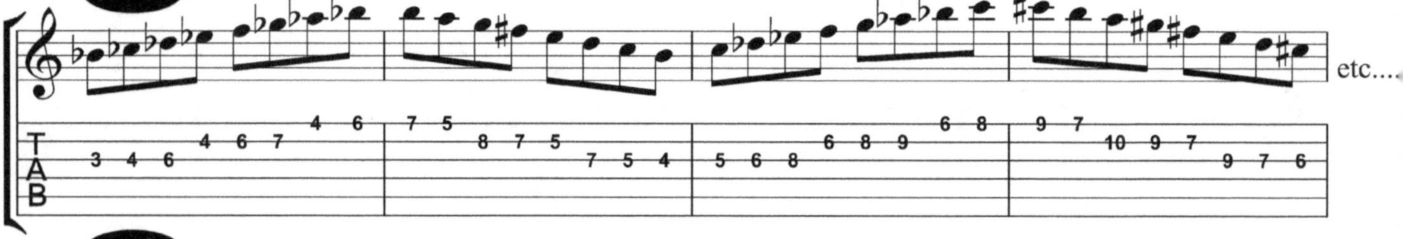

ex. 4

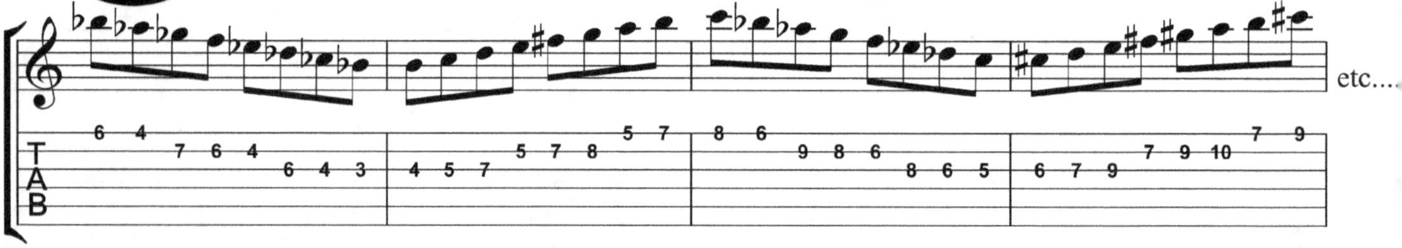

ex. 5

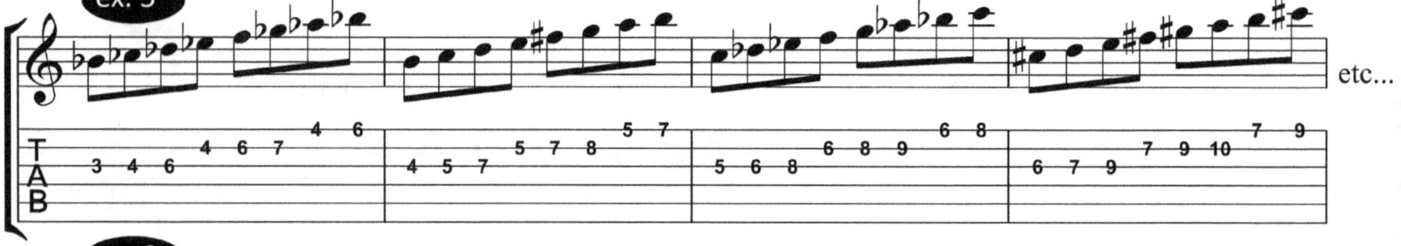

ex. 6

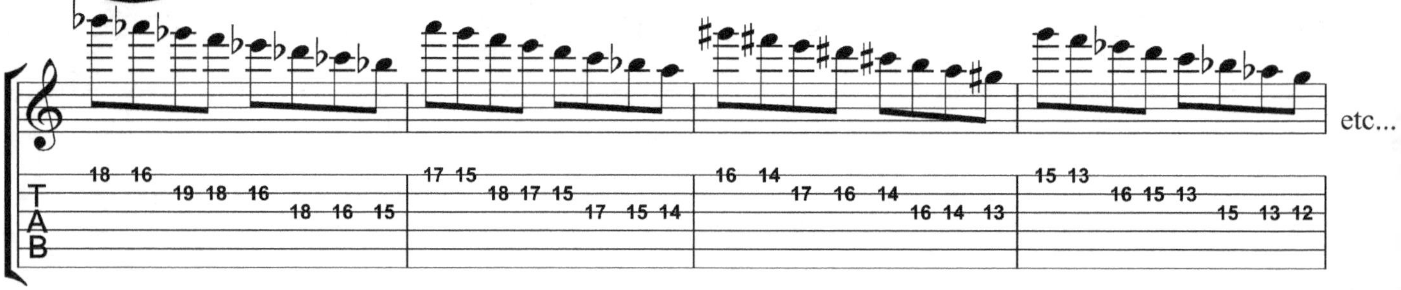

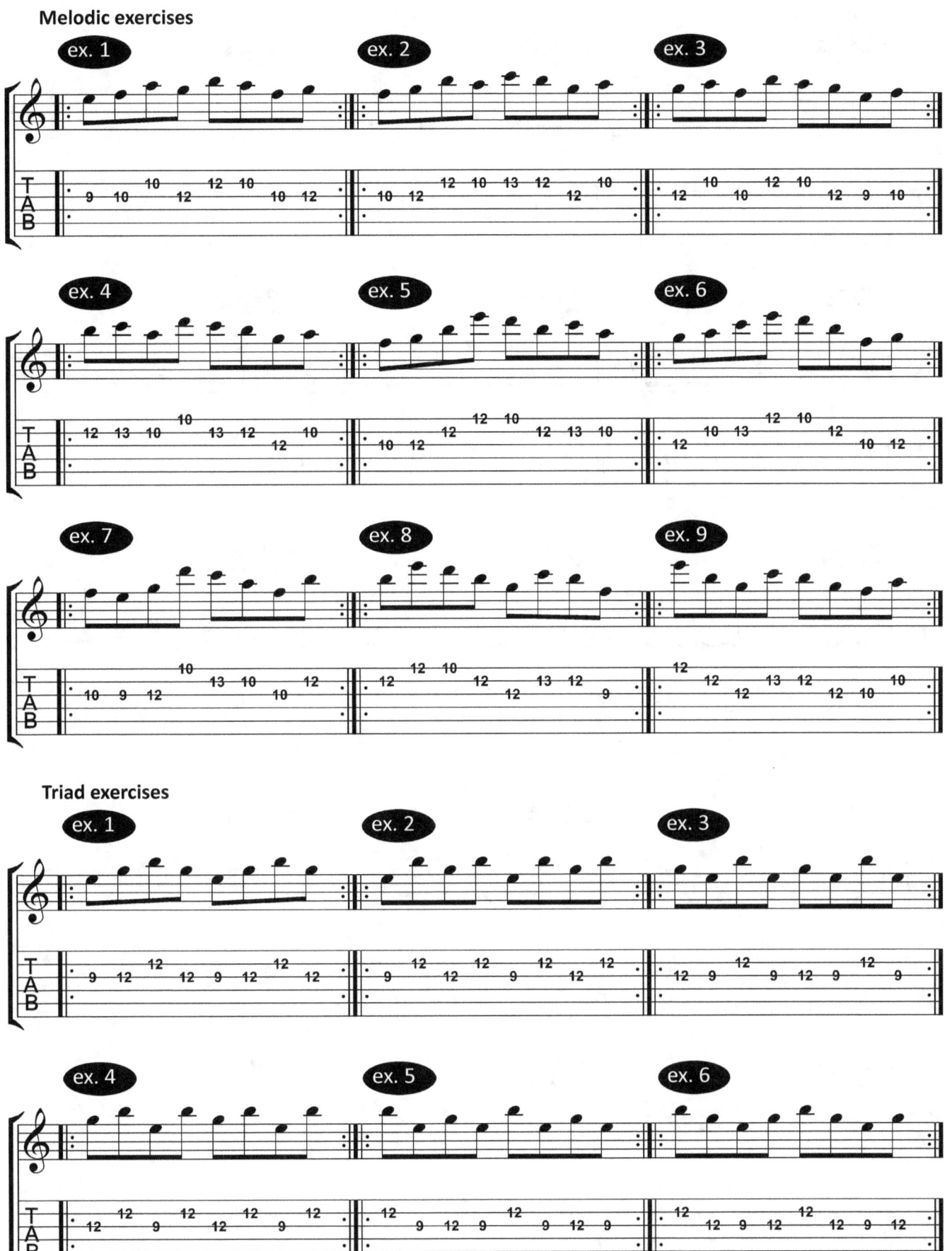

Chapter 4 the modes of the major scale - phrygian

7th chord exercises

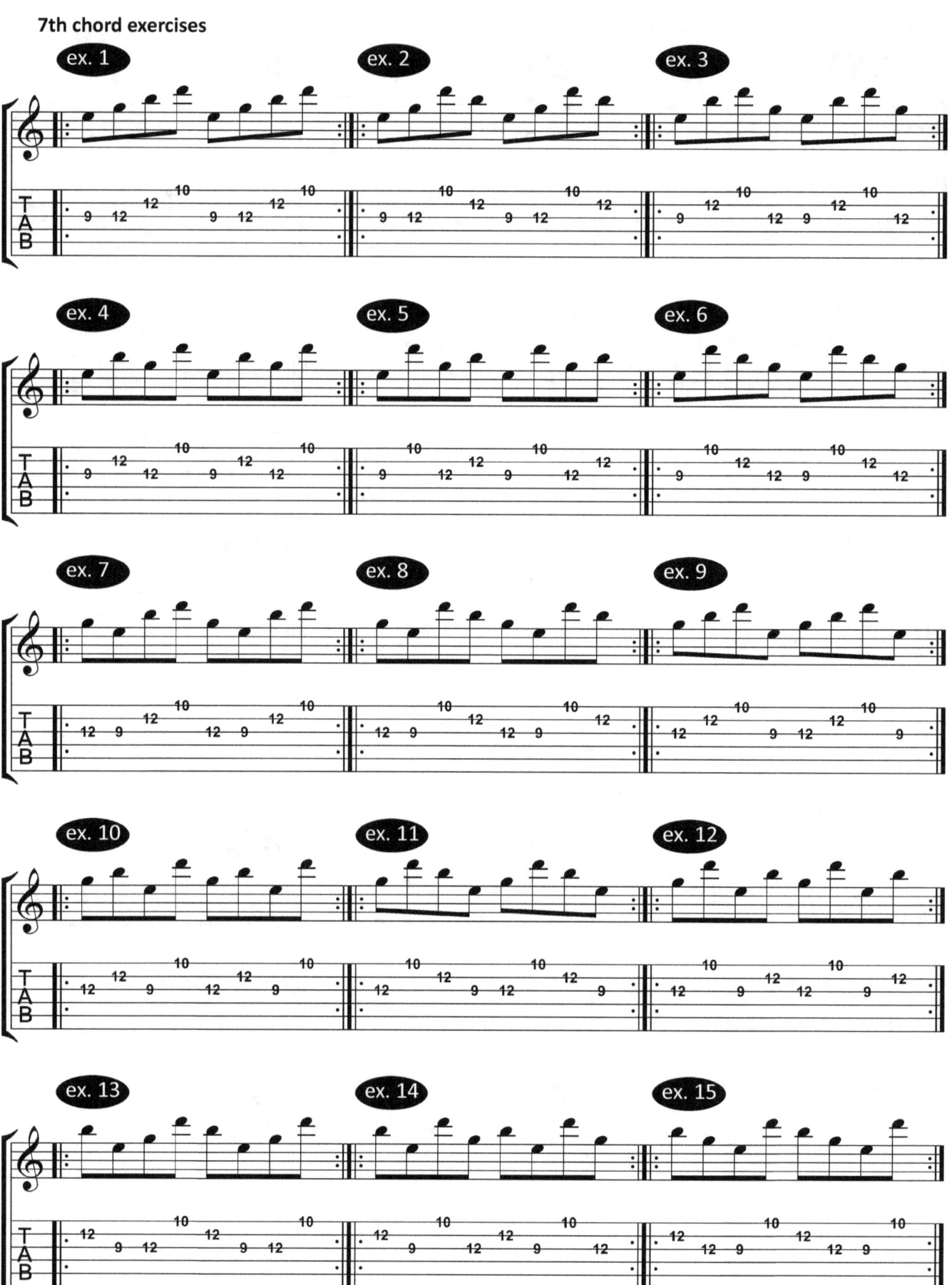

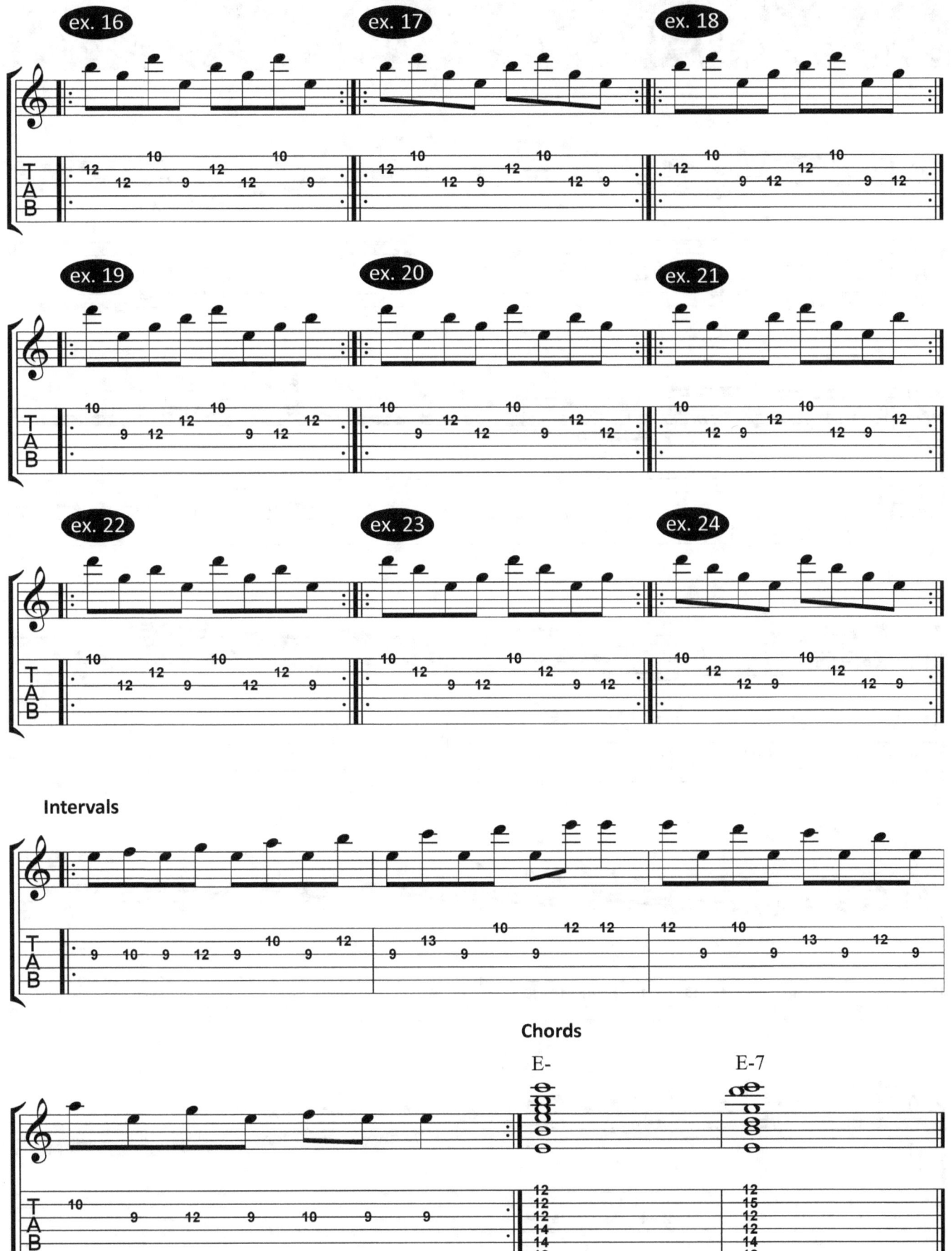

Chapter 4 the modes of the major scale - phrygian

Phrygian in 2 octaves with shapes 1 + 2

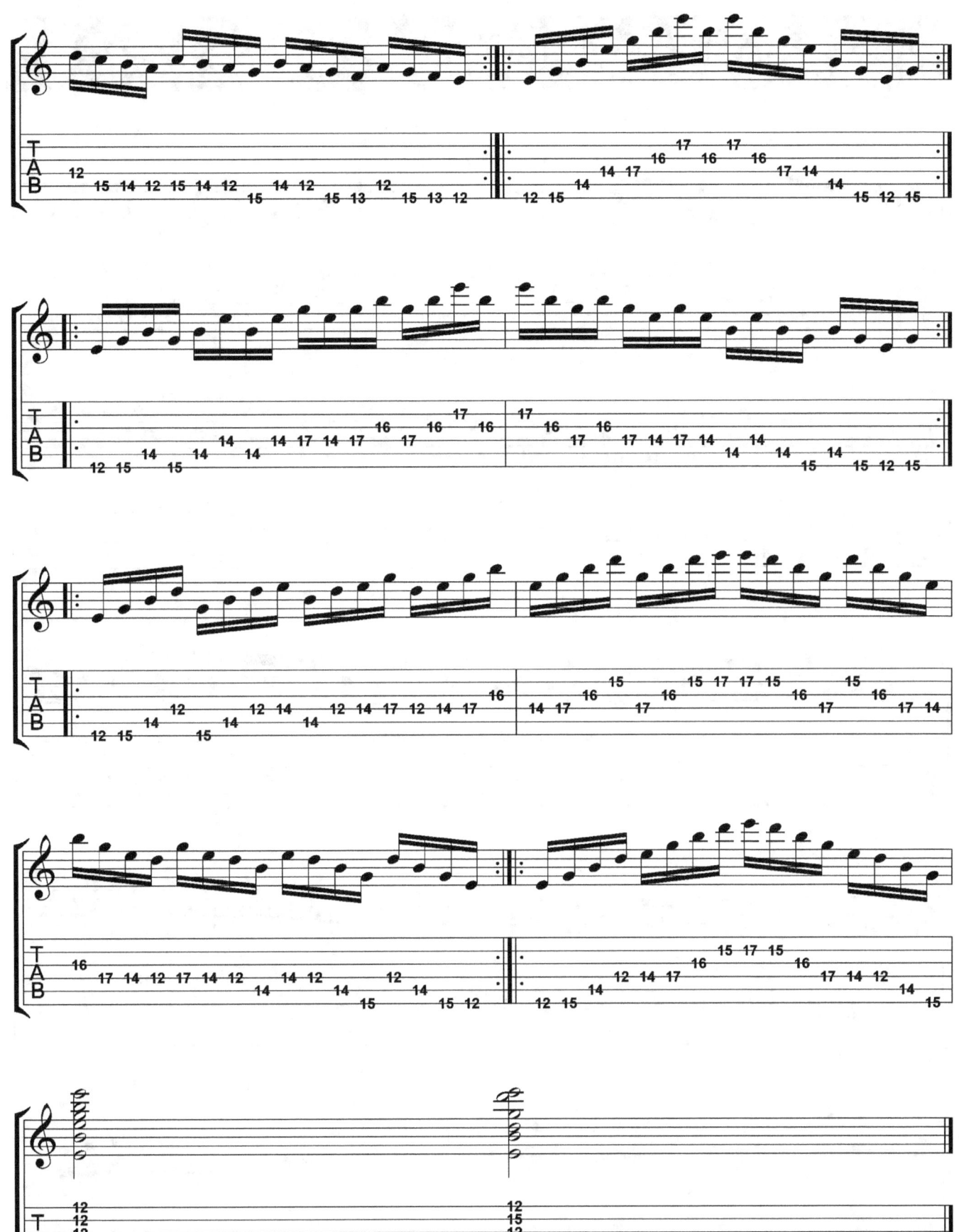

Chapter 4   the modes of the major scale - phrygian

Phrygian in 2 octaves with shapes 1 + 3

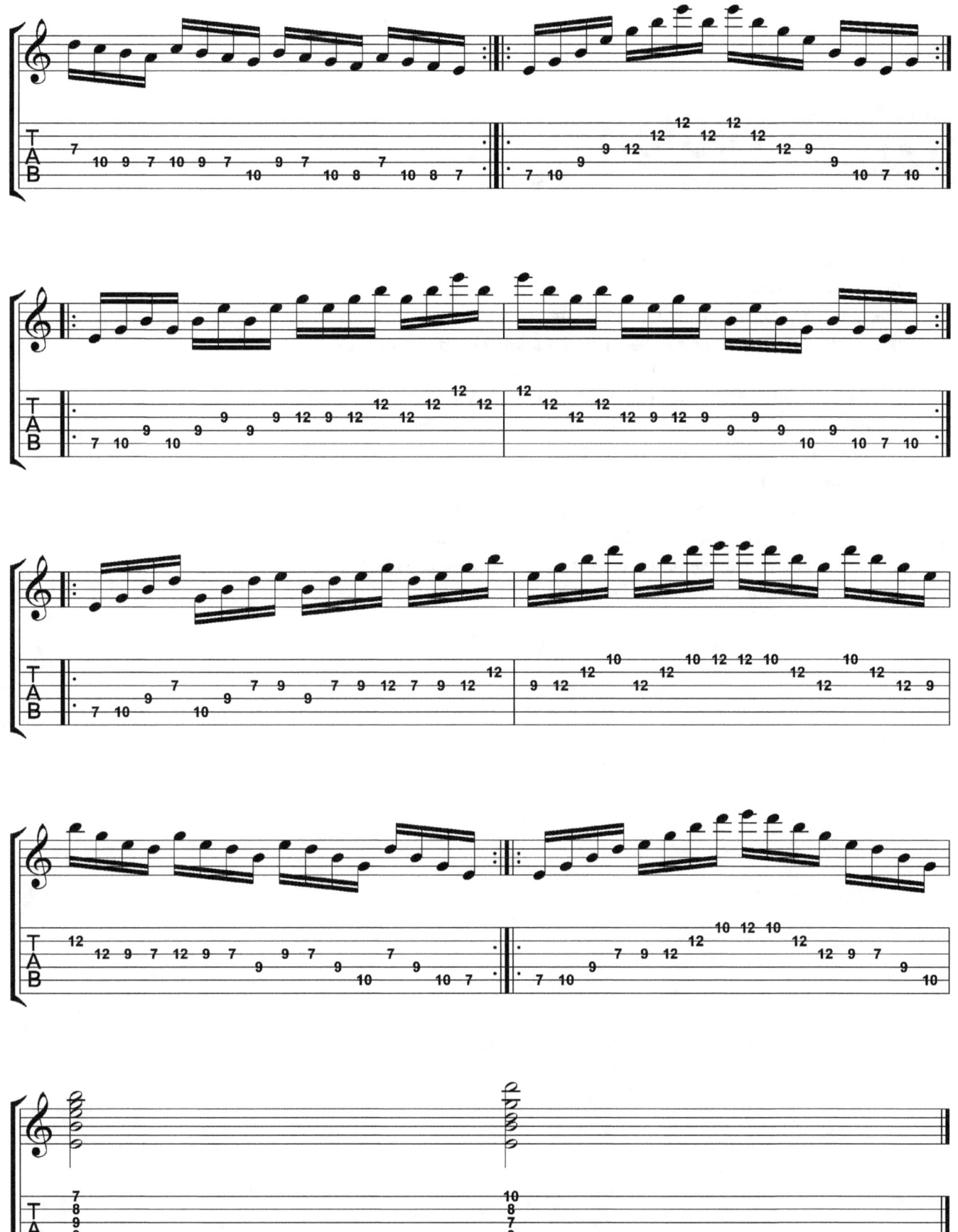

Chapter 4 the modes of the major scale - phrygian

Lydian
4th mode of the Major scale

General formula: W-W-W-H-W-W-H

Scale: Major seventh with an augmented fourth

Tetrachords: Lydian - major

Characteristic note of the mode: the augmented fourth ♯4

The intervals that are formed between the tonic and each scale degree: I-II = 2, I-III = 3, I-IV = ♯4, I-V = 5, I-VI = 6, I-VII = 7

The diatonic half steps are found on the scale degrees IV-V and VII-I

Triad: Major IV

Seventh chord: Major 7 IVmaj7, IV Δ7, IVM7

Extensions: 9, ♯11, 13

Generally: The Lydian mode is a major scale because it contains a major third, but its characteristic note is the augmented fourth which gives it a "grayish" sound, and therefore, it is used in jazz music as a first choice in major chords with a major 7 instead of the Ionian mode.

Lydian shape 1

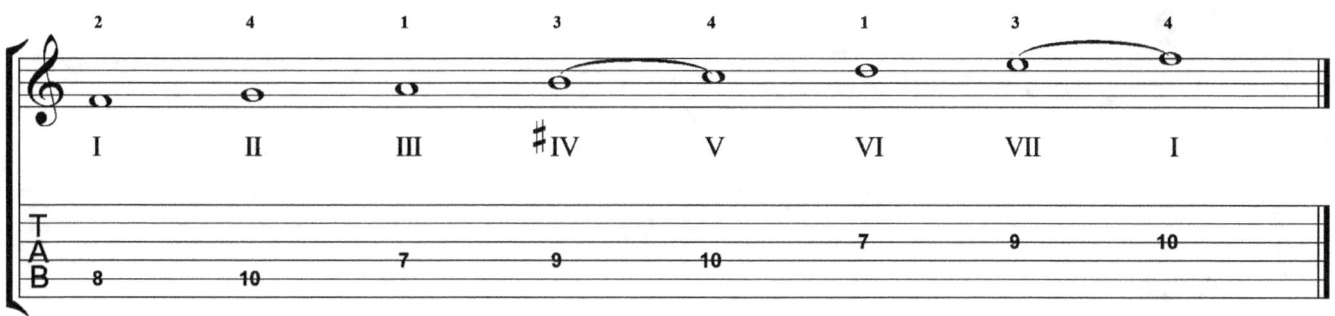

Tetrachords

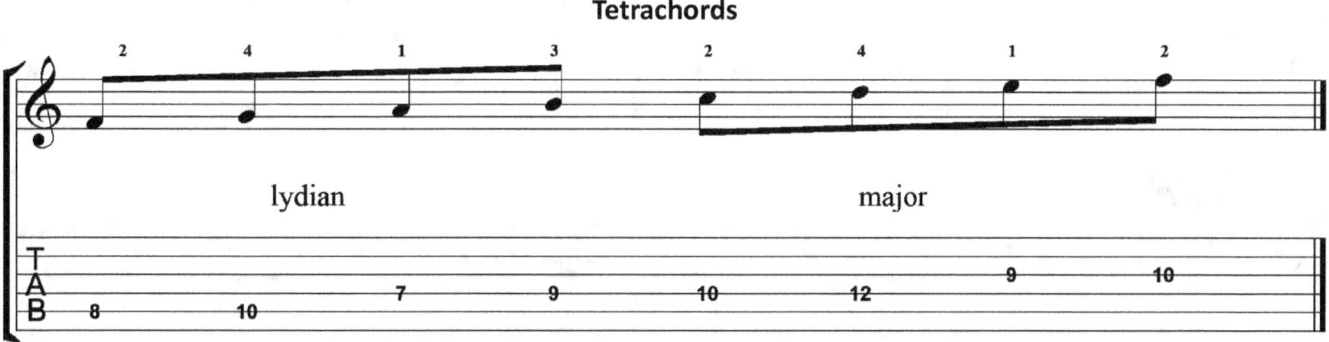

Intervals

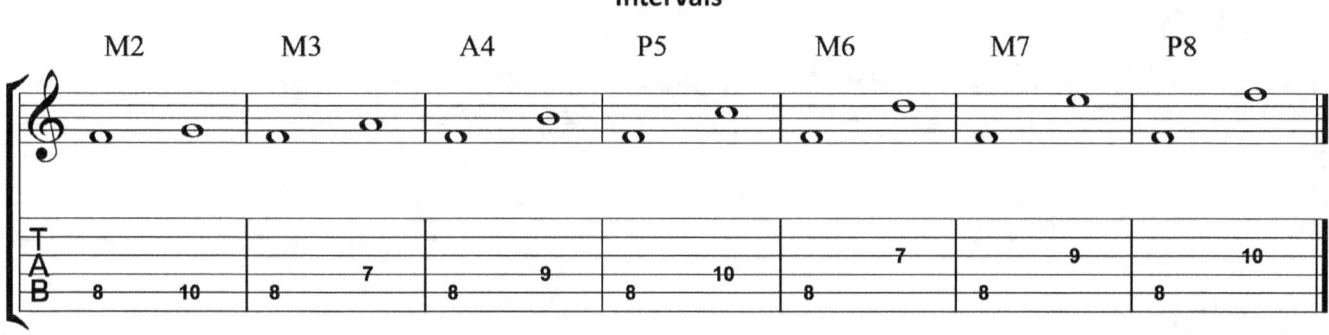

triad: major 7th chord: IVmaj7

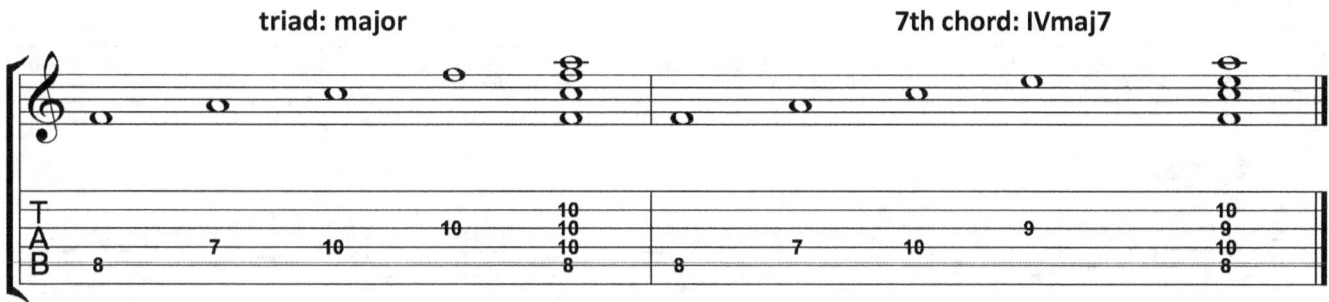

Chapter 4 the modes of the major scale - lydian

Lydian mode studies - shape 1

Mode exercises

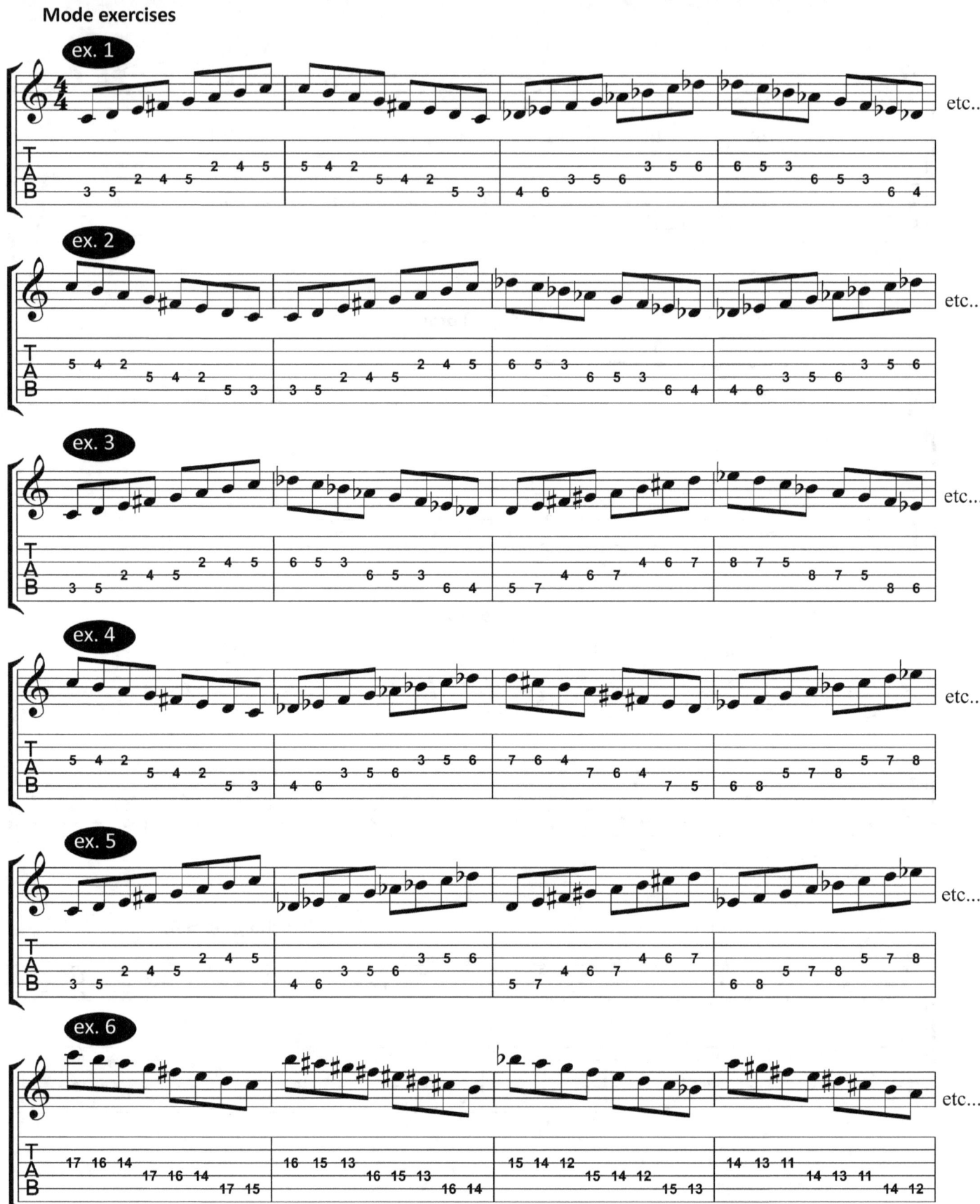

Melodic exercises

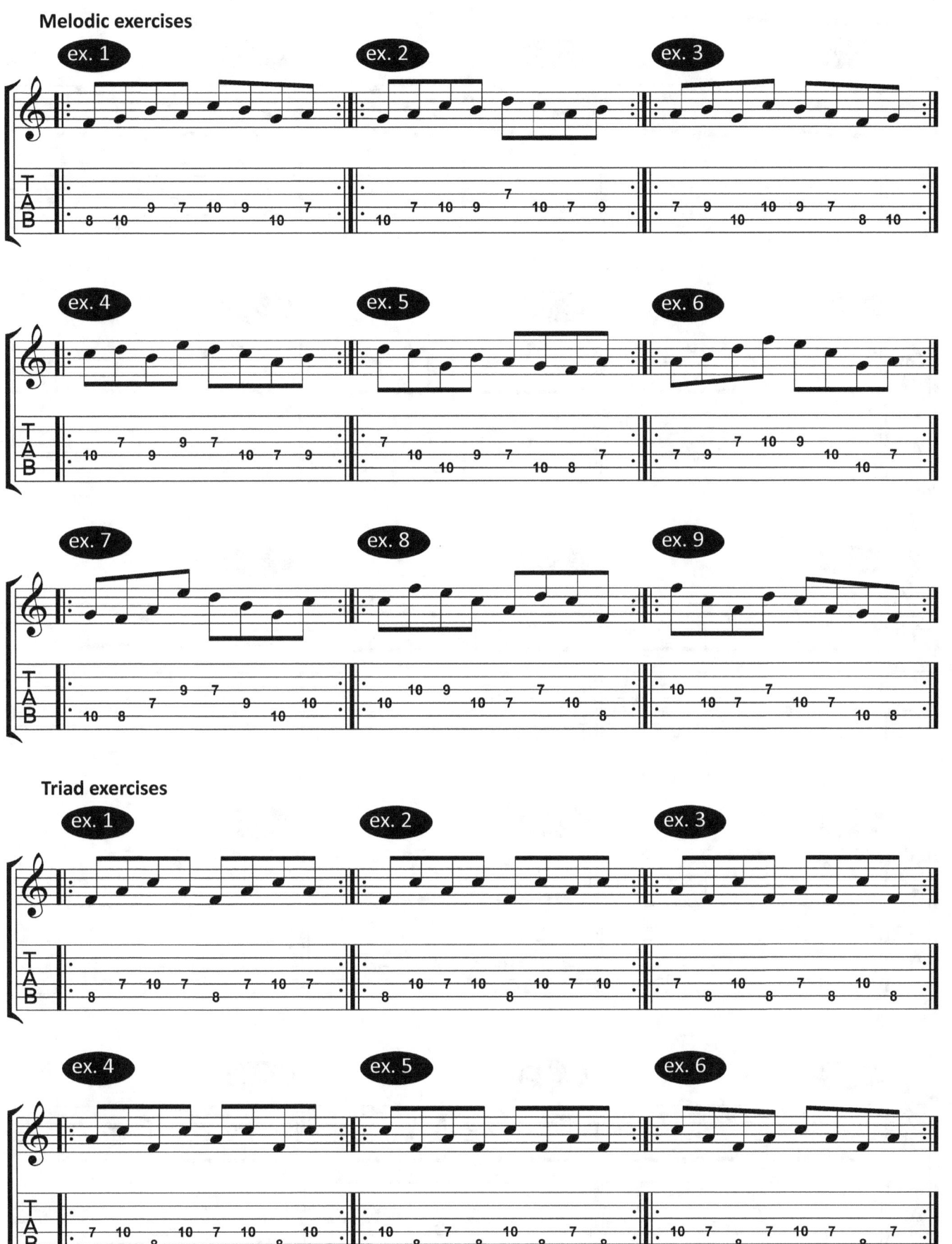

Chapter 4 the modes of the major scale - lydian

7th chord exercises

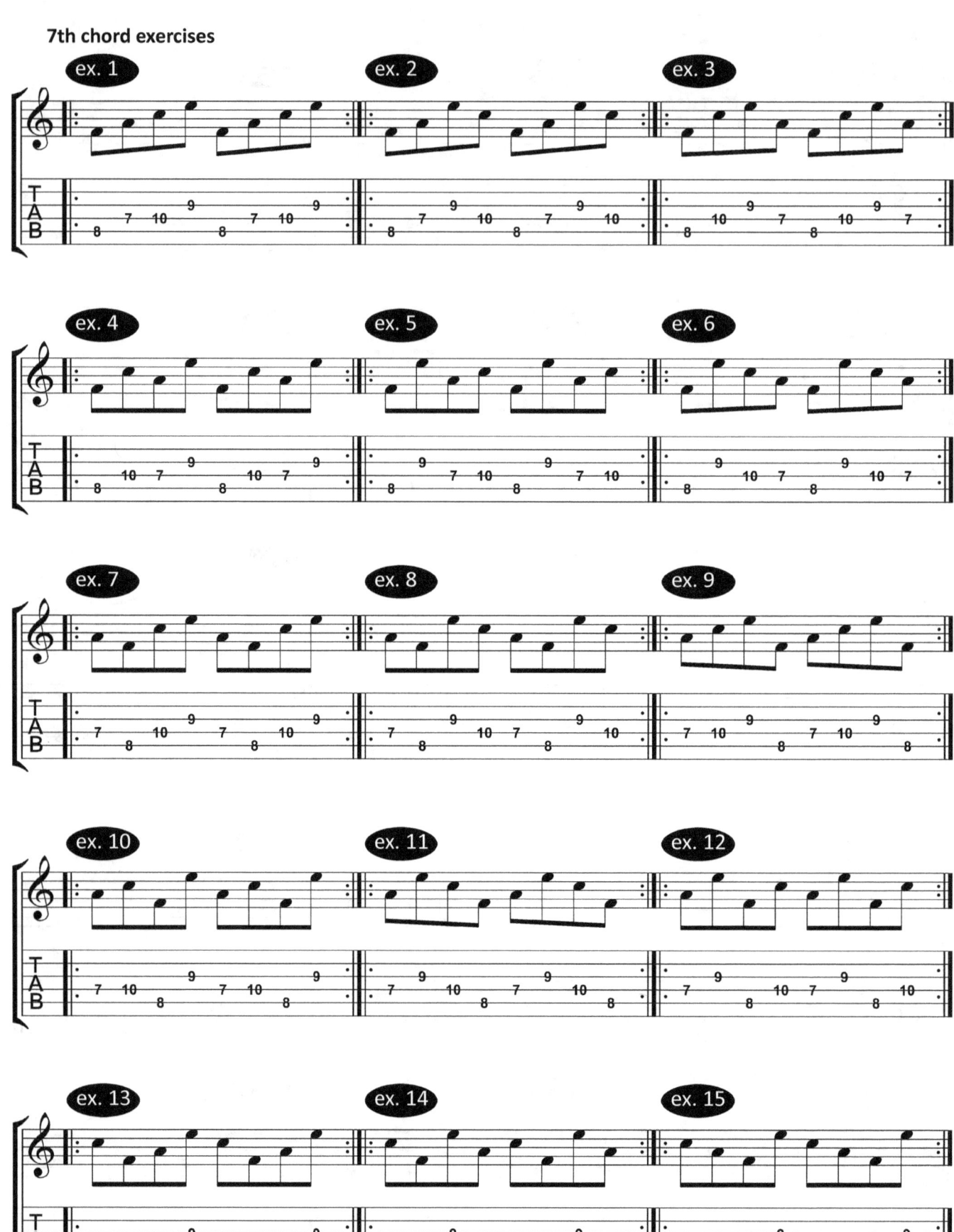

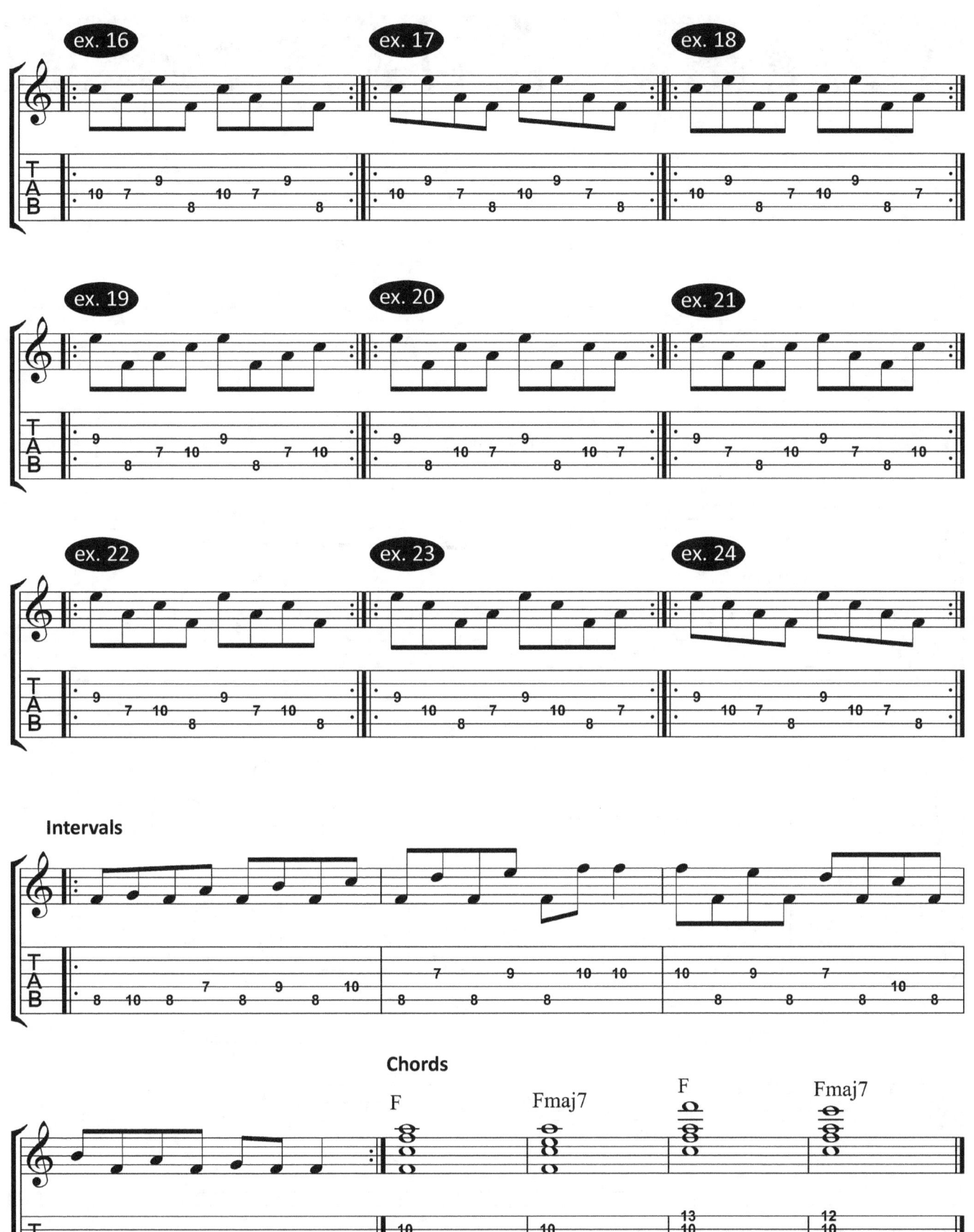

Chapter 4 the modes of the major scale - lydian

Lydian shape 2

Tetrachords

lydian   major (shape 3)

Intervals

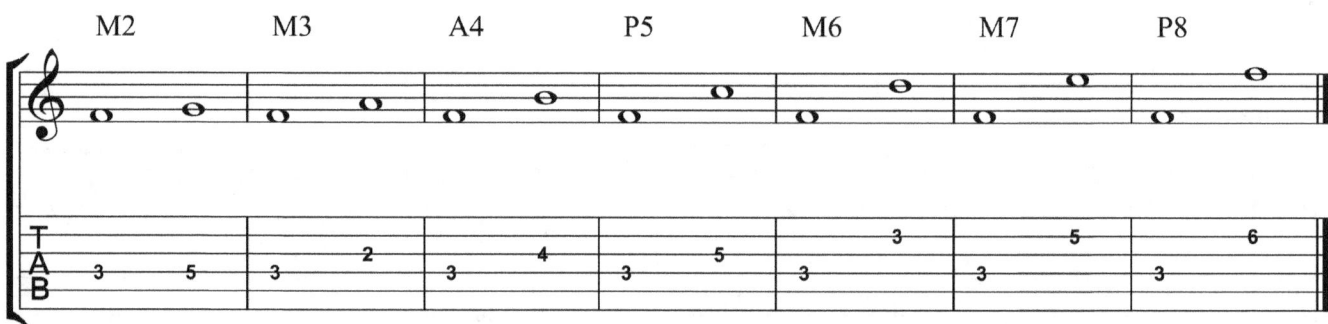

triad: major   7th chord: Imaj7

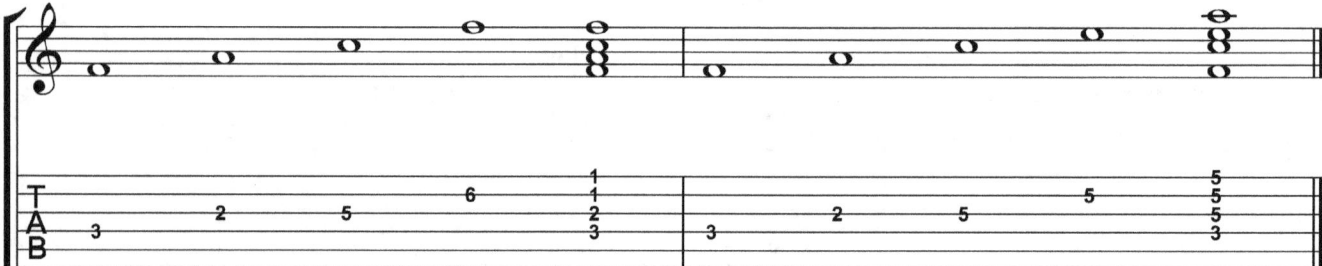

Lydian mode studies - shape 2

Mode exercises

ex. 1

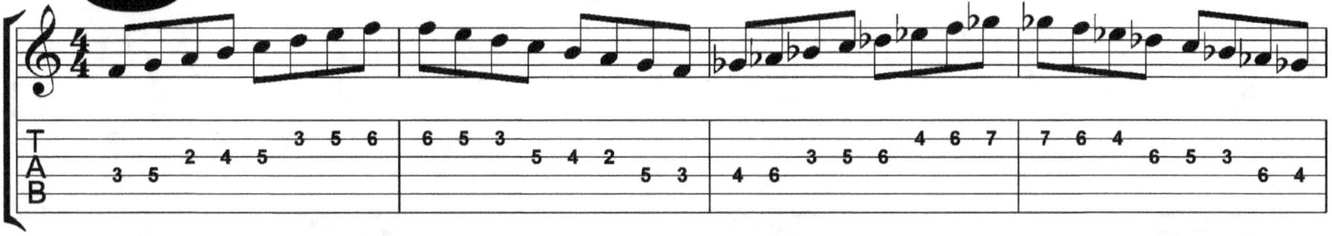

etc...

ex. 2

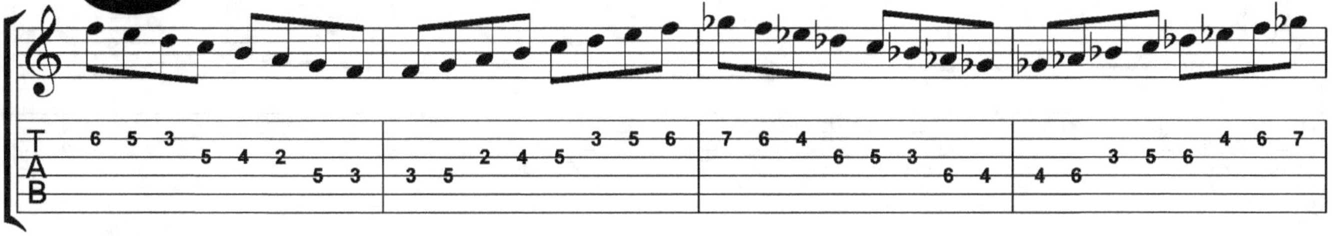

etc...

ex. 3

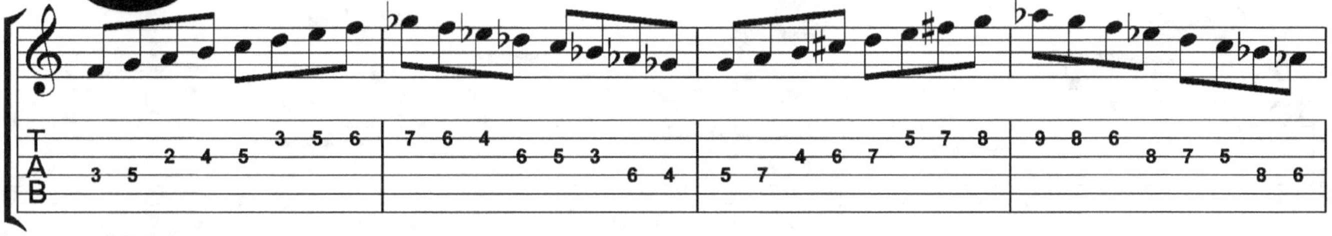

etc...

ex. 4

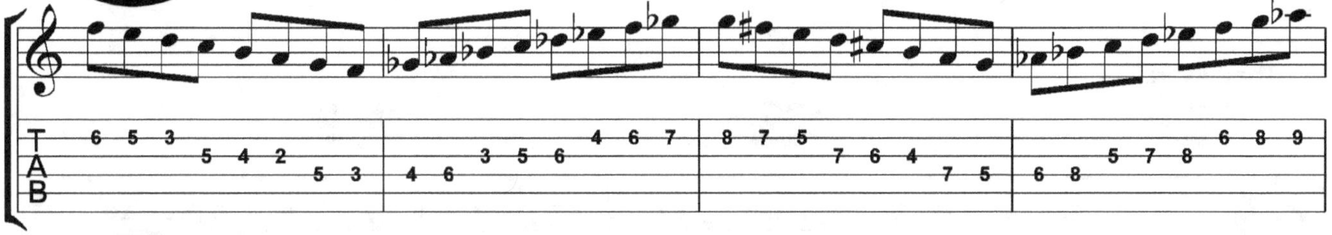

etc...

ex. 5

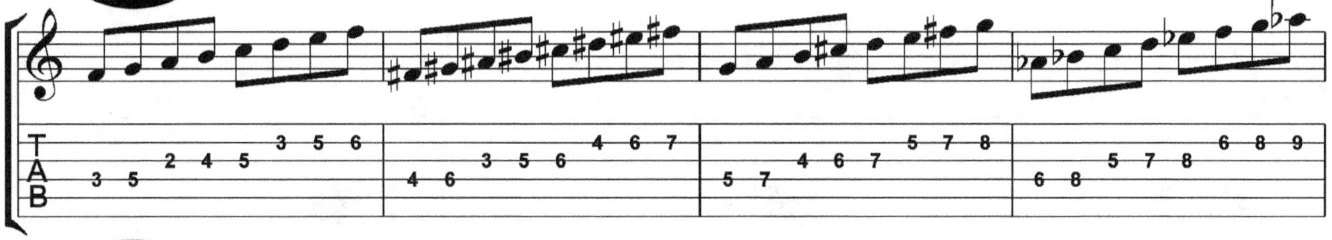

etc....

ex. 6

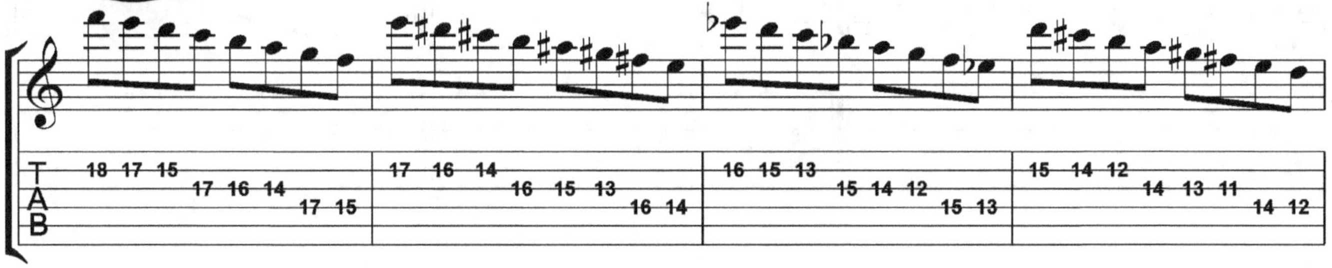

etc....

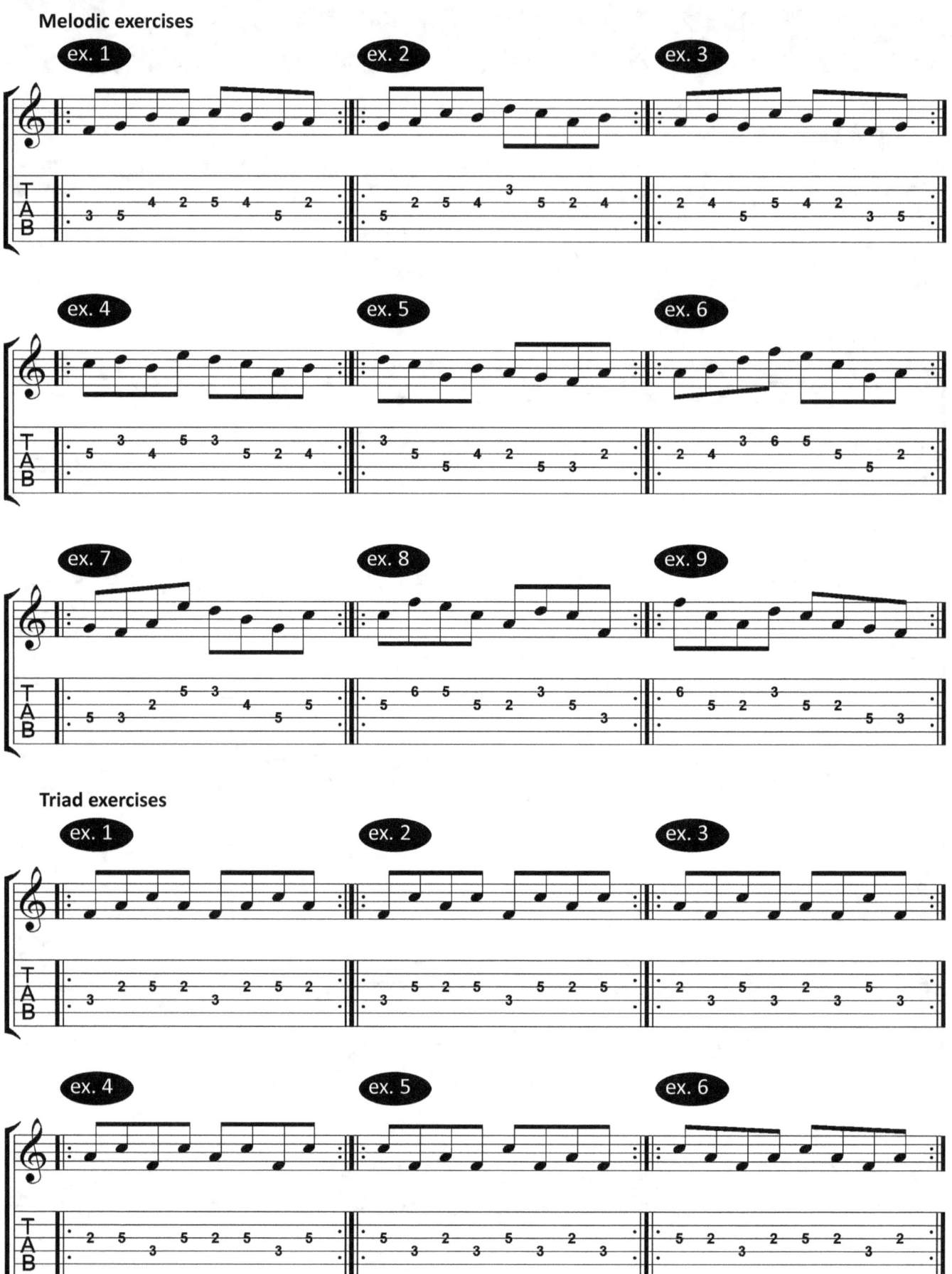

7th chord exercises

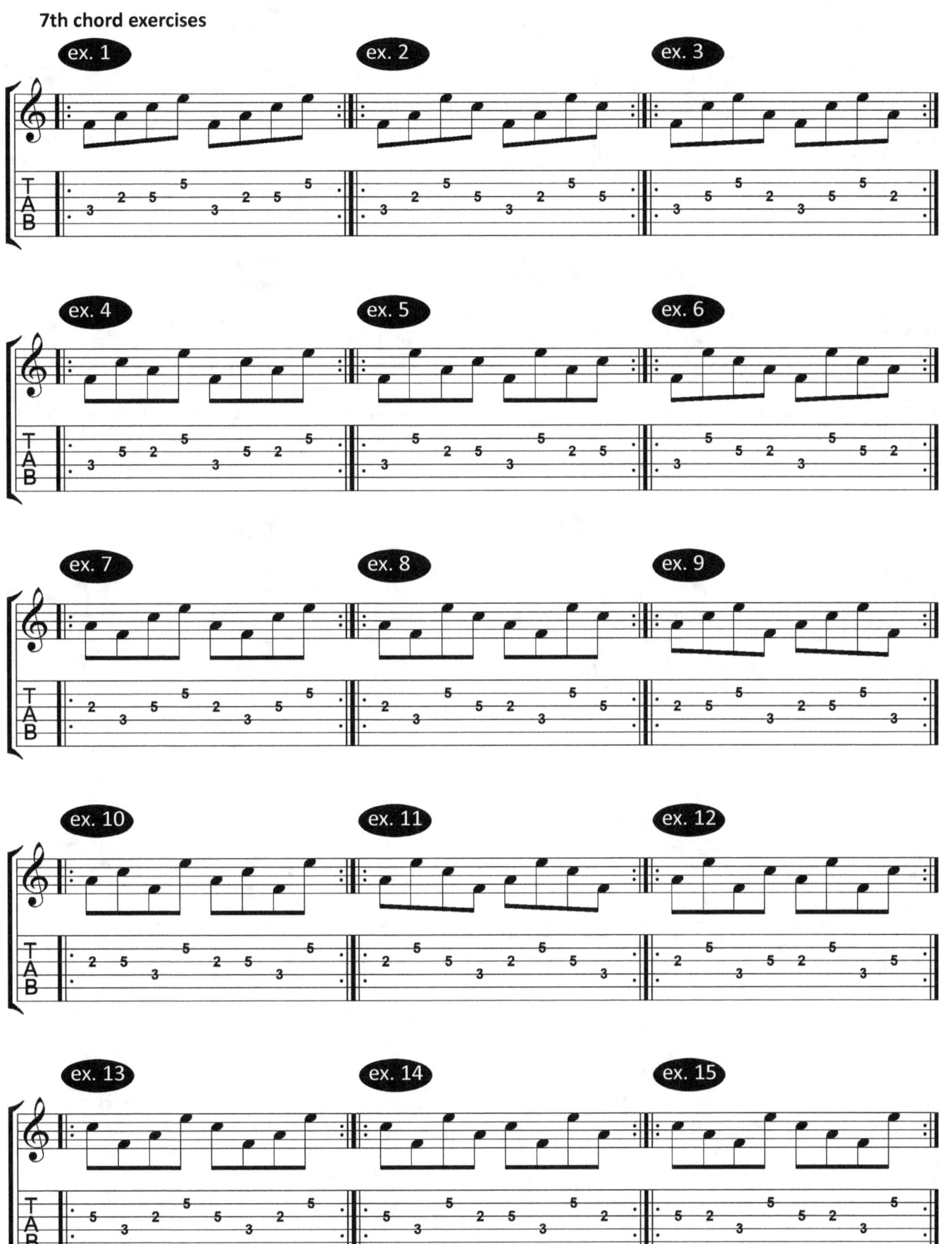

Chapter 4   the modes of the major scale - lydian

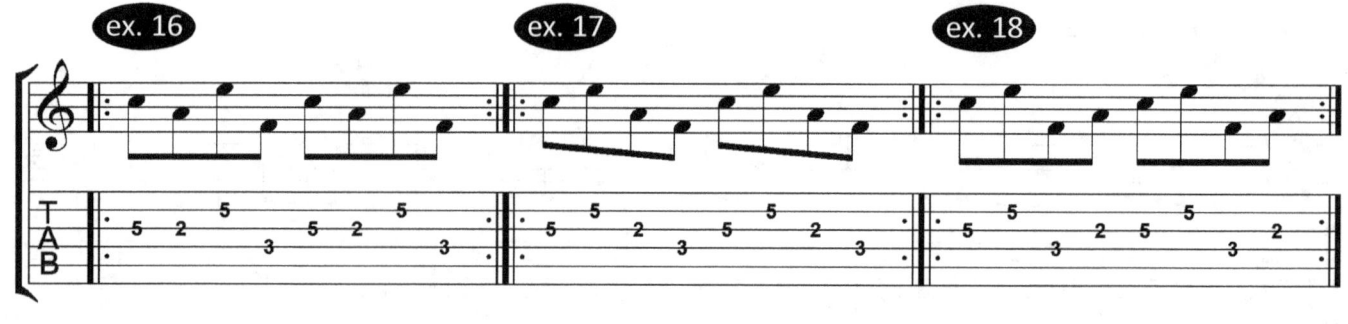

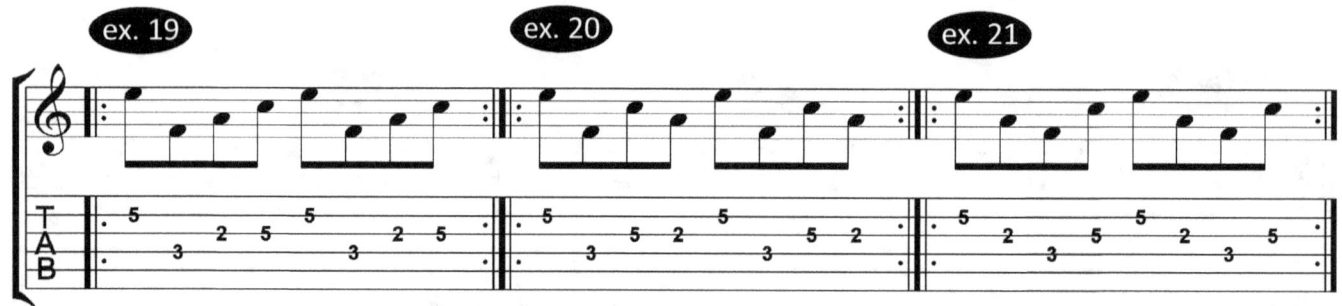

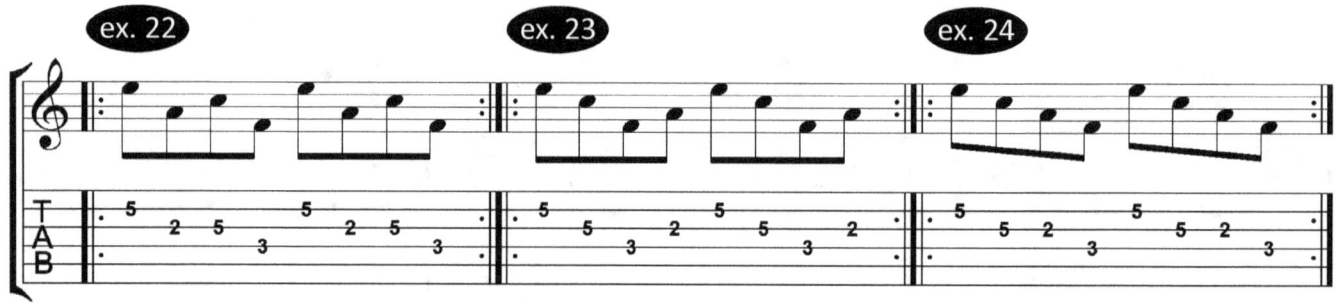

Intervals

Chords

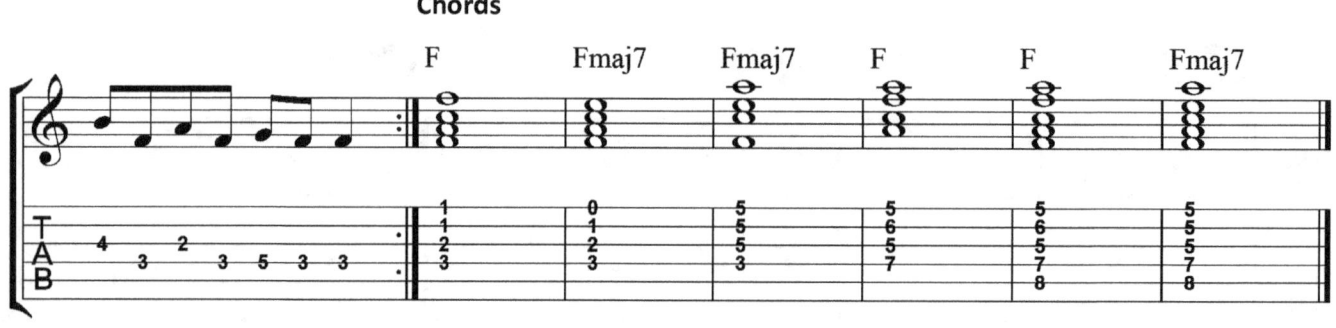

Lydian shape 3

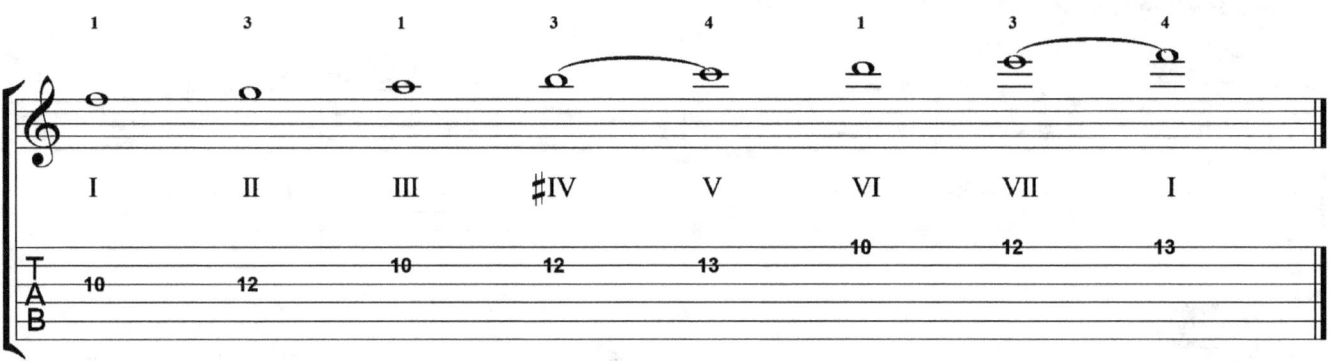

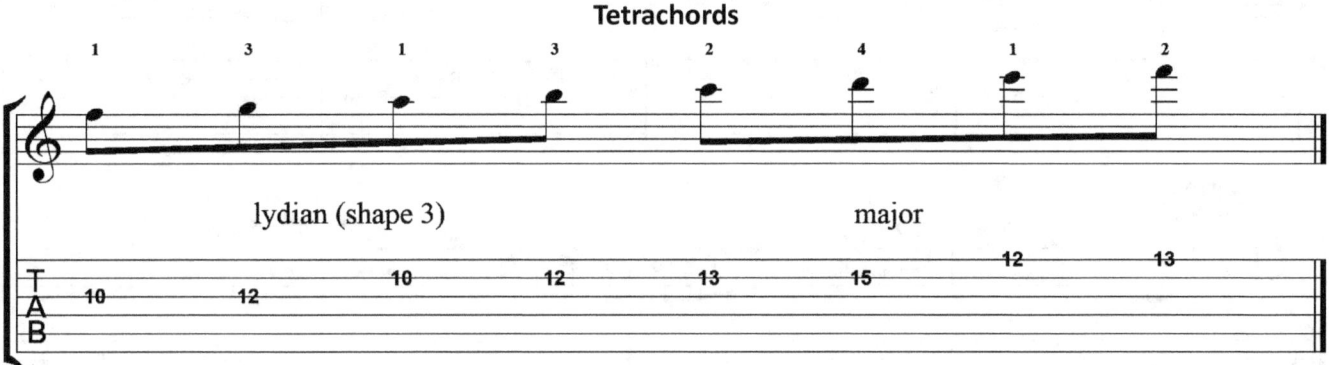

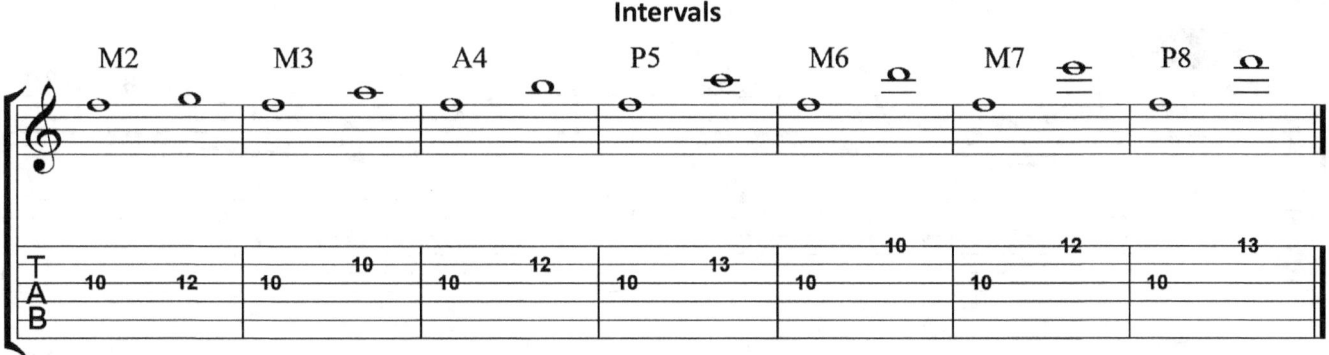

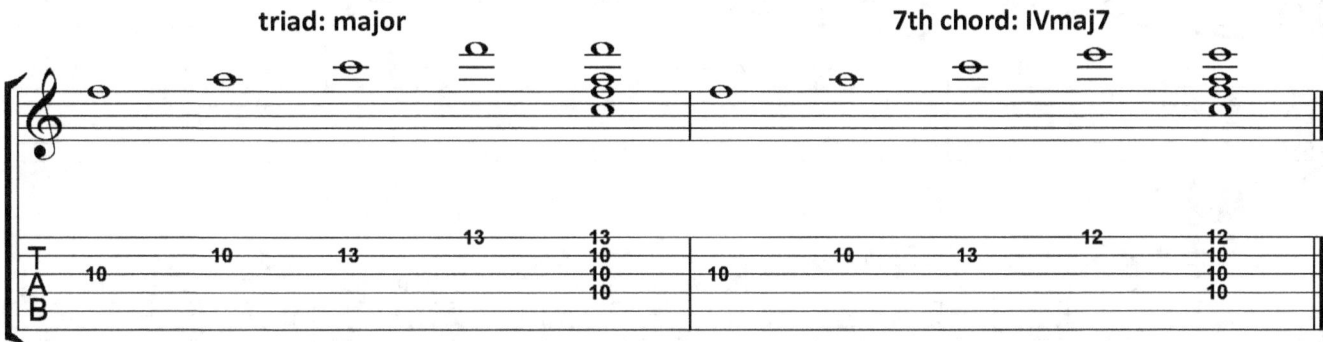

Chapter 4 the modes of the major scale - lydian

Lydian mode studies - shape 3

Mode exercises

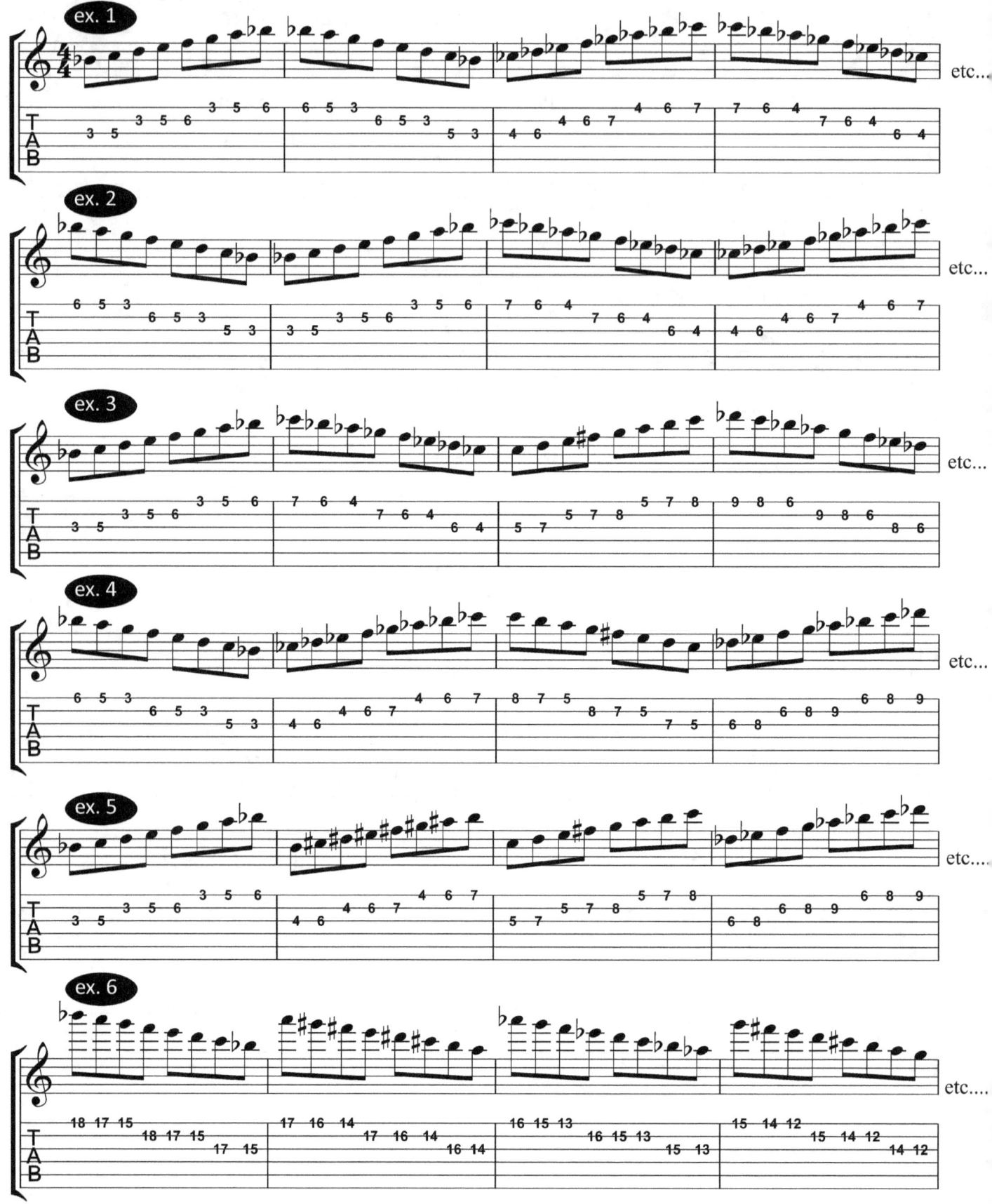

Melodic exercises

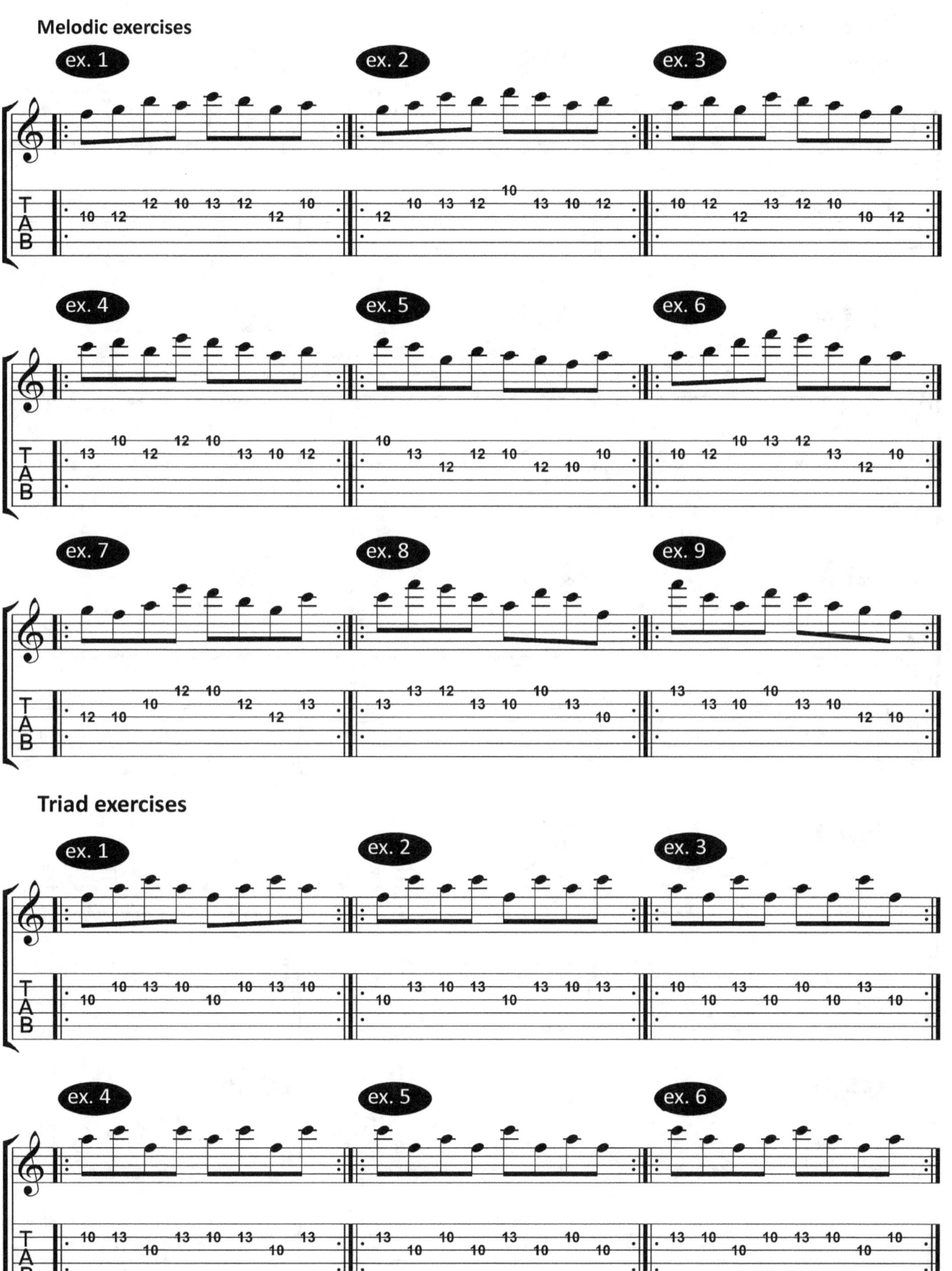

Triad exercises

Chapter 4   the modes of the major scale - lydian

7th chord exercises

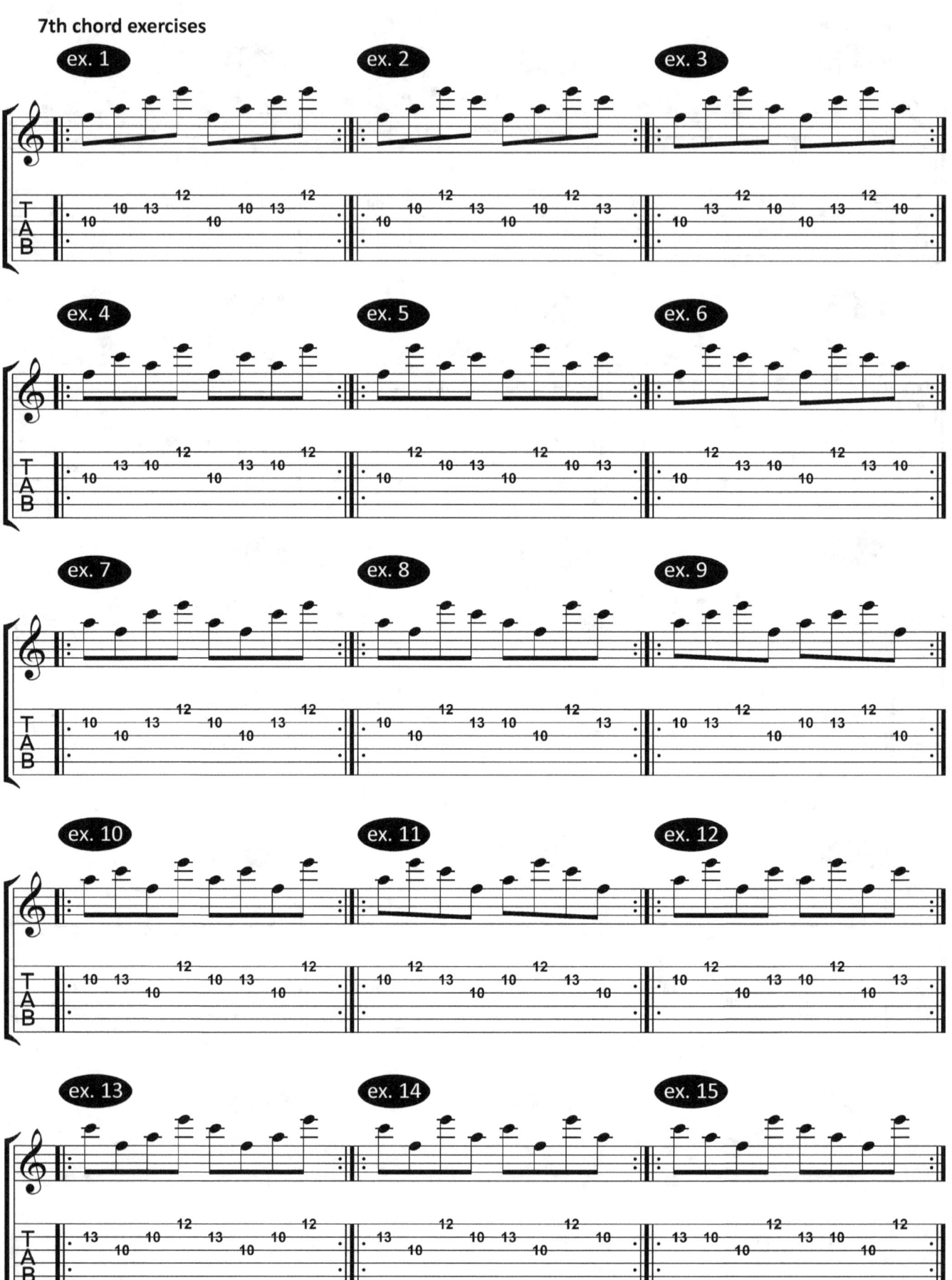

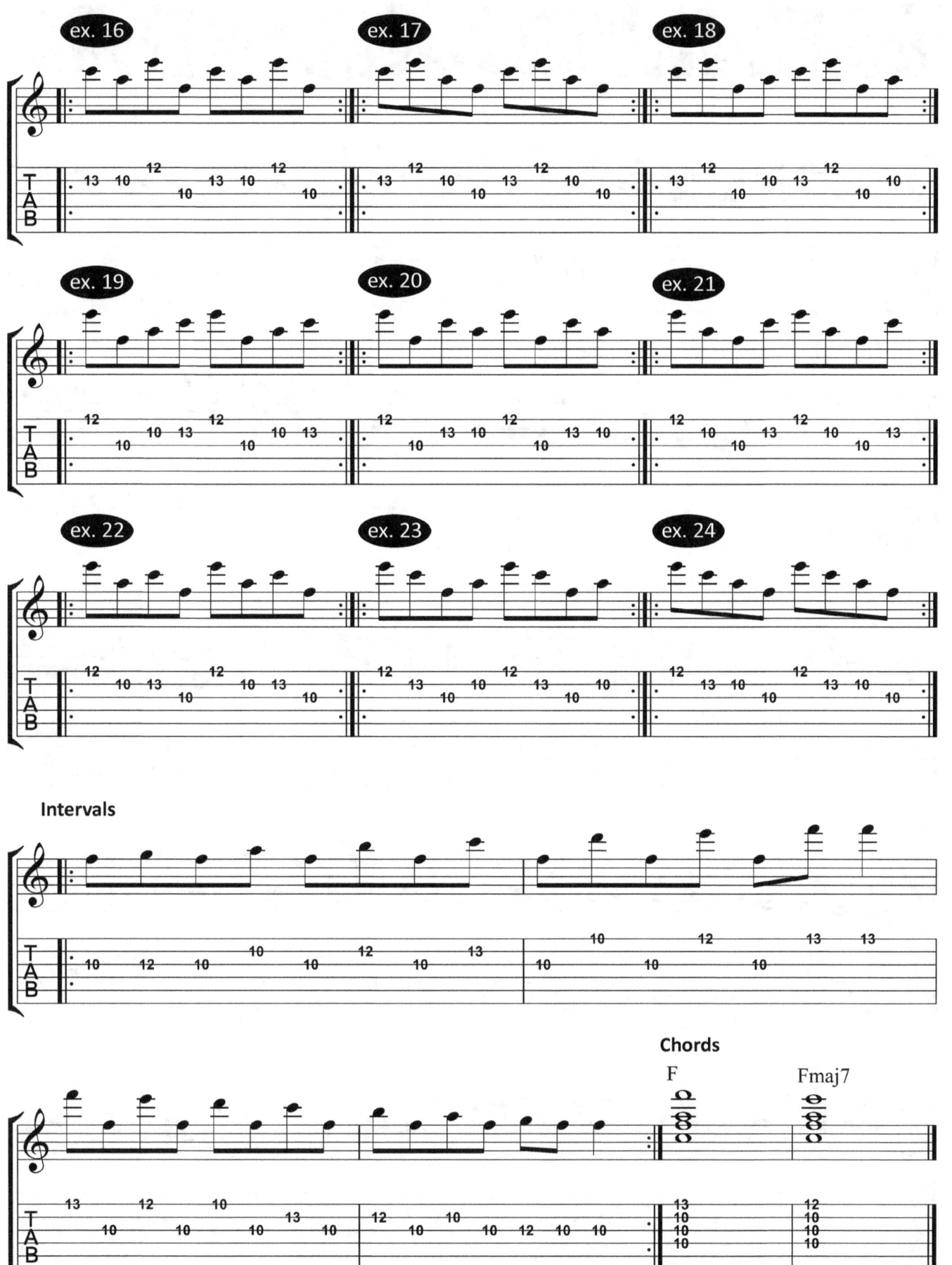

Chapter 4 the modes of the major scale - lydian

Lydian in 2 octaves with shapes 1 + 2

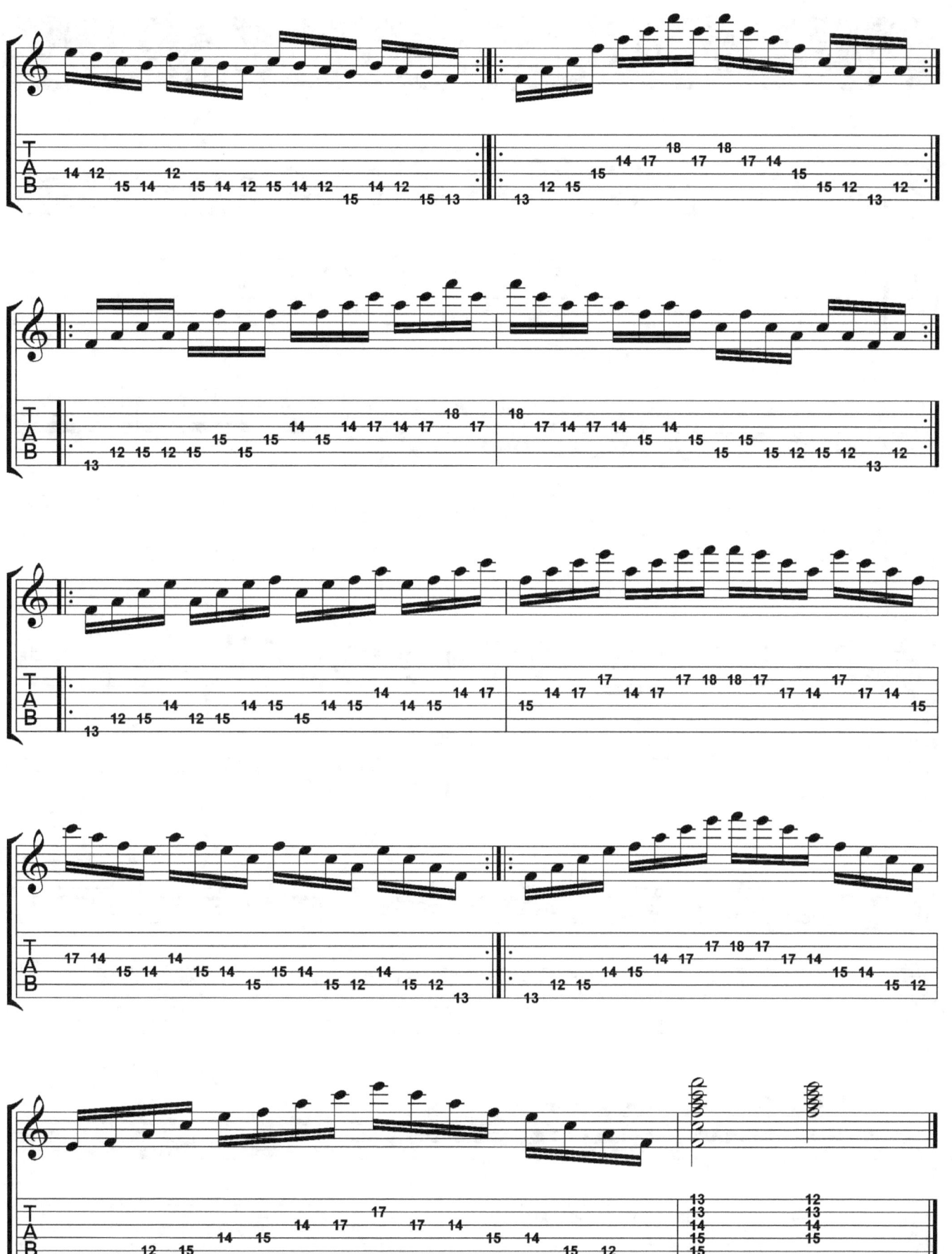

Chapter 4 the modes of the major scale - lydian

Lydian in 2 octaves with shapes 1 + 3

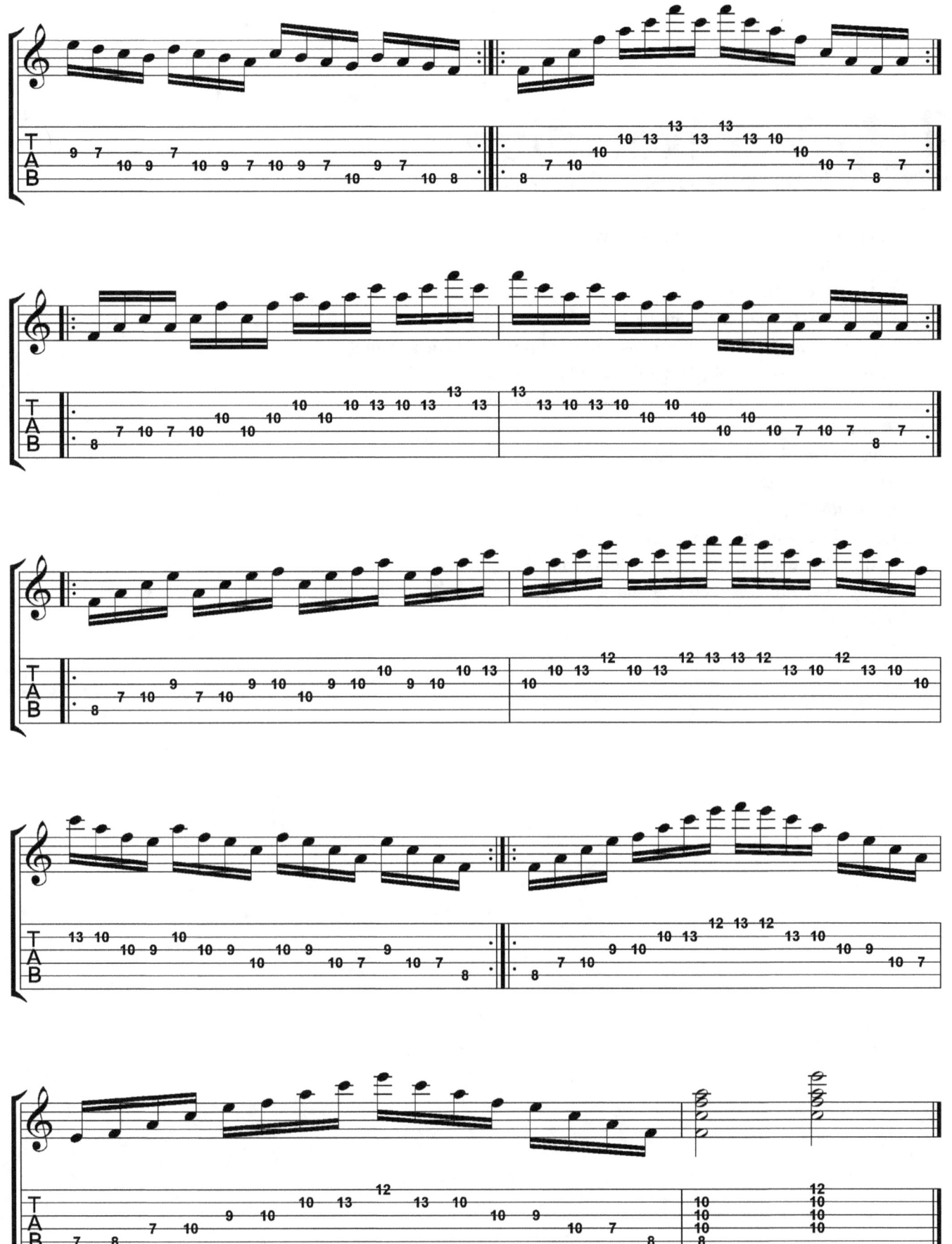

Chapter 4 the modes of the major scale - lydian

Mixolydian
5th mode of the Major scale

General formula: W-W-H-W-W-H-W

Scale: Major-minor seventh

Tetrachords: Major - minor

Characteristic note of the mode: the minor seventh ♭7

The intervals that are formed between the tonic and each scale degree: I-II = 2, I-III = 3, I-IV = 4, I-V = 5, I-VI = 6, I-VII = ♭7

The diatonic half steps are found on the scale degrees III-IV and VI-VII

Triad: Major V

Seventh chord: Major 7 V7, Vdom

Extensions: 9, 13

Generally: The Mixolydian mode is a major scale because it contains a major third, and its characteristic note is a minor seventh, as opposed to the other two major modes, the Ionian and the Lydian, which contain a major seventh. It is used over chords of V, and it gives a more "blues" tone color.

Mixolydian shape 1

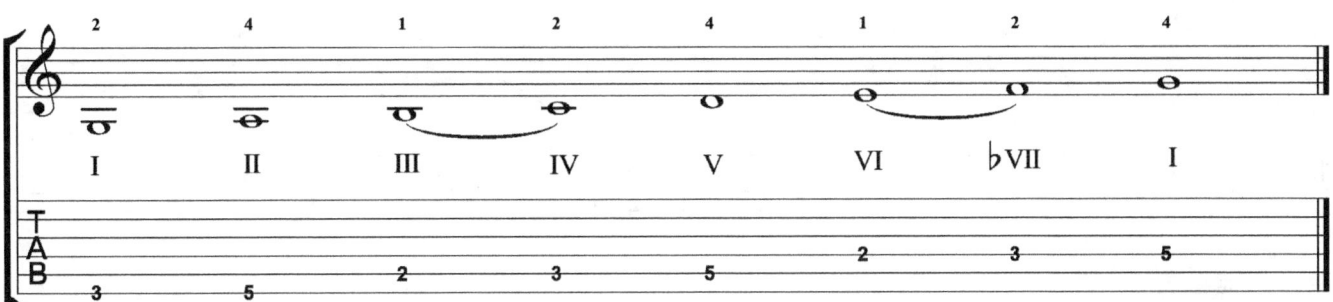

Tetrachords

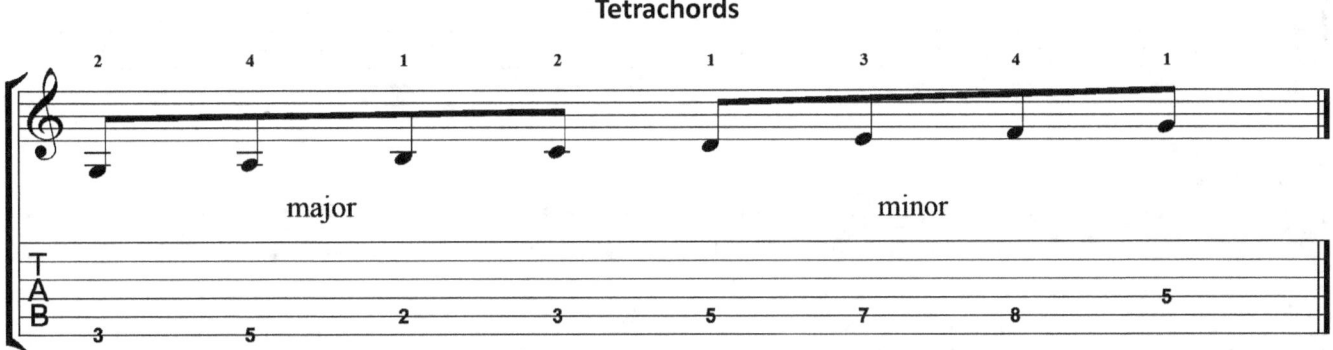

Intervals

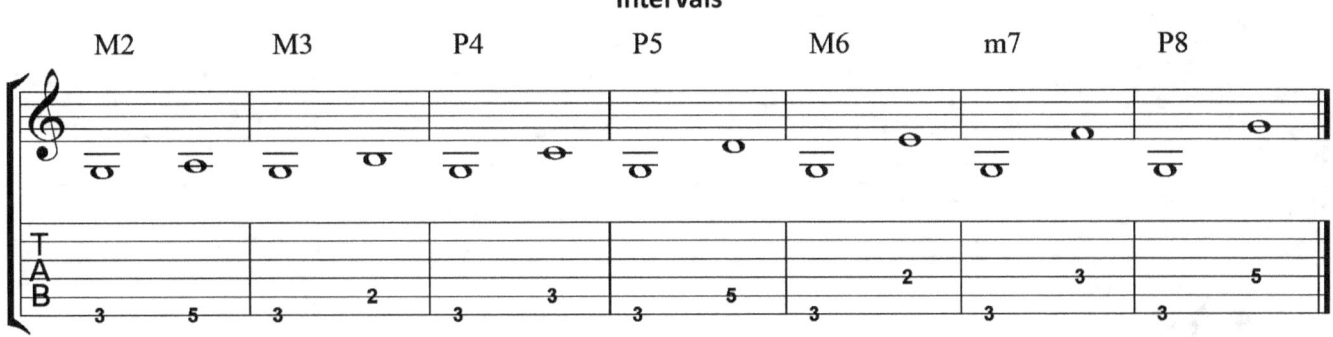

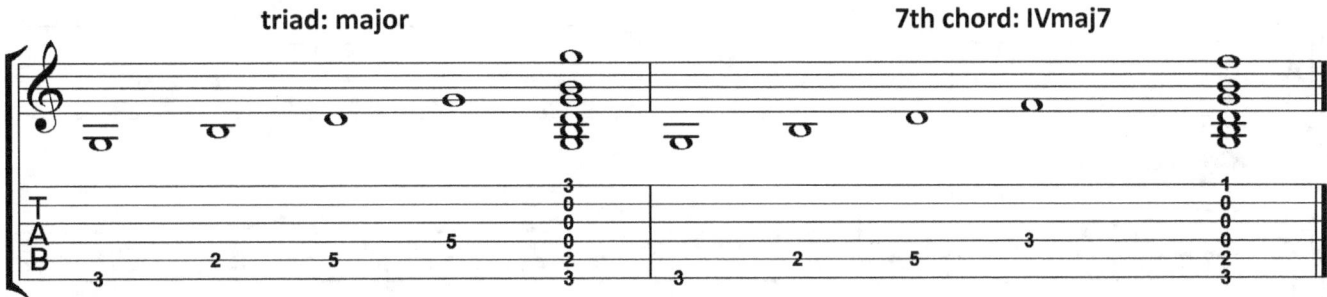

Chapter 4 the modes of the major scale - mixolydian

Mixolydian mode studies - shape 1

Mode exercises

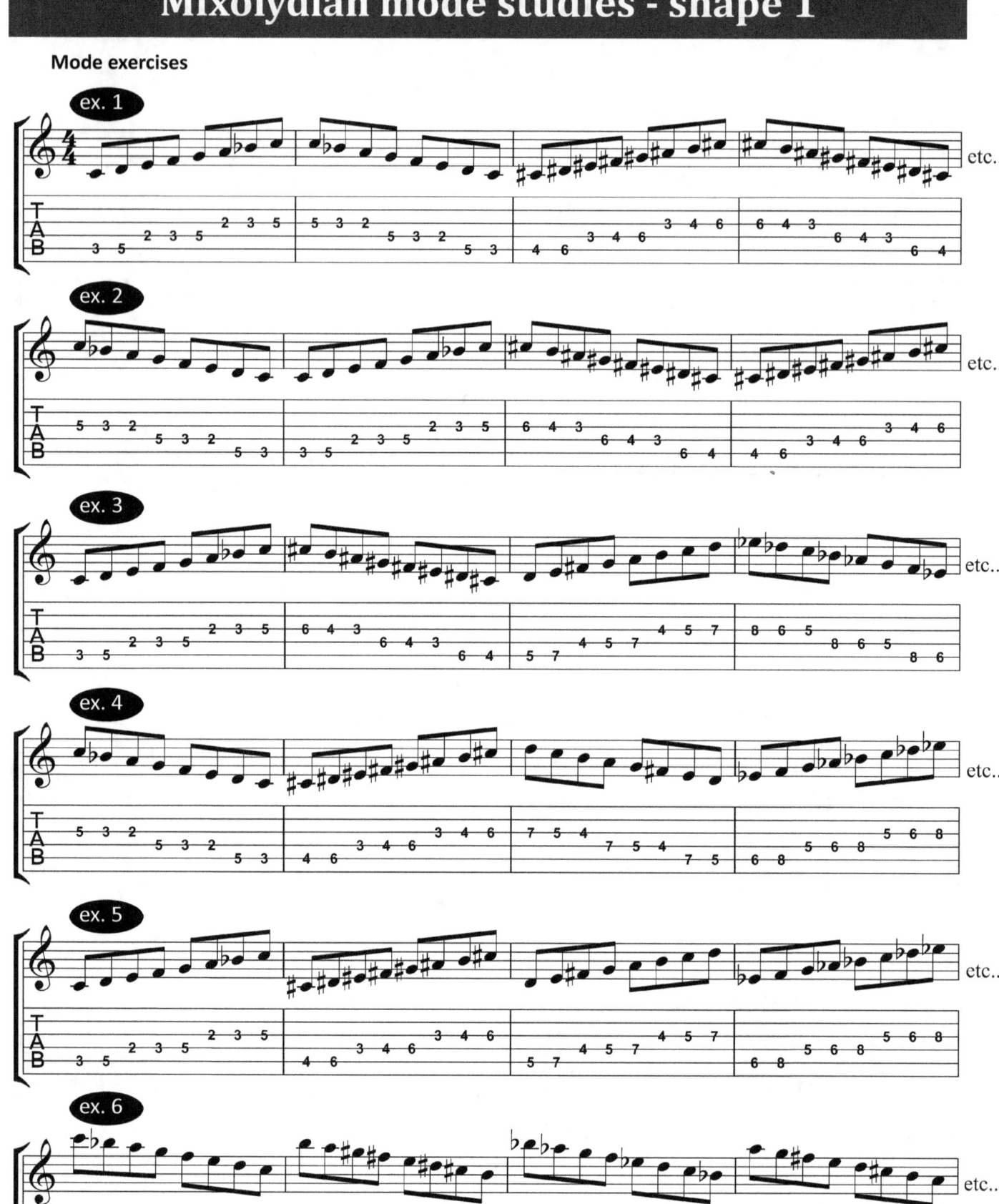

Melodic exercises

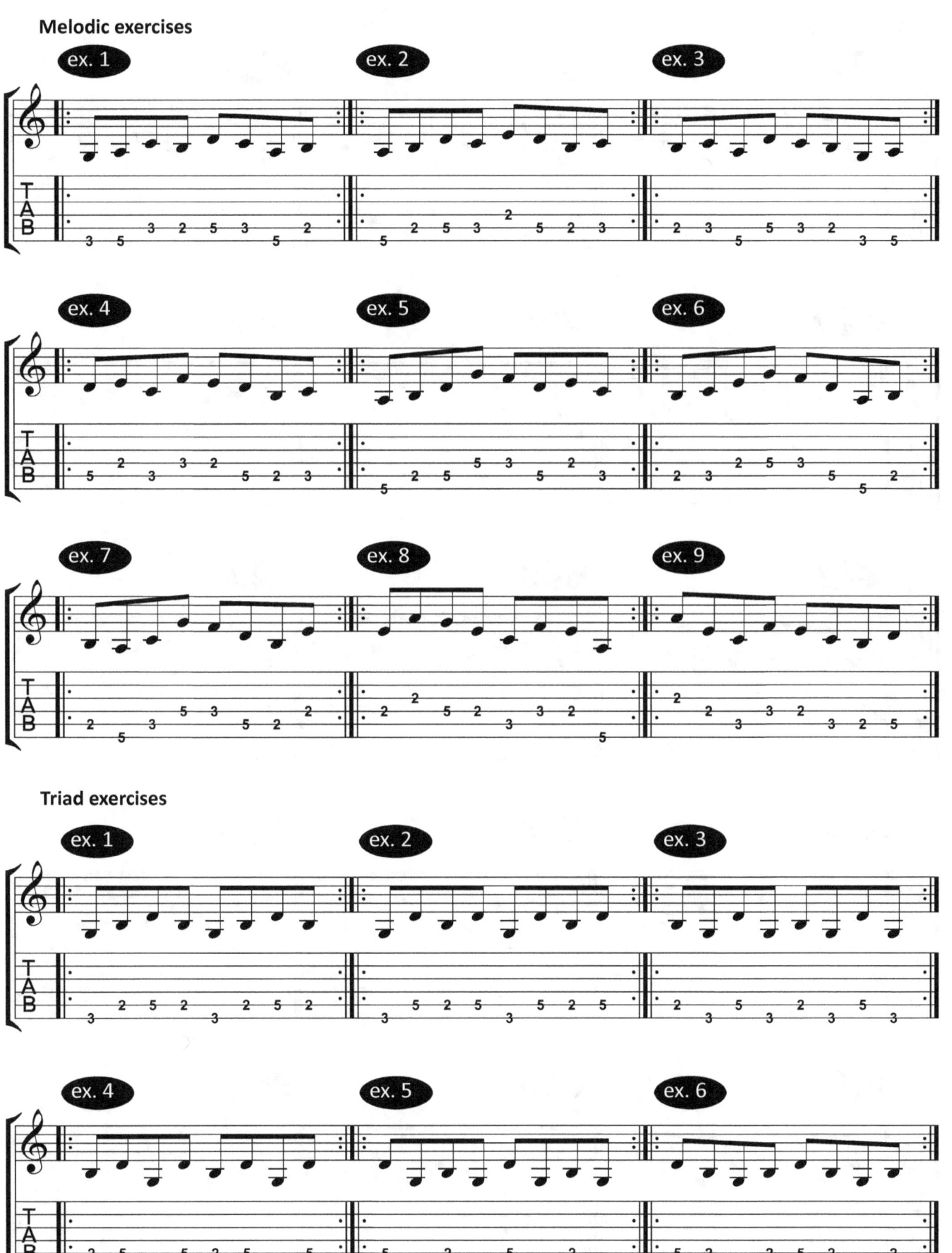

Triad exercises

Chapter 4 the modes of the major scale - mixolydian

7th chord exercises

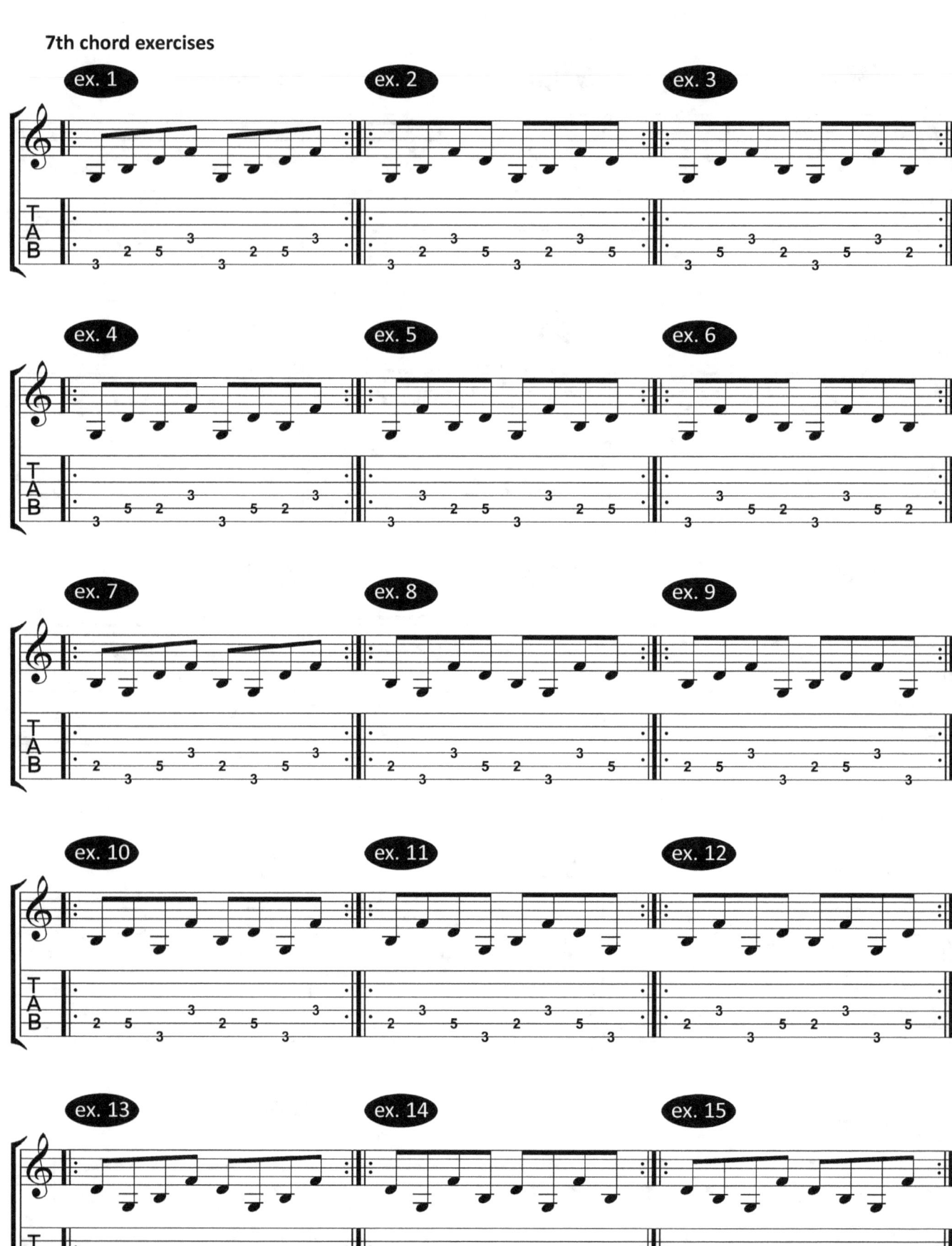

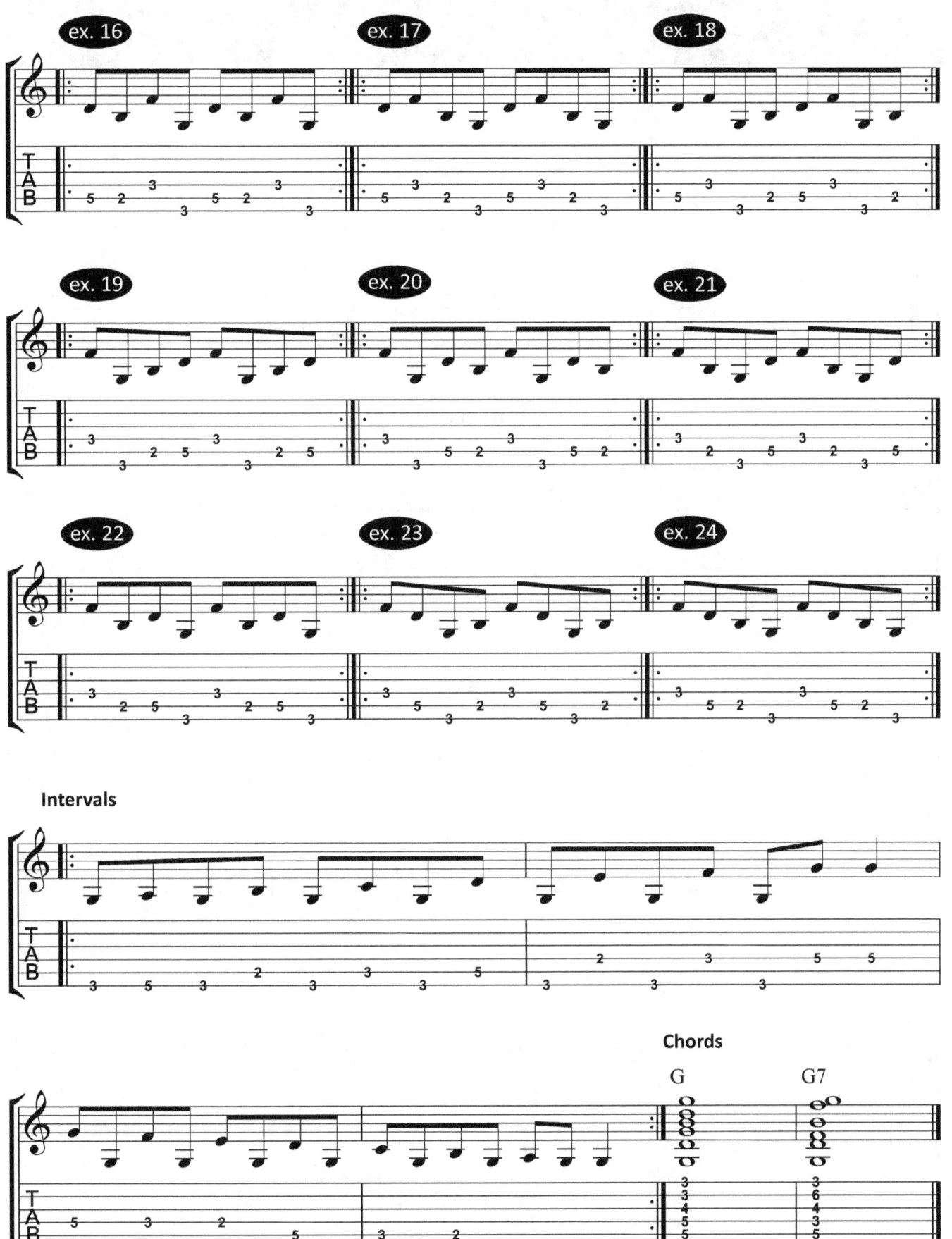

Chapter 4 the modes of the major scale - mixolydian

Mixolydian shape 2

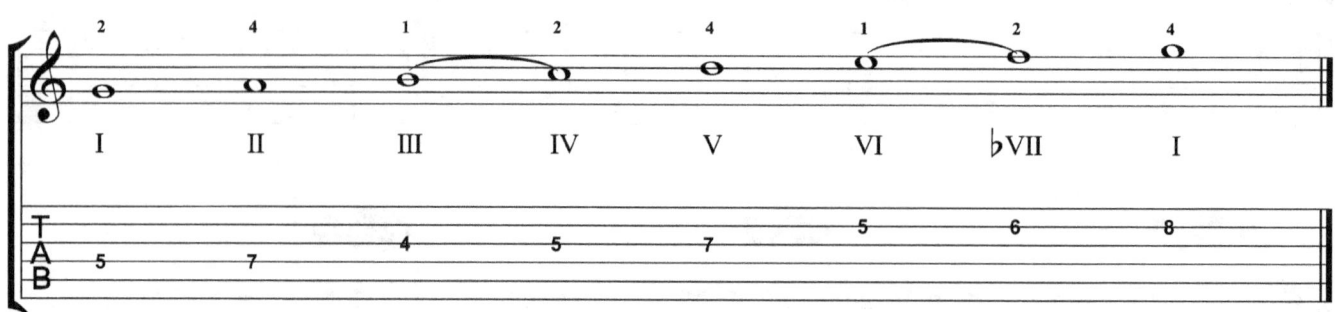

Tetrachords

Intervals

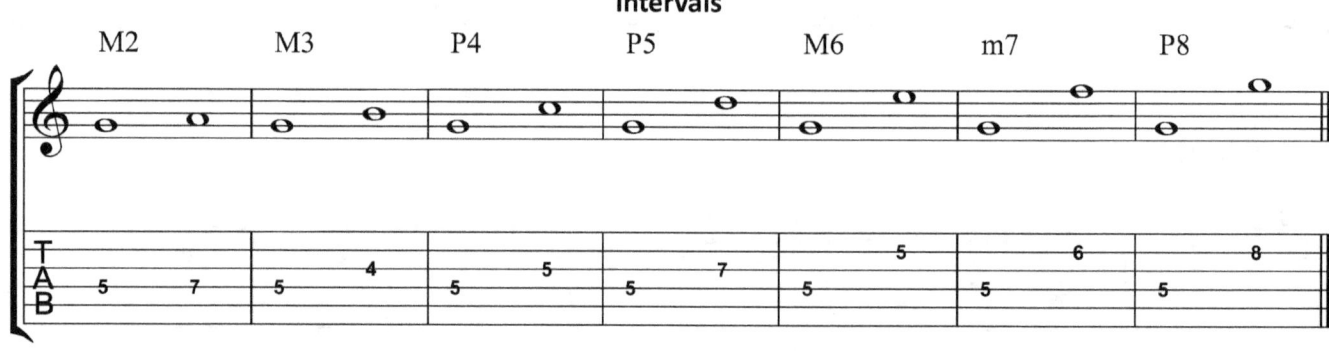

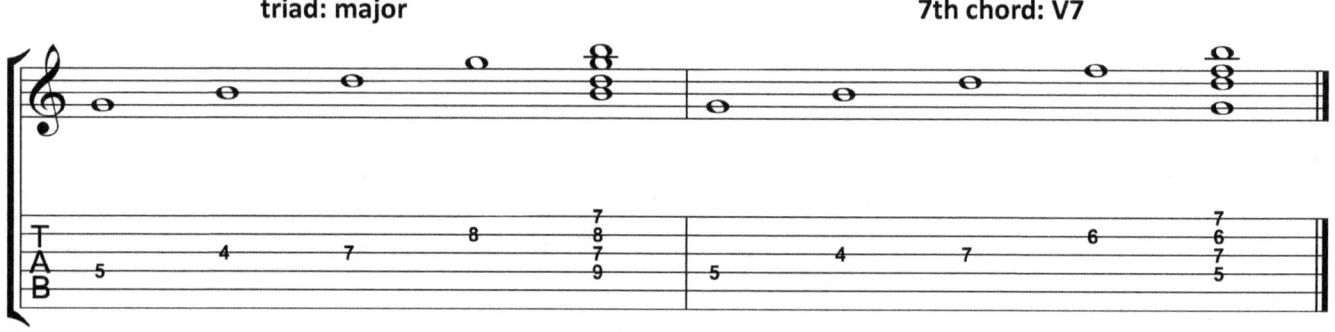

Mixolydian mode studies - shape 2

Mode exercises

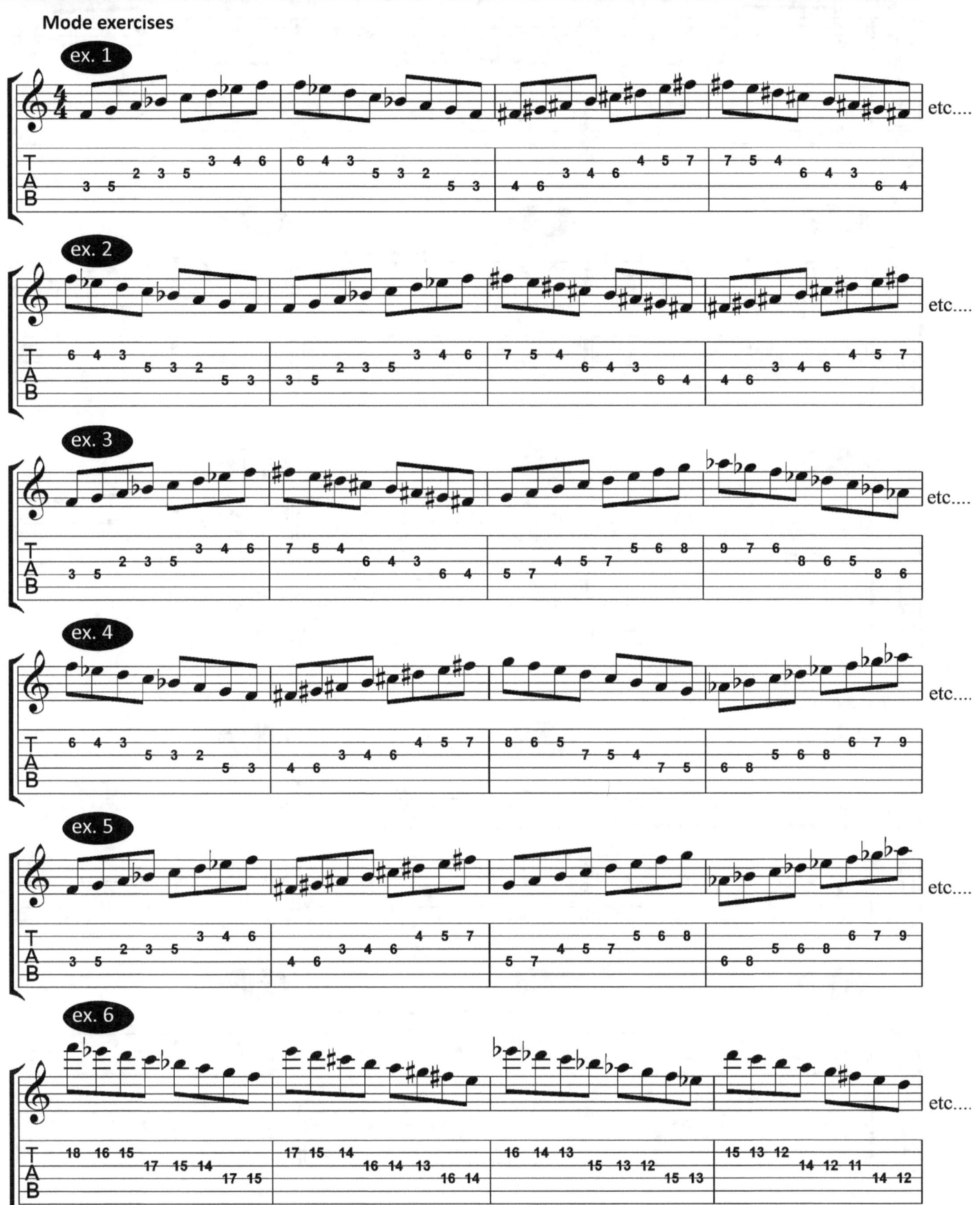

Chapter 4 the modes of the major scale - mixolydian

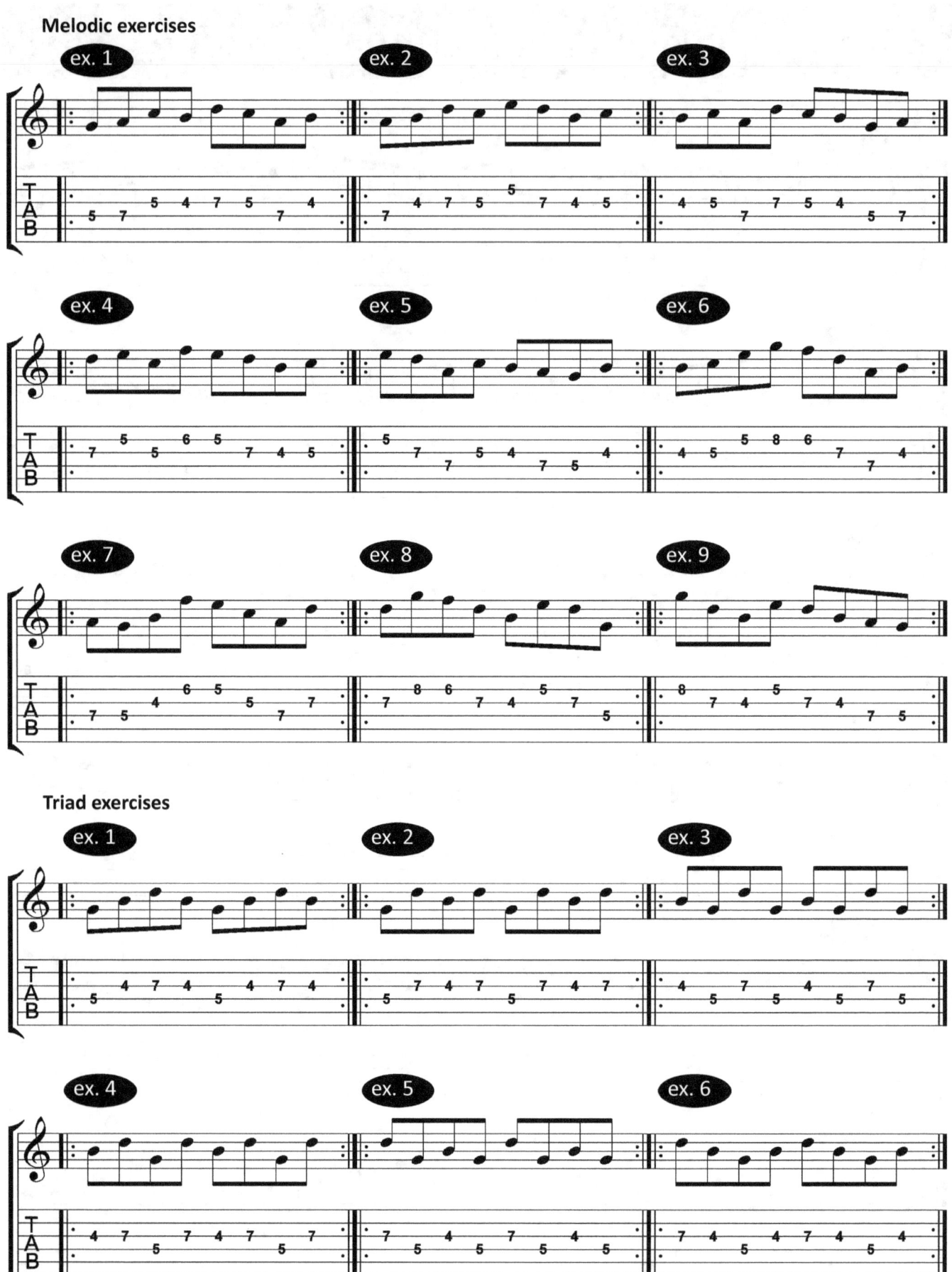

7th chord exercises

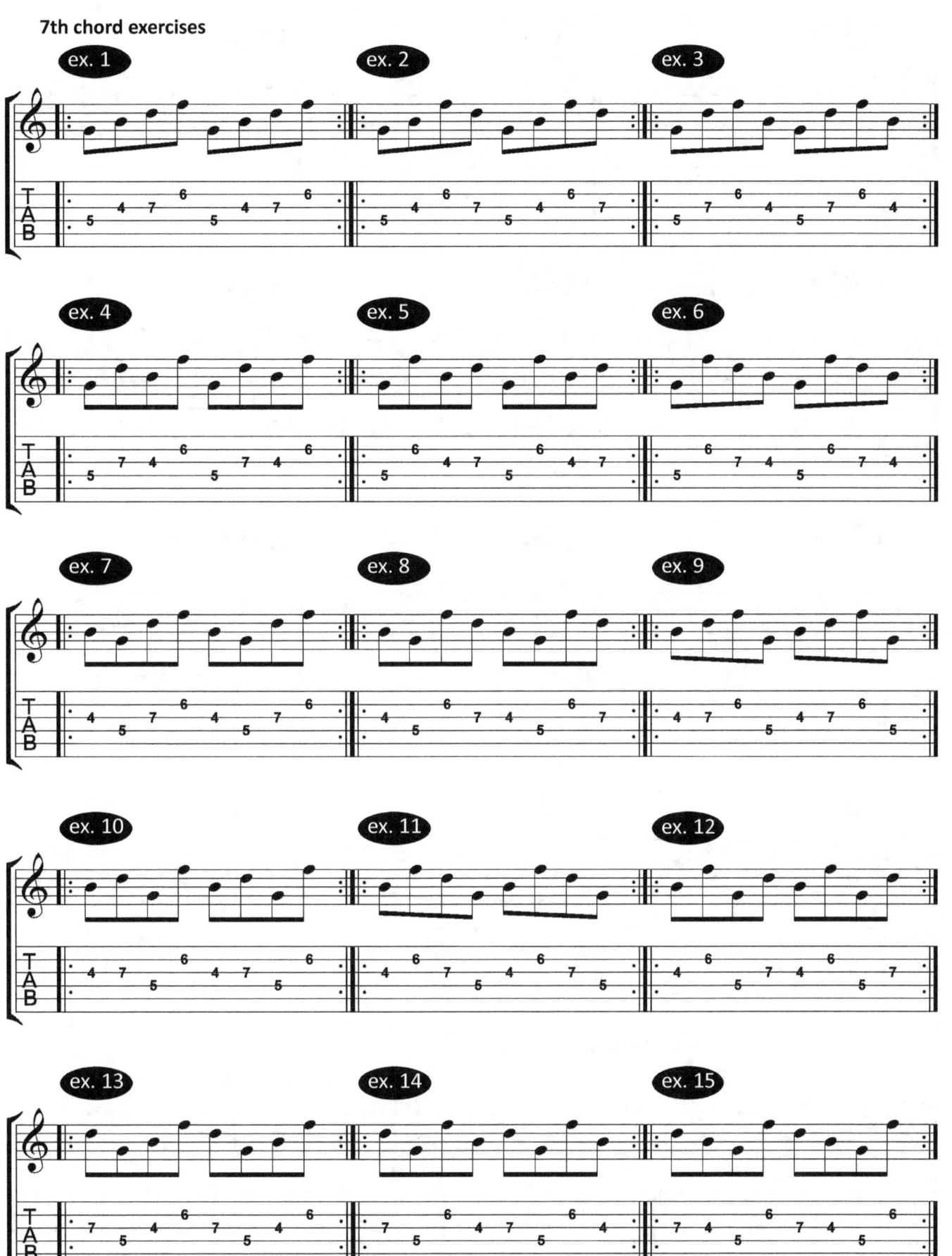

Chapter 4 the modes of the major scale - mixolydian

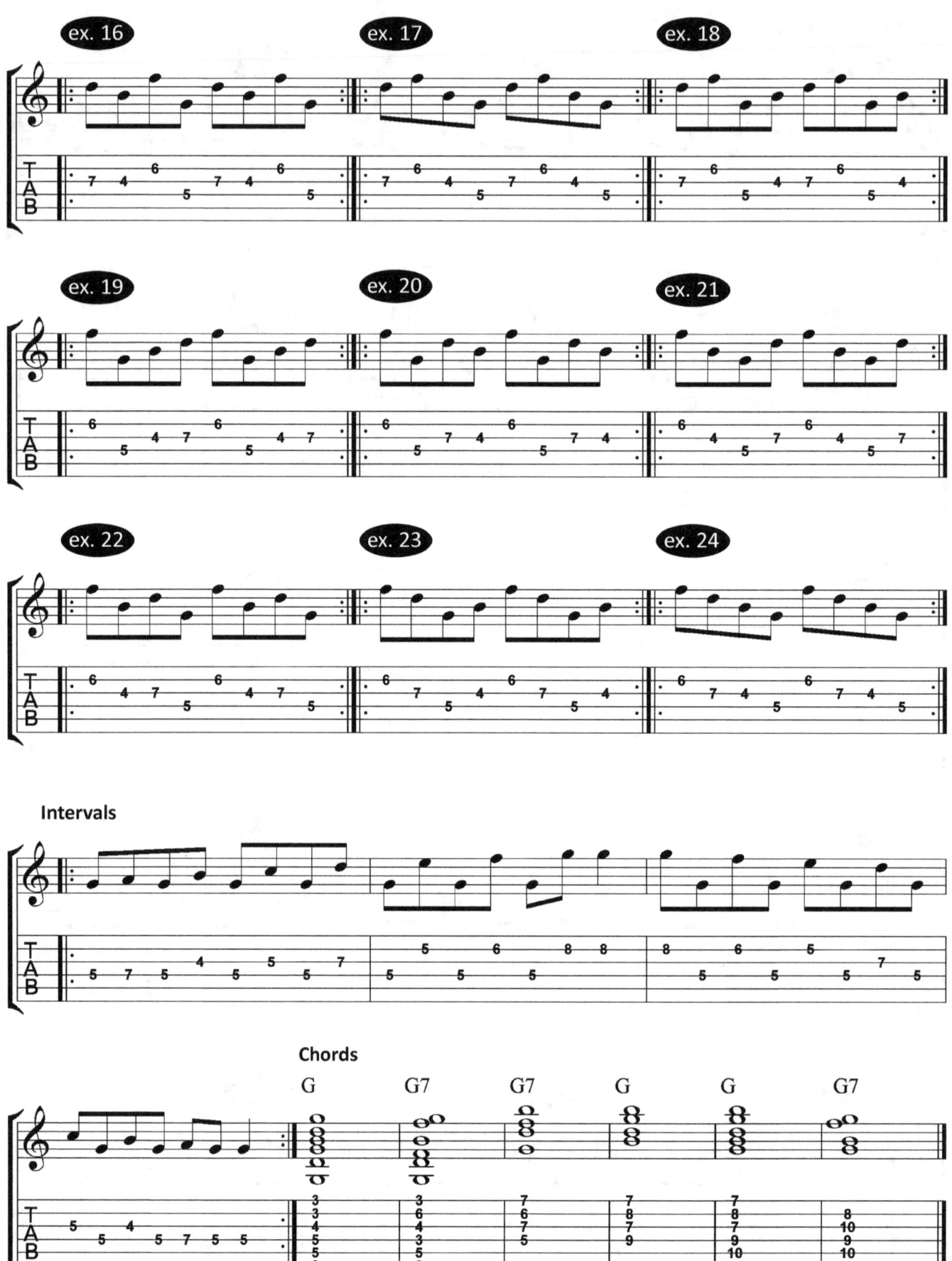

Mixolydian shape 3

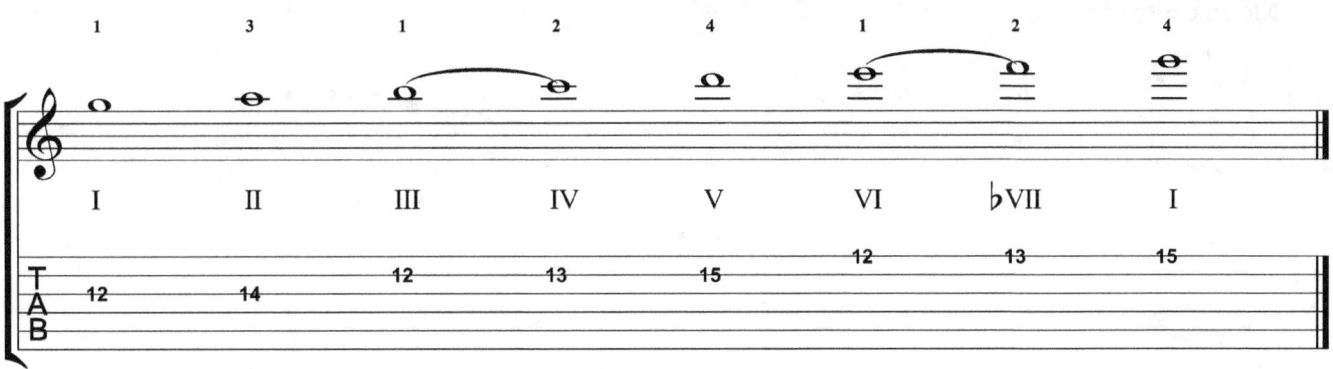

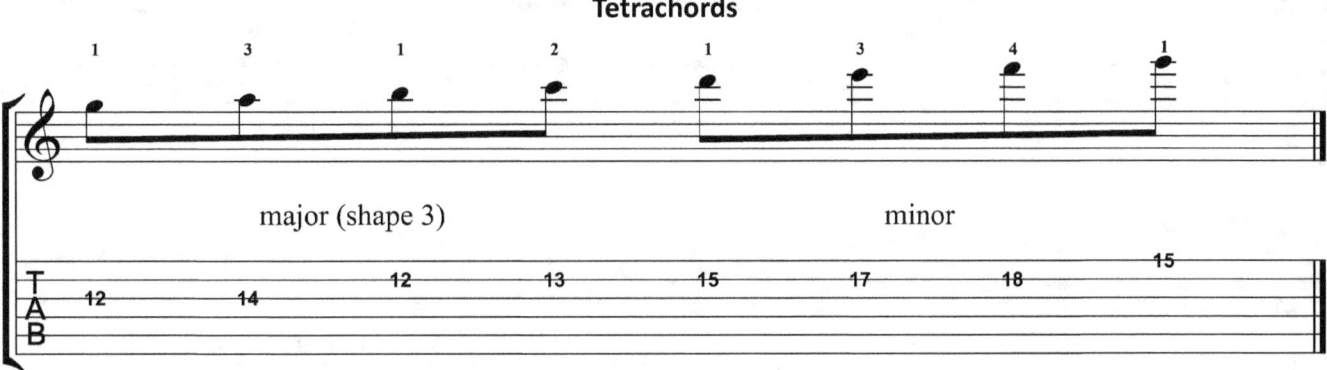

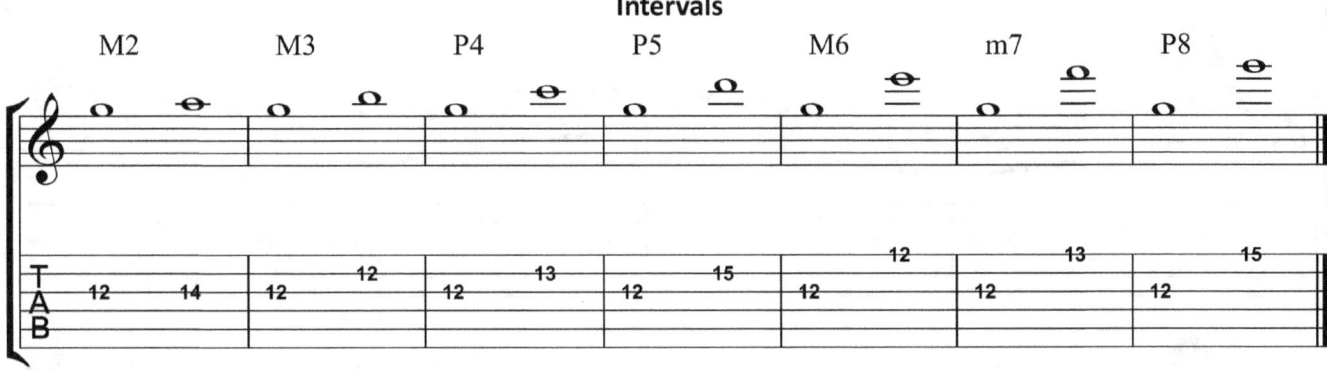

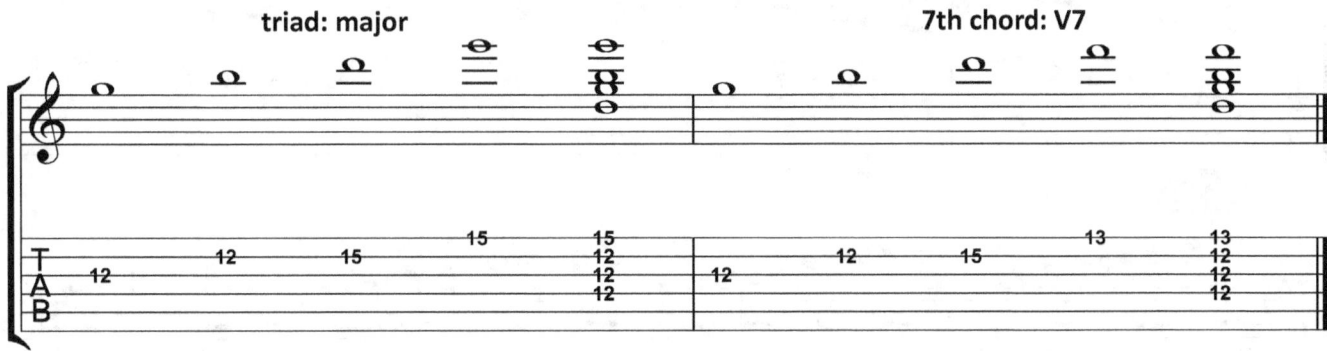

Mixolydian mode studies - shape 3

Mode exercises

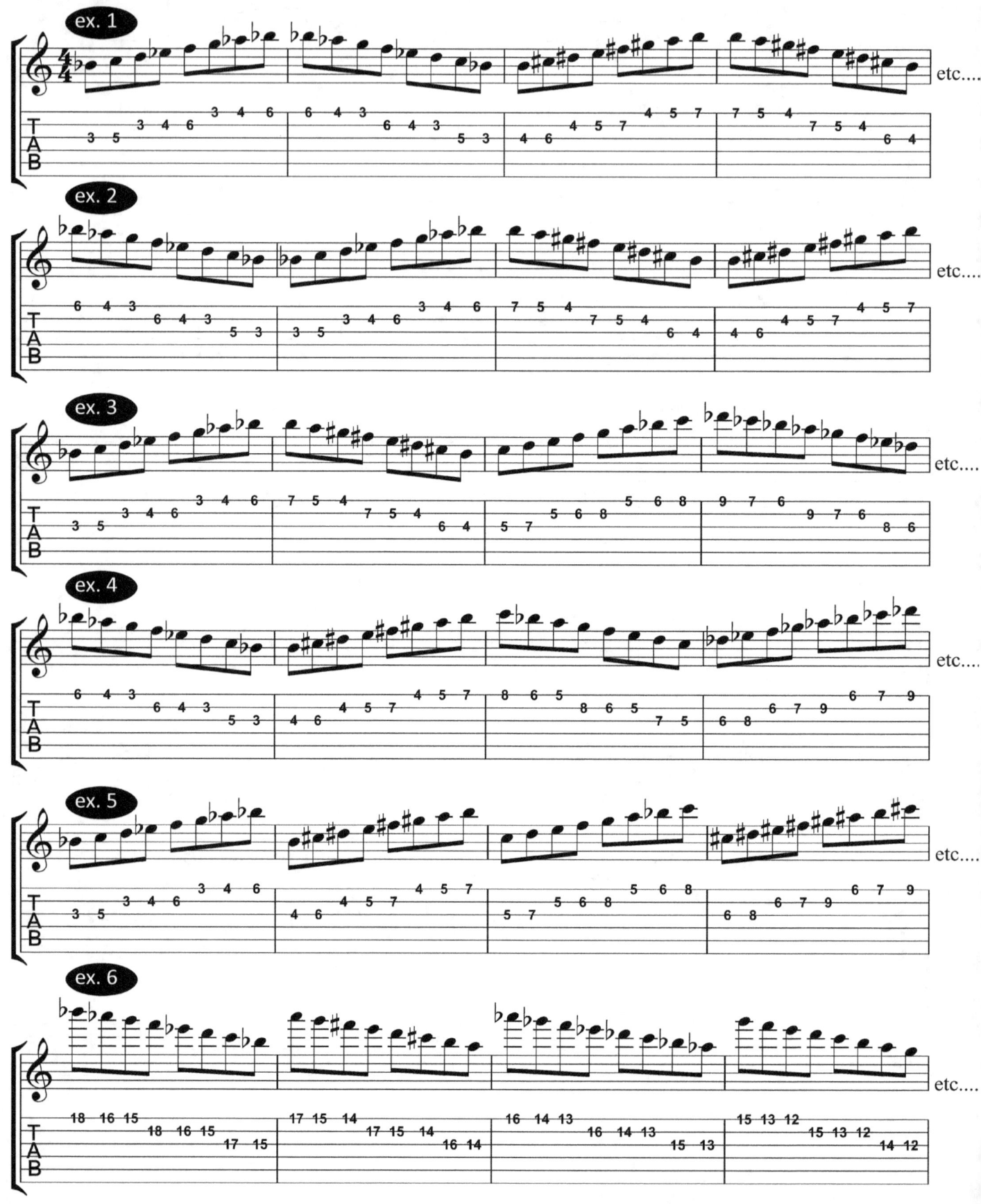

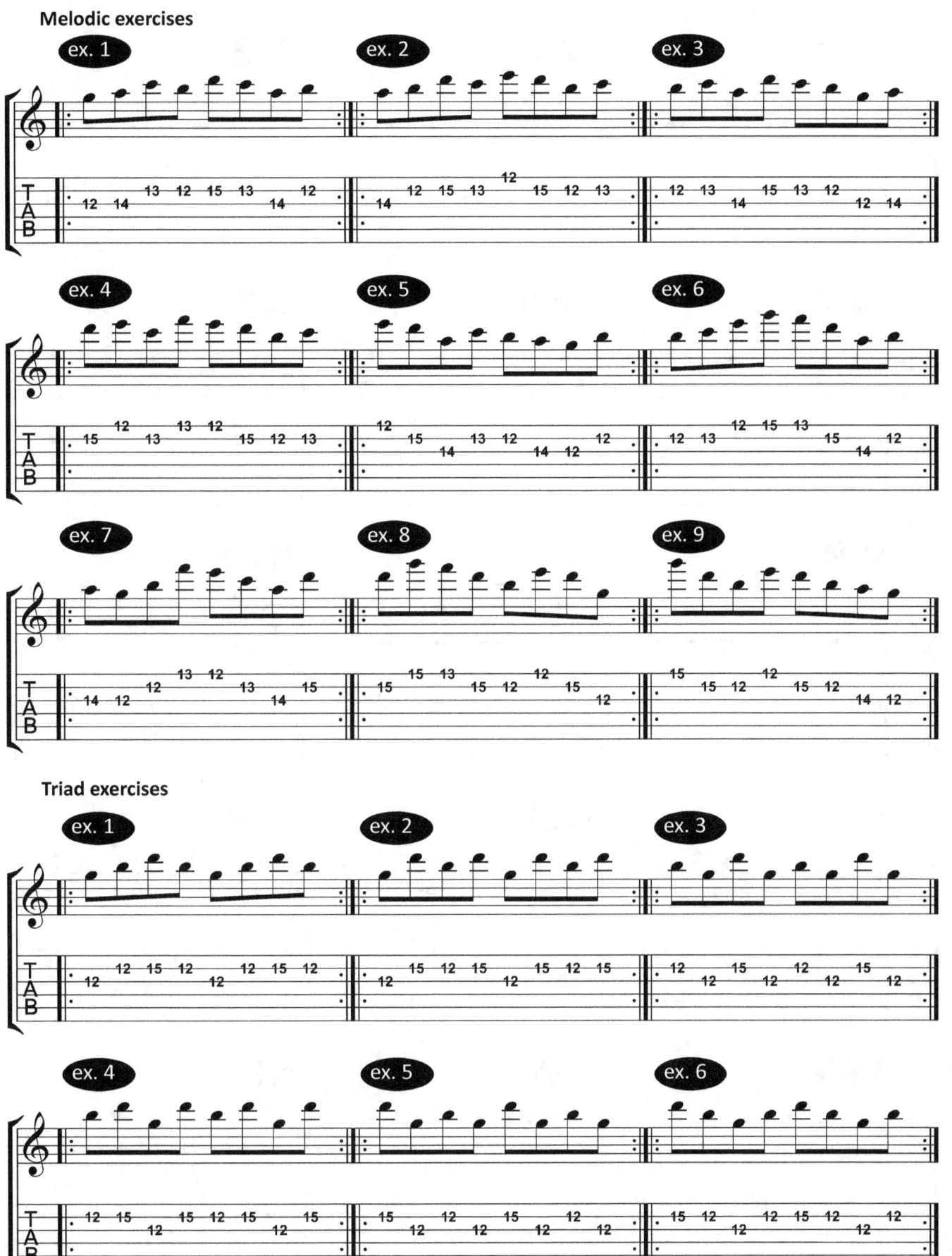

Chapter 4   the modes of the major scale - mixolydian

7th chord exercises

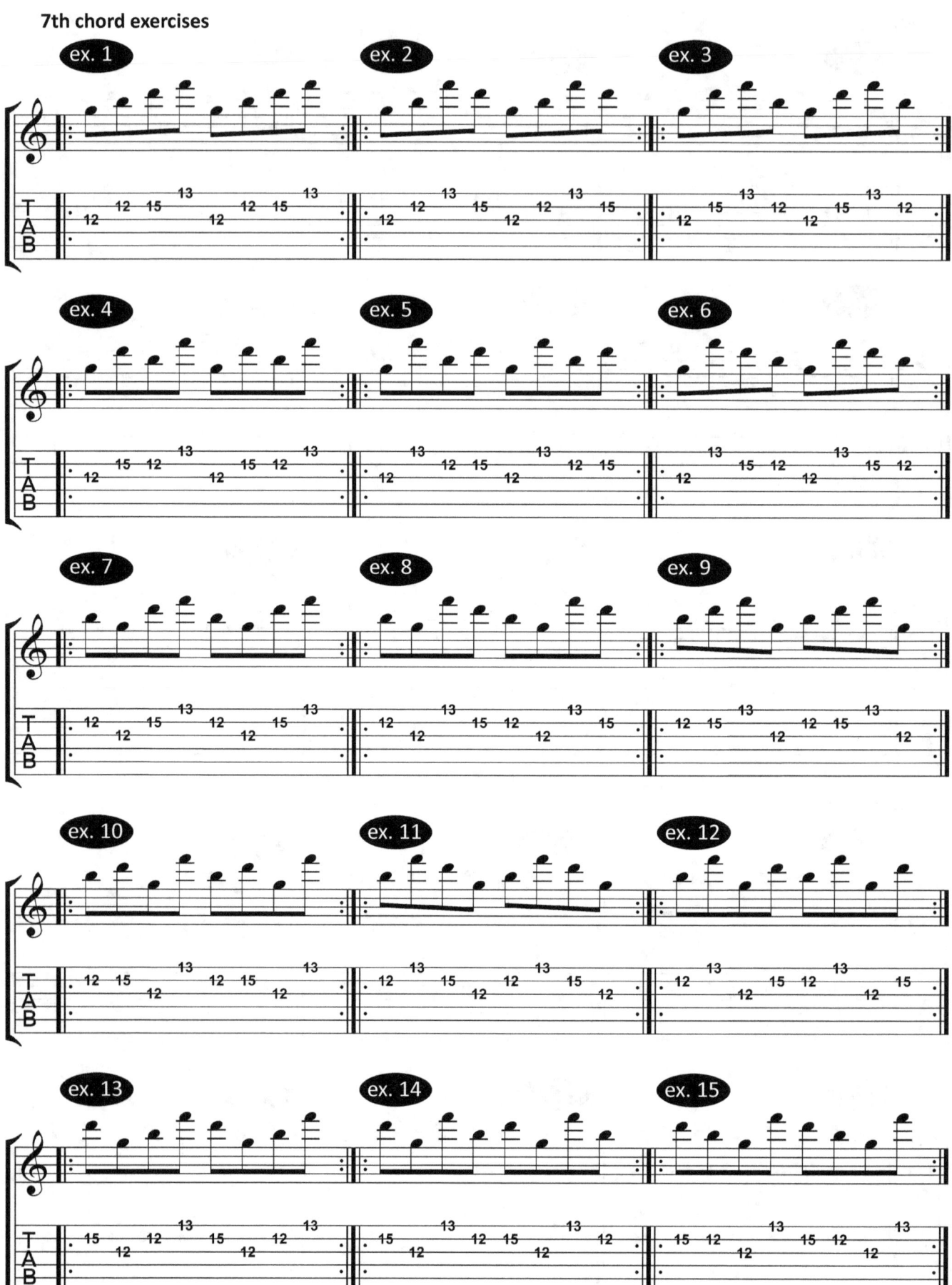

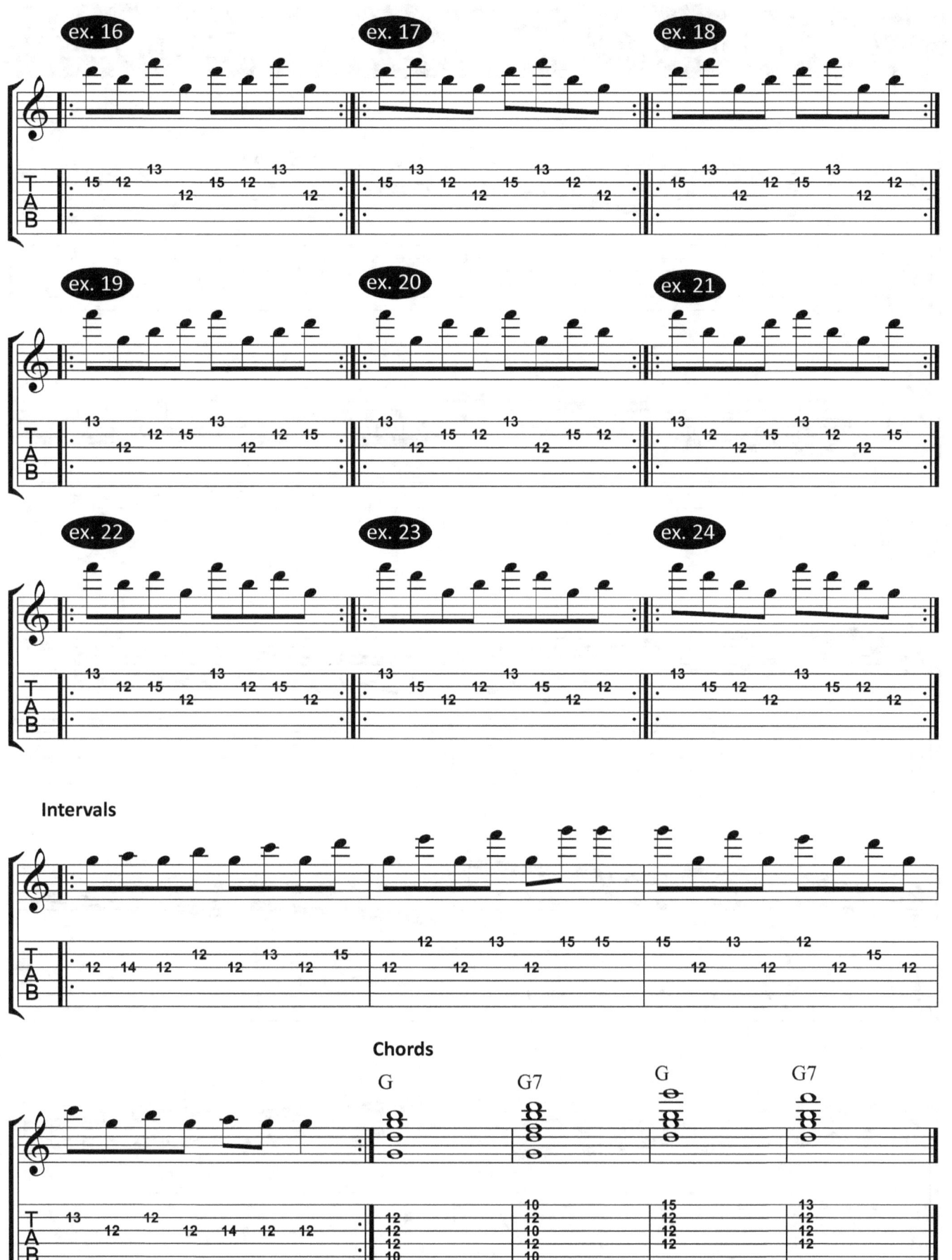

Chapter 4 the modes of the major scale - mixolydian

Mixolydian in 2 octaves with shapes 1 + 2

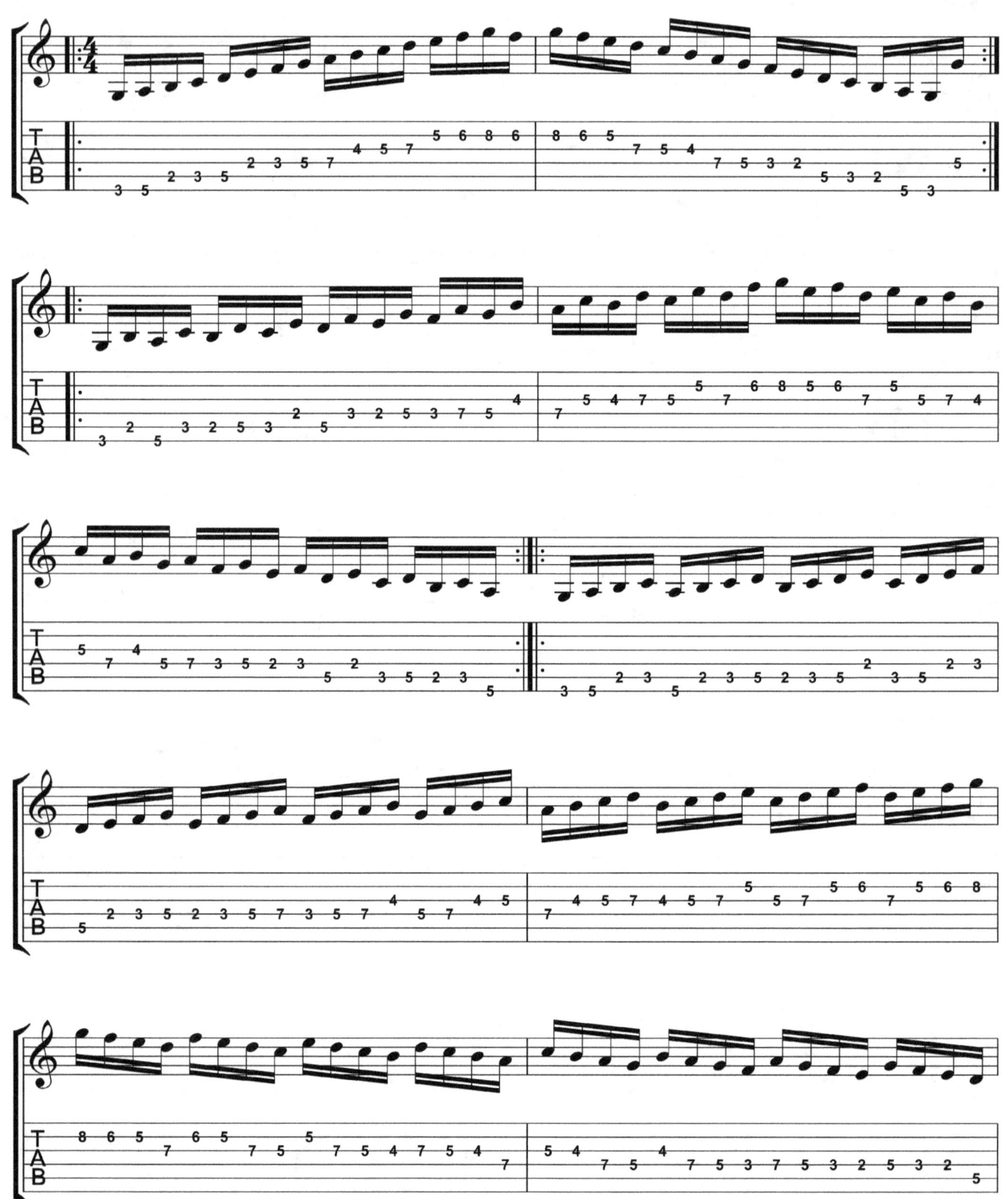

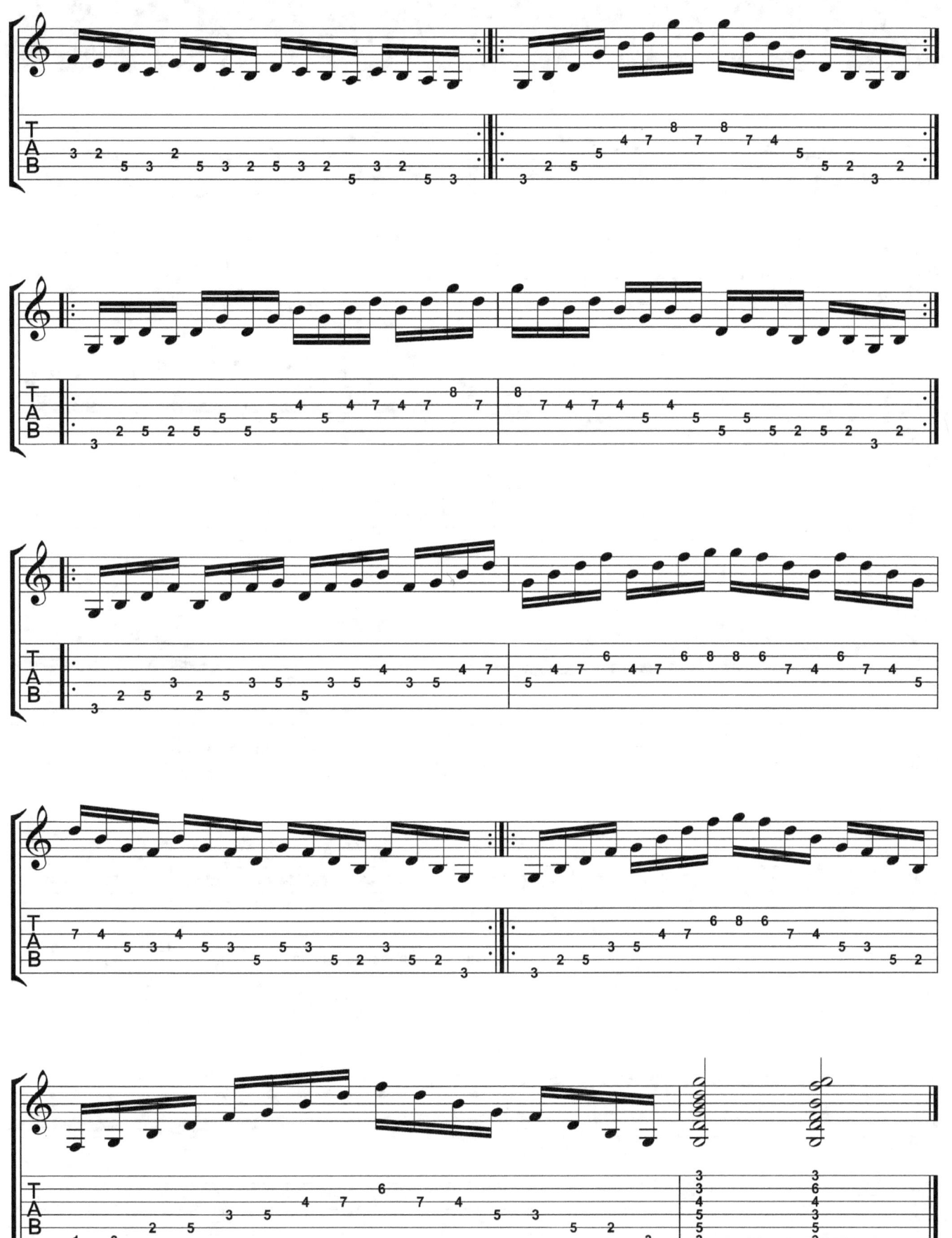

Chapter 4   the modes of the major scale - mixolydian

Mixolydian in 2 octaves with shapes 1 + 3

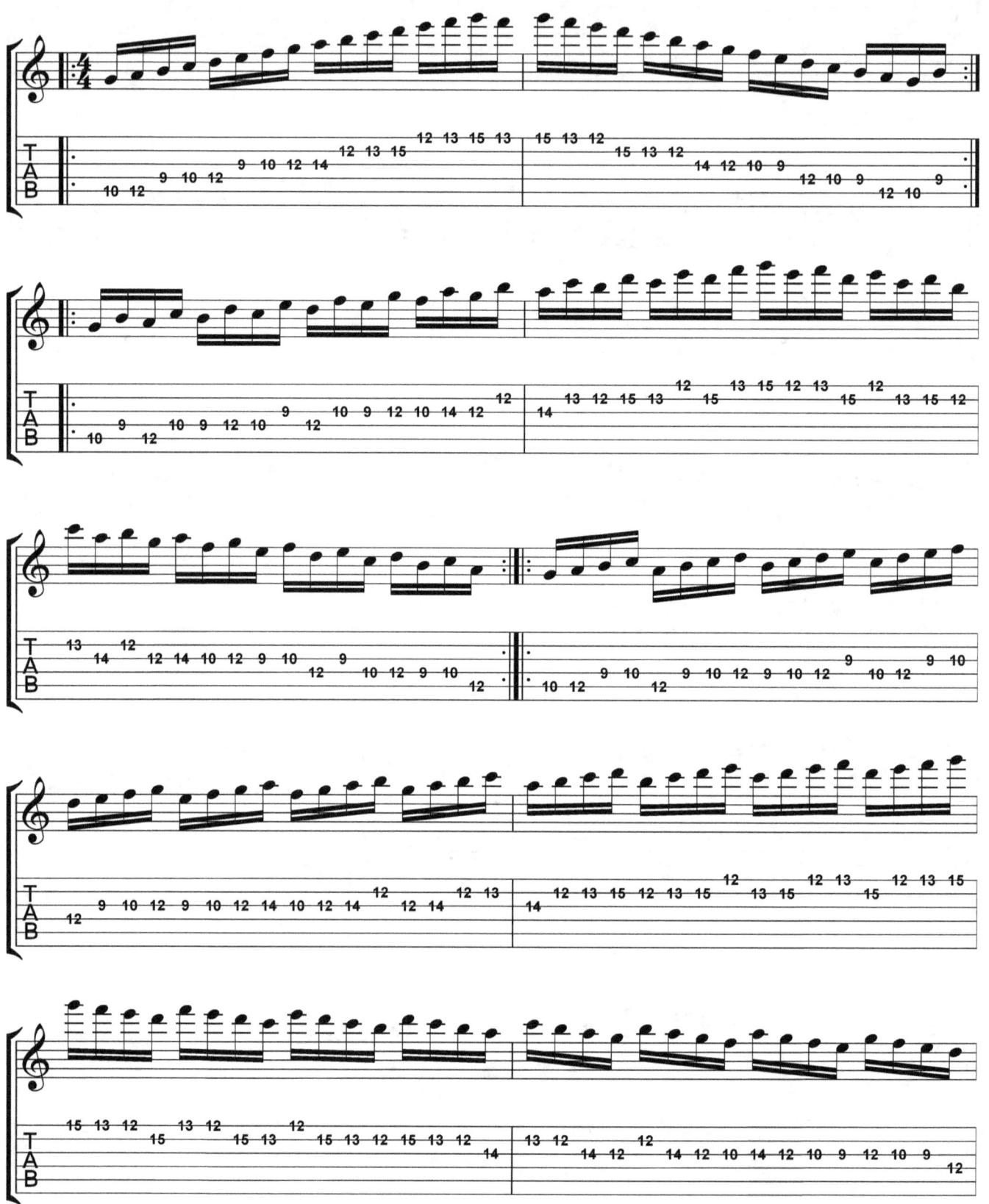

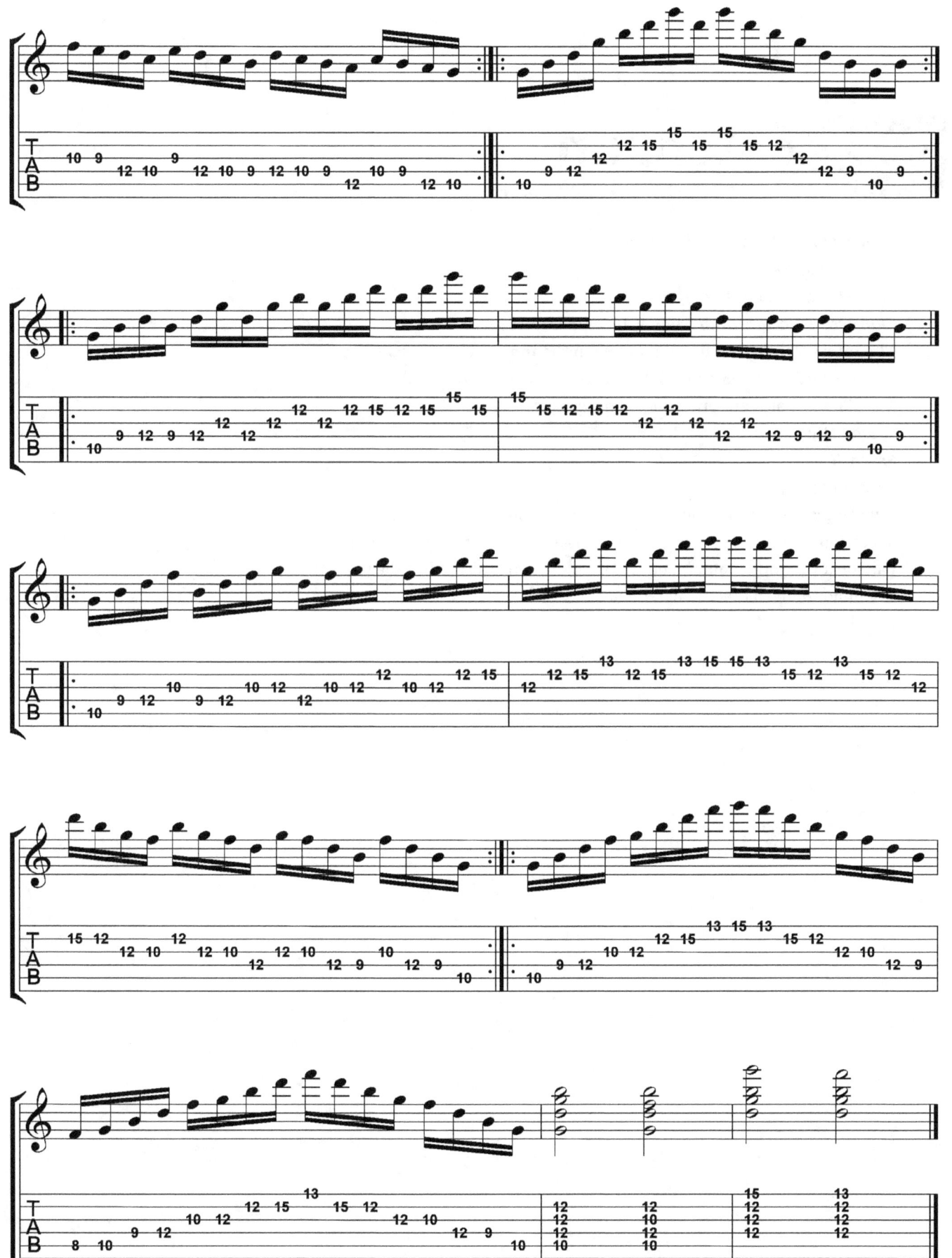

Chapter 4 the modes of the major scale - mixolydian

Aeolian
6th mode of the Major scale

General formula: W-H-W-W-H-W-W

Scale: Minor seventh (Natural minor)

Tetrachords: Minor - Phrygian

Characteristic note of the mode: the minor third ♭3

The intervals that are formed between the tonic and each scale degree: I-II = 2, I-III = ♭3, I-IV = 4, I-V = 5, I-VI = ♭6, I-VII = ♭7

The diatonic half steps are found on the scale degrees II-III and V-VI

Triad: Minor vi-

Seventh chord: Minor 7th vi-7

Extensions: 9, 11

Generally: The Aeolian mode is the natural minor scale. It has a balanced sound as far as its structure, and it is a point of reference and comparison for the other minor modes of the system. It is also called the relative minor of the mother Major scale.

Aeolian shape 1

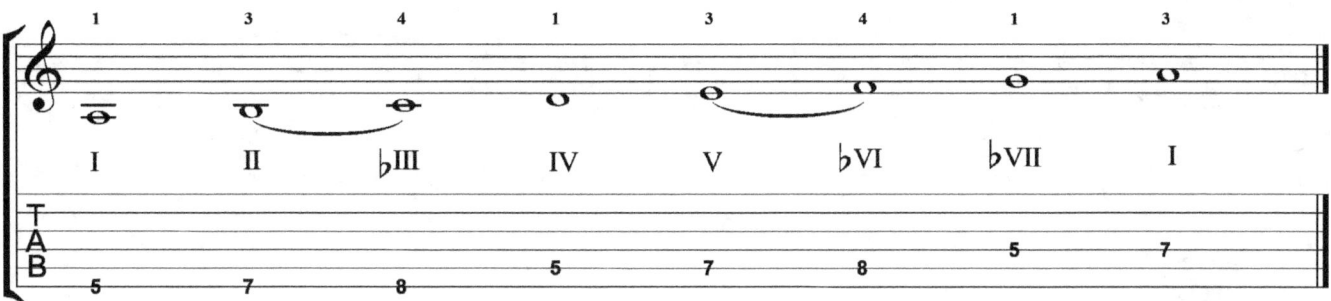

Tetrachords

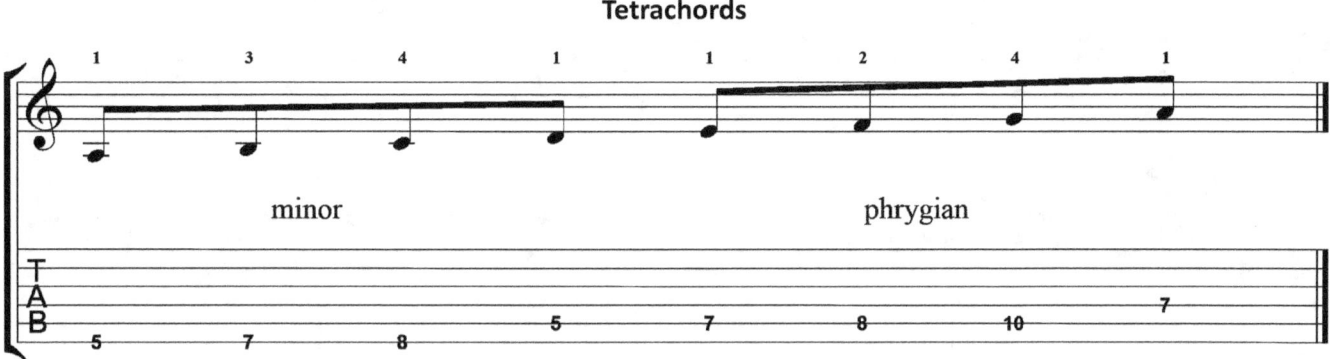

Intervals

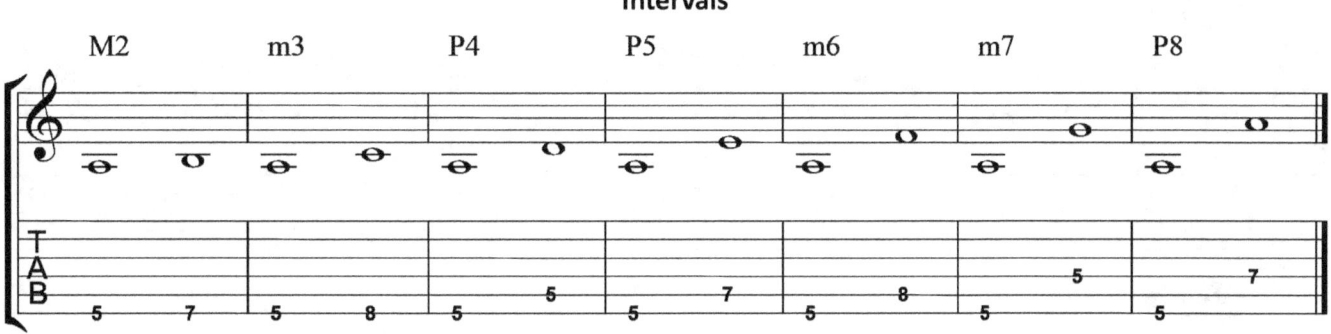

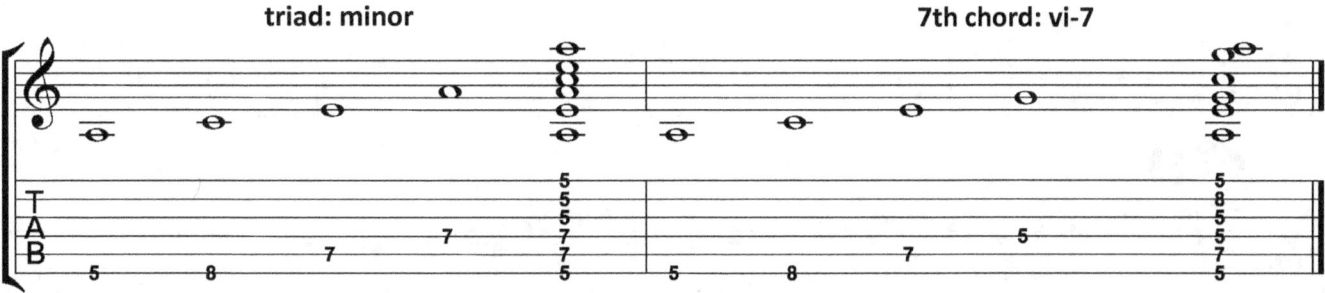

Chapter 4   the modes of the major scale - aeolian

Aeolian mode studies - shape 1

Mode exercises

ex. 1

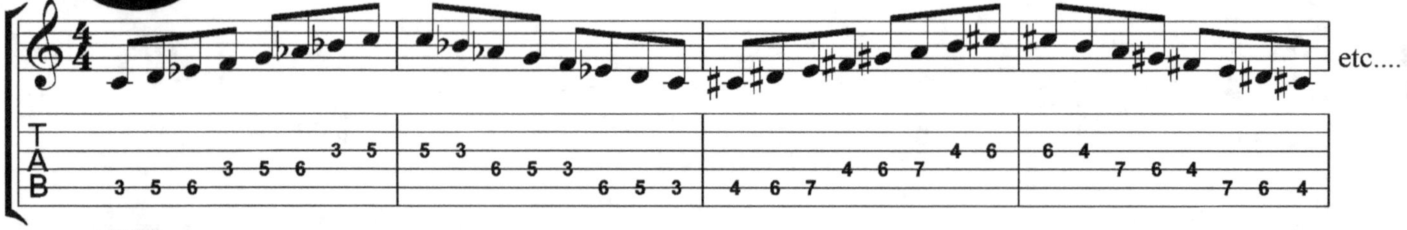

ex. 2

ex. 3

ex. 4

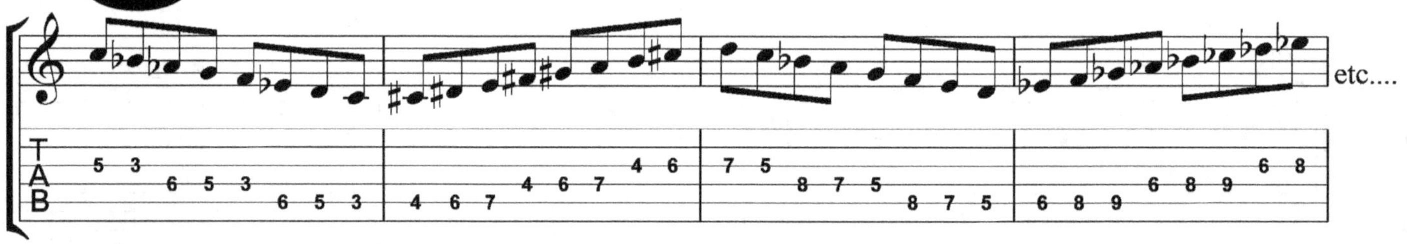

ex. 5

ex. 6

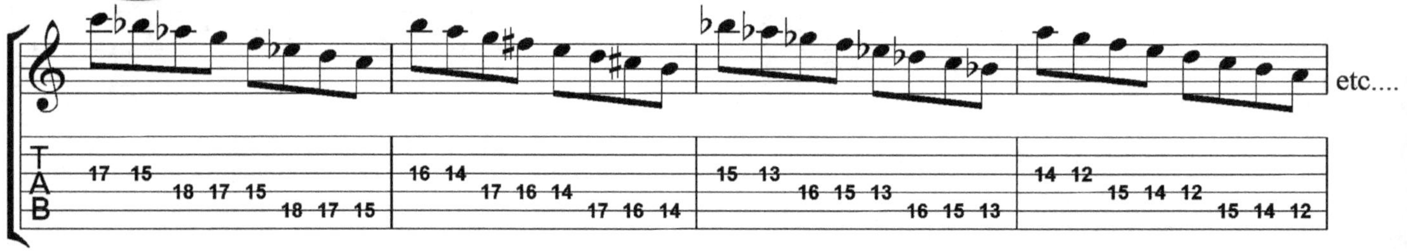

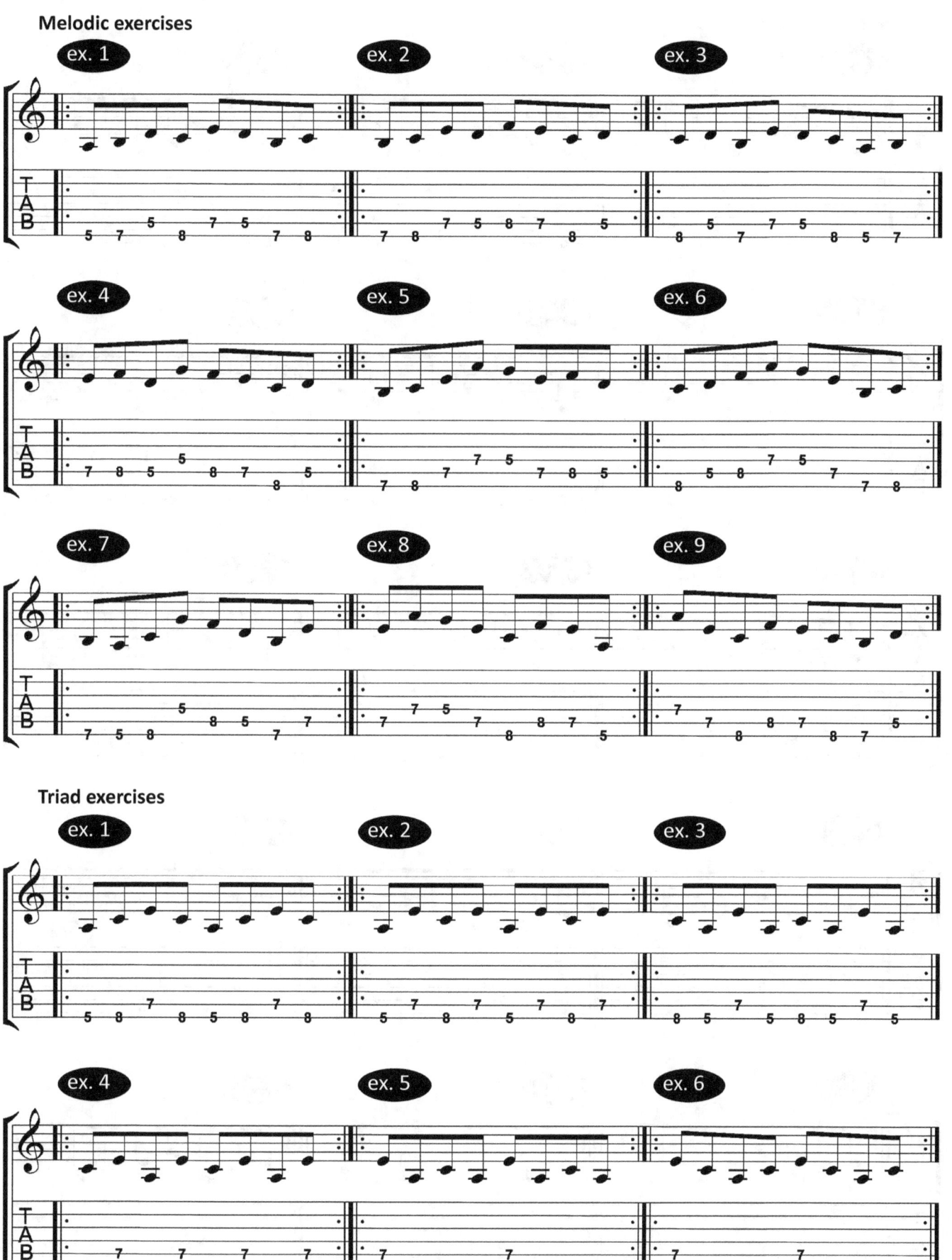

Chapter 4 the modes of the major scale - aeolian

7th chord exercises

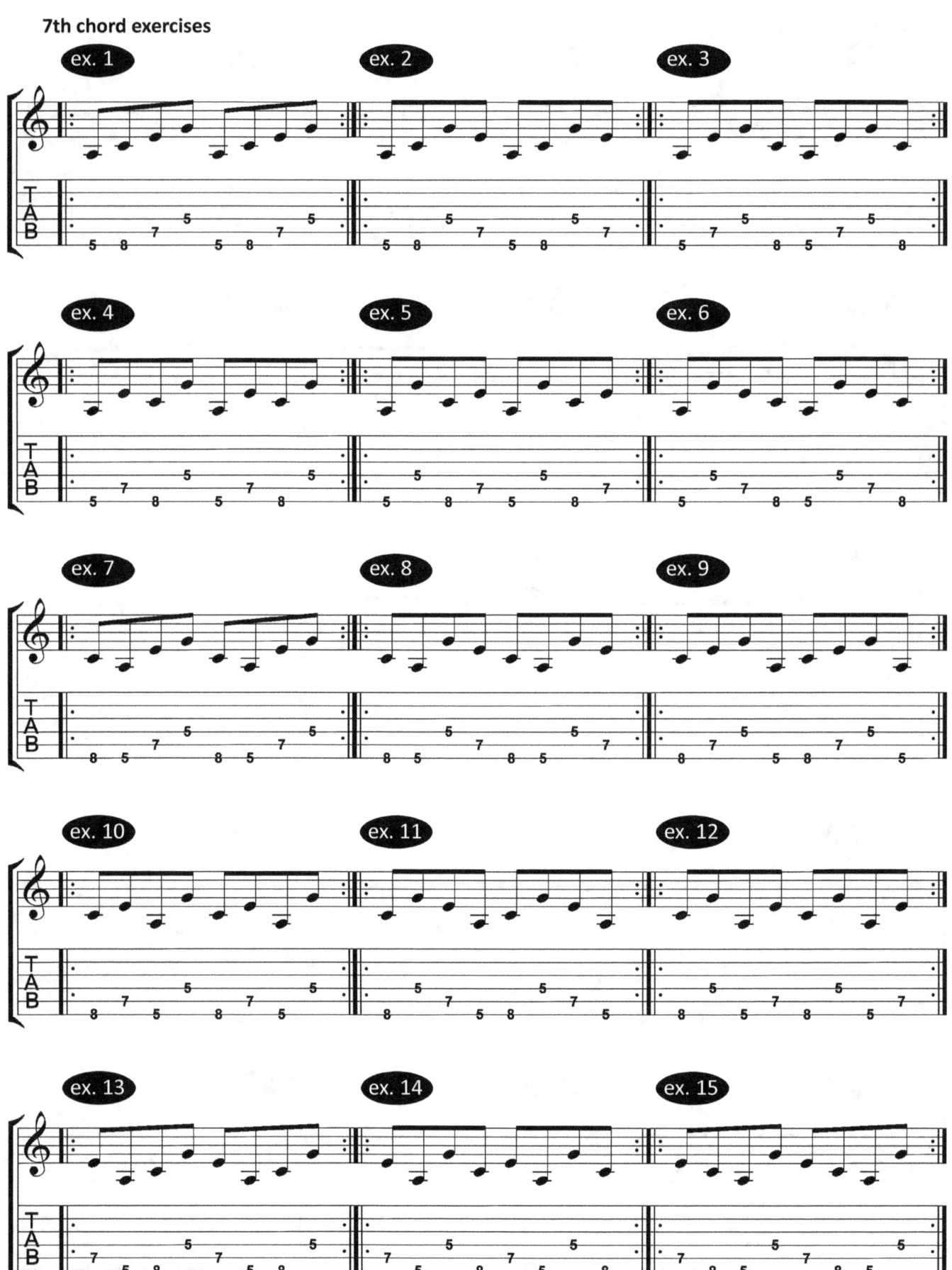

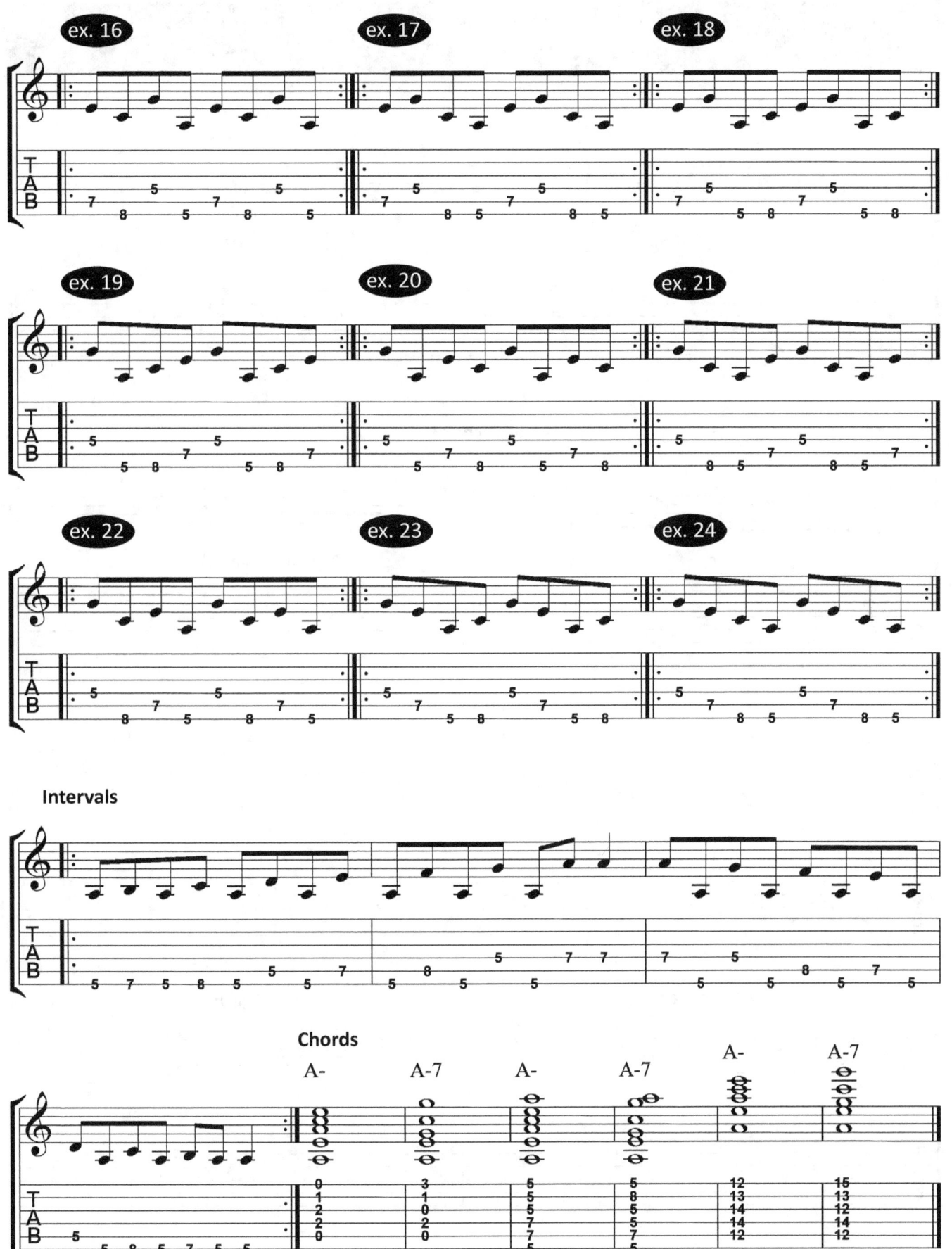

Chapter 4 the modes of the major scale - aeolian

Aeolian shape 2

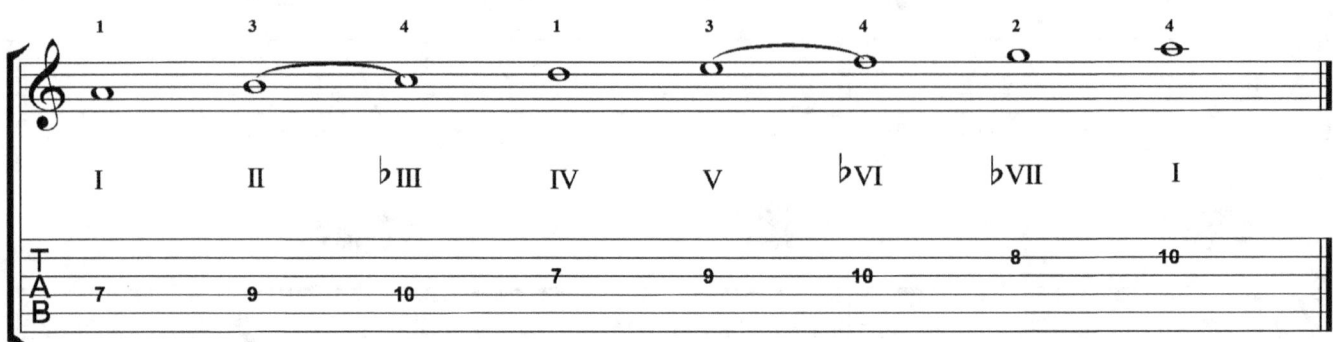

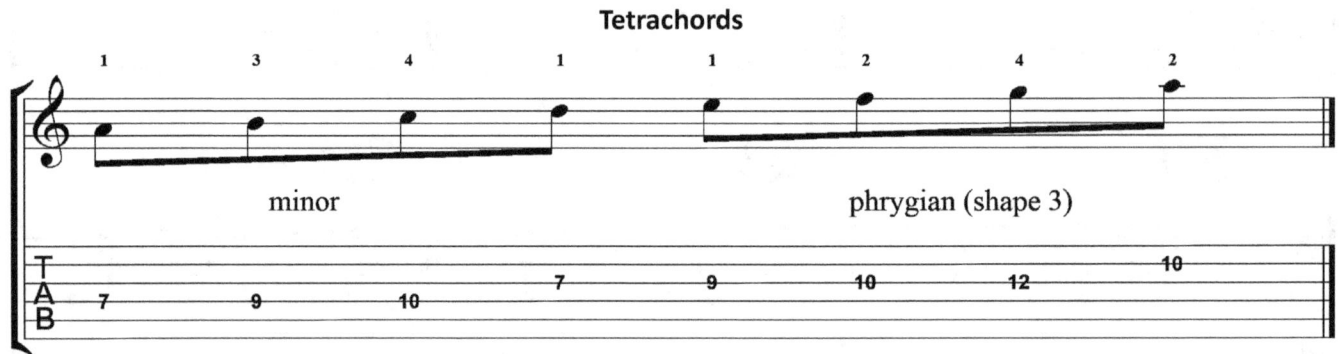

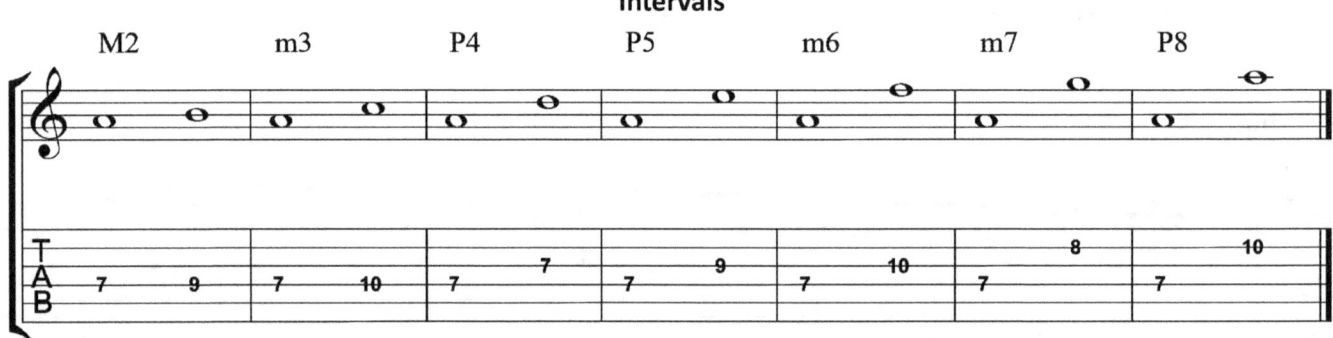

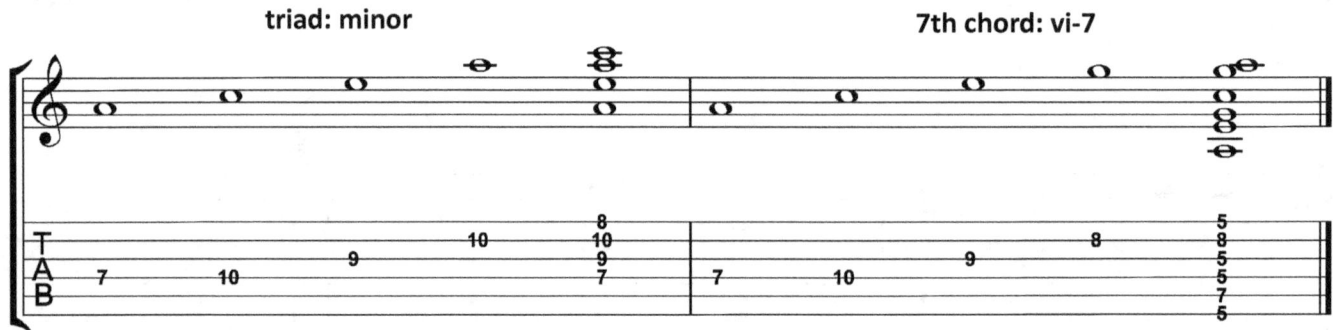

Aeolian mode studies - shape 2

Mode exercises

Chapter 4   the modes of the major scale - aeolian

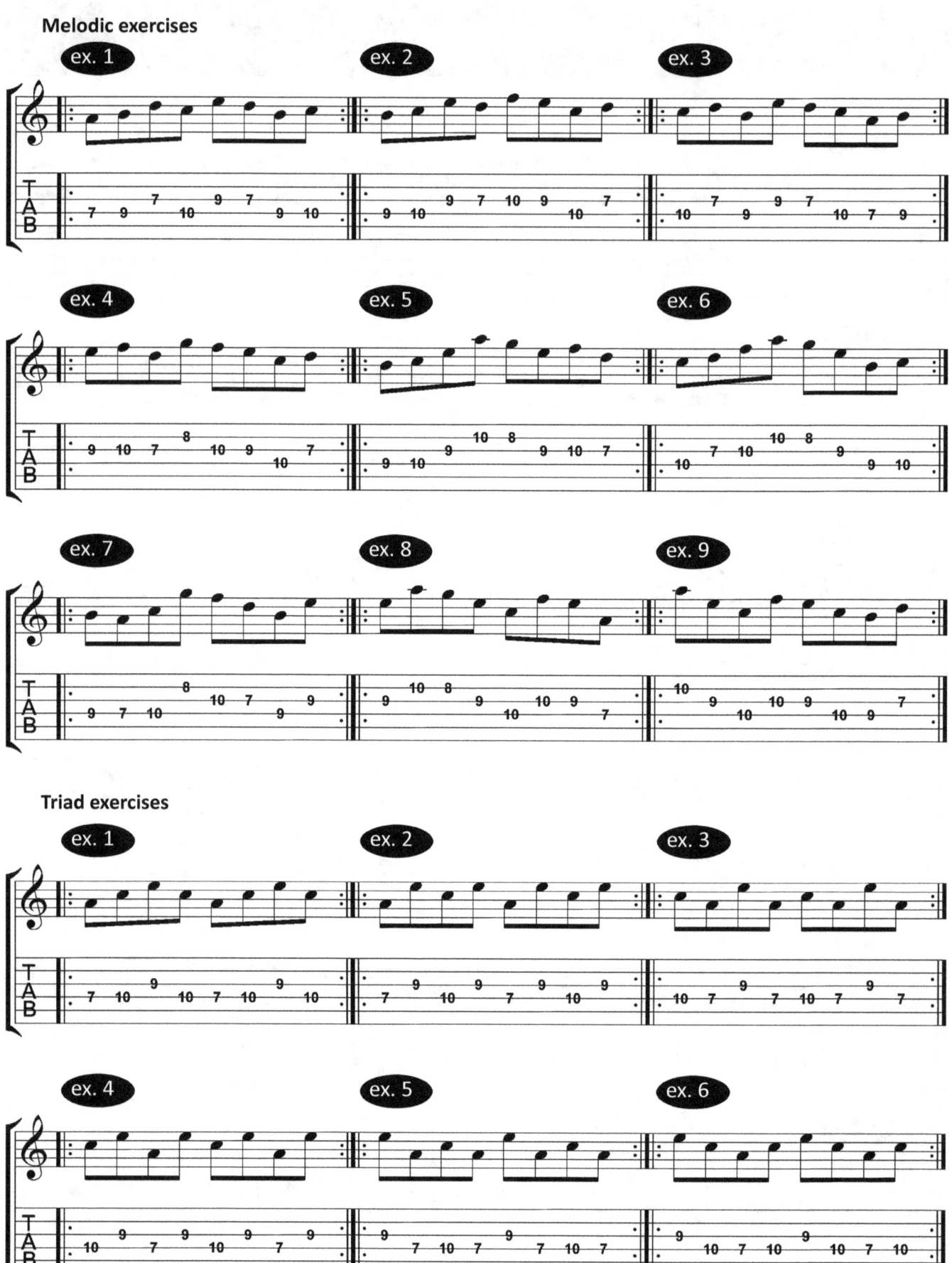

7th chord exercises

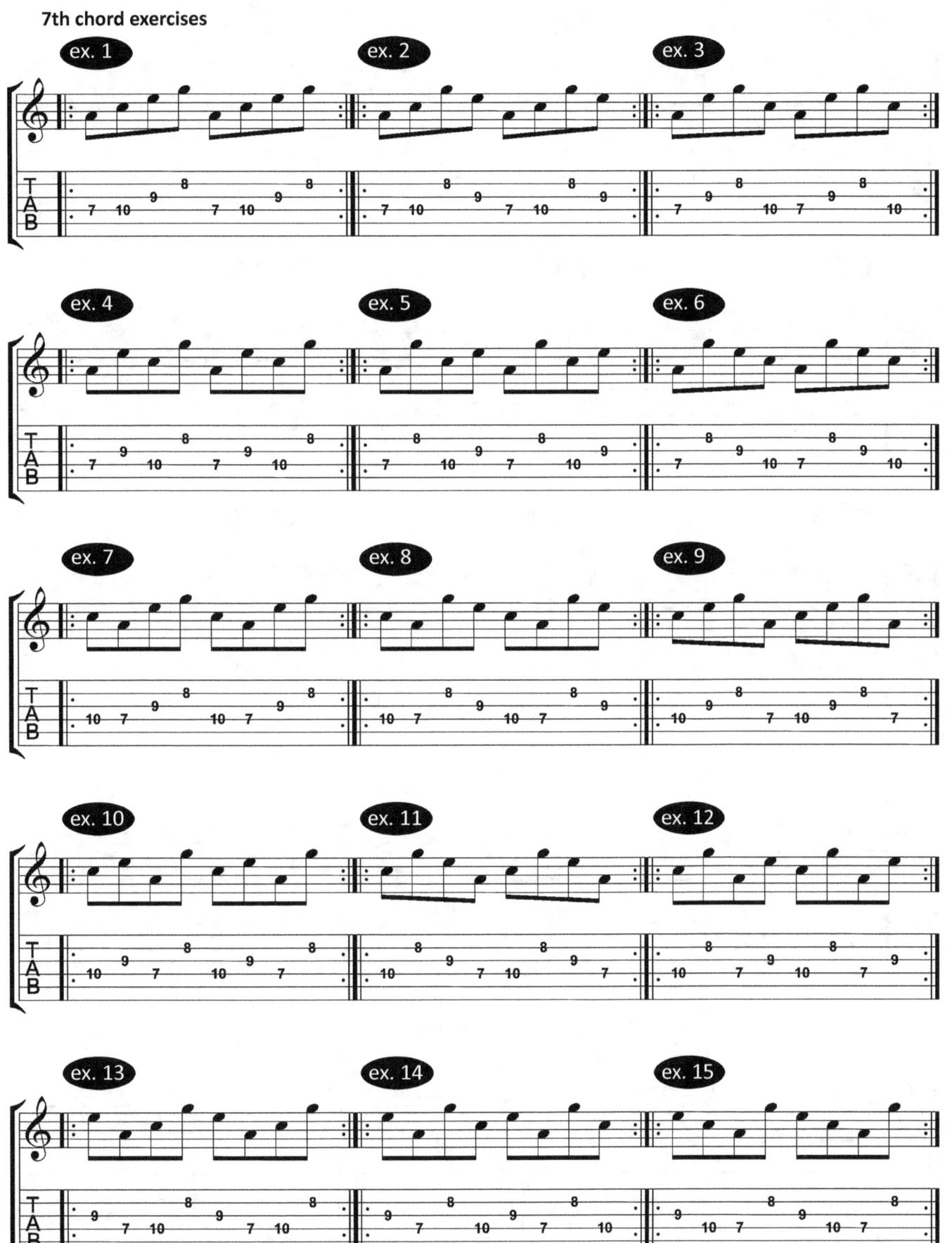

Chapter 4   the modes of the major scale - aeolian

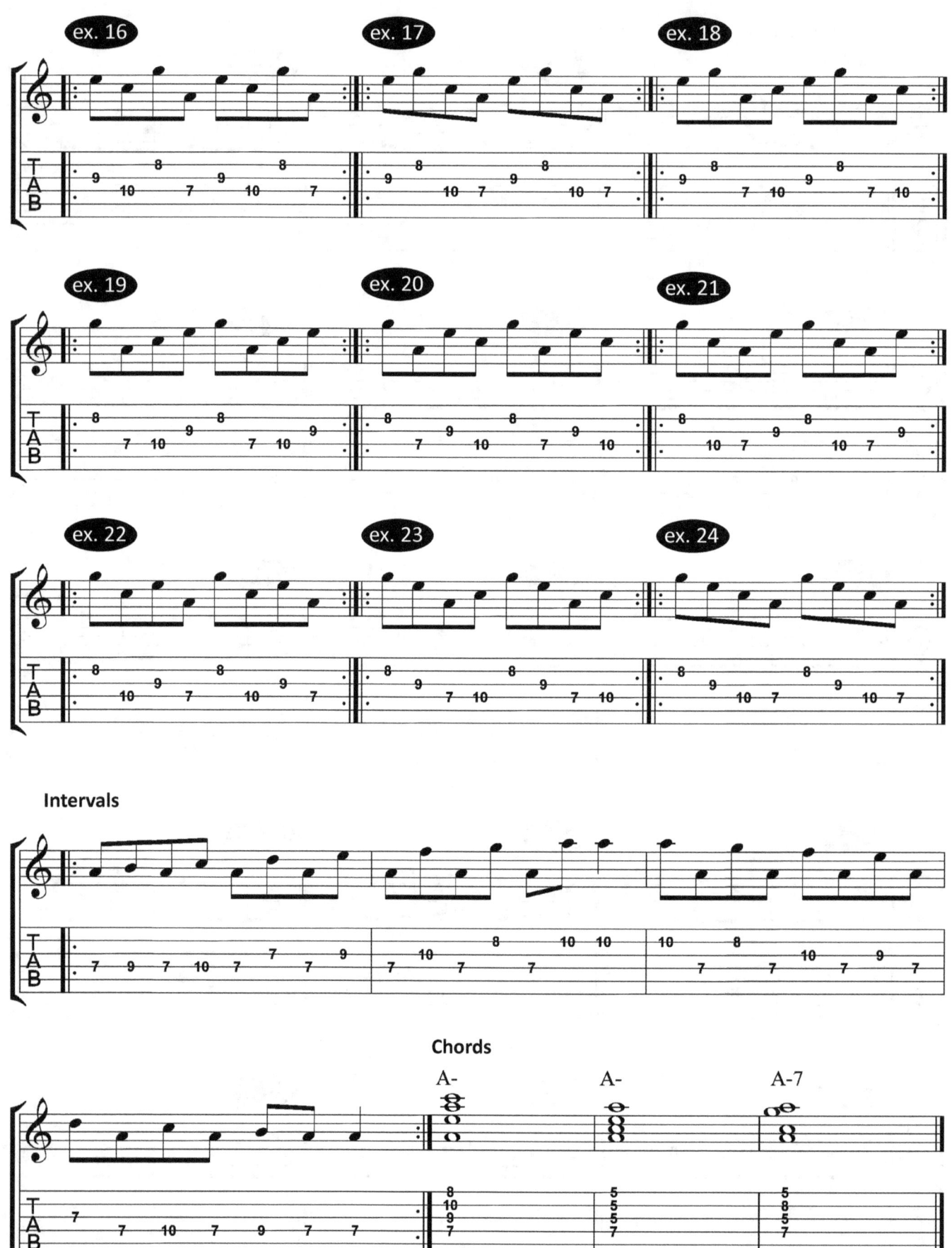

Aeolian shape 3

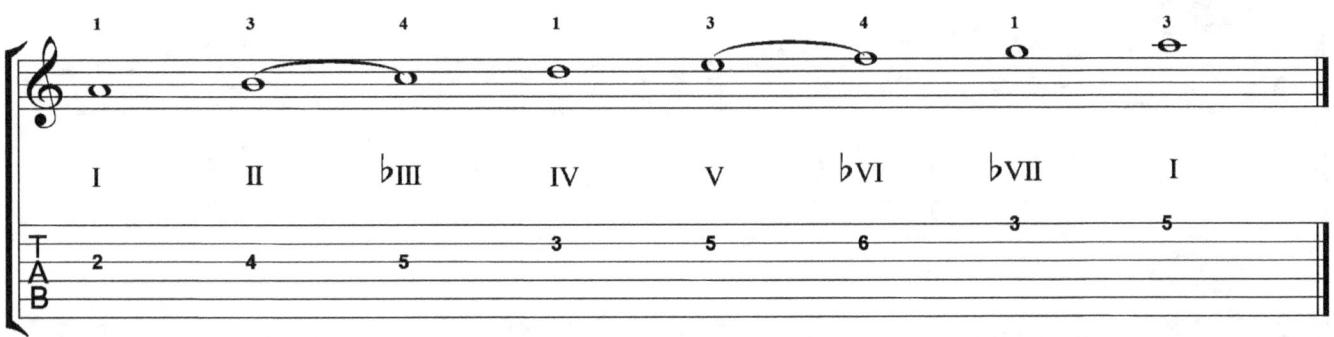

Tetrachords

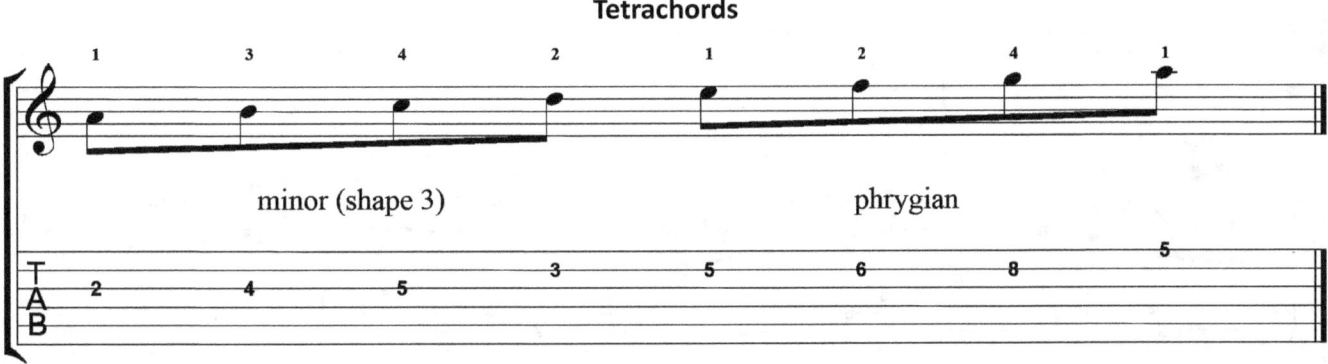

minor (shape 3)   phrygian

Intervals

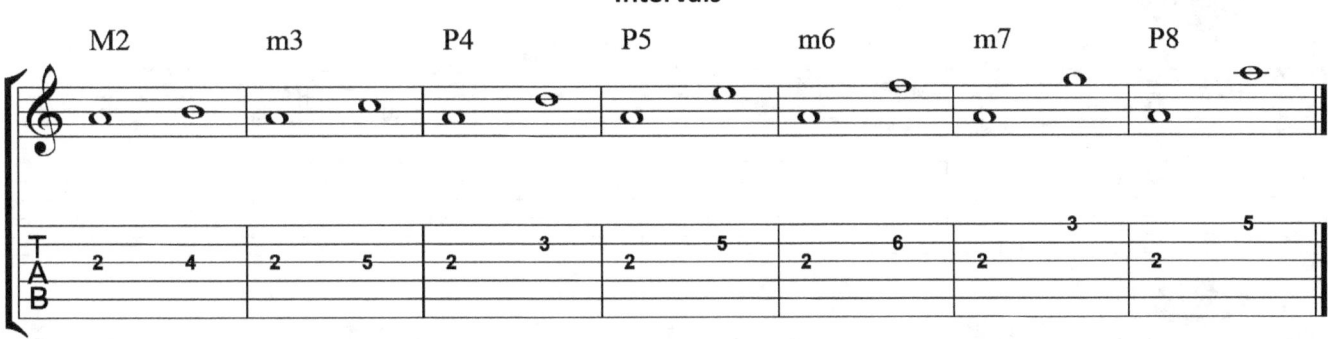

triad: minor   7th chord: vi-7

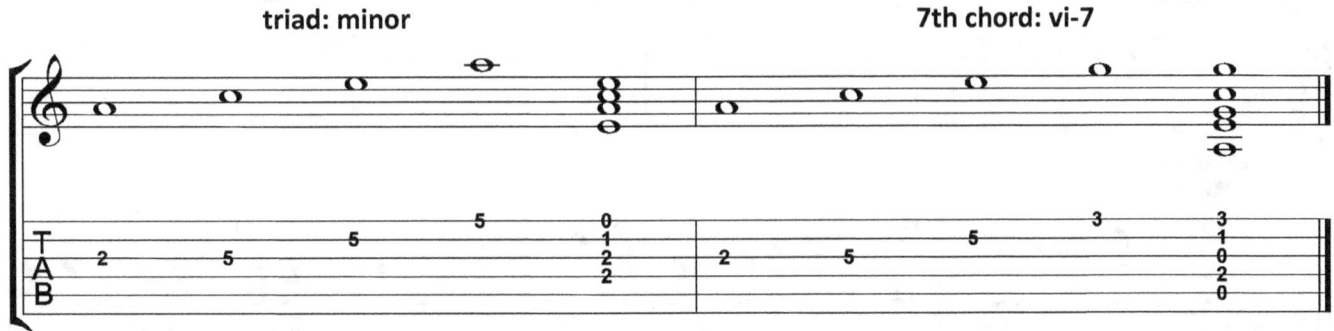

Chapter 4   the modes of the major scale - aeolian

Aeolian mode studies - shape 3

Mode exercises

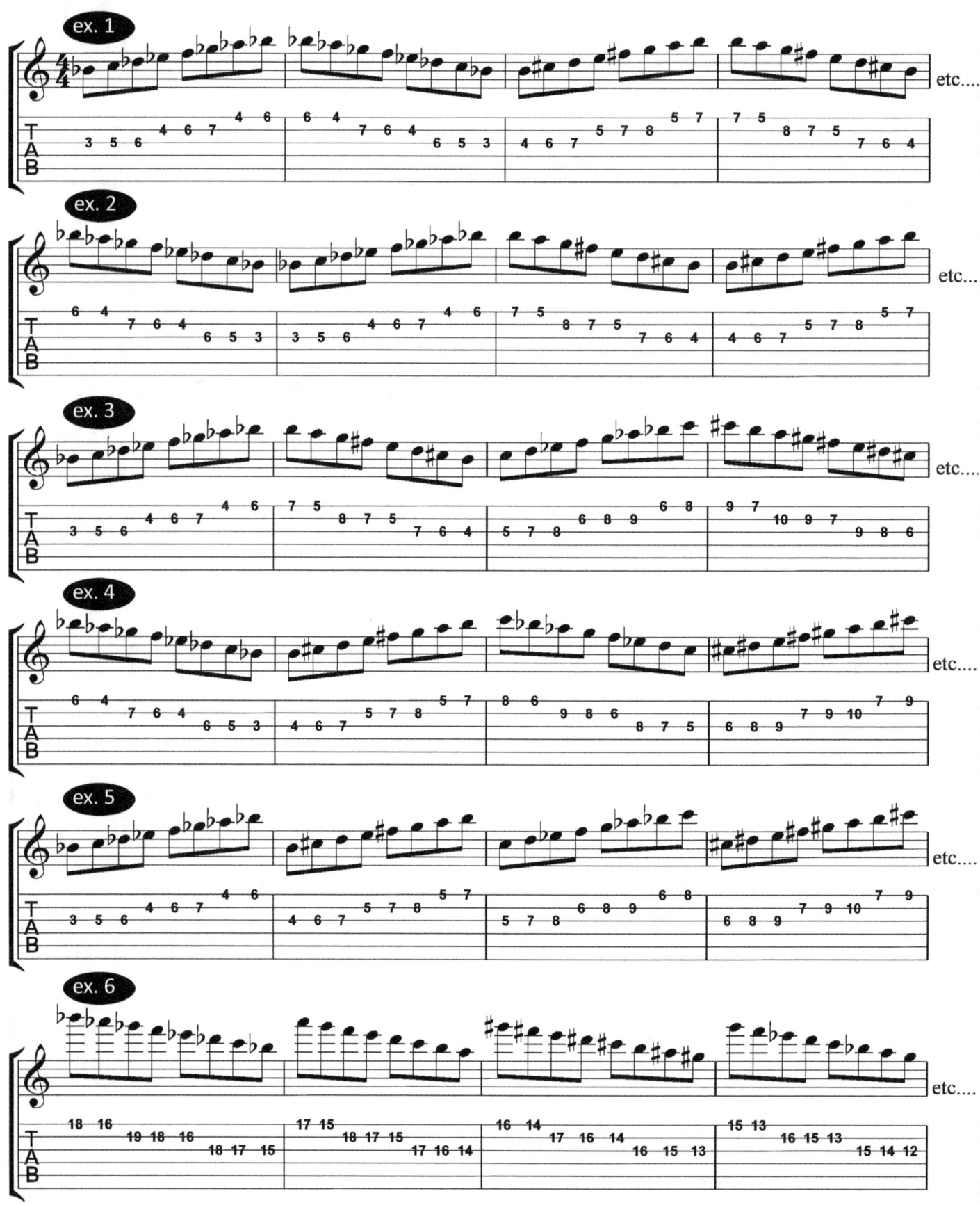

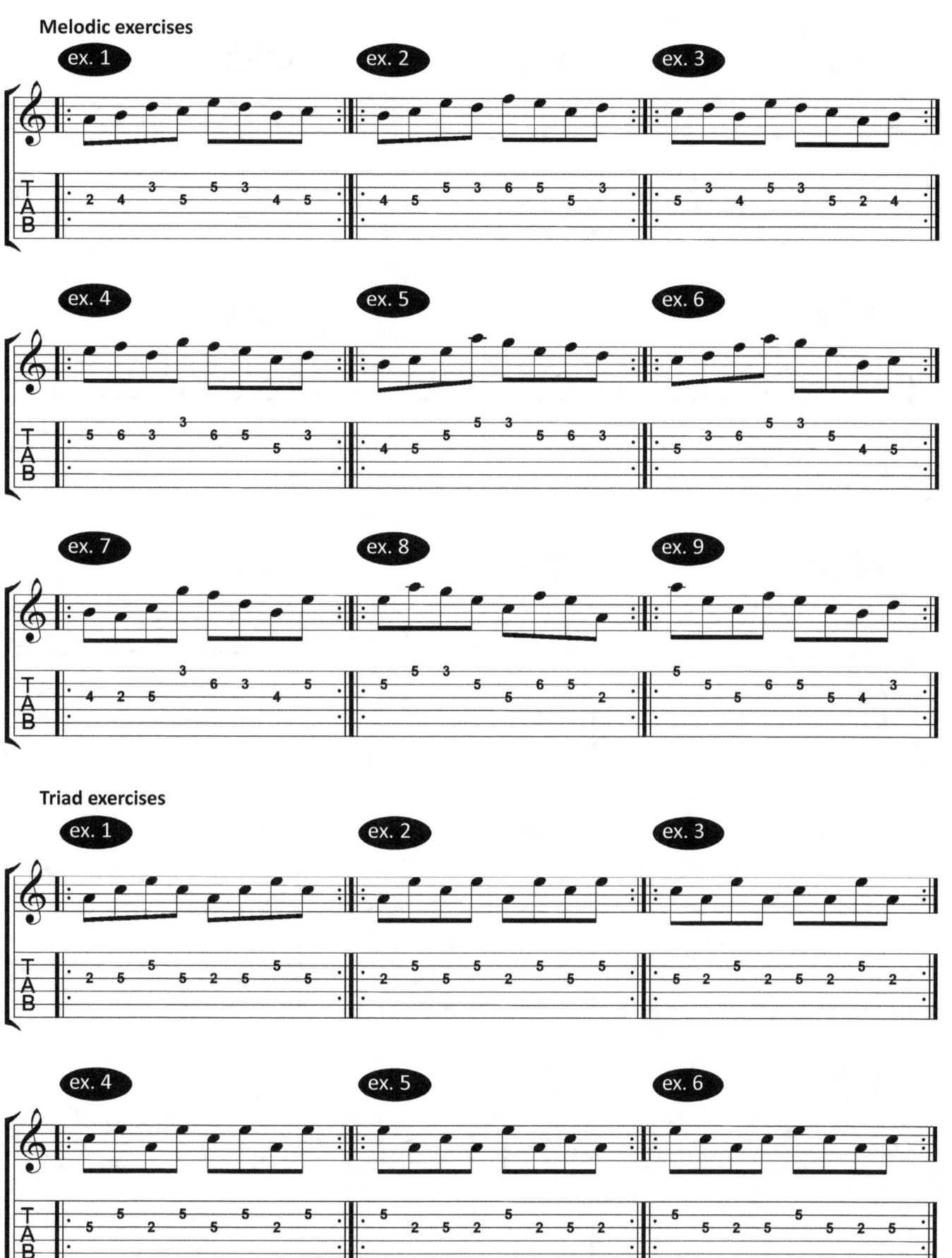

Chapter 4 the modes of the major scale - aeolian

7th chord exercises

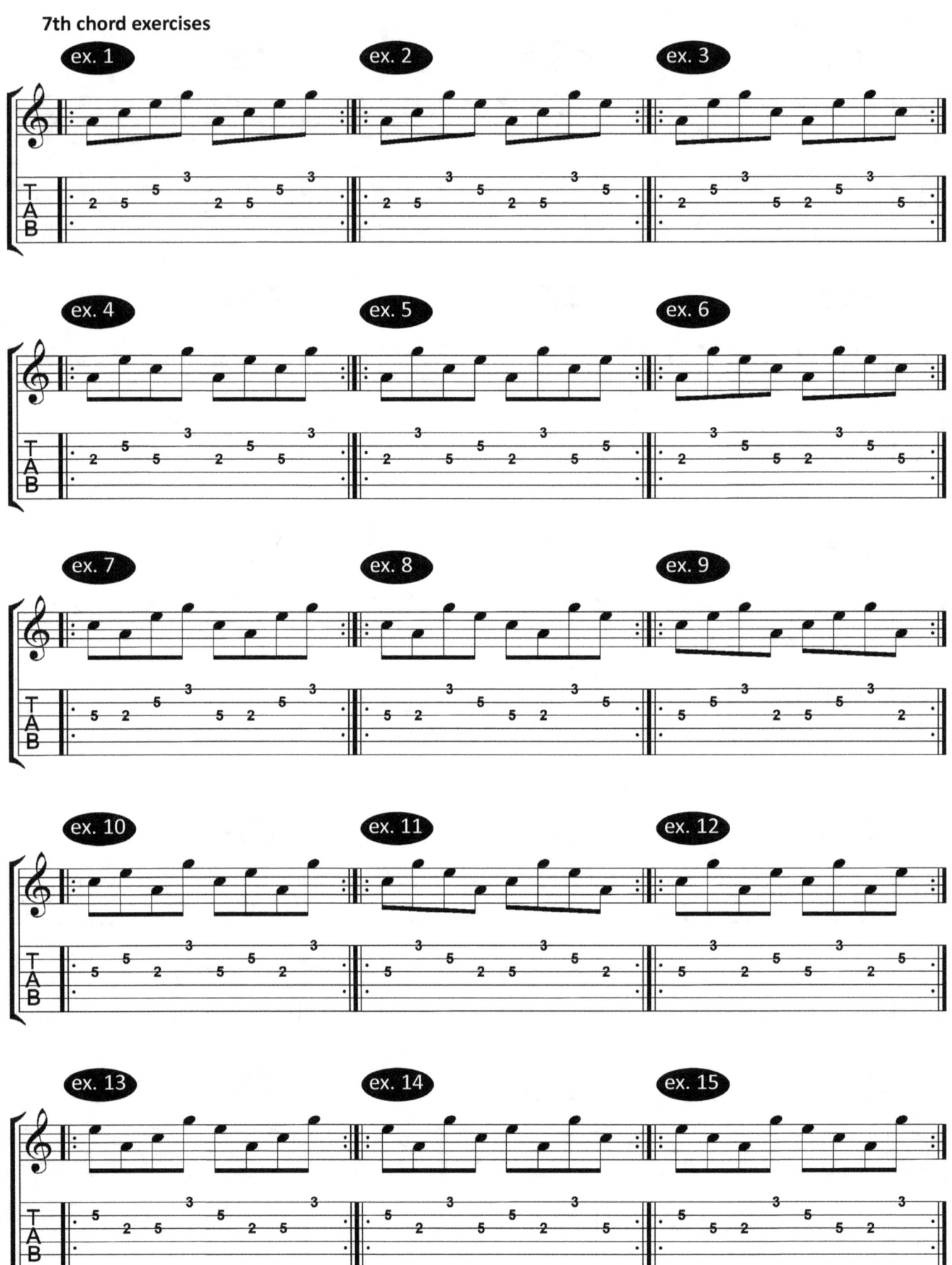

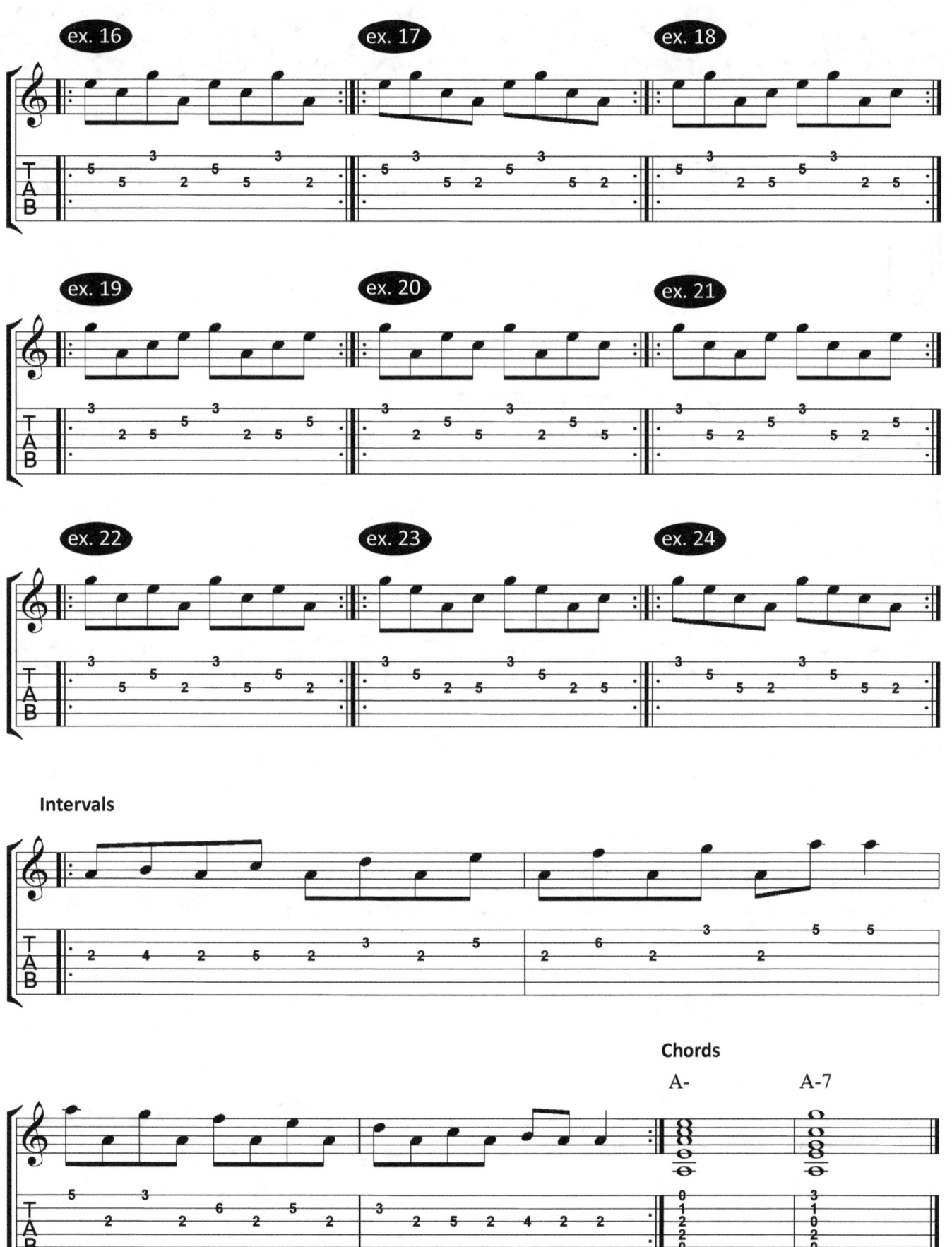

Chapter 4 the modes of the major scale - aeolian

Aeolian in 2 octaves with shapes 1 + 2

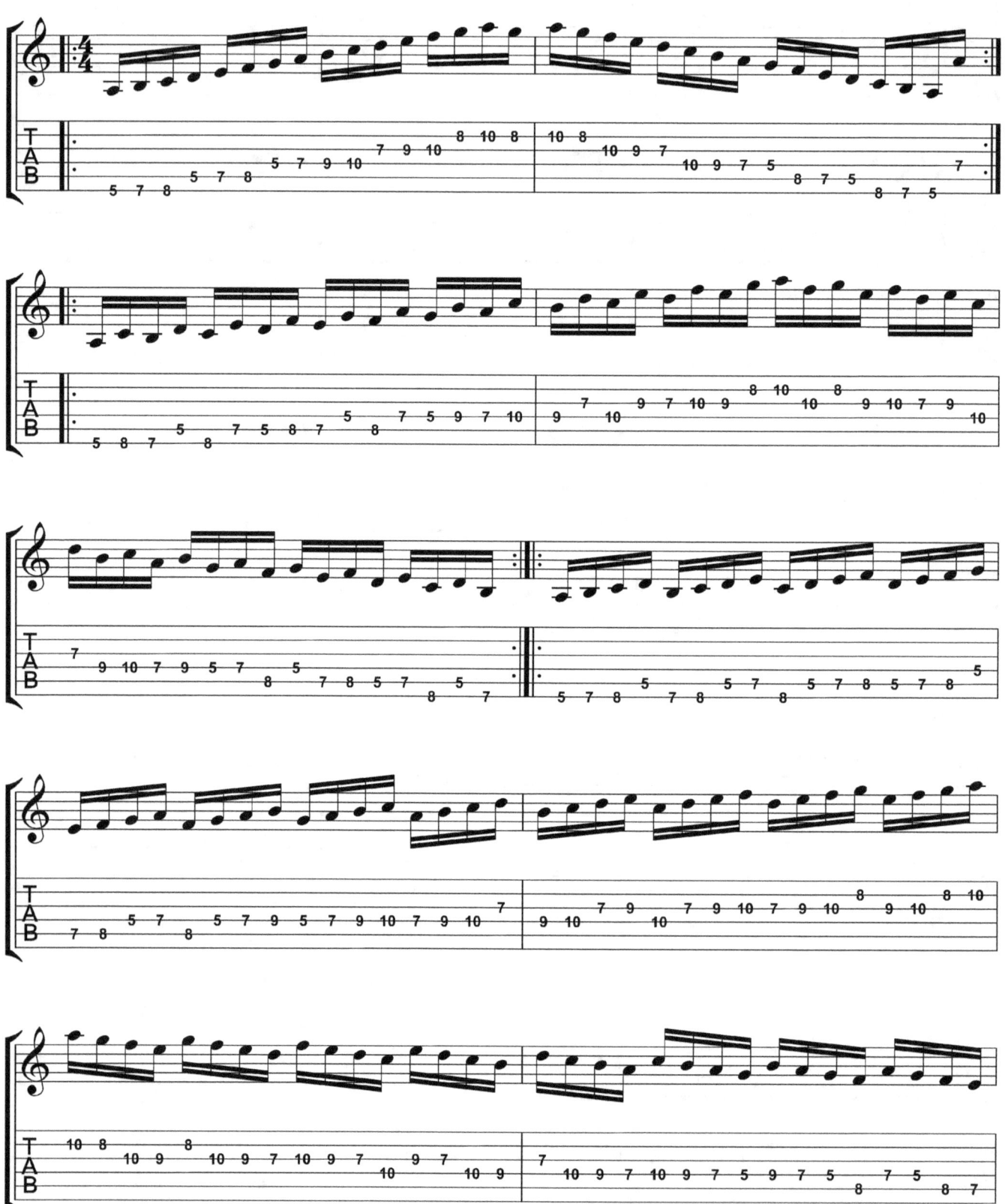

Chapter 4 the modes of the major scale - aeolian

Aeolian in 2 octaves with shapes 1 + 3

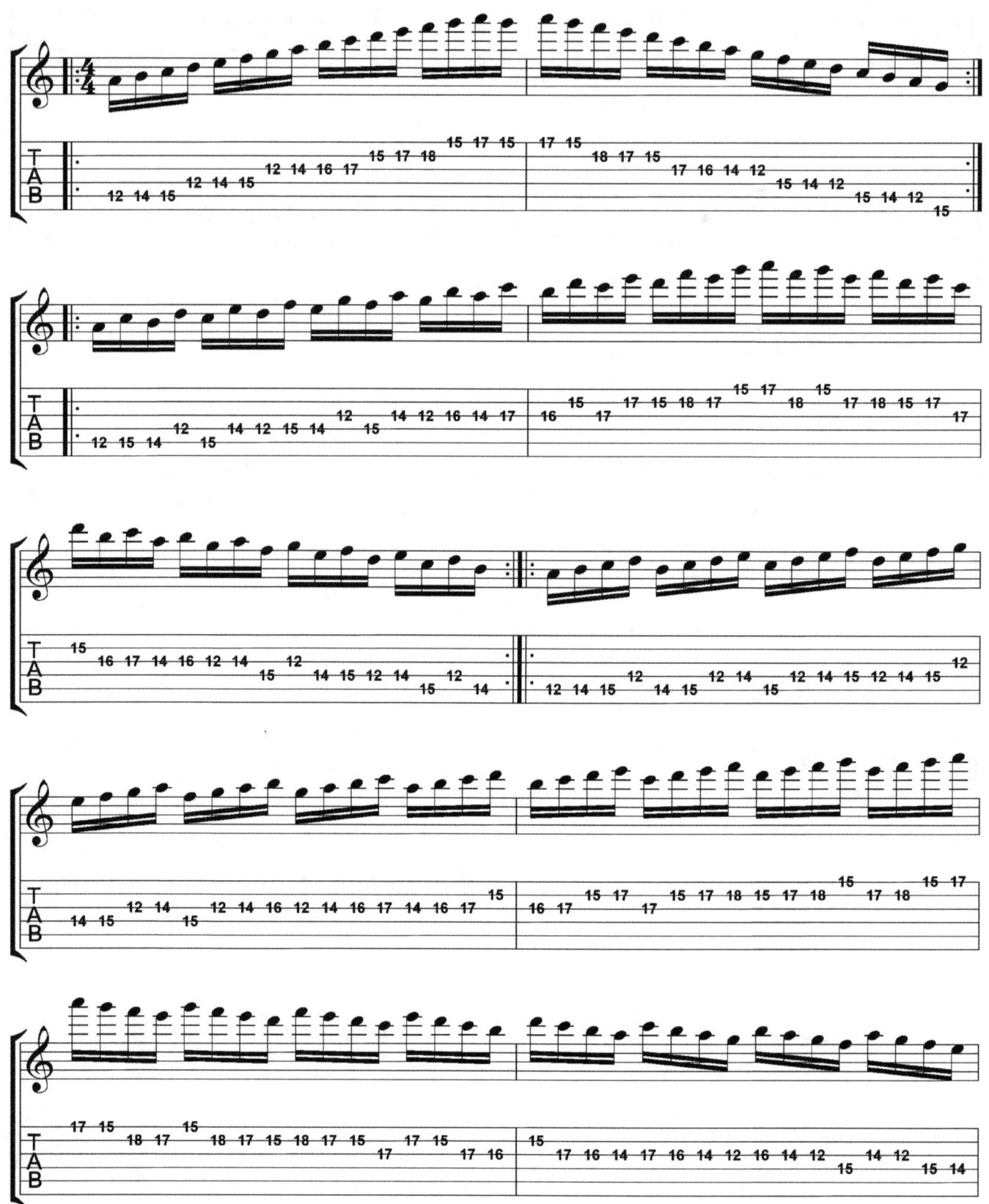

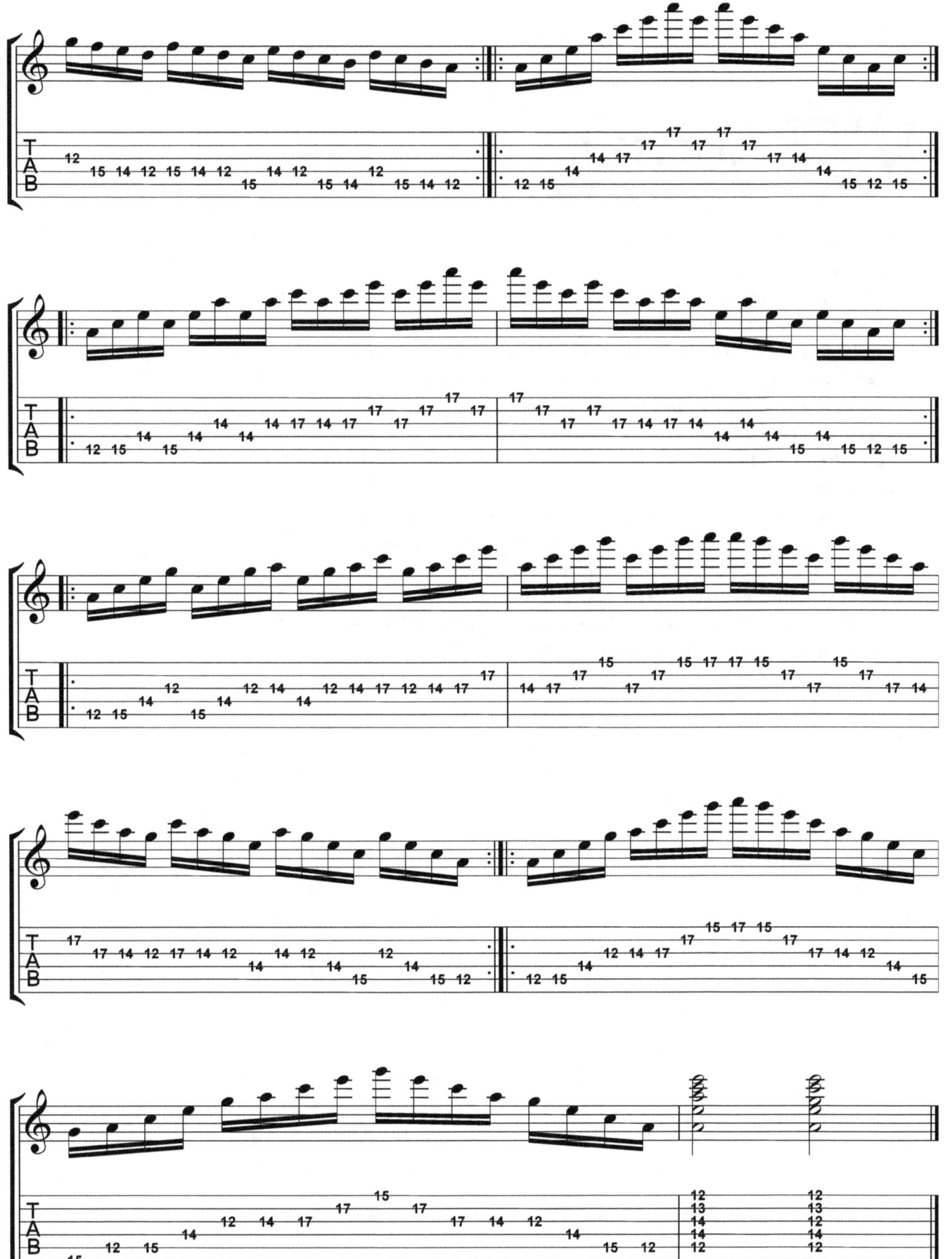

Chapter 4 the modes of the major scale - aeolian

Locrian
7th mode of the Major scale

General formula: H-W-W-H-W-W-W

Scale: Half-diminished

Tetrachords: Phrygian - Lydian

Characteristic note of the mode: the diminished fifth ♭5

The intervals that are formed between the tonic and each scale degree: I-II = ♭2, I-III = ♭3, I-IV = 4, I-V = ♭5, I-VI = ♭6, I-VII = ♭7

The diatonic half steps are found on the scale degrees I-II and IV-V

Triad: Diminished viio

Seventh chord: Minor 7th with ♭5 vii-7(♭5)

Extensions: ♭13

Generally: The Locrian mode is a scale that has its own unique sound color. That happens because it contains a minor third and therefore is considered a minor scale, but it also contains a ♭5 which gives it a different sound from the minor scales that we have examined so far. In addition, it contains a ♭9 which gives it an even more unique sound. It is commonly used in the harmonic progression ii-7(♭5) - V7 - i-7.

Locrian shape 1

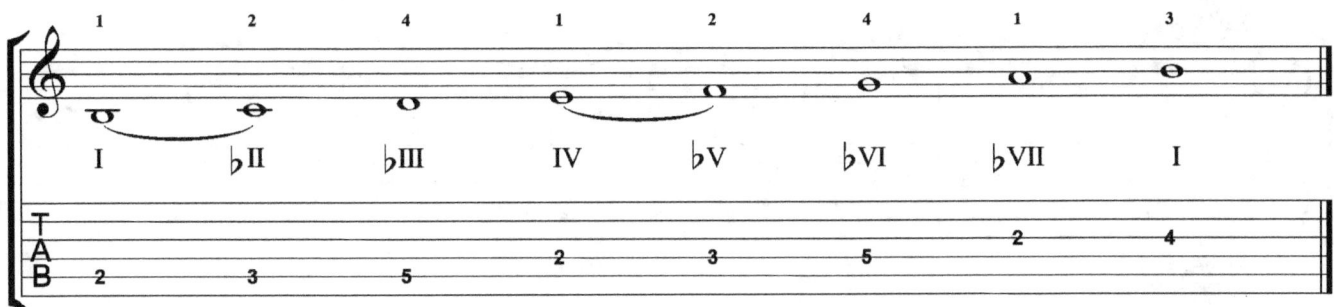

Tetrachords

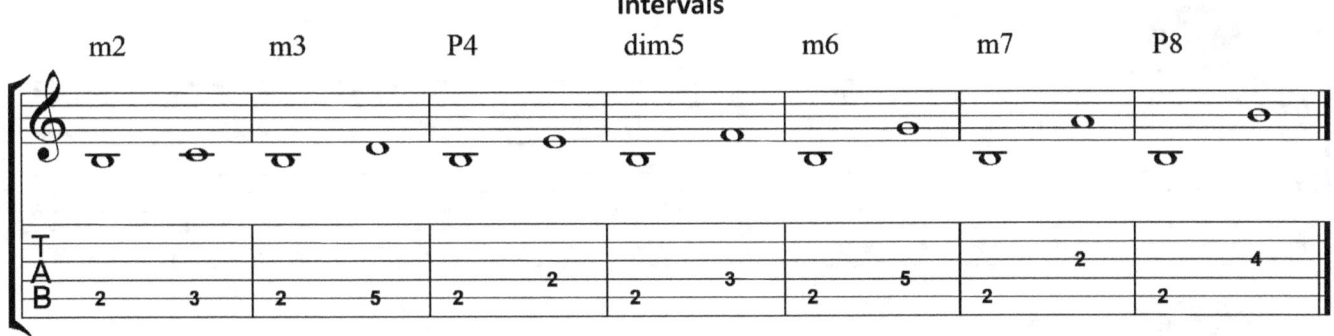

Intervals

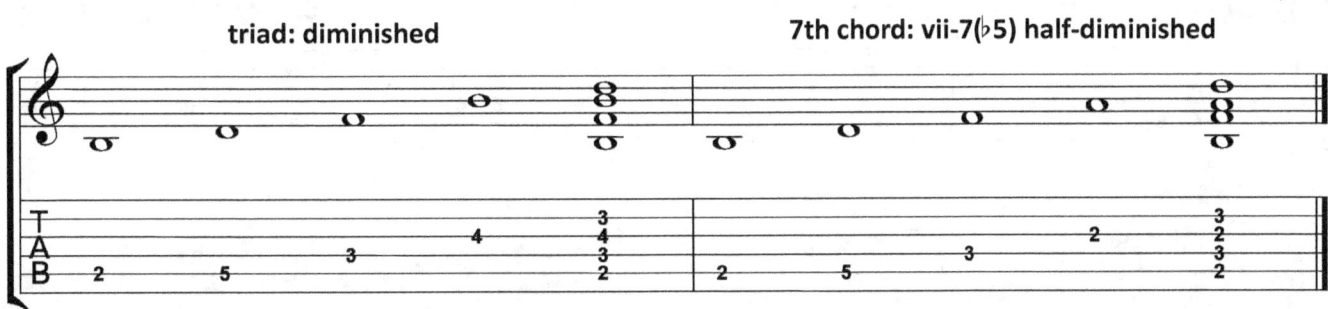

Locrian mode studies - shape 1

Mode exercises

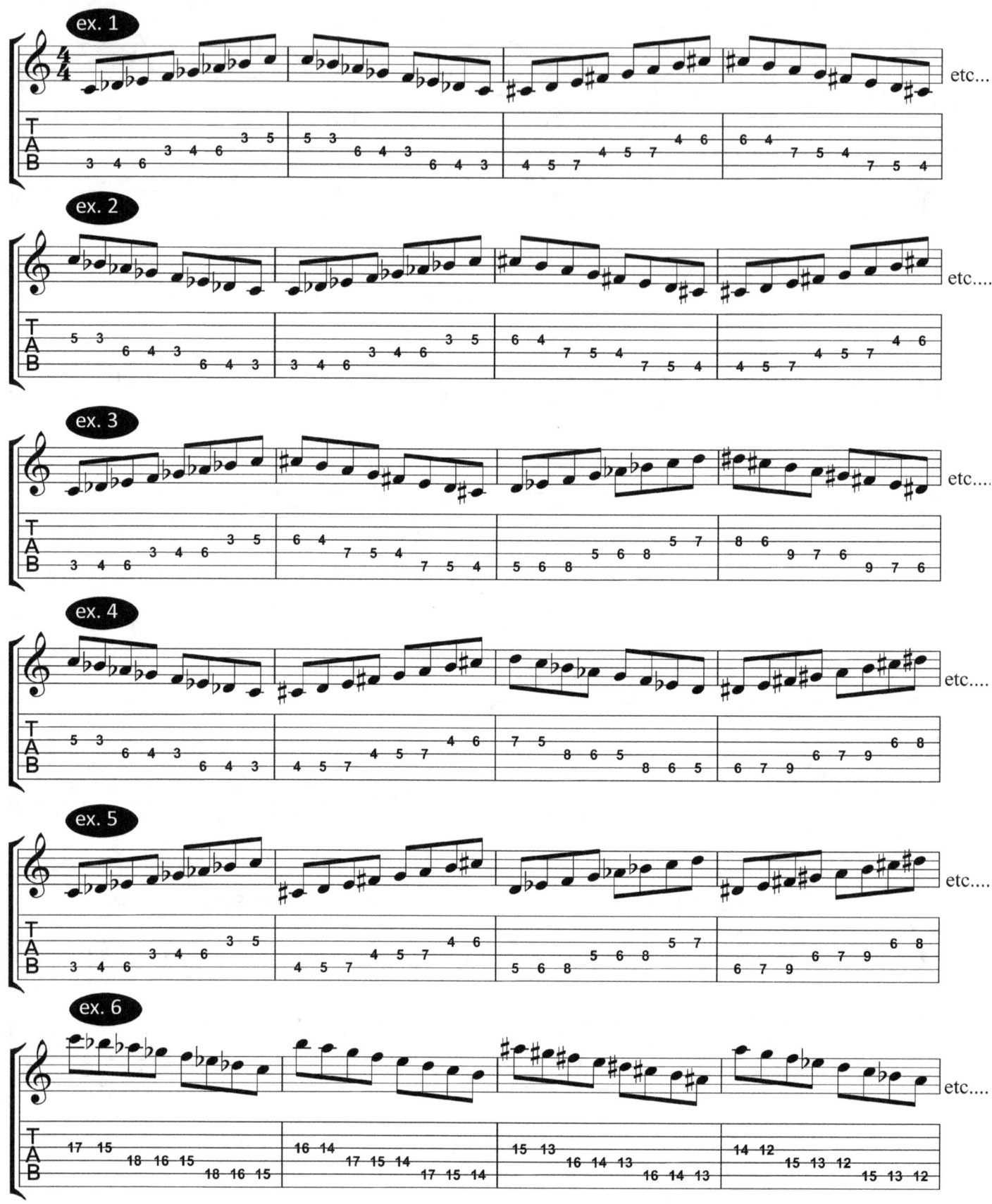

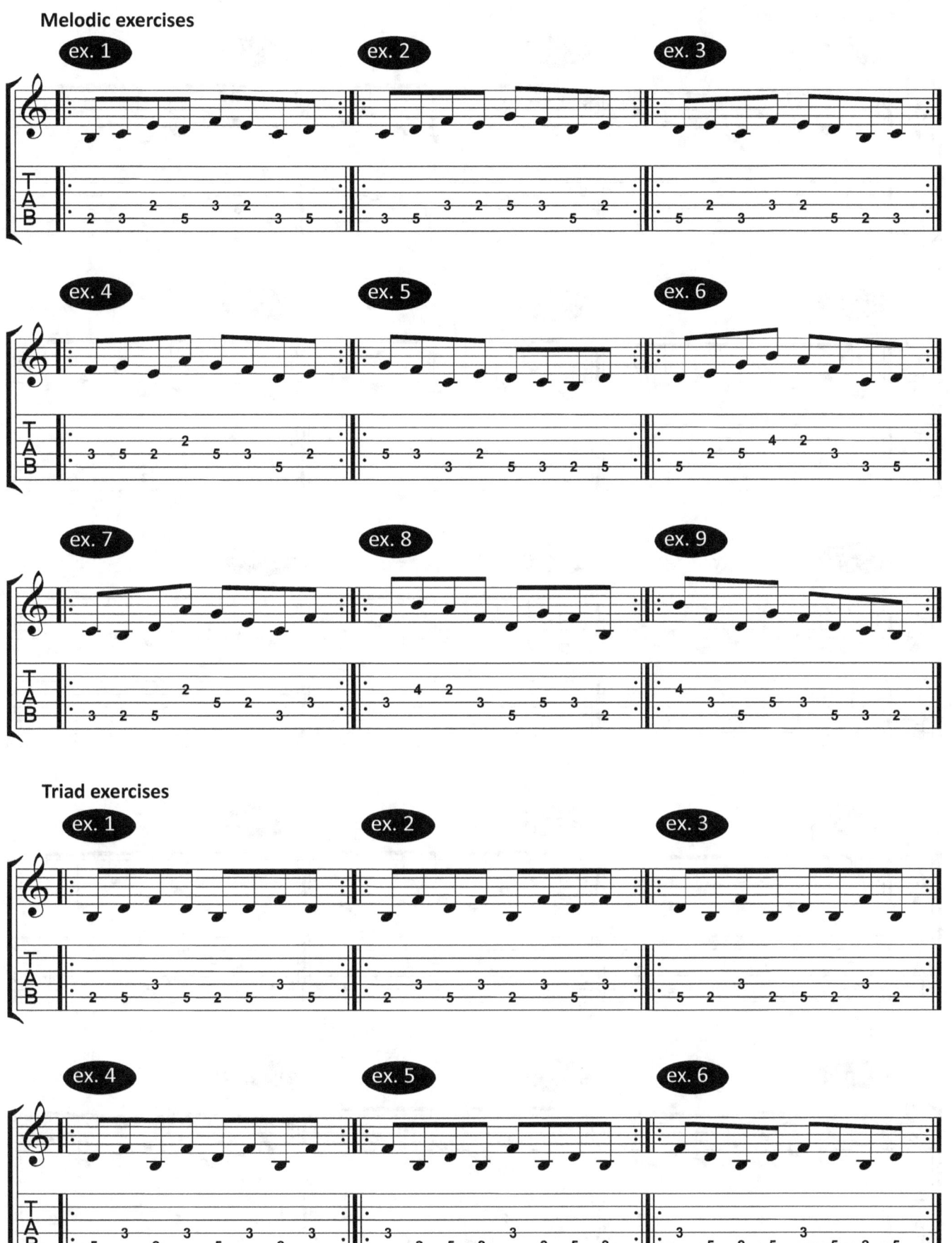

Chapter 4 the modes of the major scale - locrian

7th chord exercises

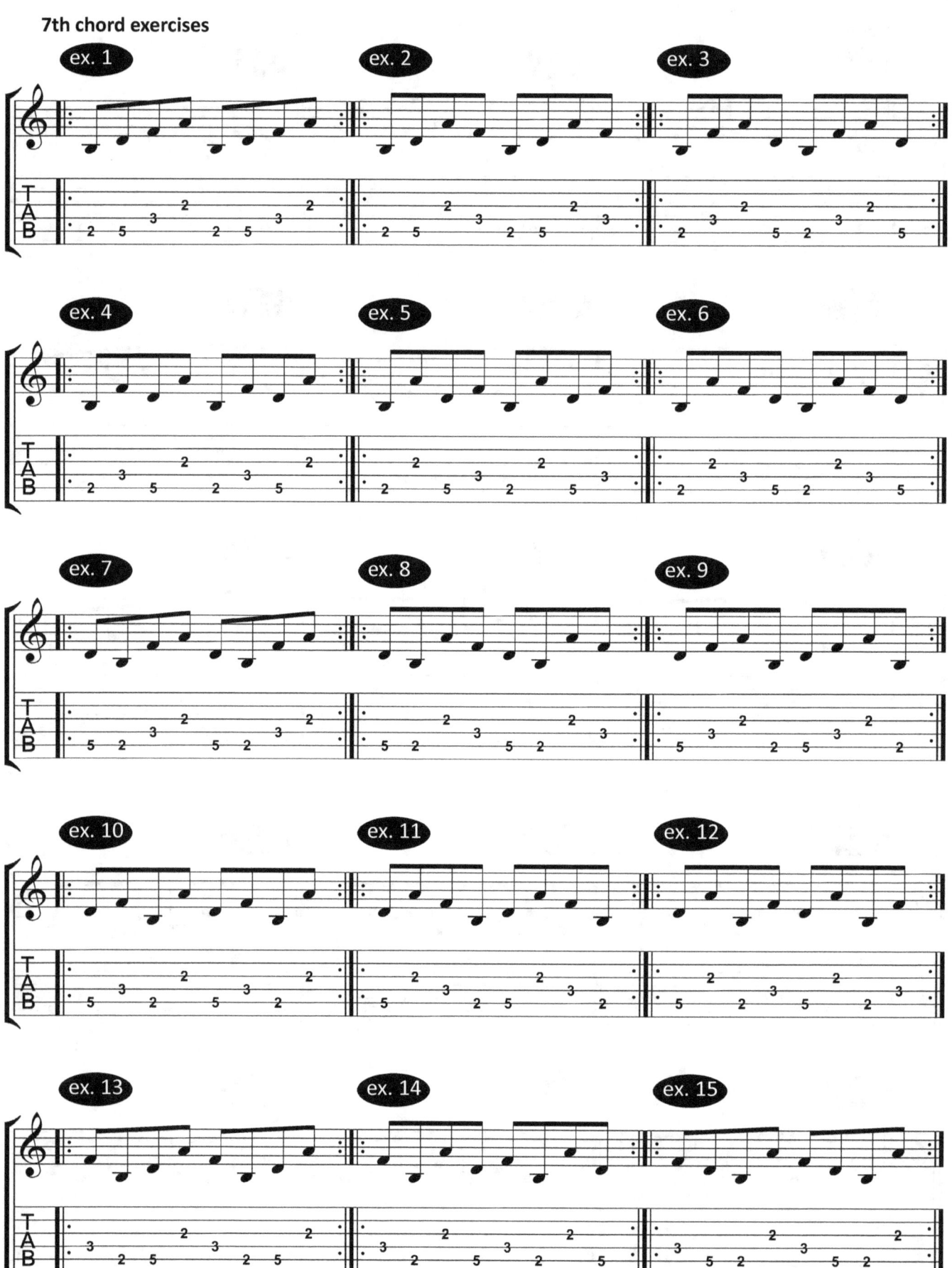

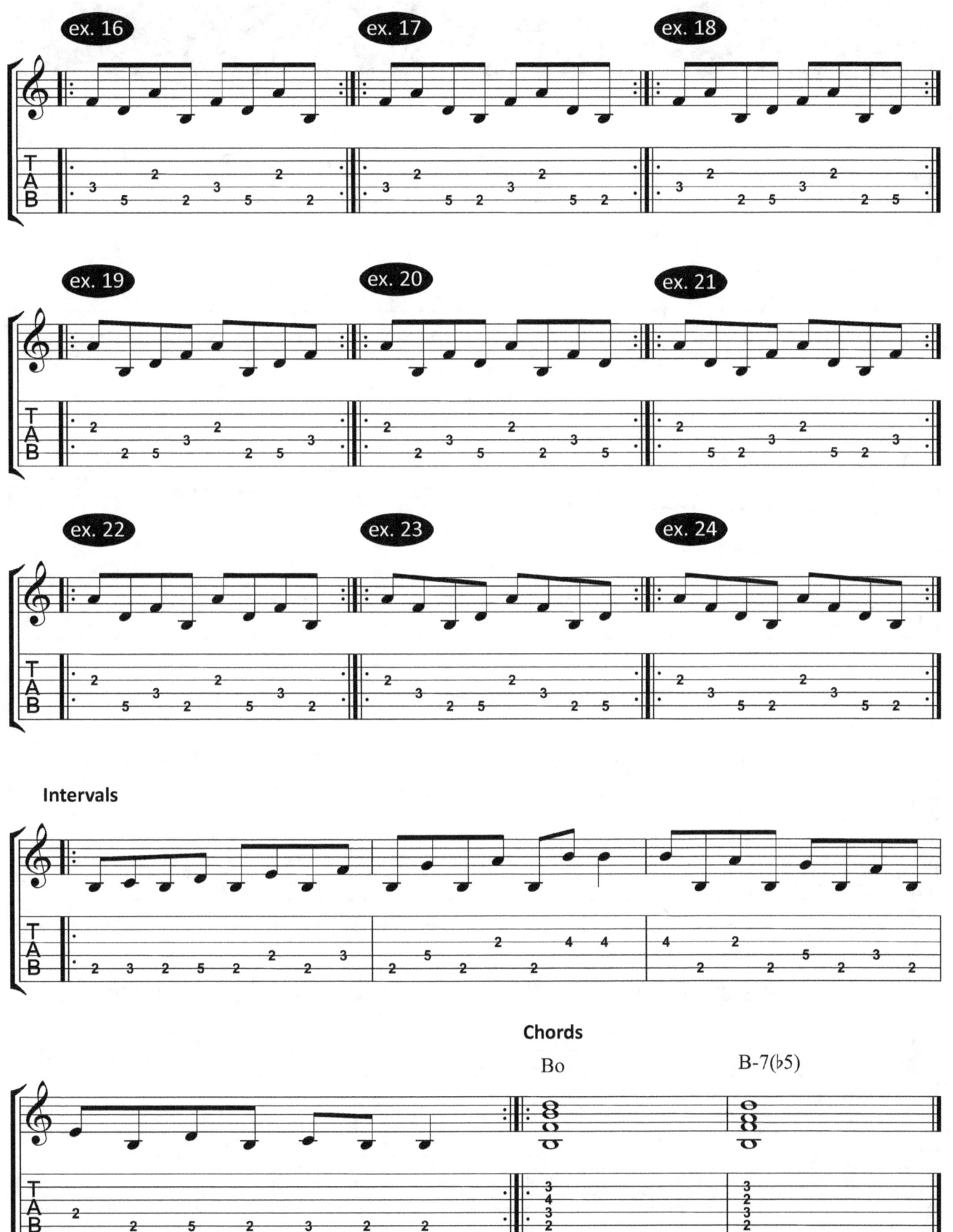

Chapter 4   the modes of the major scale - locrian

Locrian shape 2

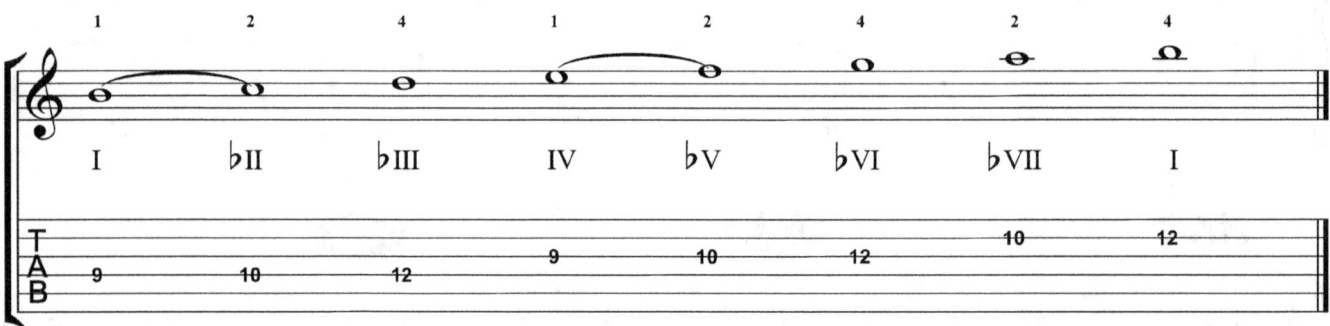

Tetrachords

Intervals

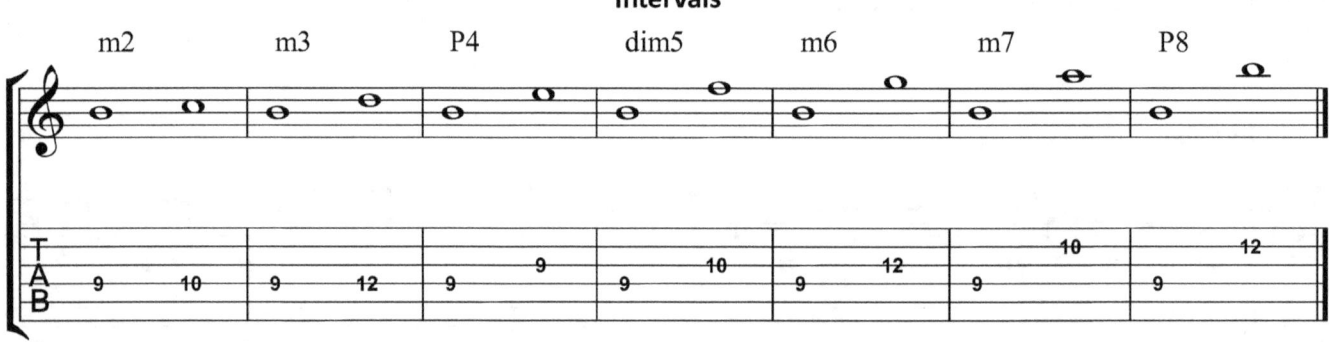

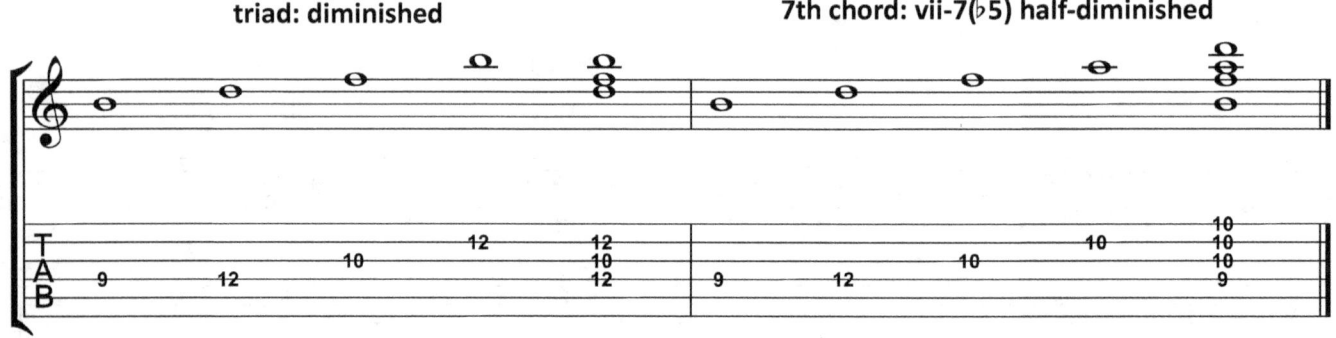

Locrian mode studies - shape 2

Mode exercises

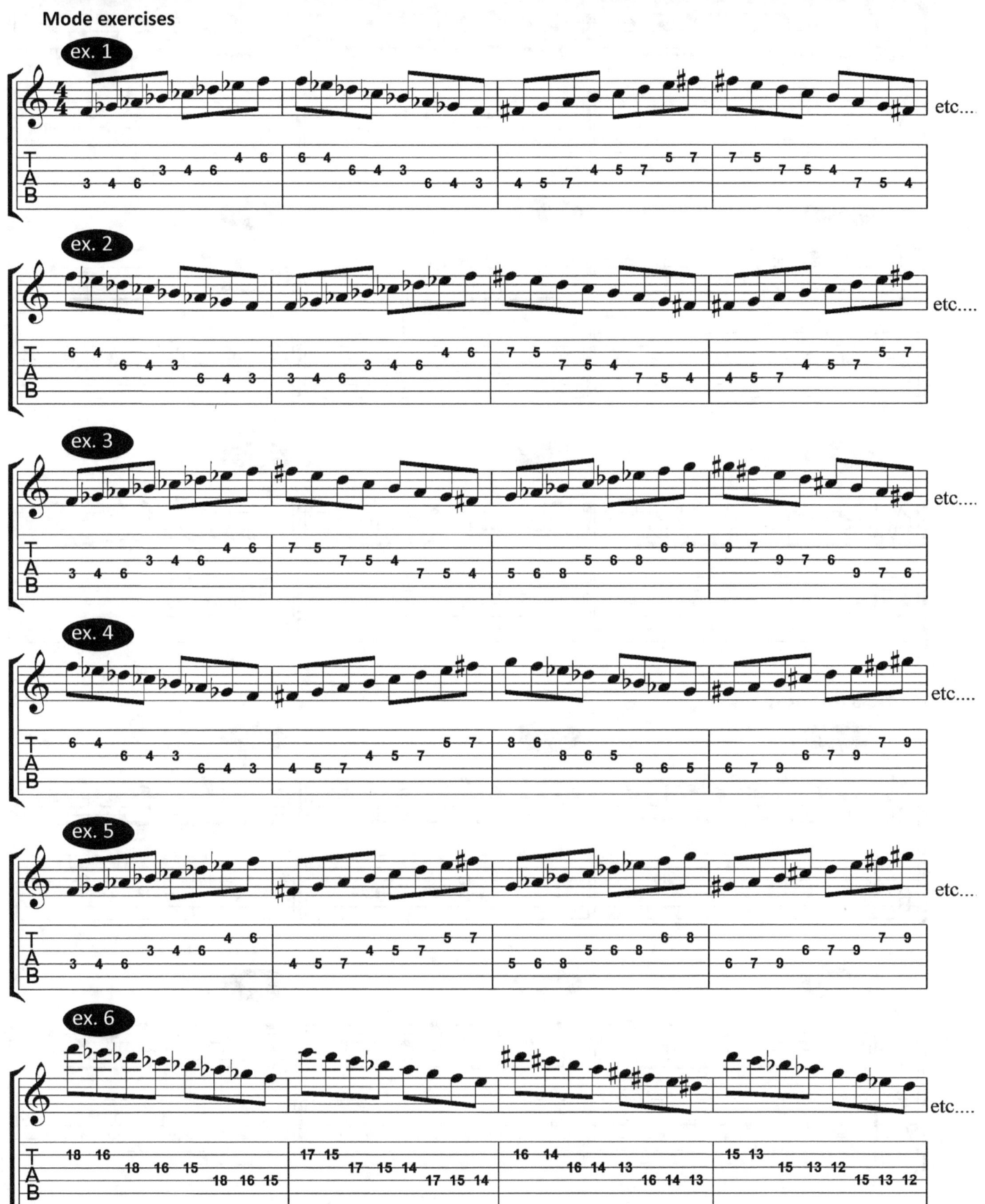

Chapter 4 the modes of the major scale - locrian

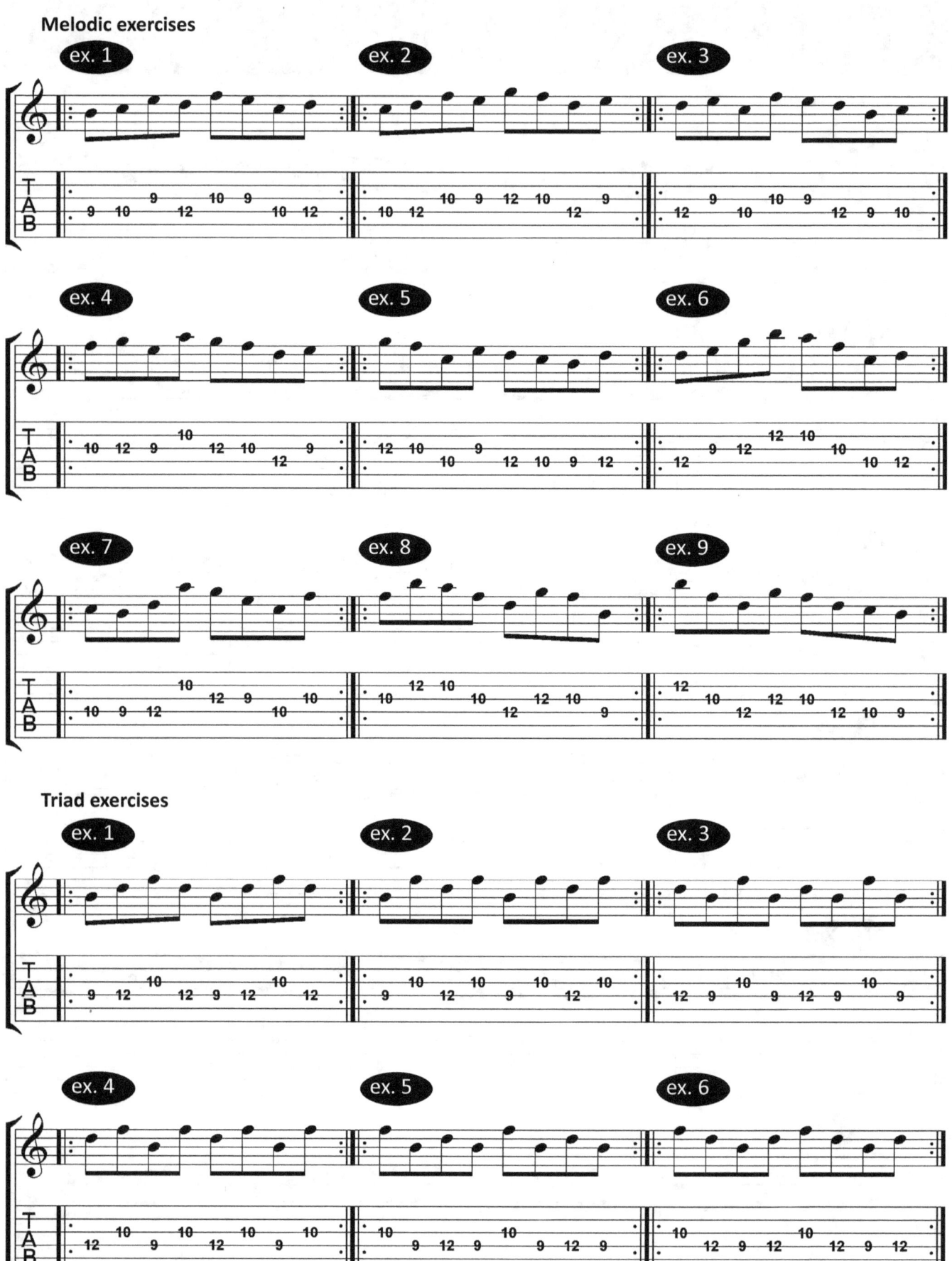

7th chord exercises

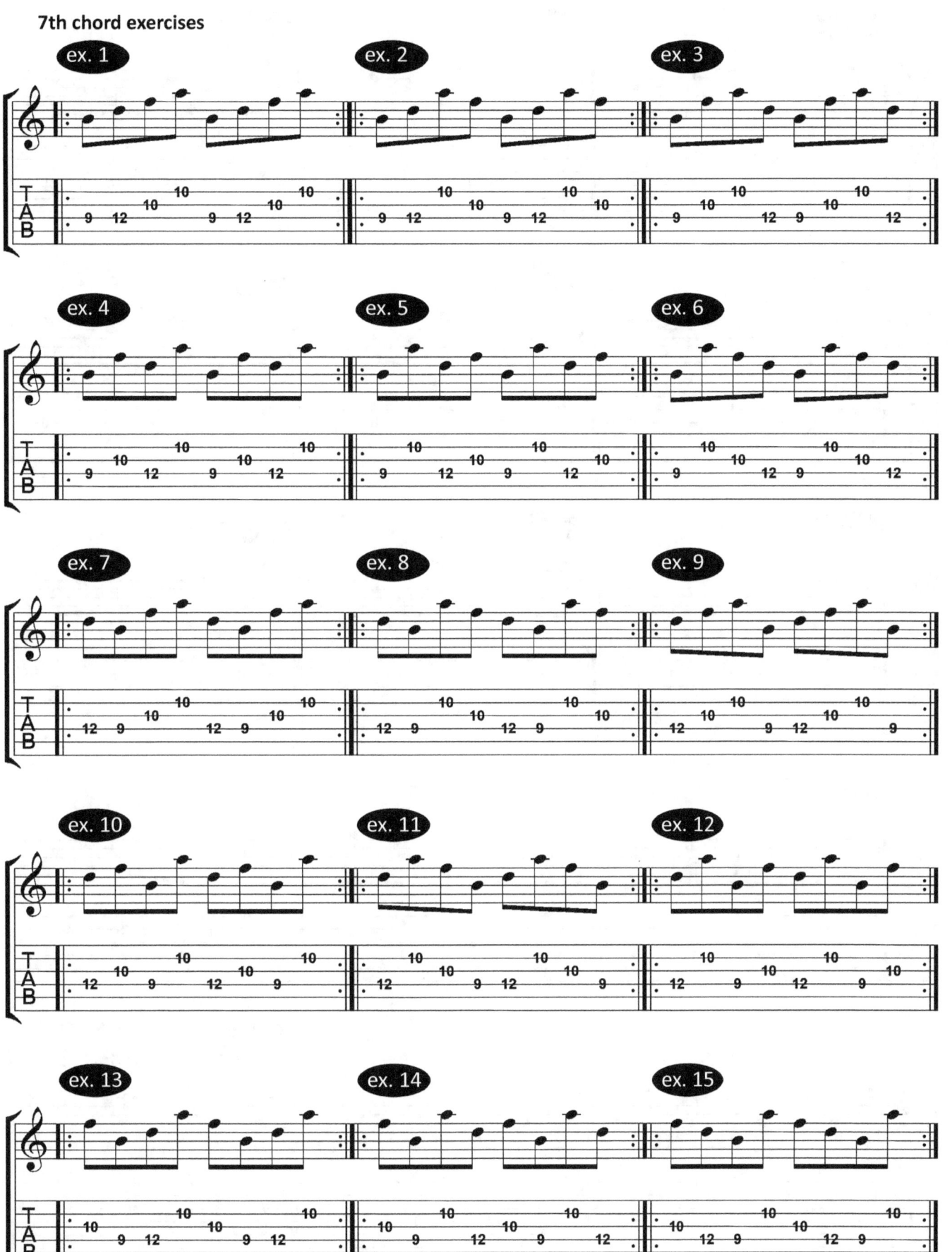

Chapter 4   the modes of the major scale - locrian

167

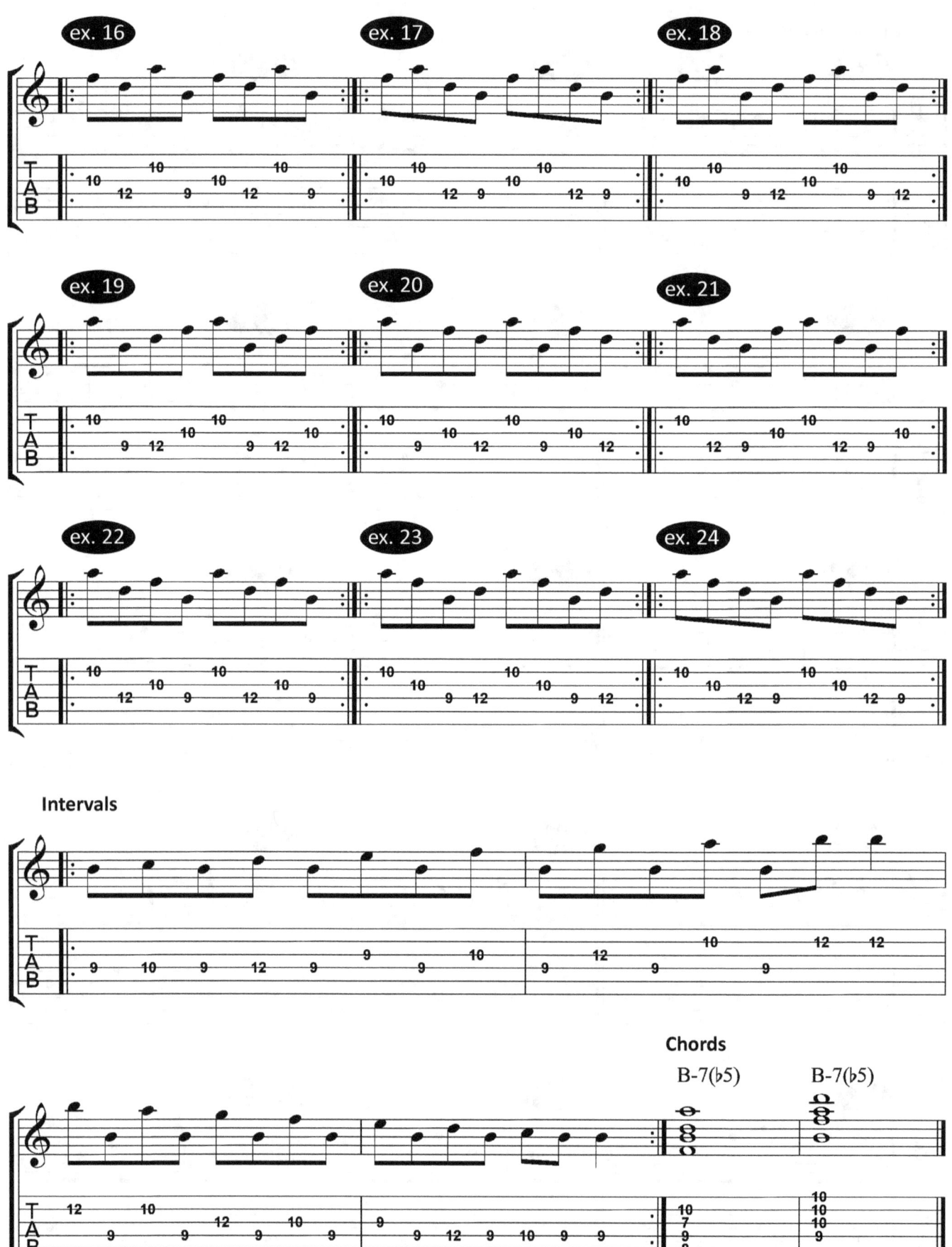

168 The complete guitar book 1

Locrian shape 3

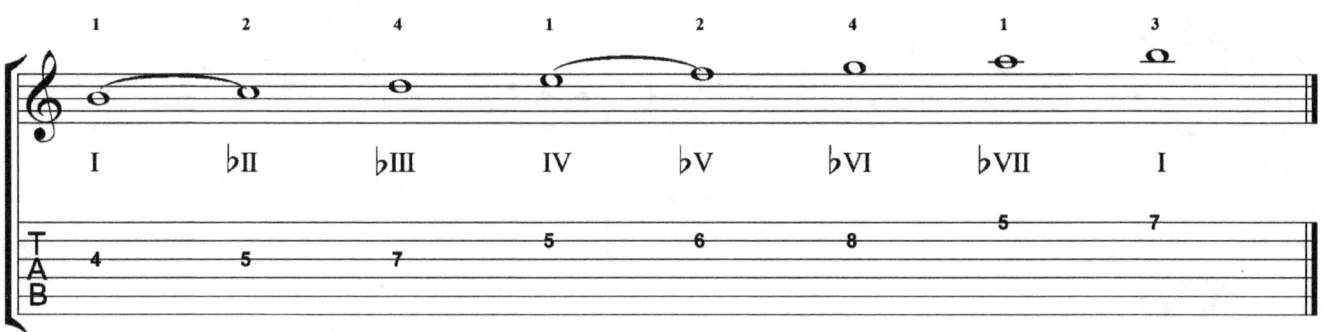

Tetrachords

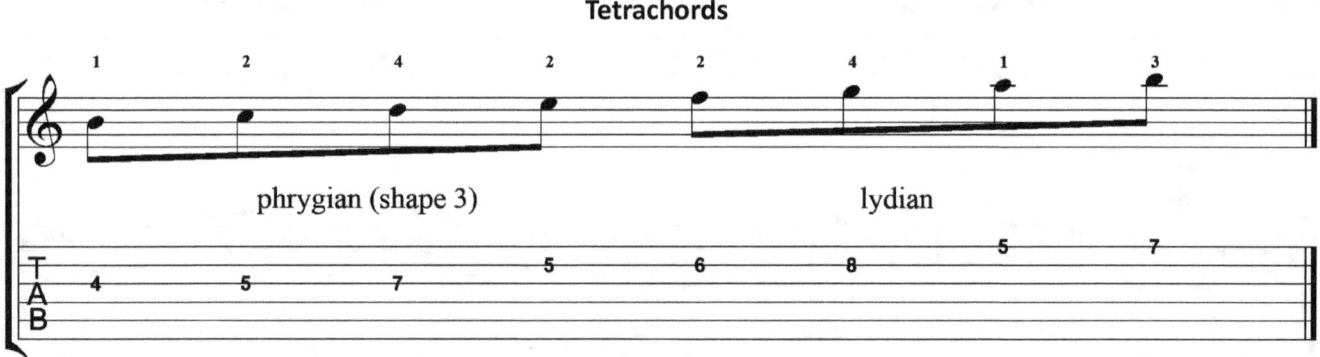

Intervals

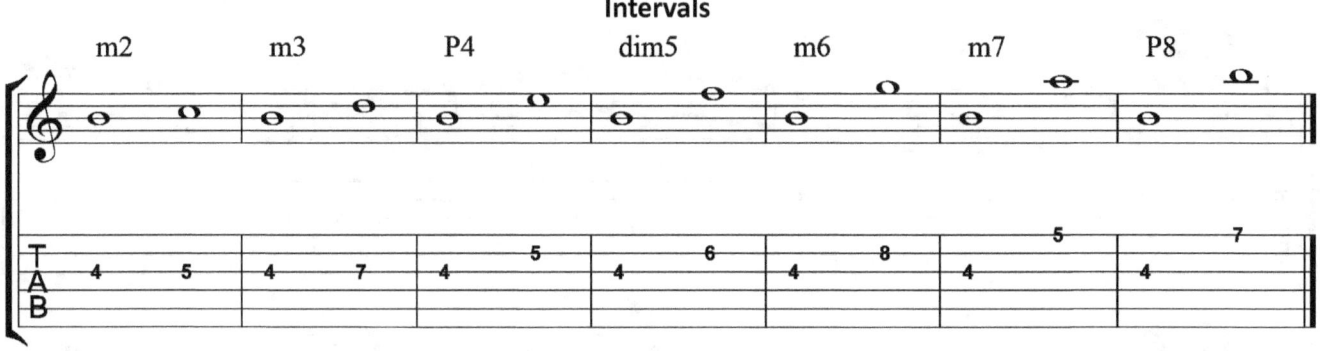

triad: diminished   7th chord: vii-7(♭5) half-diminished

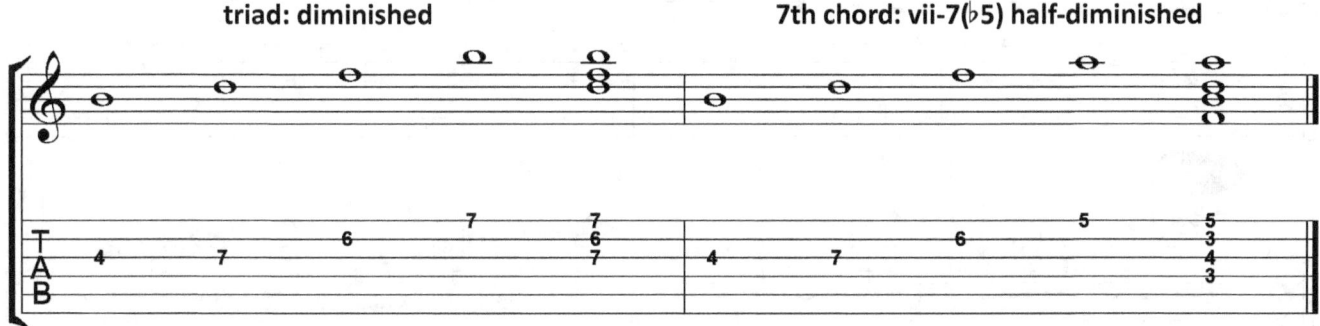

Chapter 4   the modes of the major scale - locrian

Locrian mode studies - shape 3

Mode exercises

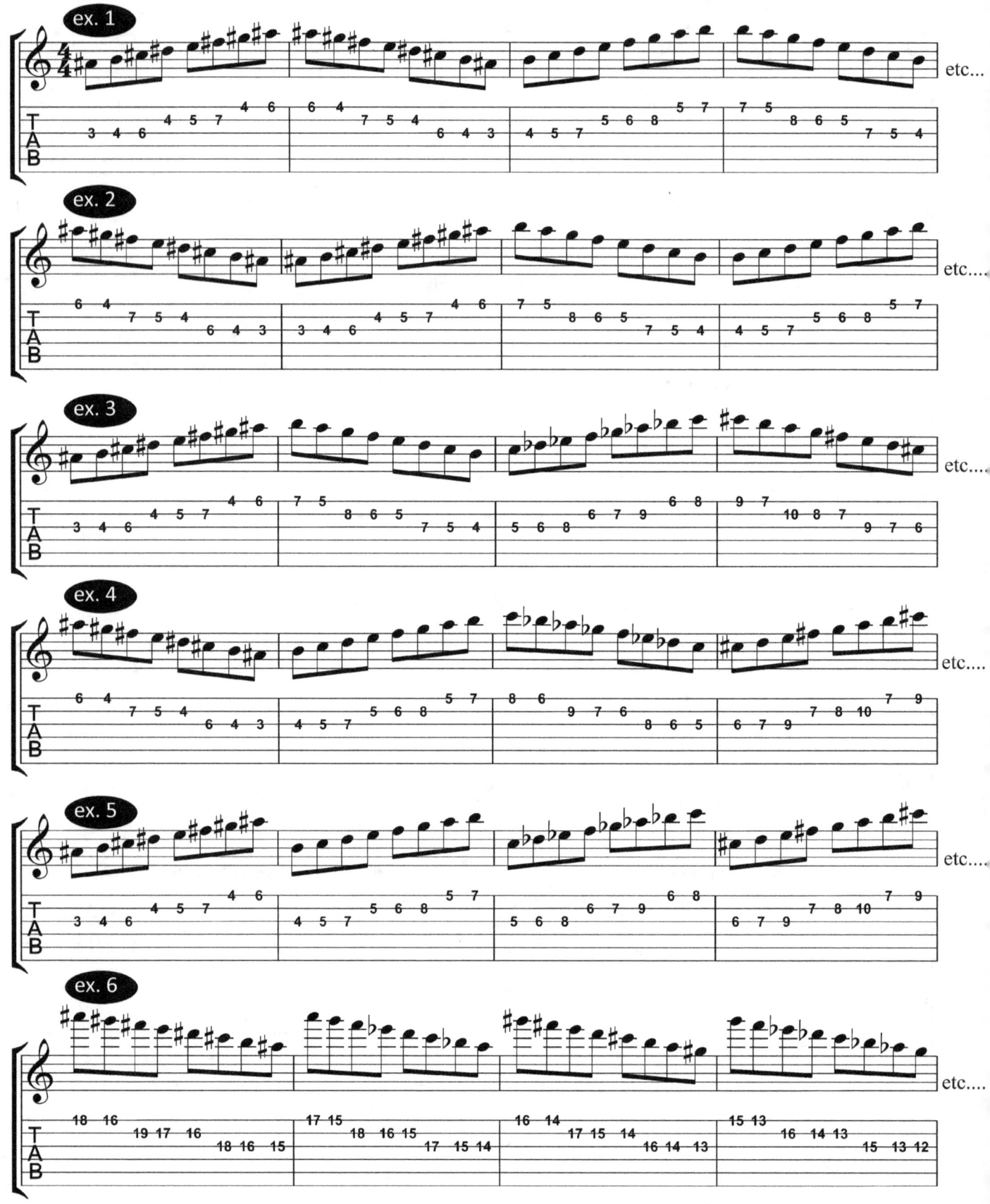

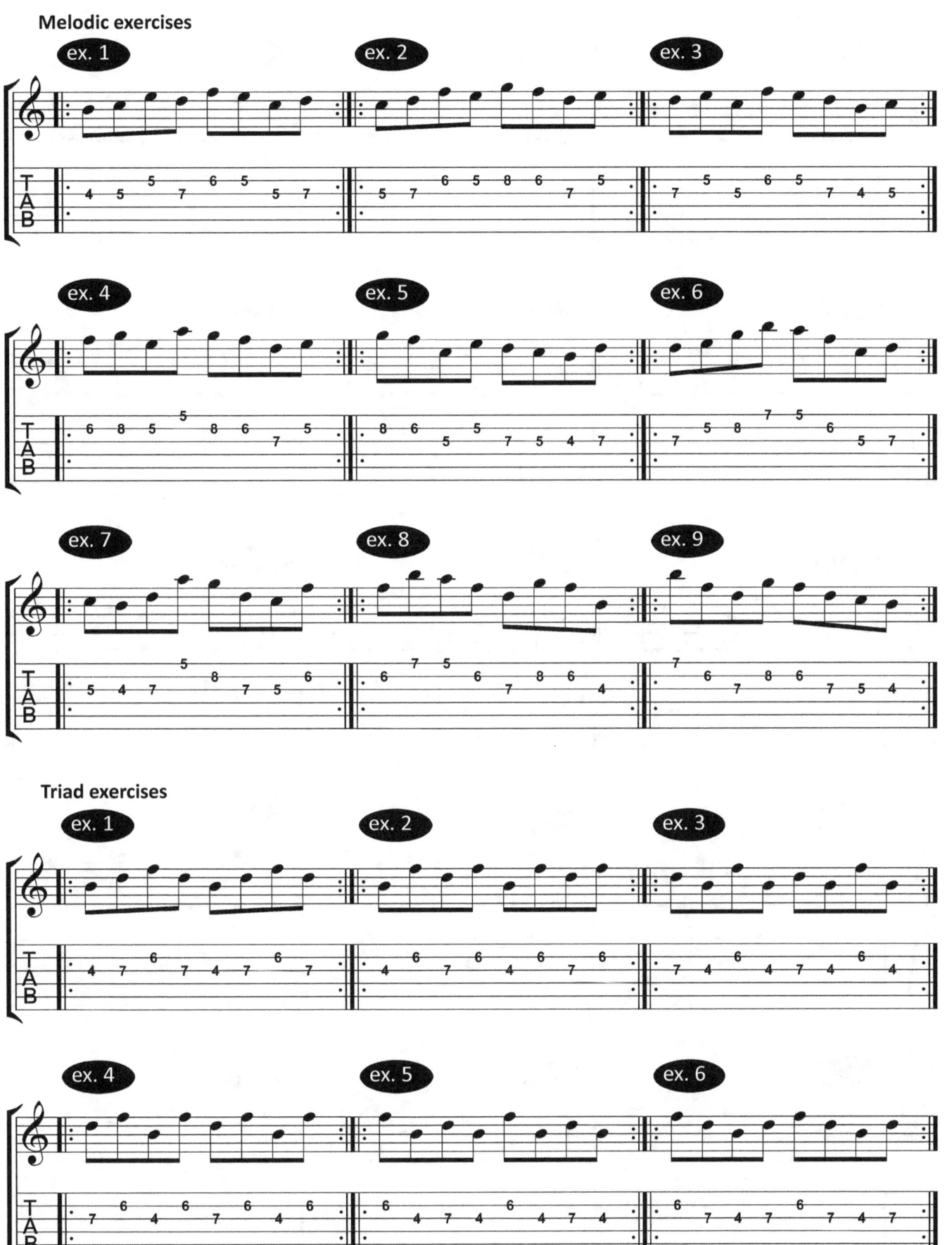

Chapter 4 the modes of the major scale - locrian

7th chord exercises

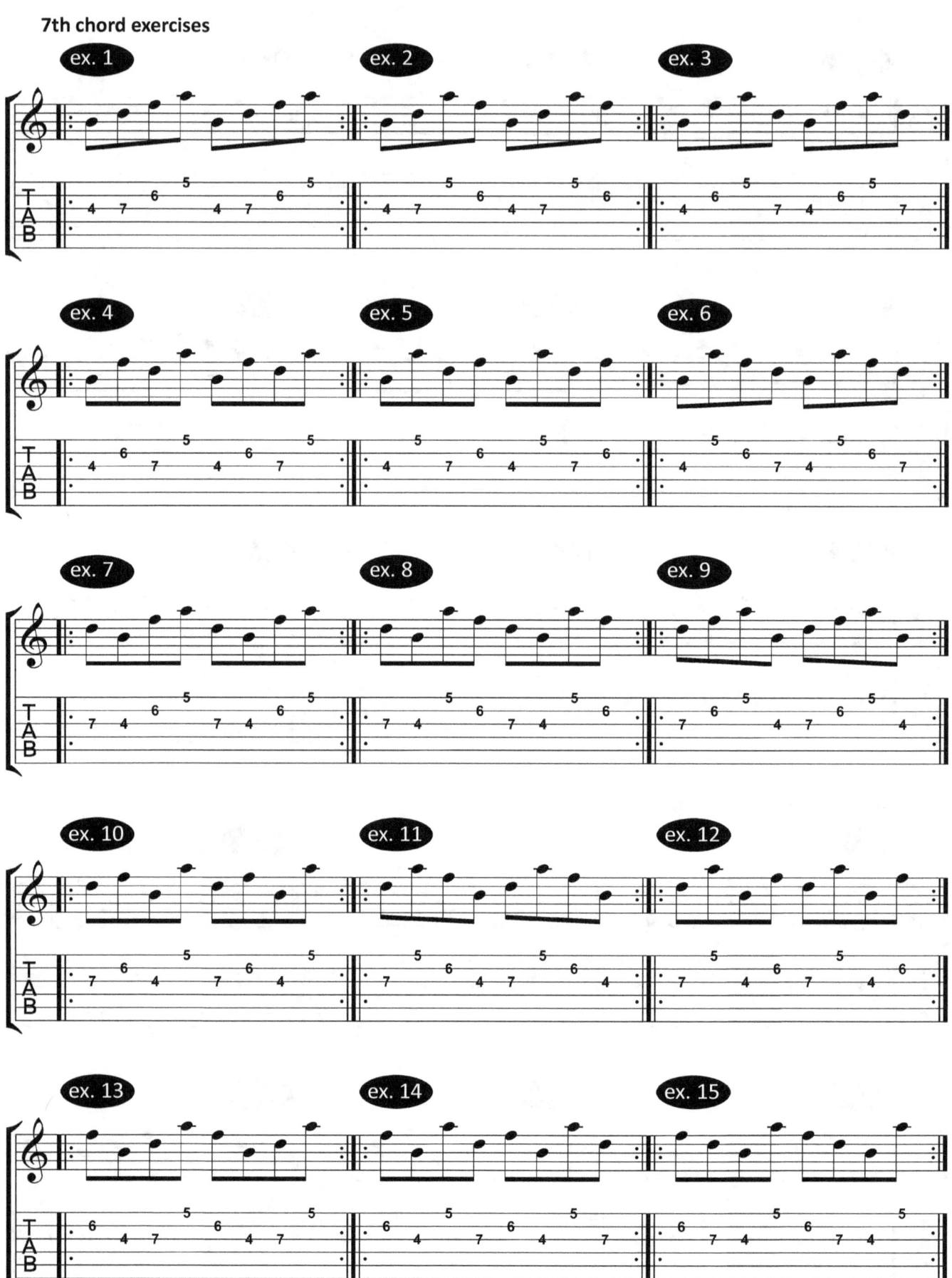

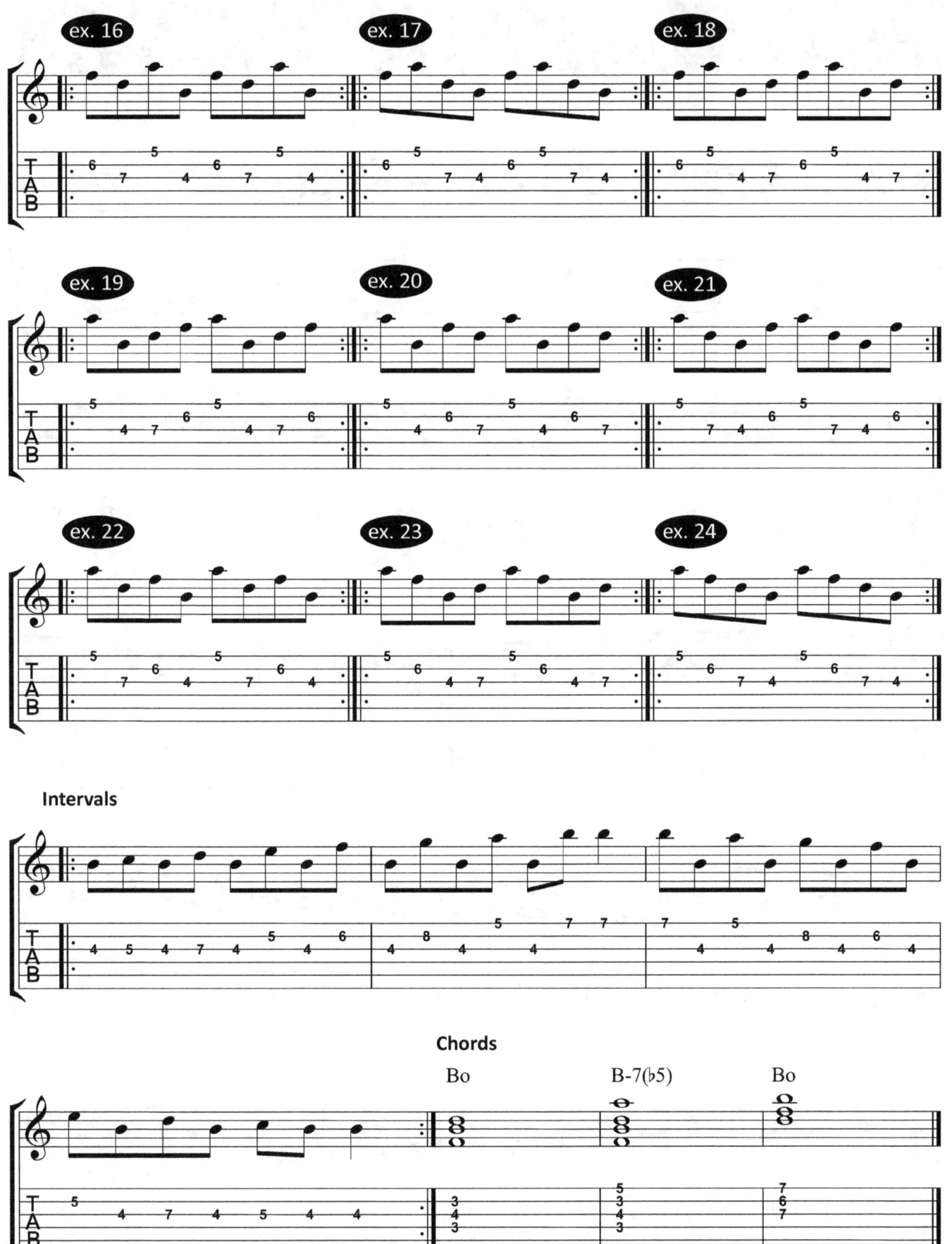

Intervals

Chords

Chapter 4 the modes of the major scale - locrian

Locrian in 2 octaves with shapes 1 + 2

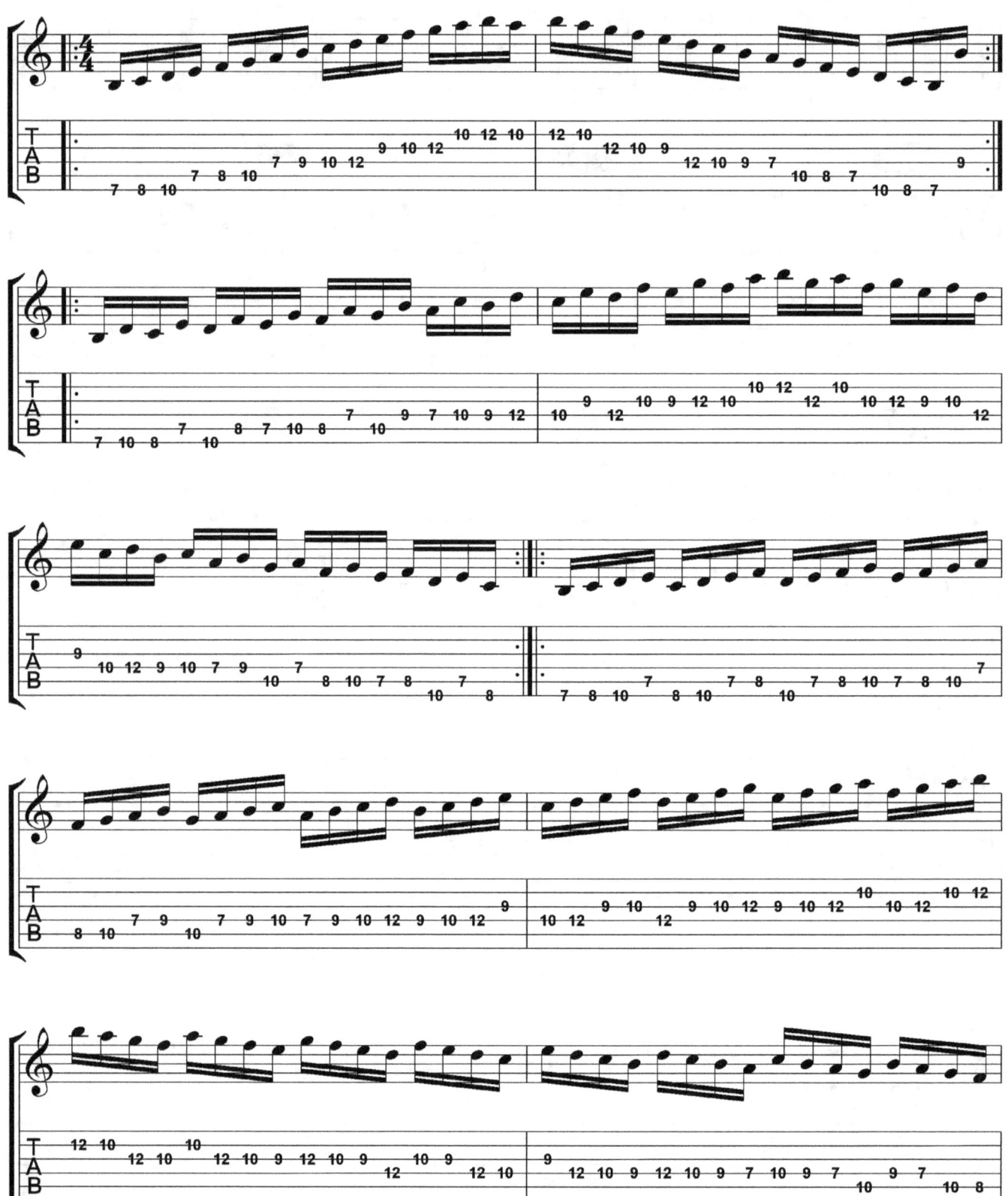

174   The complete guitar book 1

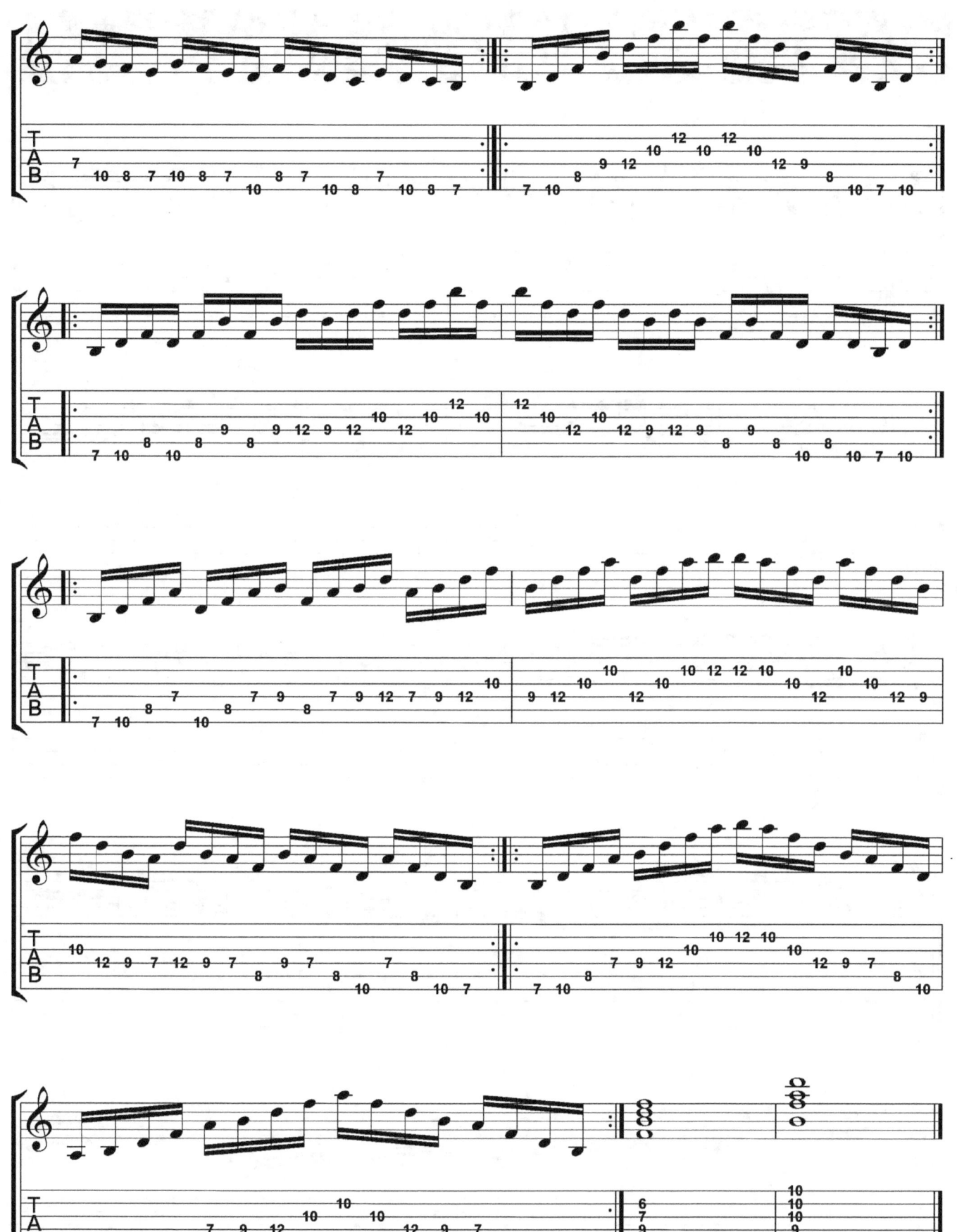

Chapter 4 the modes of the major scale - locrian

Locrian in 2 octaves with shapes 1 + 3

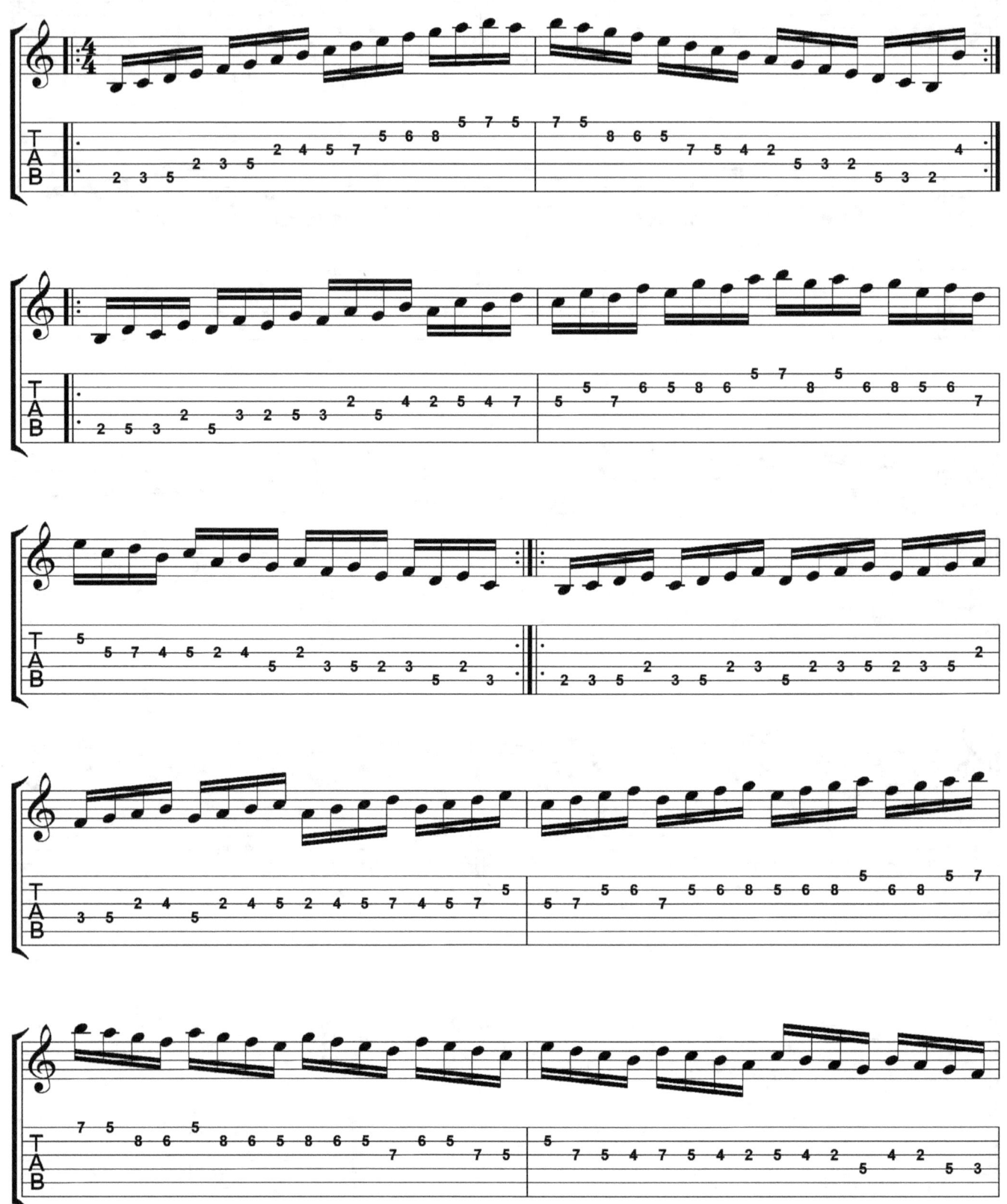

Chapter 4 the modes of the major scale - locrian

Chapter 5
horizontal construction of the modes

In this chapter we will study how the 7 modes of each major mother scale are constructed by placing each one on the respective scale degree it represents in horizontal construction on the fingerboard. That way, the progression of the exercise includes sub-parts of study which present the complete construction of the modes and the diatonic chords of the key center.

Study guidelines for this chapter
- There are repeat signs that separate each part of the exercise from the next part.
- You should play each exercise part several times before moving on to the next part.
- At the end, you should play the entire exercise without the repeats.

The exercise is presented in 3 key centers in order to study all 3 shapes. For shape 1 it is constructed in C major, for shape 2 in F major, and for shape 3 in B♭ major.

Horizontal mode studies in C major - shape 1

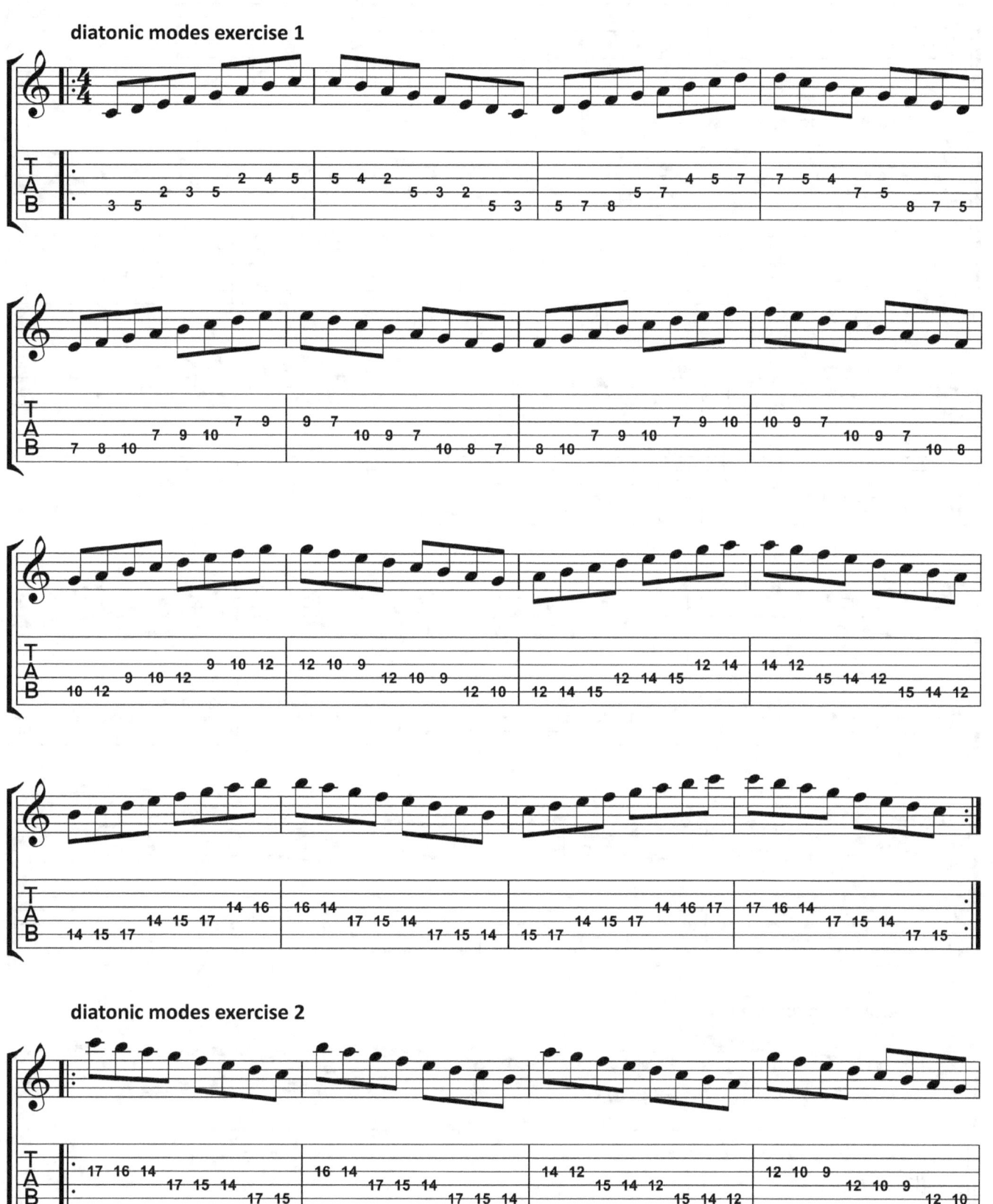

Chapter 5   horizontal construction of the modes

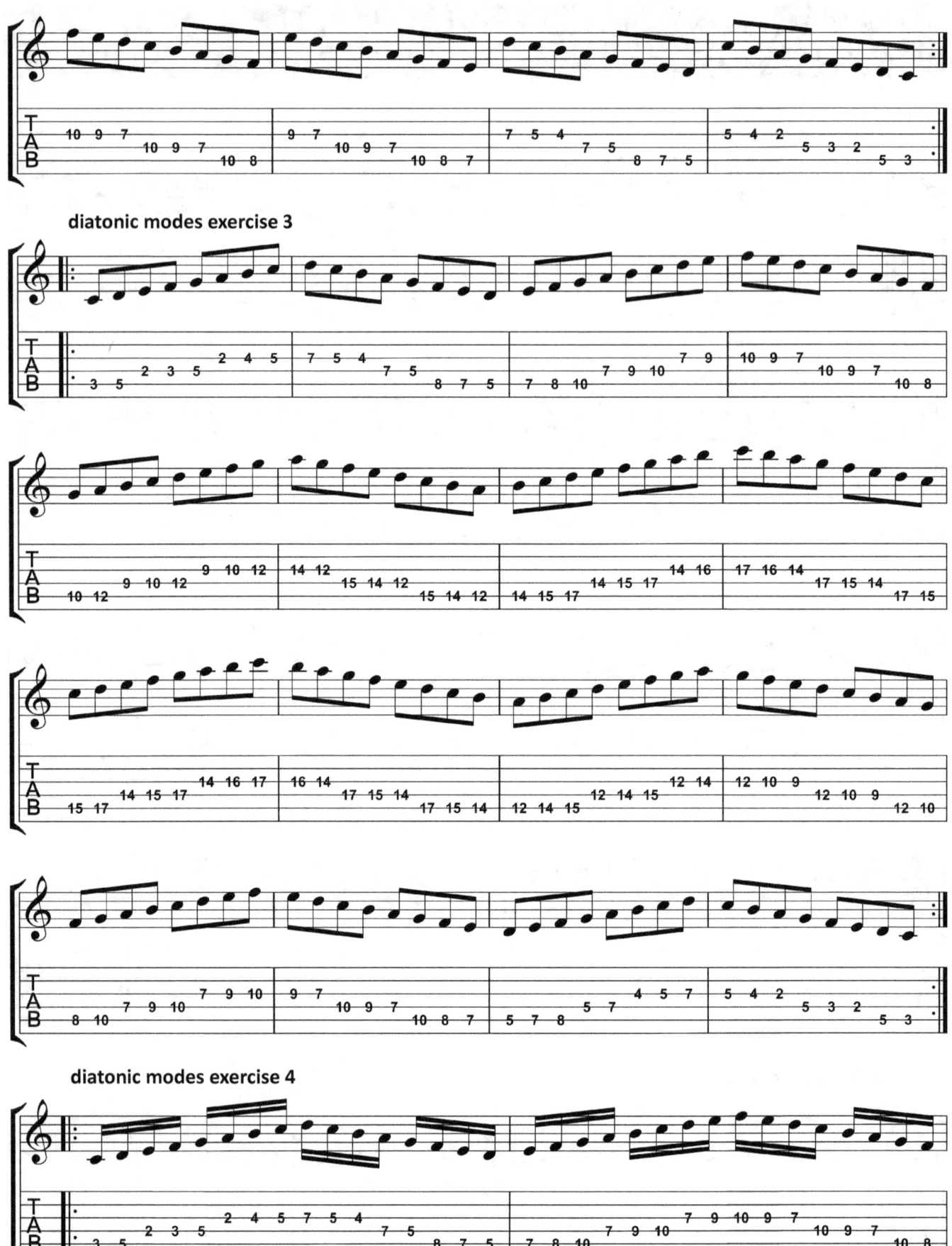

diatonic modes exercise 3

diatonic modes exercise 4

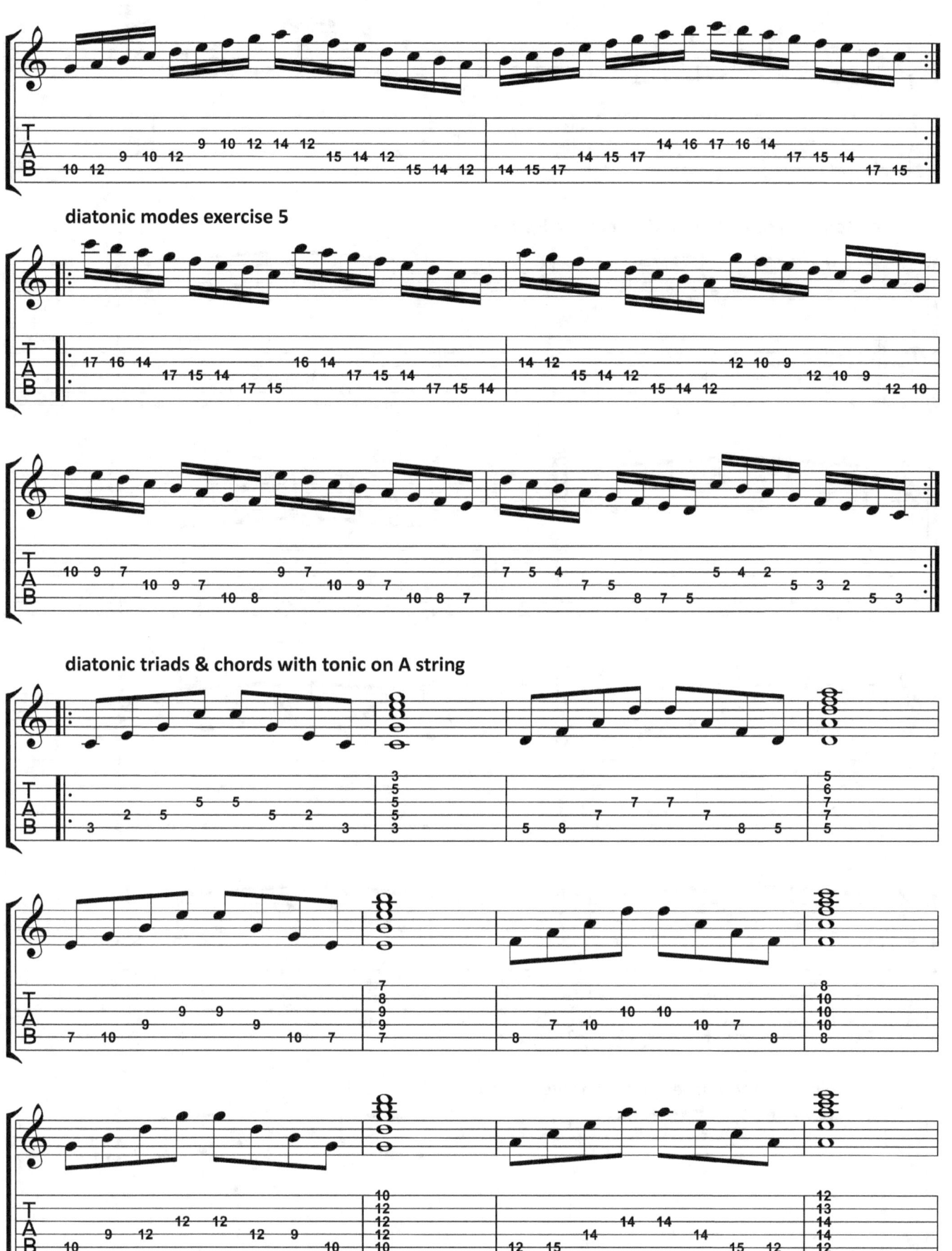

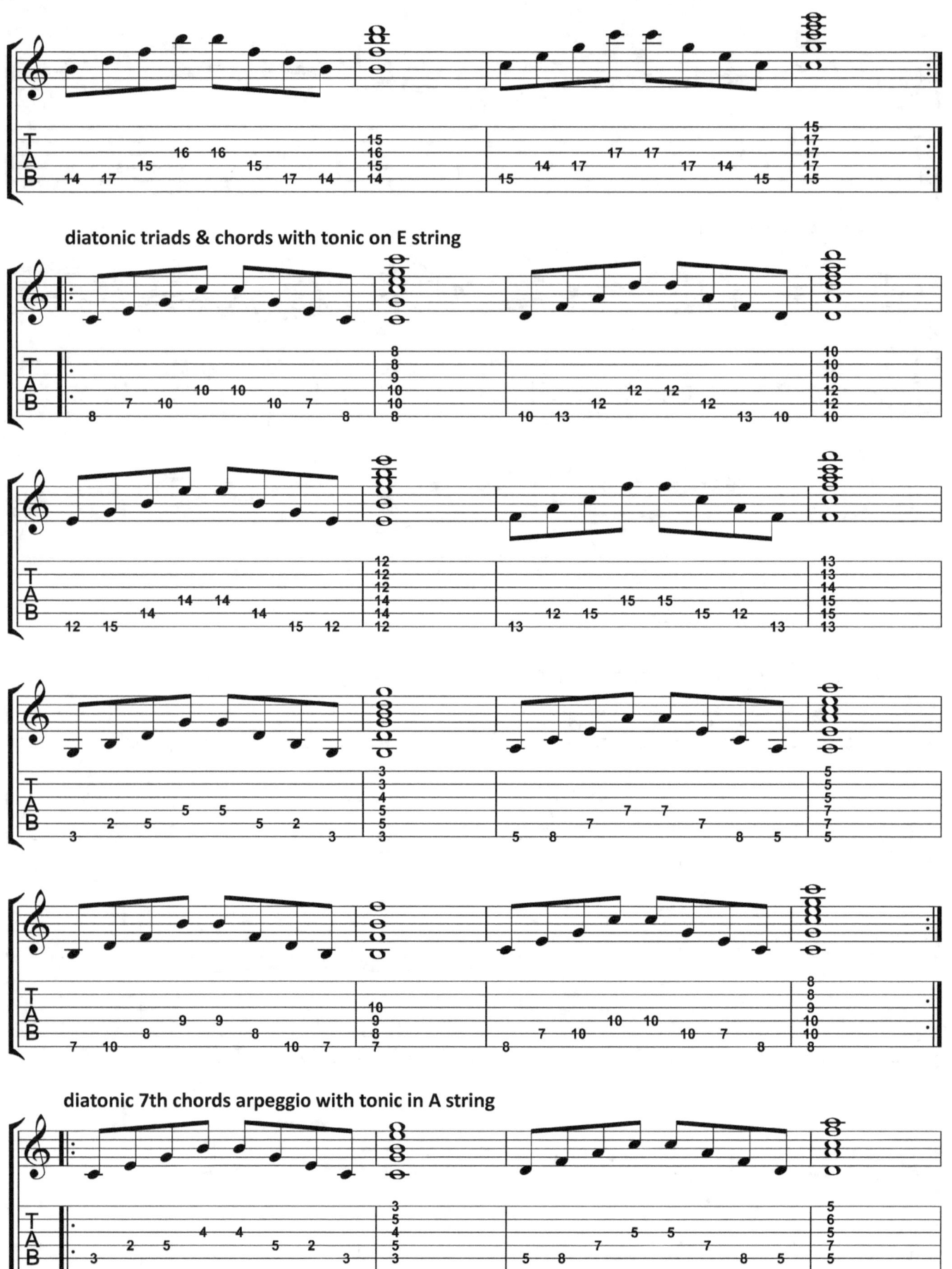

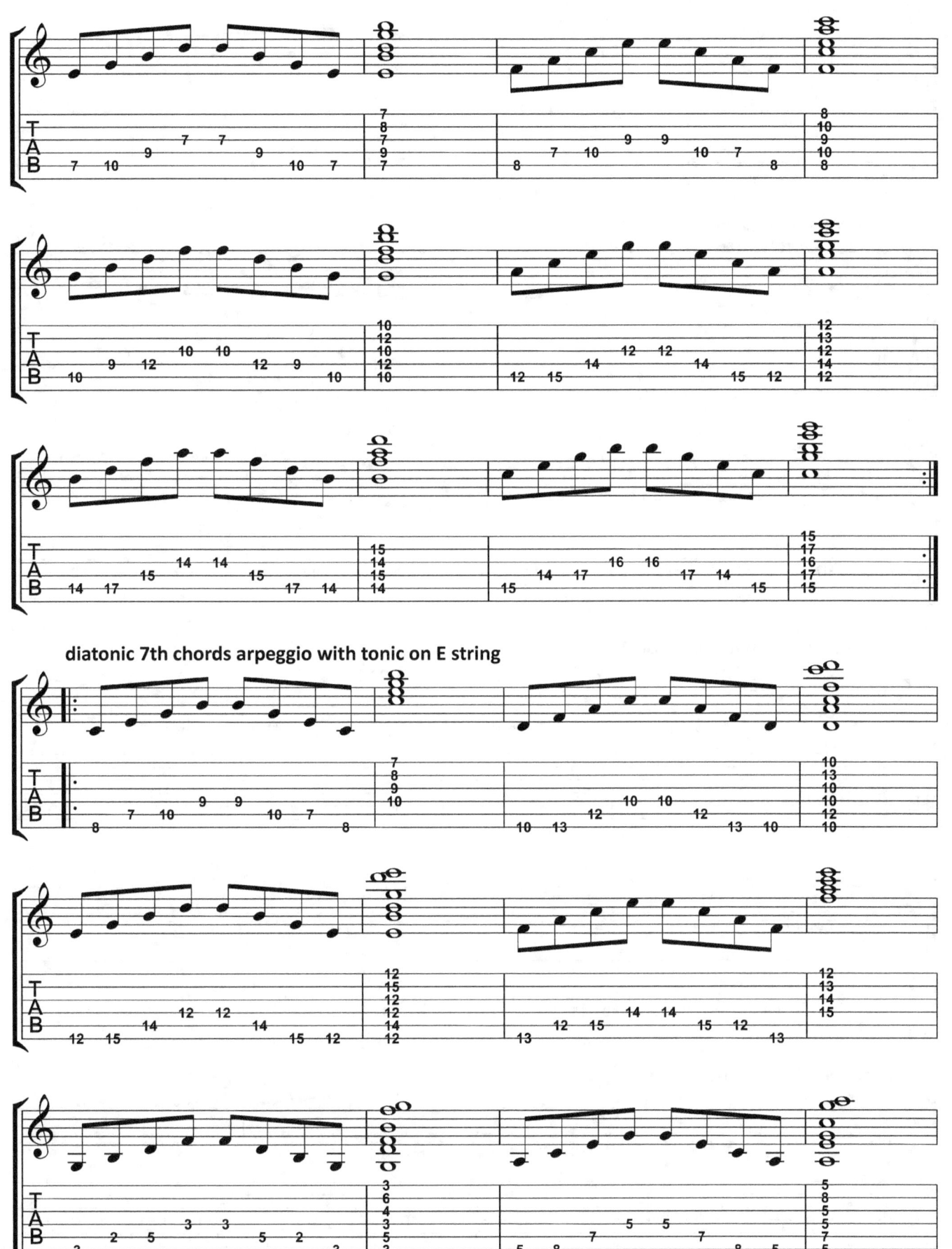

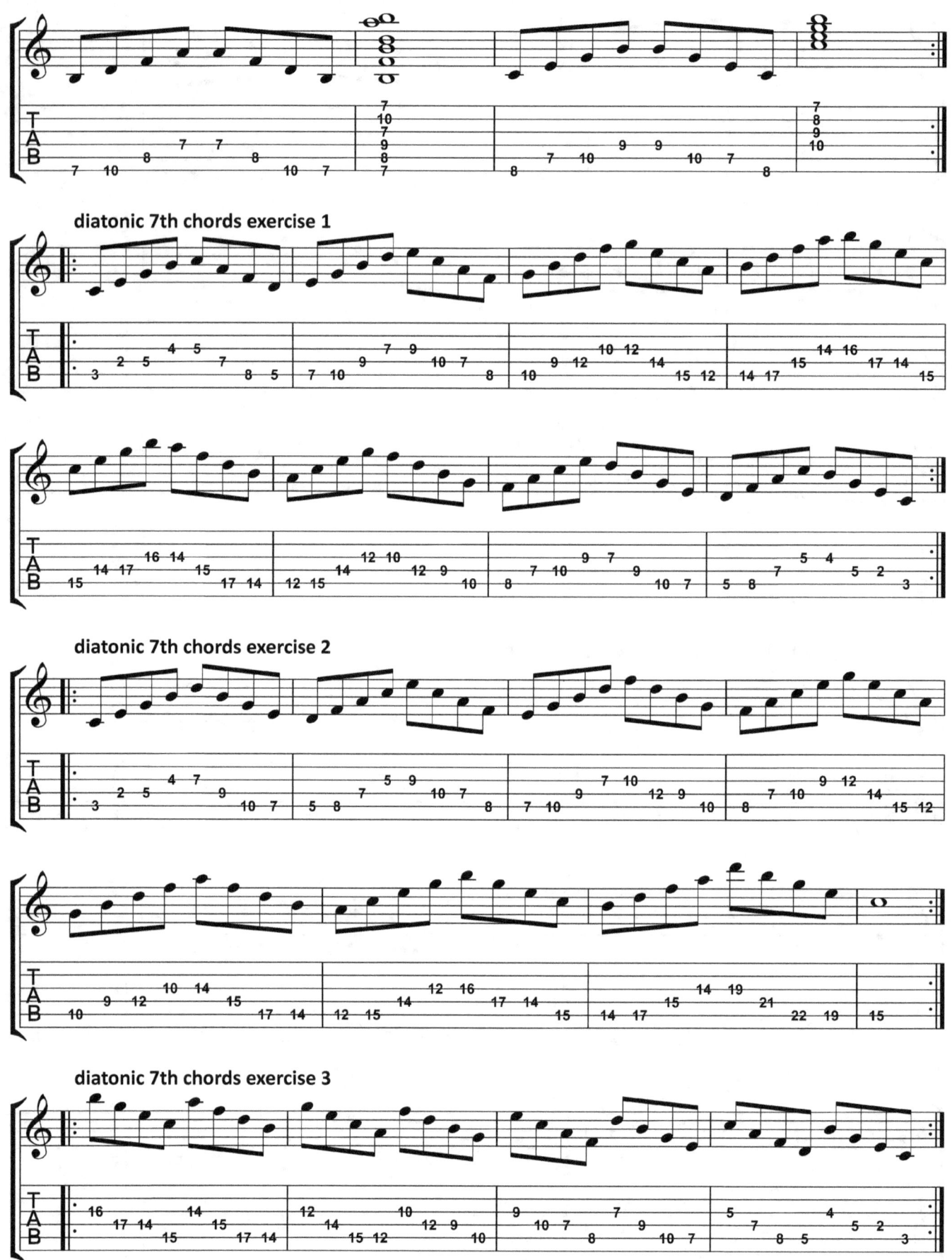

diatonic modes melodic exercise 1 on 2 strings

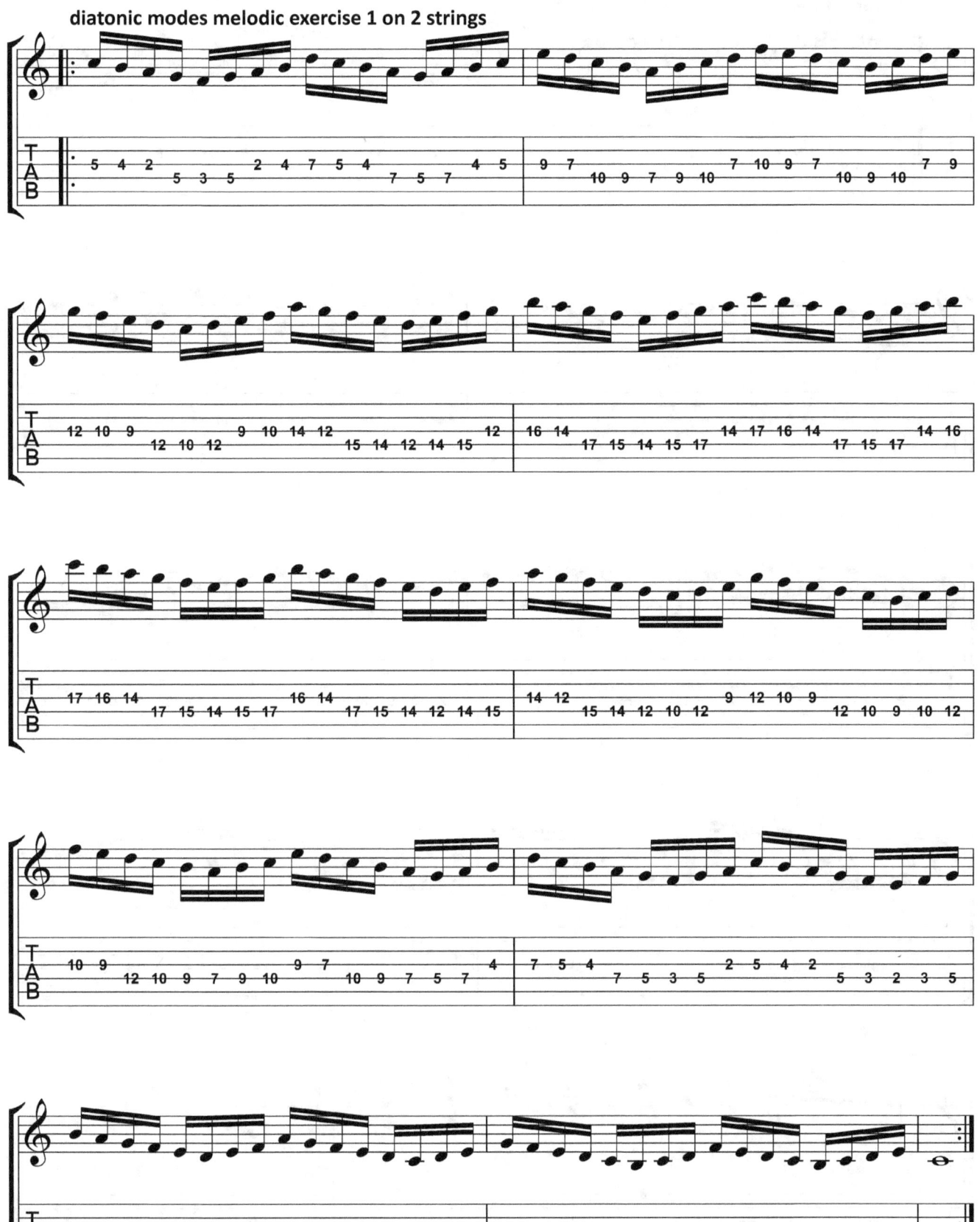

Chapter 5 horizontal construction of the modes

diatonic modes melodic exercise 2 on 2 strings

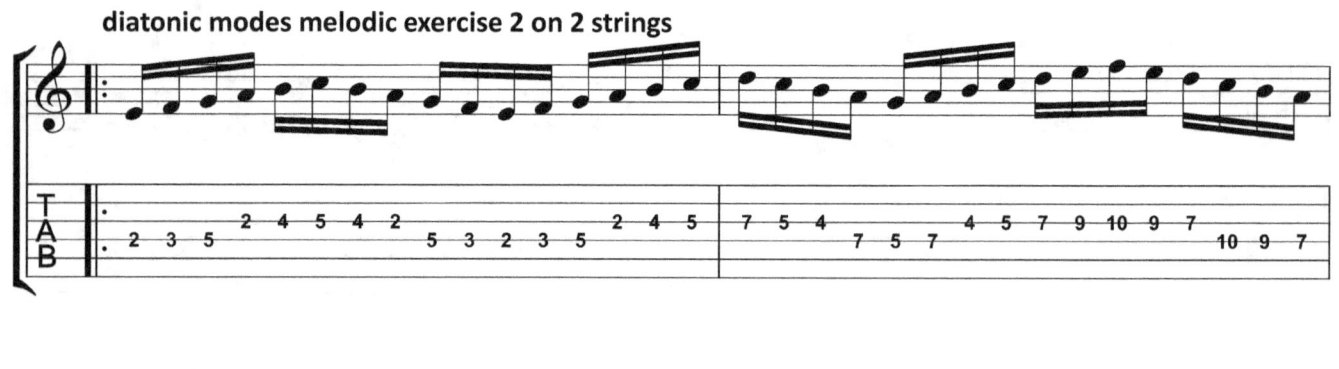
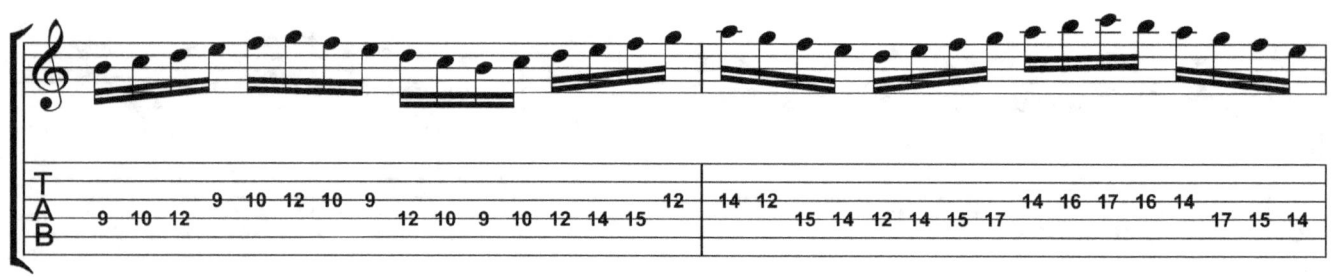

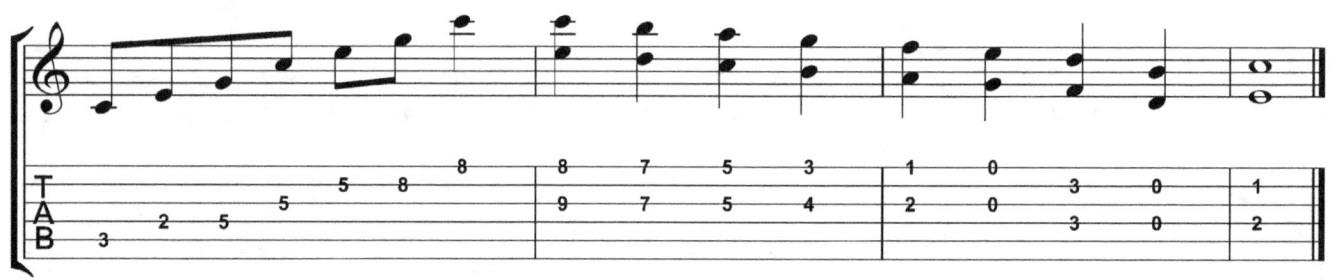

Horizontal mode studies in F major - shape 2

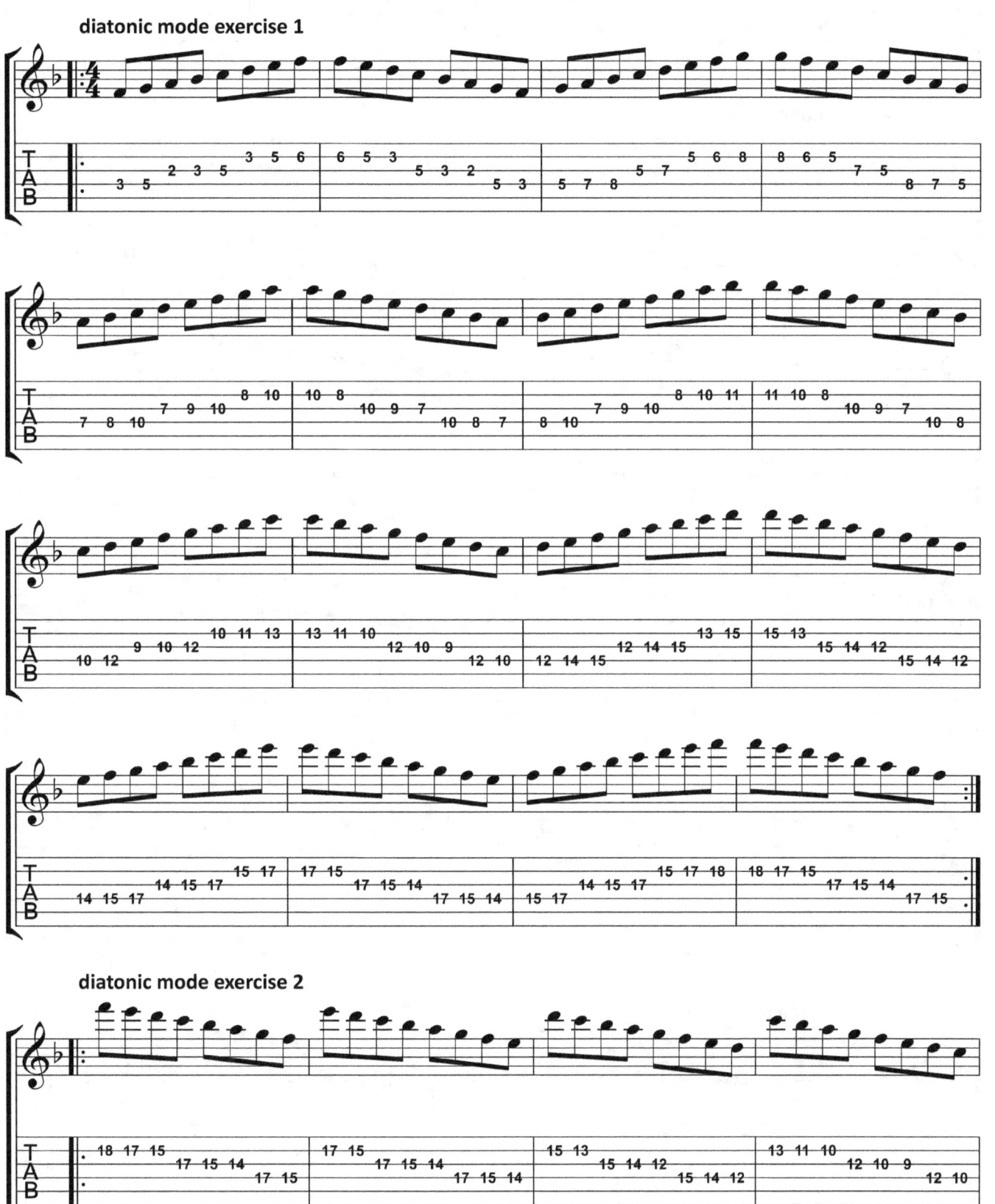

Chapter 5 horizontal construction of the modes

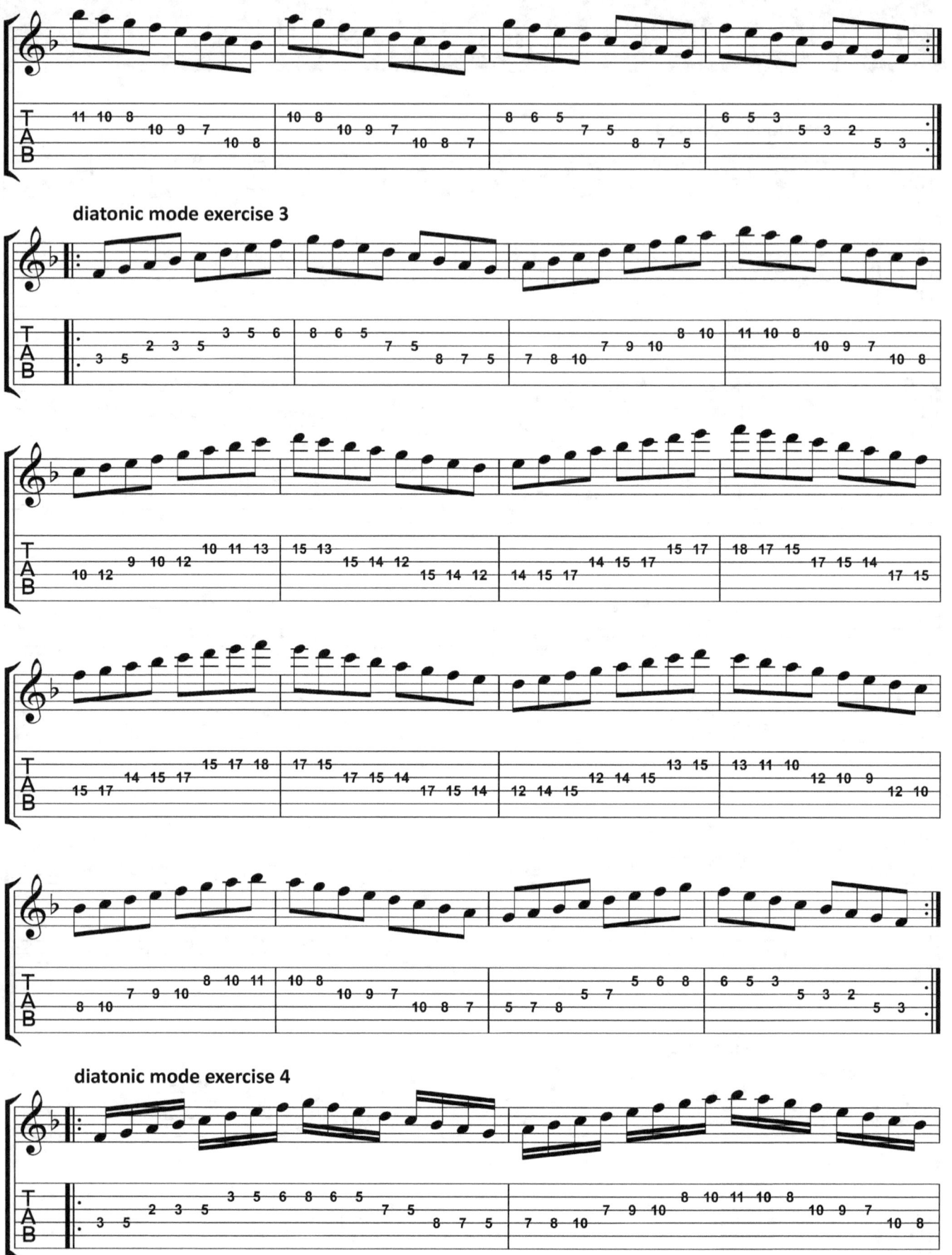

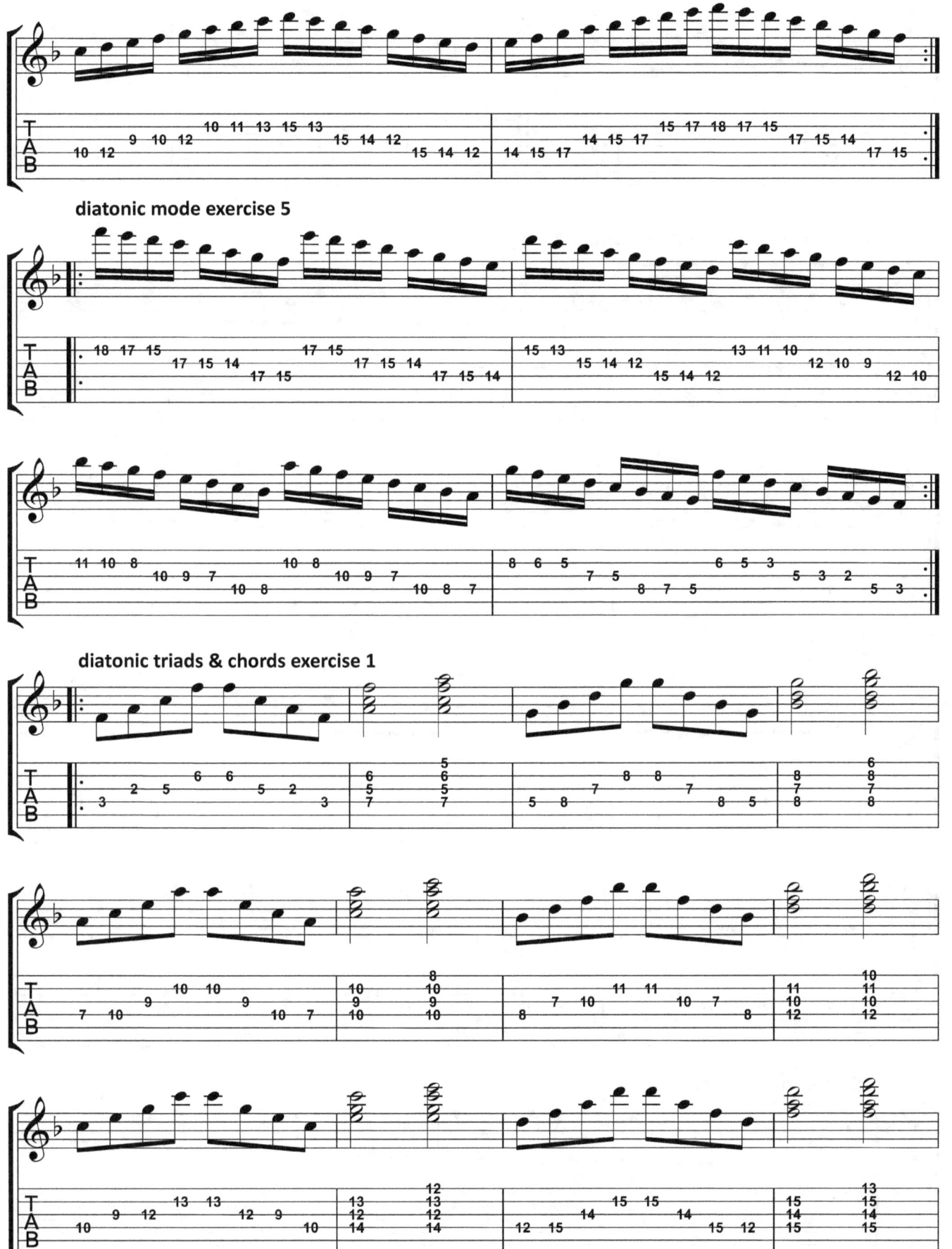

Chapter 5 horizontal construction of the modes

diatonic triads exercise 4

diatonic 7th chords exercise 1

Chapter 5 *horizontal construction of the modes*

diatonic 7th chords exercise 2

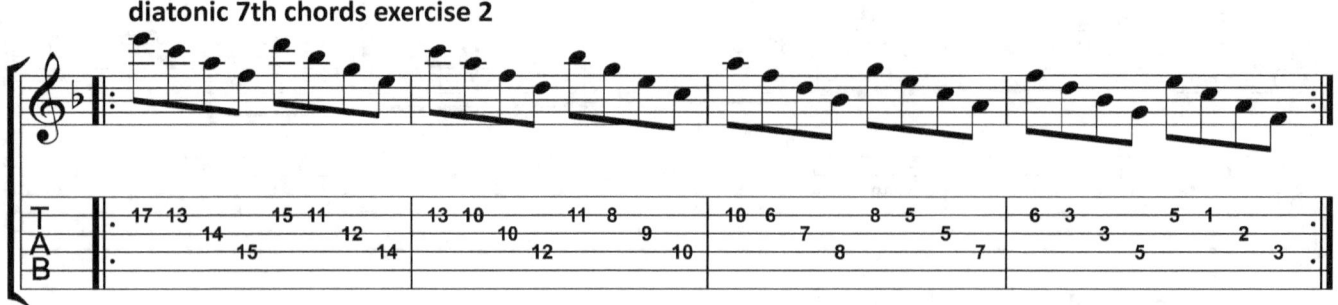

diatonic 7th chords exercise 3

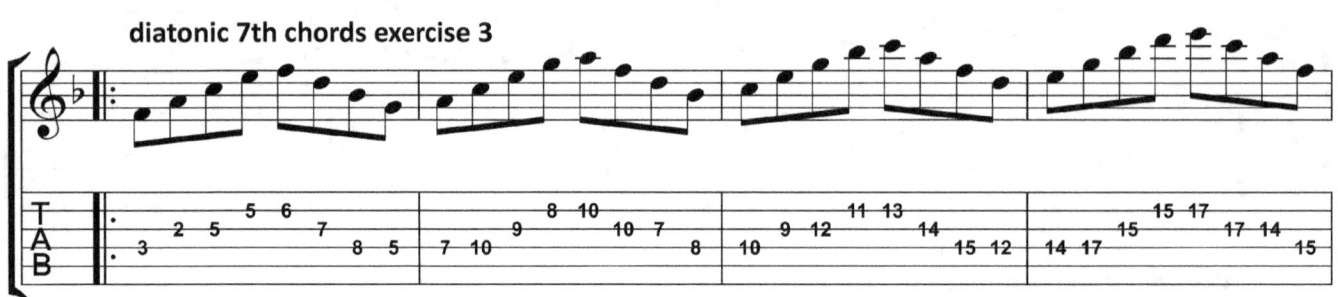

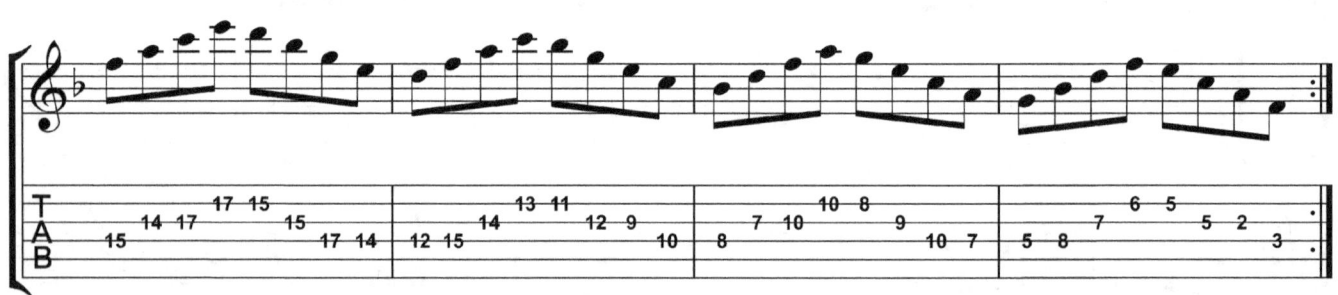

diatonic 7th chords exercise 4

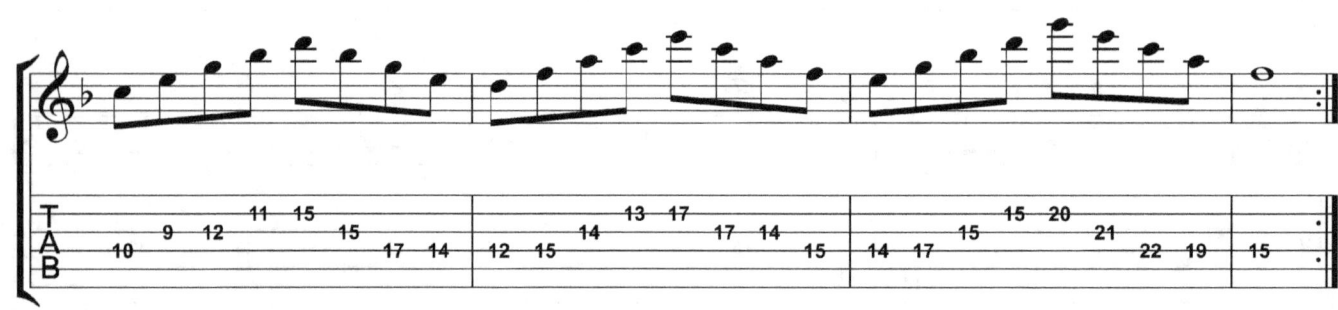

diatonic modes exercise 1 on 2strings

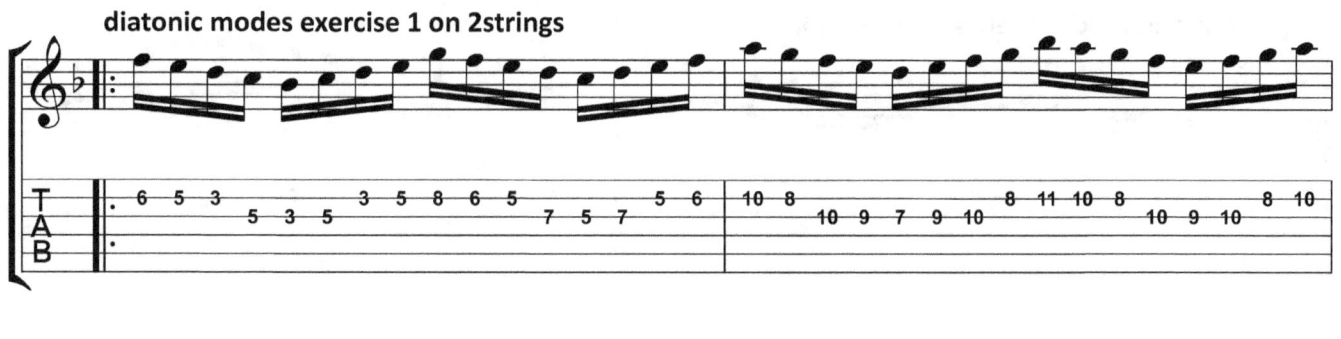
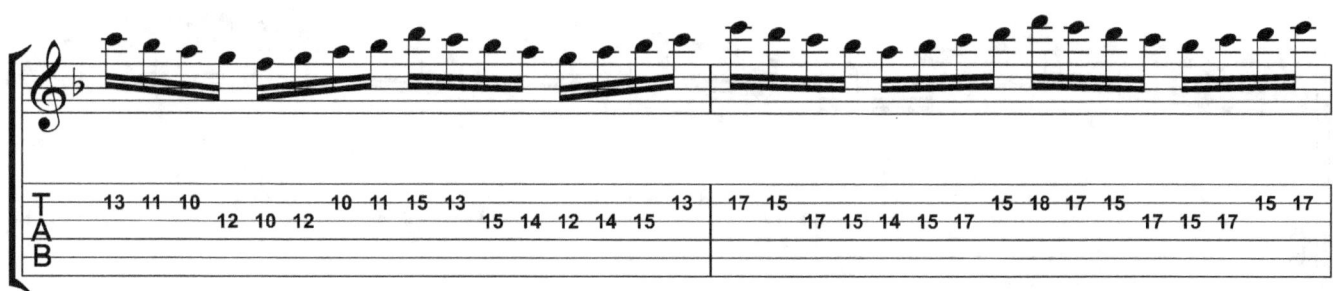
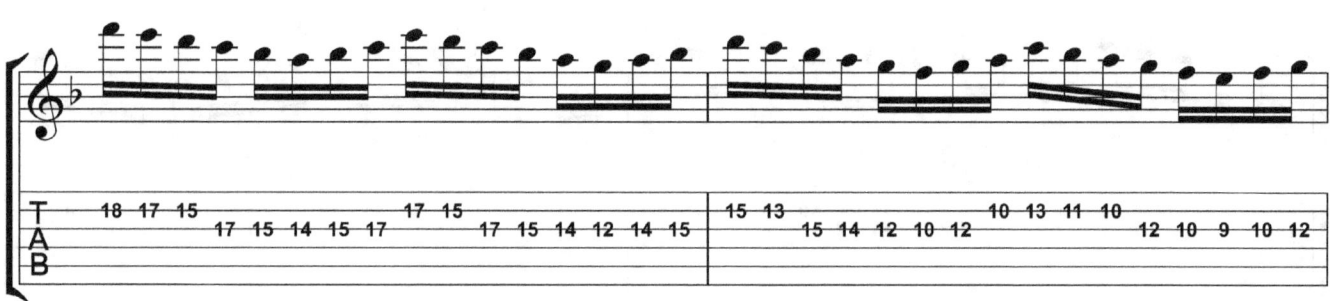

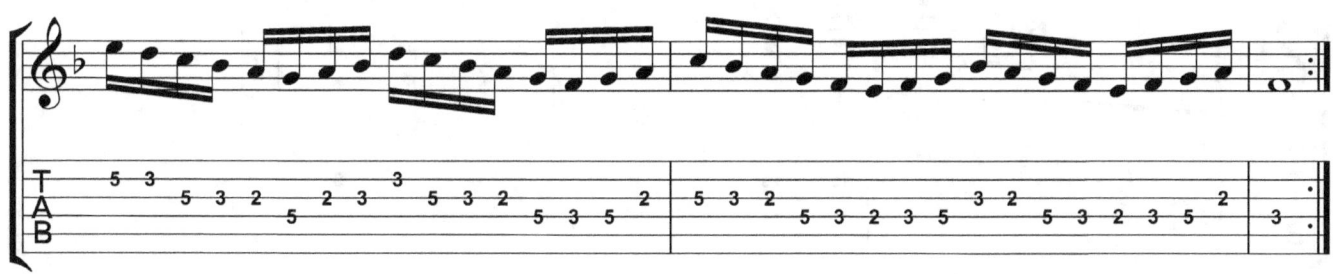

Chapter 5   horizontal construction of the modes

diatonic modes exercise 2 on 2strings

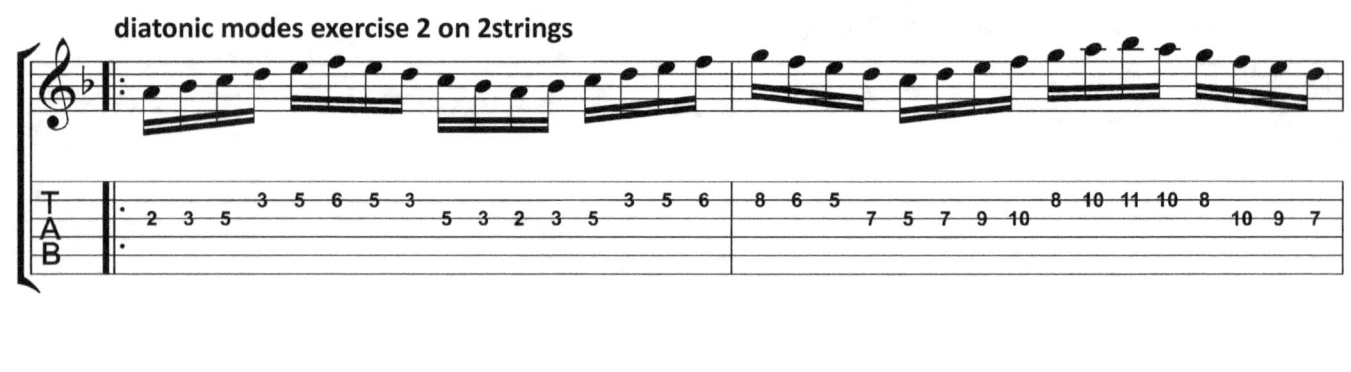
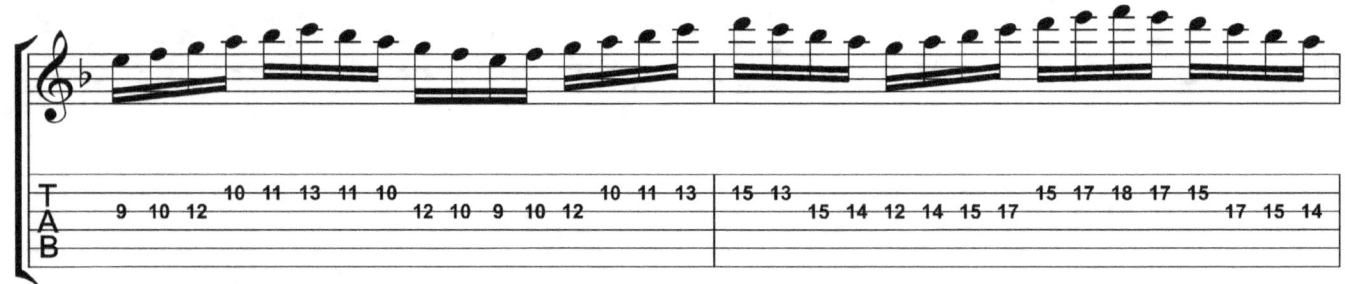
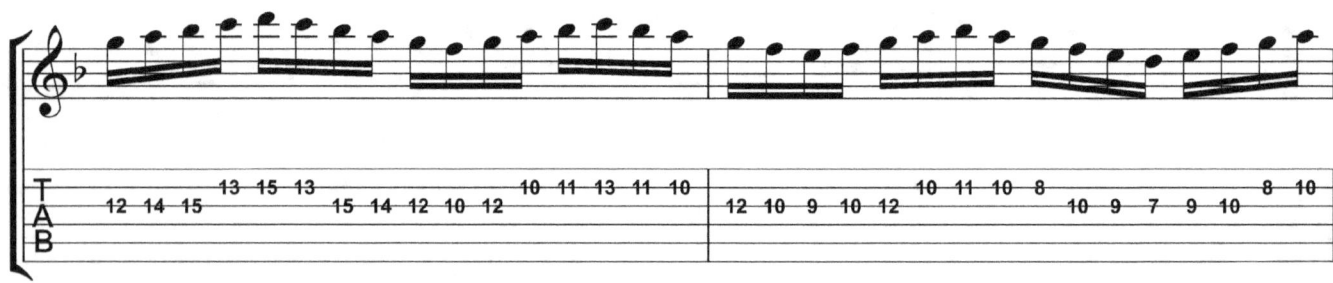

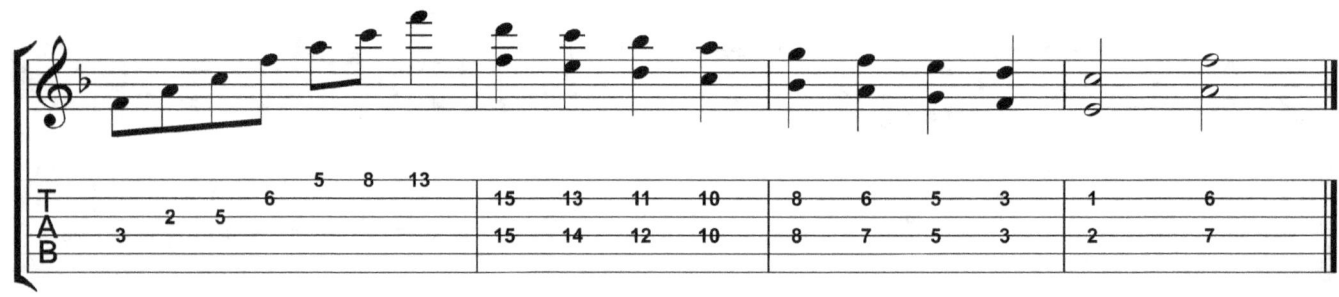

Horizontal mode studies in B♭ major - shape 3

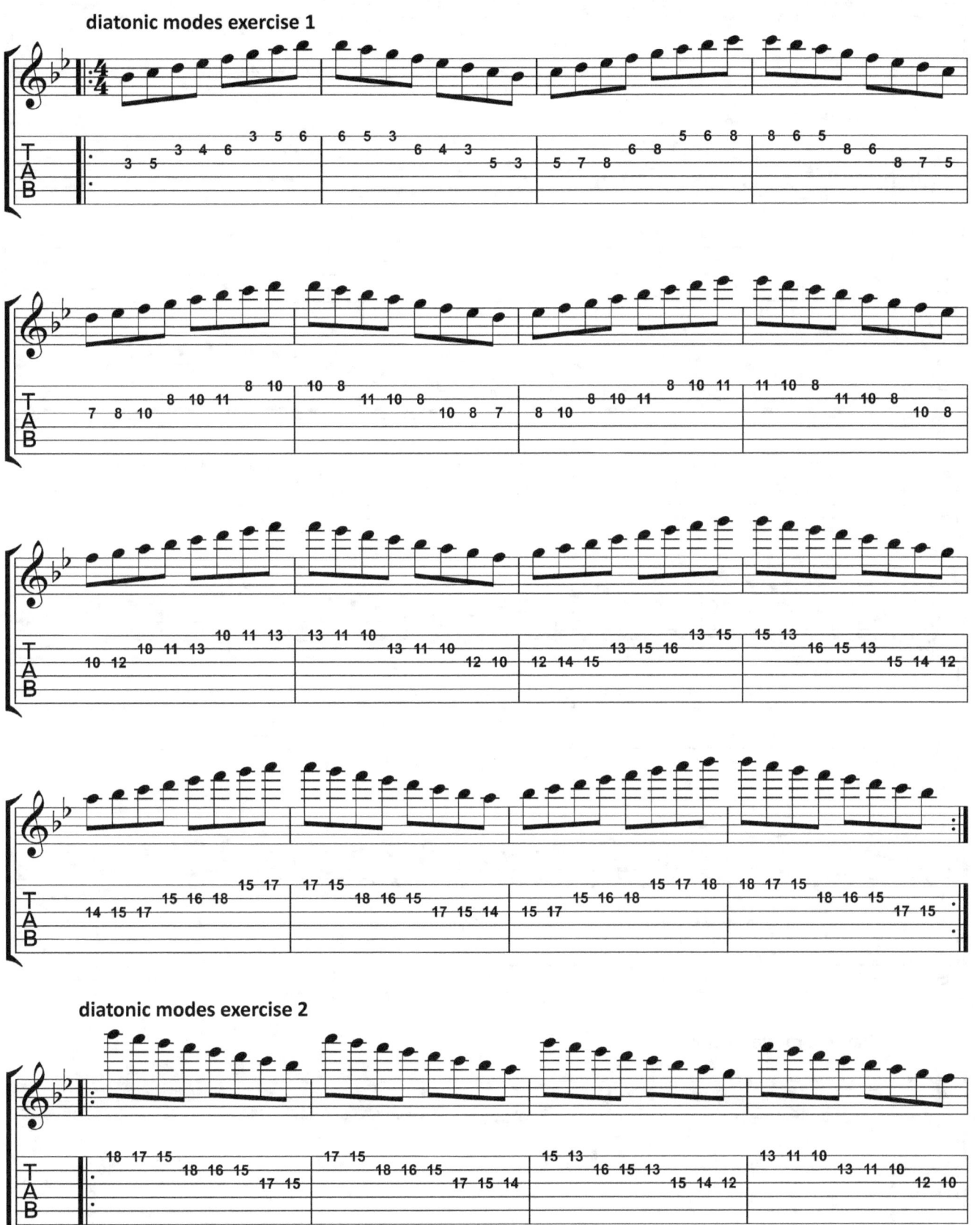

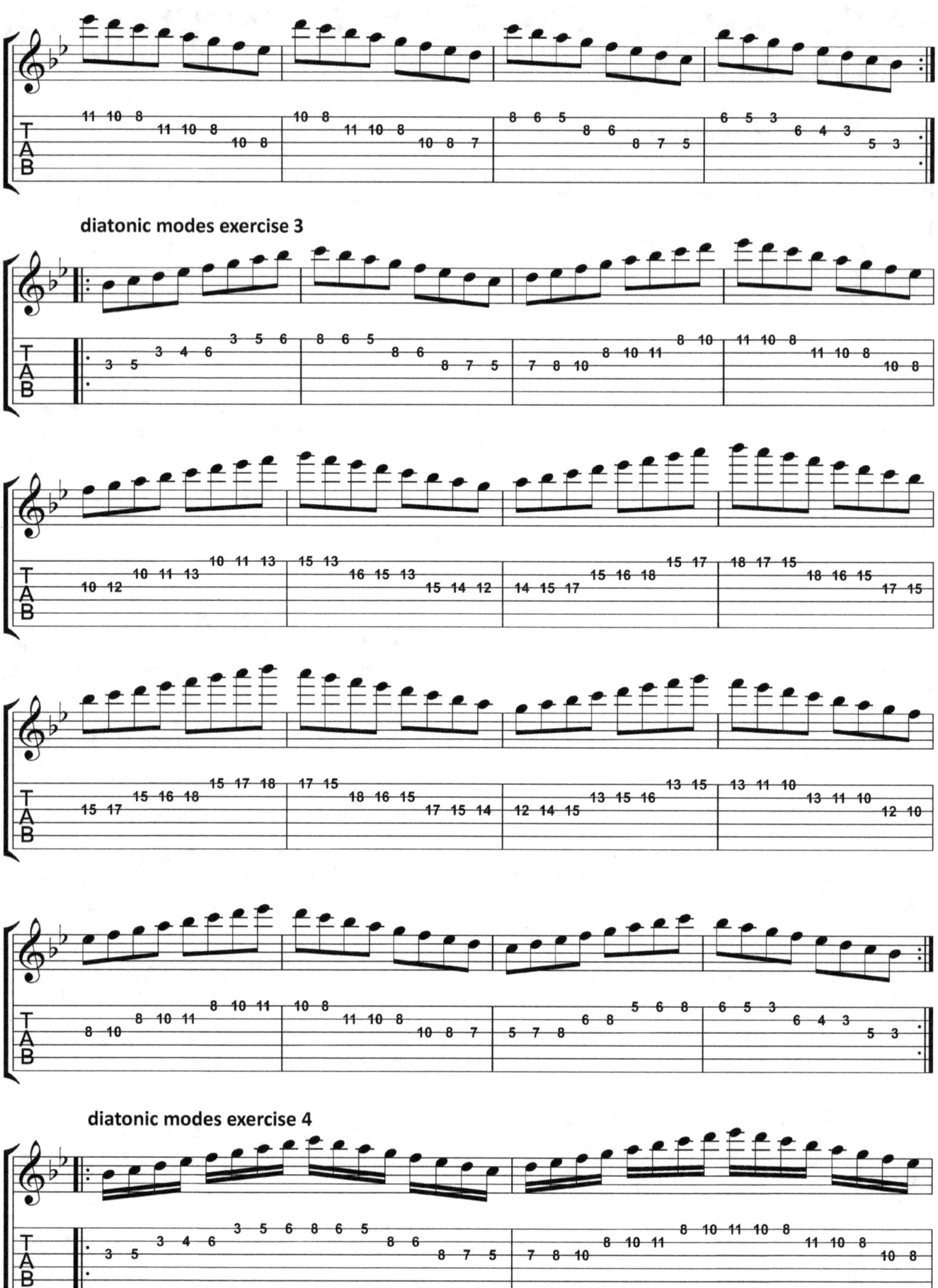

diatonic modes exercise 3

diatonic modes exercise 4

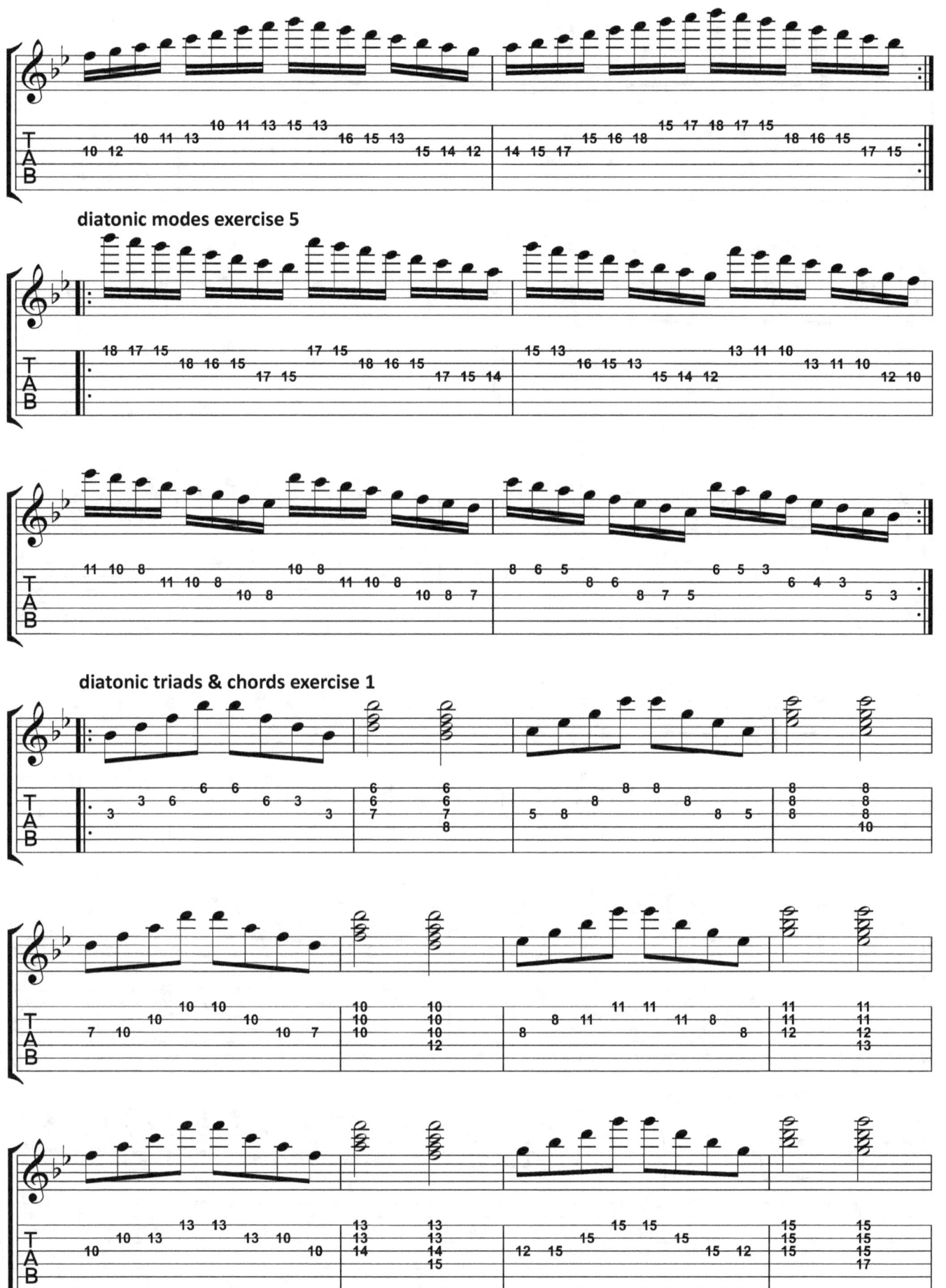

Chapter 5 horizontal construction of the modes

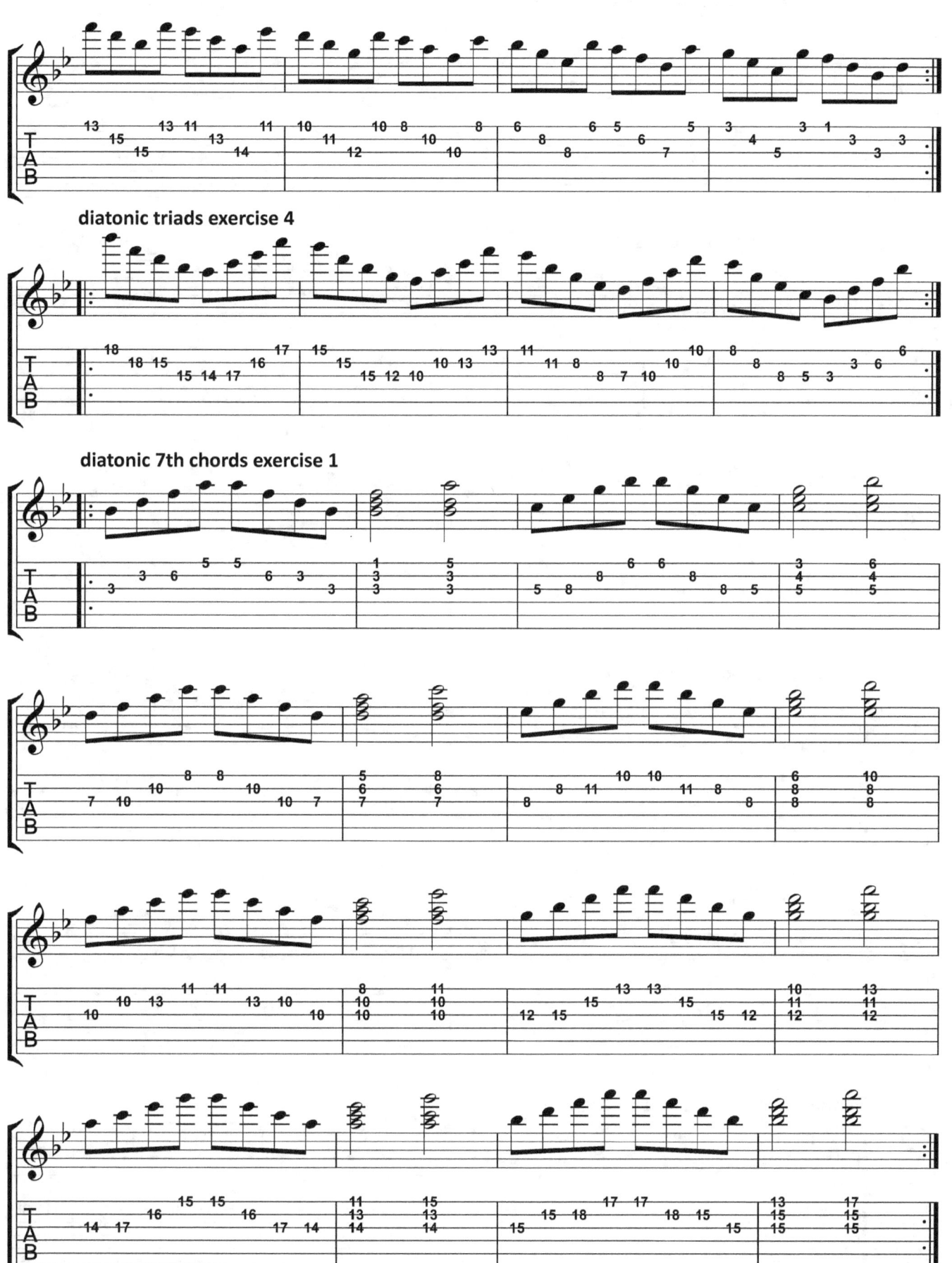

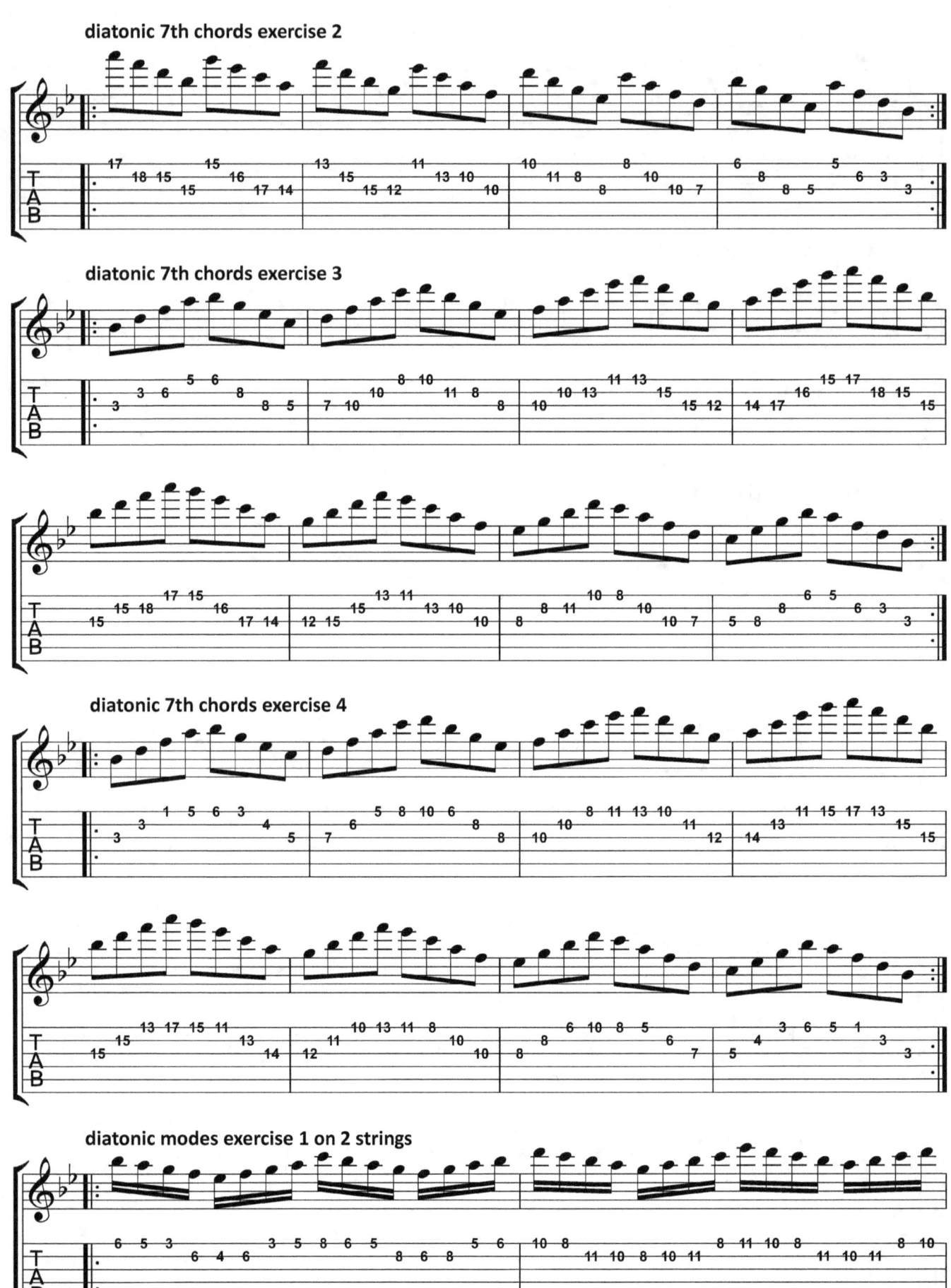

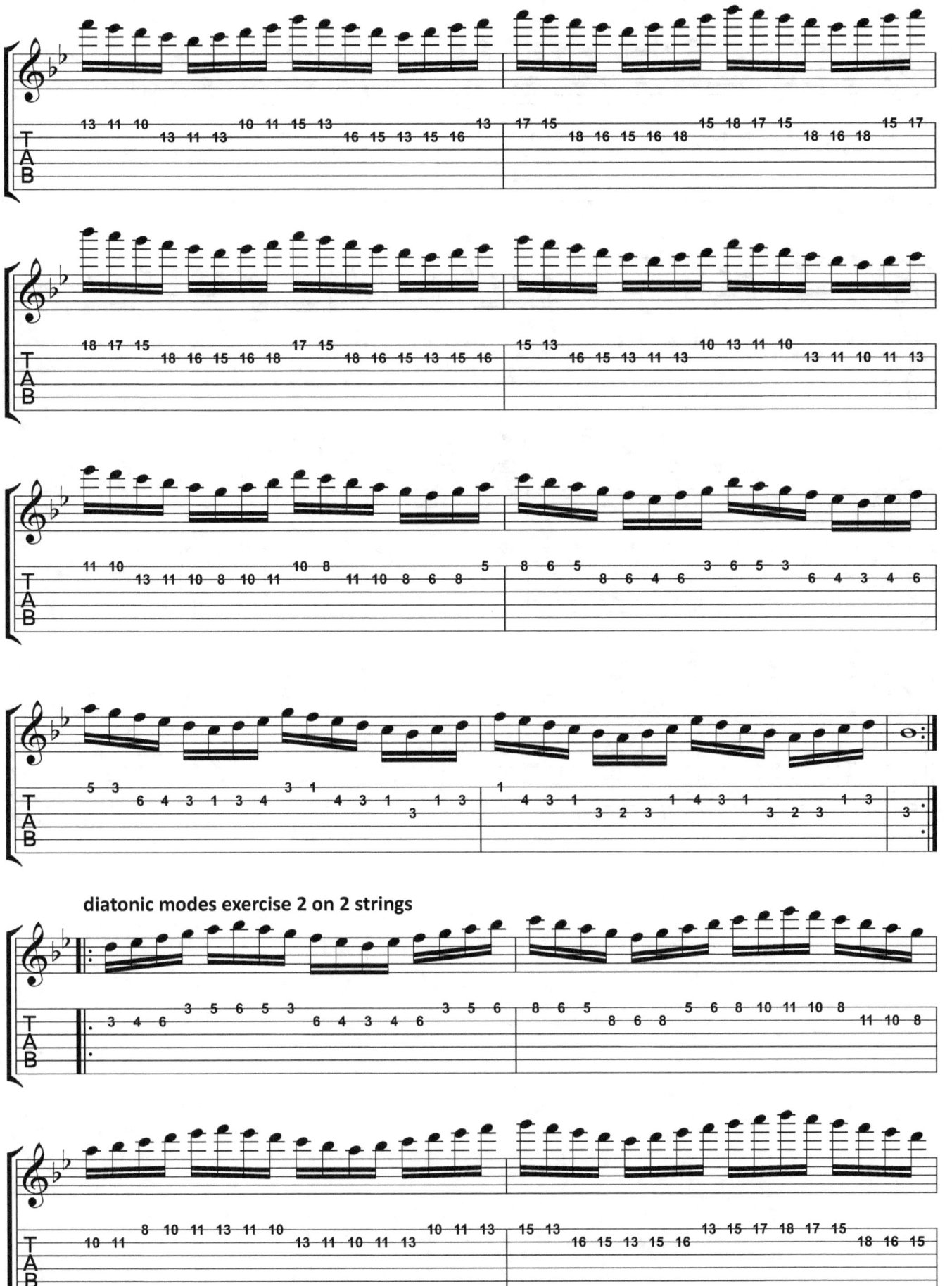

Chapter 5 horizontal construction of the modes

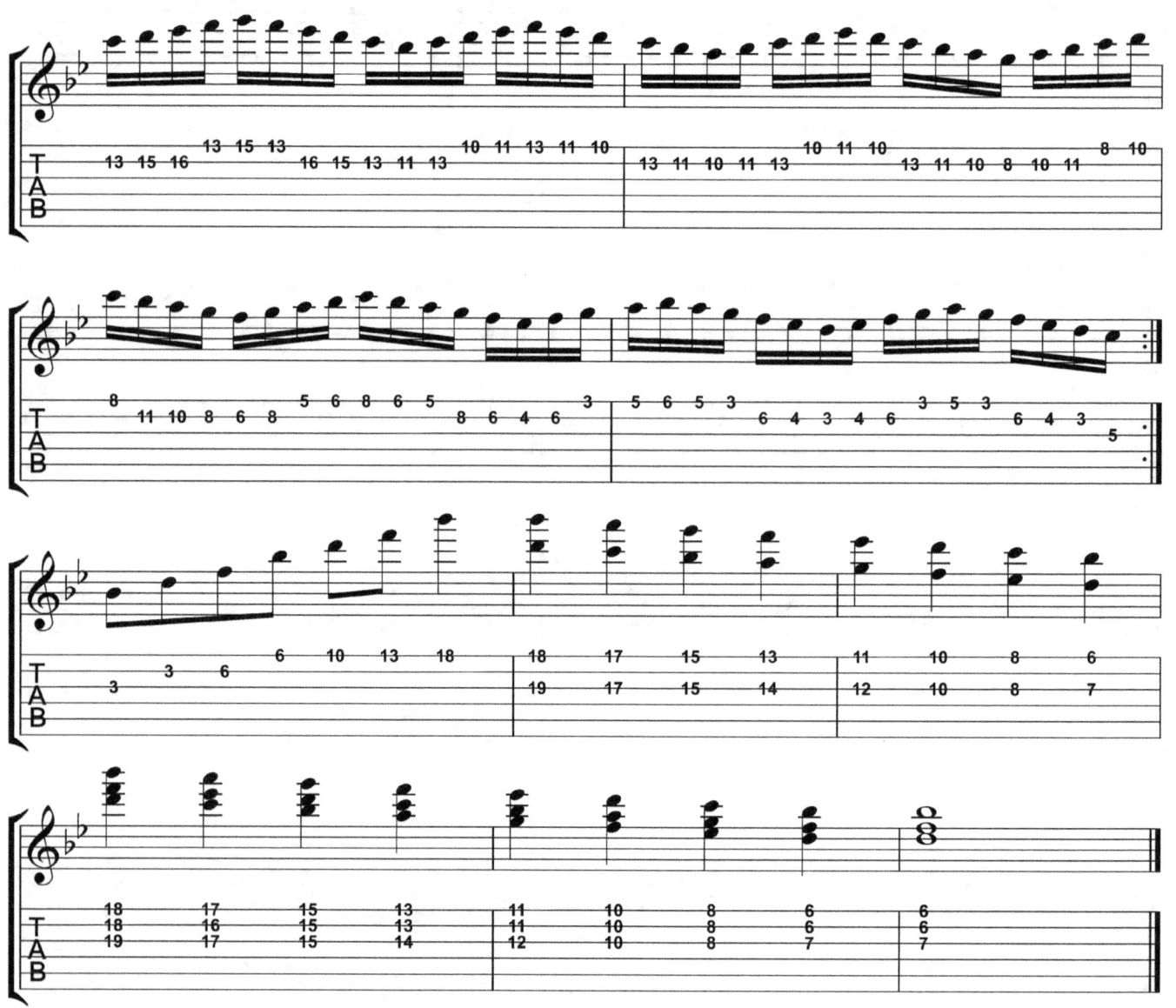

Chapter 6
the modes vertically

In this chapter we will examine the vertical positioning of the modes on the fingerboard. This means that we will find in every position, within four or five frets, how many complete modes we can construct without moving horizontally on the fingerboard, but moving only vertically on all the strings.

Position 7-1
The first position is position 7-1, which is the position where we find the 7th and 1st modes of a key center on the low string of the guitar, the E string. For example, if we want to find the first position of the C key center, we find the note B and next to it the note C, which are respectively the 7th and 1st degrees of the C key center. Based on this, we find what other complete mode we can play in the same position, but using only one of the three shapes we have learned and no other fingering. From there we see that we are able to play the 7th and the 1st mode with the tonic on the E string (shape 1), the 3rd and the 4th mode with the tonic on the A string (shape 1), the 6th mode with the tonic on the D string (shape 2), and finally the 2nd mode with the tonic on the G string (shape 3).

Position 2
In position 2 we find the 2nd mode with the tonic note on the E string (shape 1), the 5th mode with the tonic on the A string (shape 1), the 7th and 1st mode with the tonic on the D string (shape 2), and finally the 3rd and 4th mode with the tonic on the G string (shape 3).

Position 3-4
In position 3-4 we find the 3rd and 4th modes with the tonic on the E string (shape 1), the 6th mode with the tonic on the A string (shape 1), the 2nd mode with the tonic on the D string (shape 2), and finally the 5th mode with the tonic on the G string (shape 3).

Position 5
In position 5 we find the 5th mode with the tonic on the E string (shape 1), the 2nd mode with the tonic on the A string (shape 1), the 5th mode with the tonic on the D string (shape 2), and finally the 7th and 1st modes with the tonic on the G string (shape 3).

Position 6

In position 6 we find the 6th mode with the tonic on the E string (shape 1), the 2nd mode with the tonic on the A string (shape 1), the 5th mode with the tonic on the D string (shape 2), and finally the 7th and the 1st mode with the tonic on the G string (shape 3).

Secret scales

In the progression of the exercises and once we recognize for each position the modes that we used for its structure, we will see that we are able to play all of the remaining modes but with a different shape and fingering from the one we have learned so far. Those are the "secret scales and chords" as I like to call them because even though we have studied them in the exercises that we have already covered for each position, we had not recognized them until now, which will lead us to the complete construction of each position with all the modes and their diatonic chords.

Based on the appearance of all the modes and their chords in every position we will see which new fingerings we need to use for each mode.

In position 7-1 we find as secret scales the 2nd mode which starts with the fourth finger, the 5th mode which starts with the fourth finger, the 7th mode with the third finger, and the 1st mode with the fourth finger.

In position 2 we find as secret scales the 3rd mode which starts with the third finger, the 4th mode which starts with the fourth finger, the 6th mode with the fourth finger, and the 2nd mode with the fourth finger.

In position 3-4 we find as secret scales the 5th mode which starts with the fourth finger, the 7th mode which starts with the third finger, the 1st mode with the fourth finger, the 3rd mode with the third finger, and the 4th mode with the fourth finger.

In position 5 we find as secret scales the 6th mode which starts with the fourth finger, the 2nd mode which starts with the fourth finger, and the 5th mode with the fourth finger.

In position 6 we find as secret scales the 7th mode which starts with the third finger, the 1st mode which starts with the fourth finger, the 3rd mode with the third finger, the 4th mode with the fourth finger, and the 6th mode with the fourth finger.

Progression of the exercises
- The main modes that form each position, ascending and descending.
- The 7th chord arpeggios of the main modes, ascending and descending.
- All the notes of the position as one scale.
- The notes of the position with broken thirds.
- The notes of the position with triad arpeggios.
- All the modes found in each position, hidden modes.
- All the diatonic 7th chords, hidden chords.
- Practice of the entire position with sets of four sixteenth notes.
- The triads and 7th chords with arpeggios of the main mode(s) where each position starts.

Position 7-1 studies in C major

VII-I shape 1
III-IV shape 1
VI shape 2
II shape 3

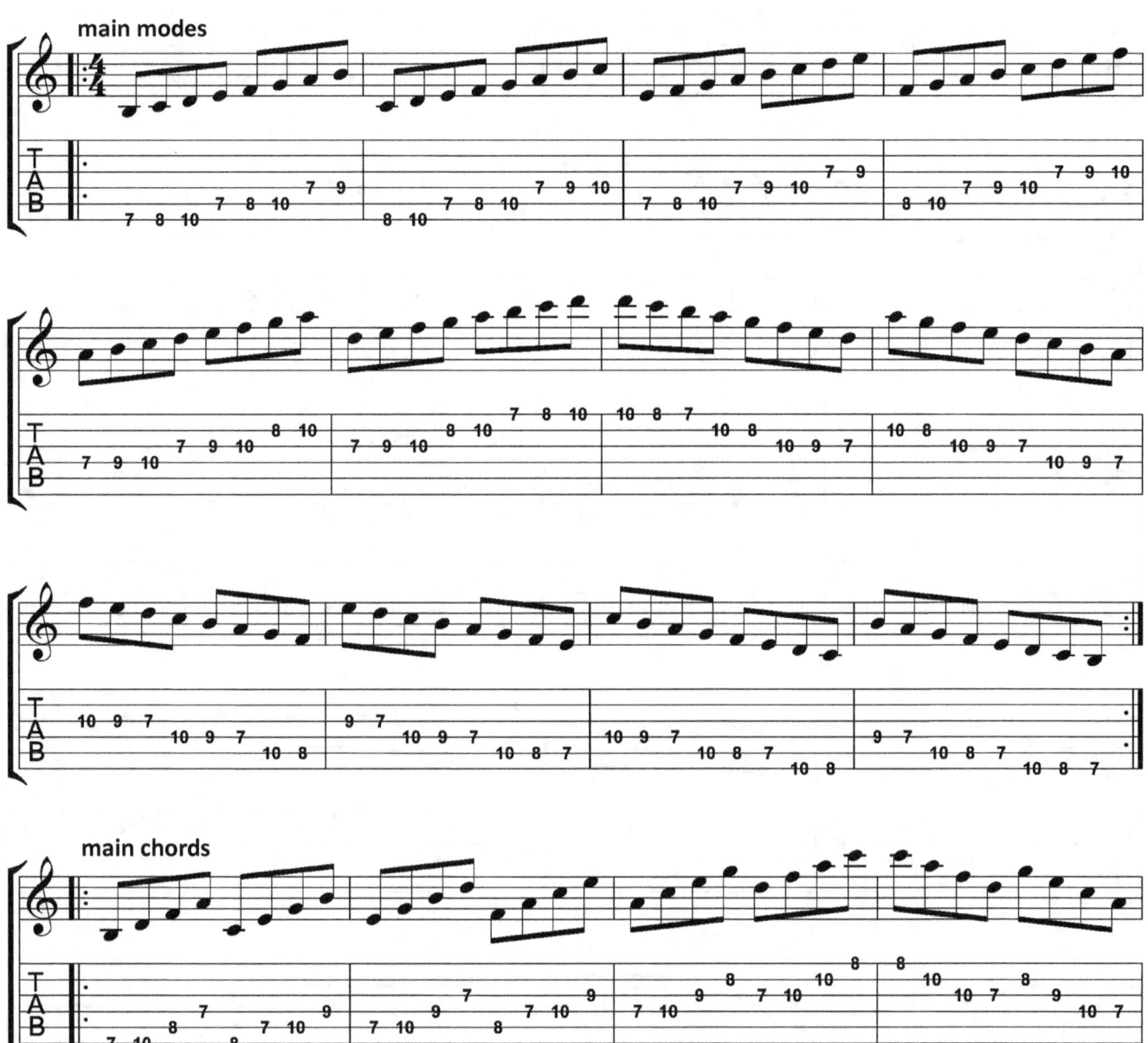

Chapter 6   the modes vertically

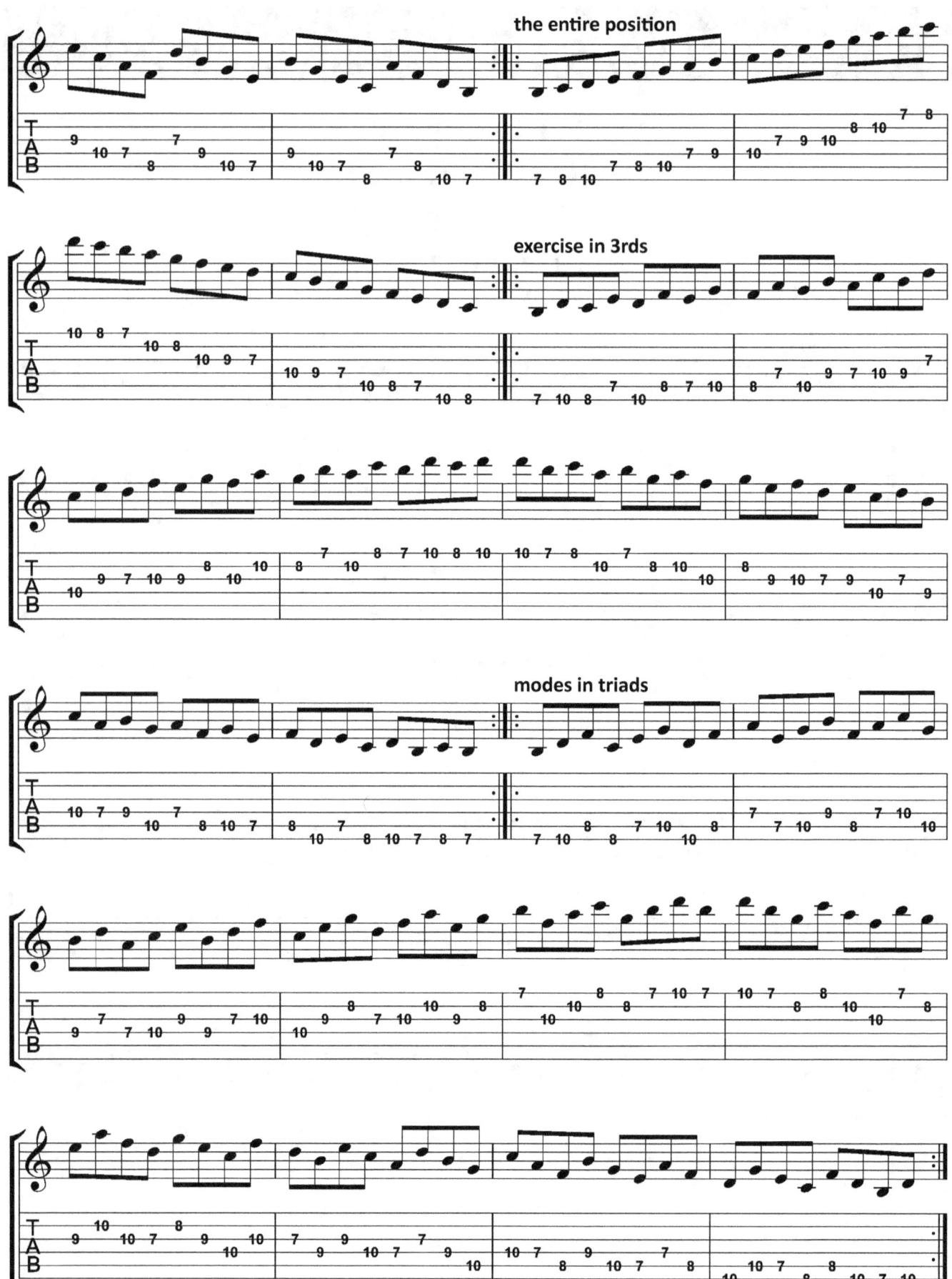

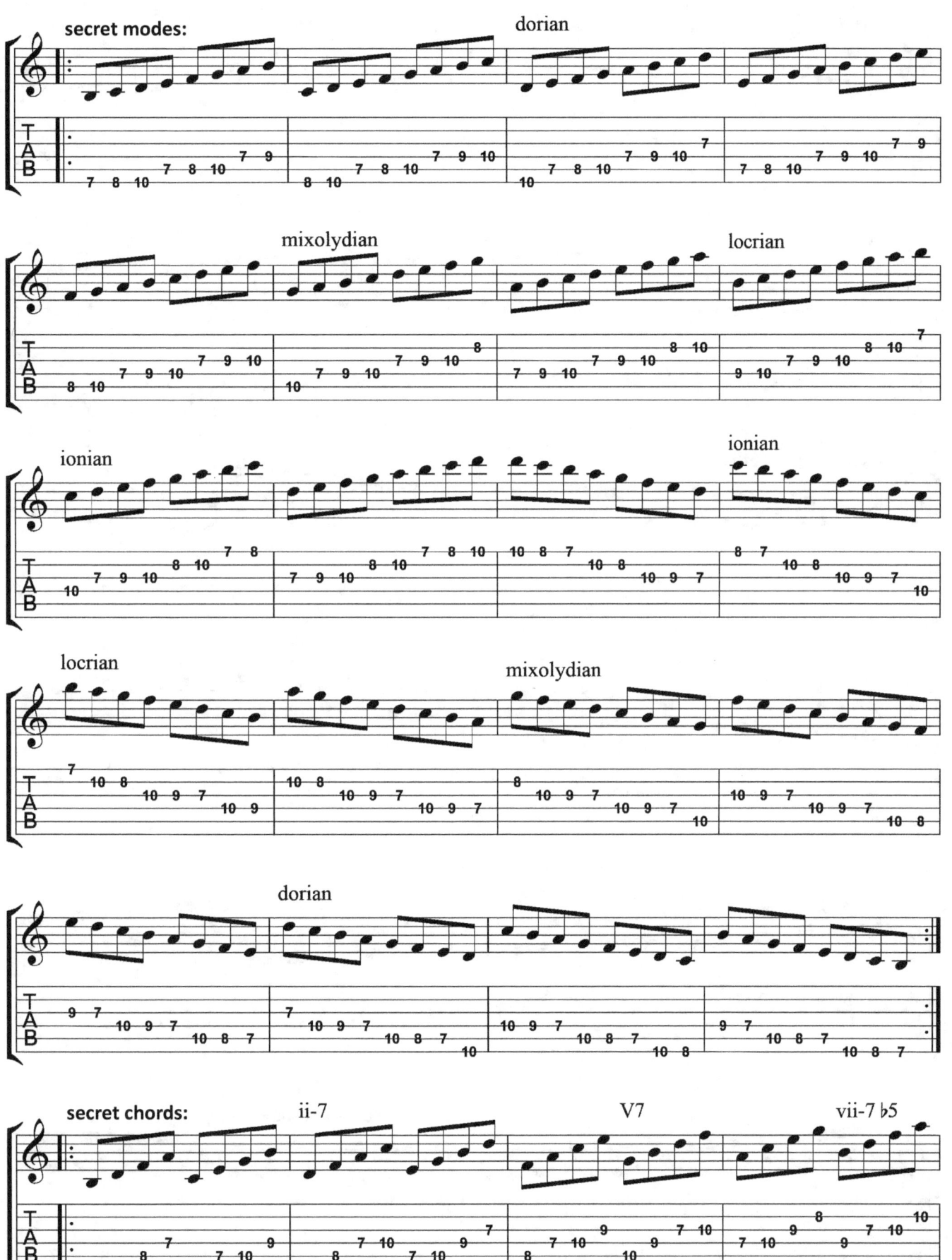

Chapter 6 the modes vertically

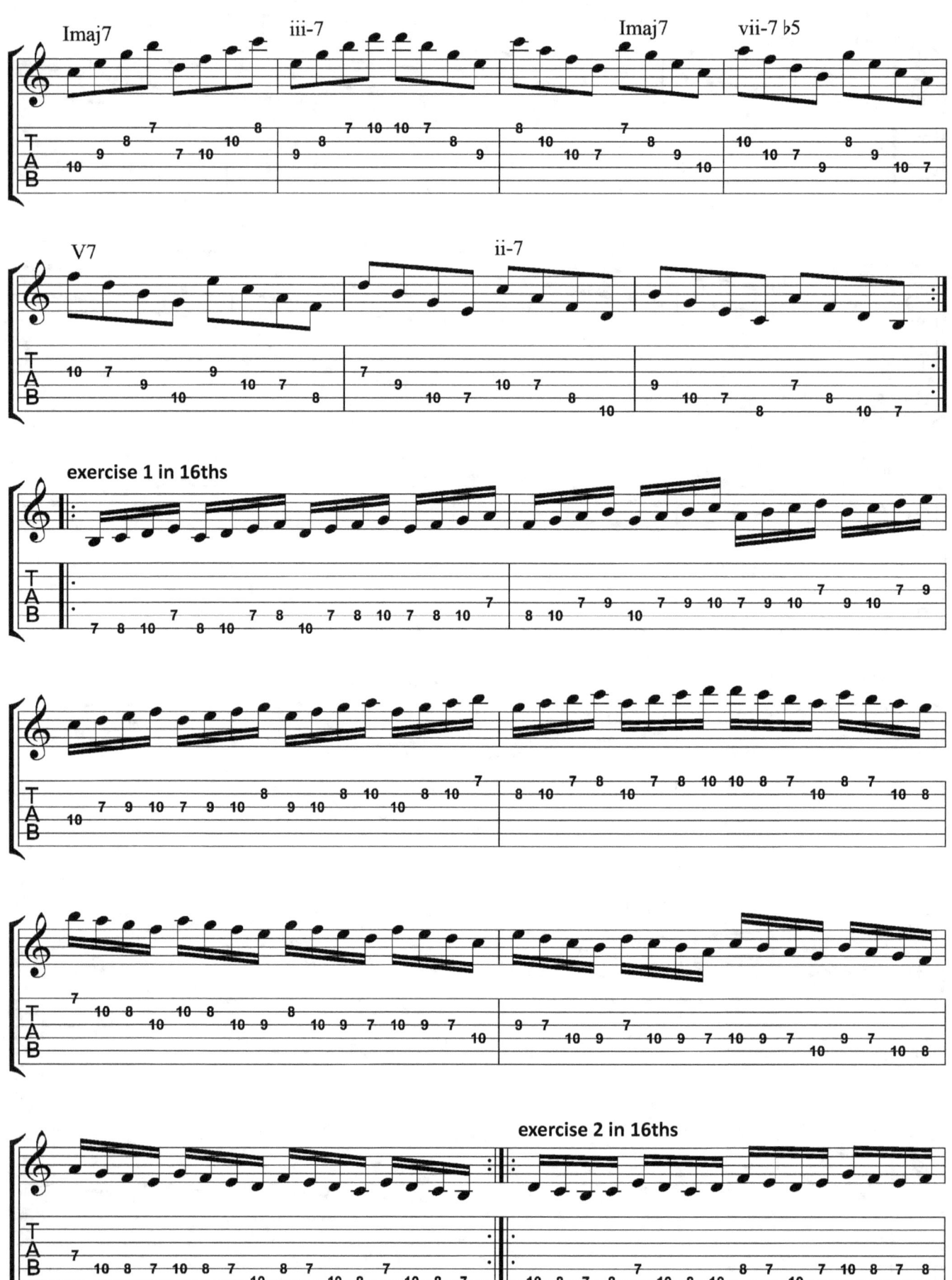

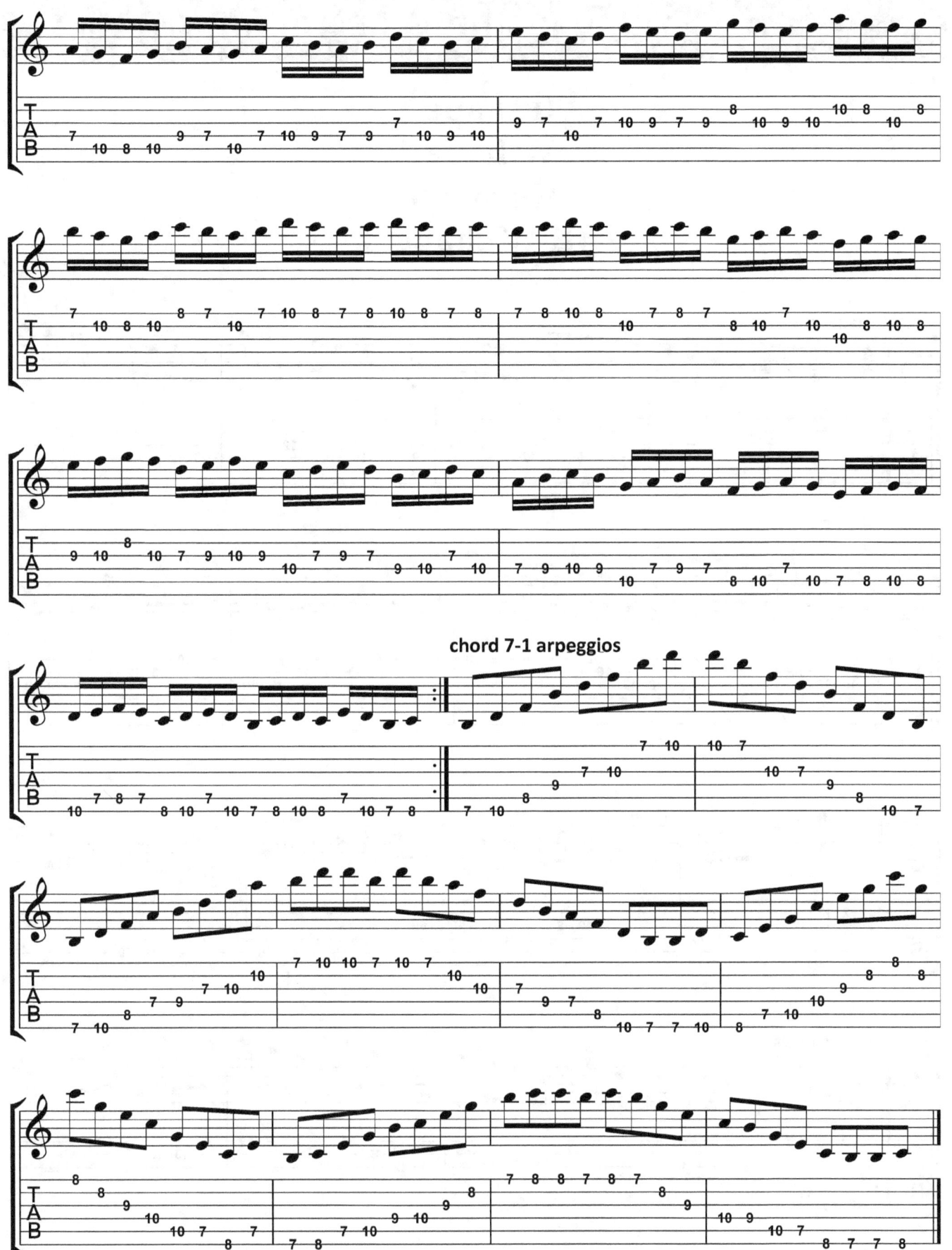

Chapter 6 the modes vertically

Position 2 studies in C major

II shape 1
V shape 1
VII-I shape 2
III-IV shape 3

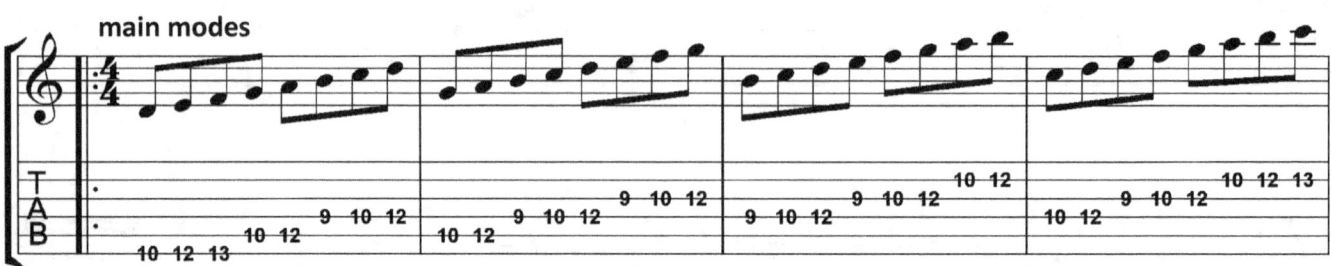

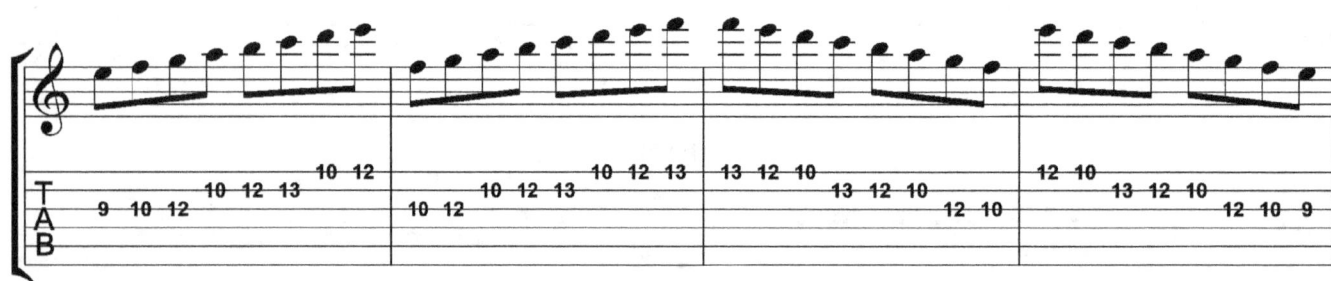

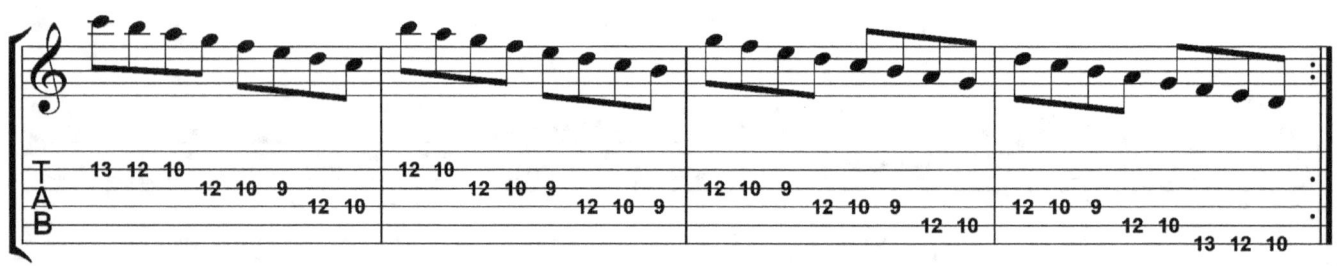

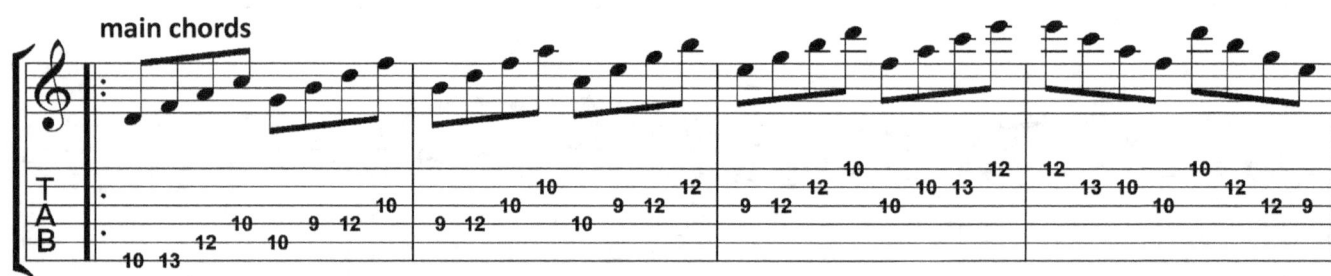

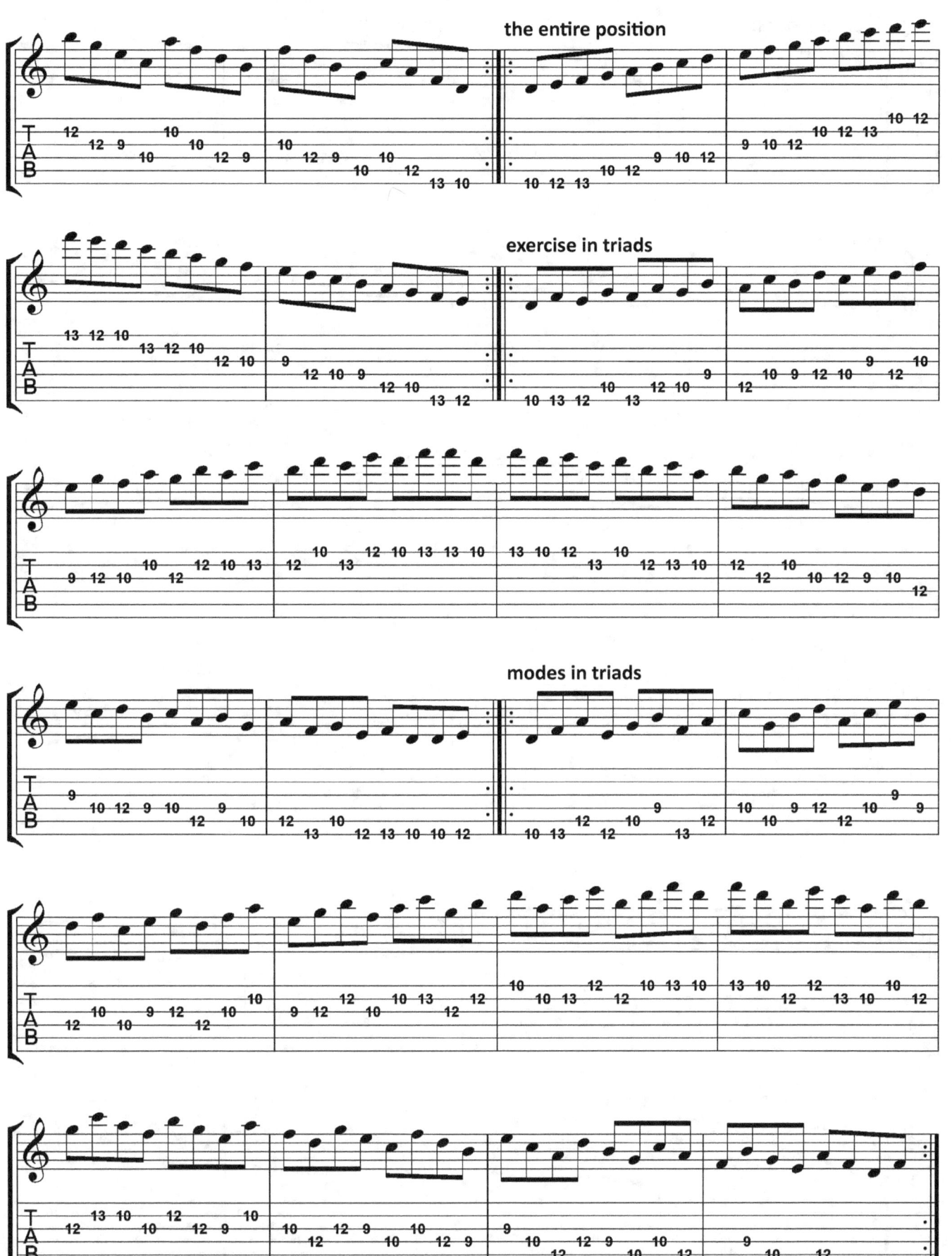

Chapter 6 the modes vertically

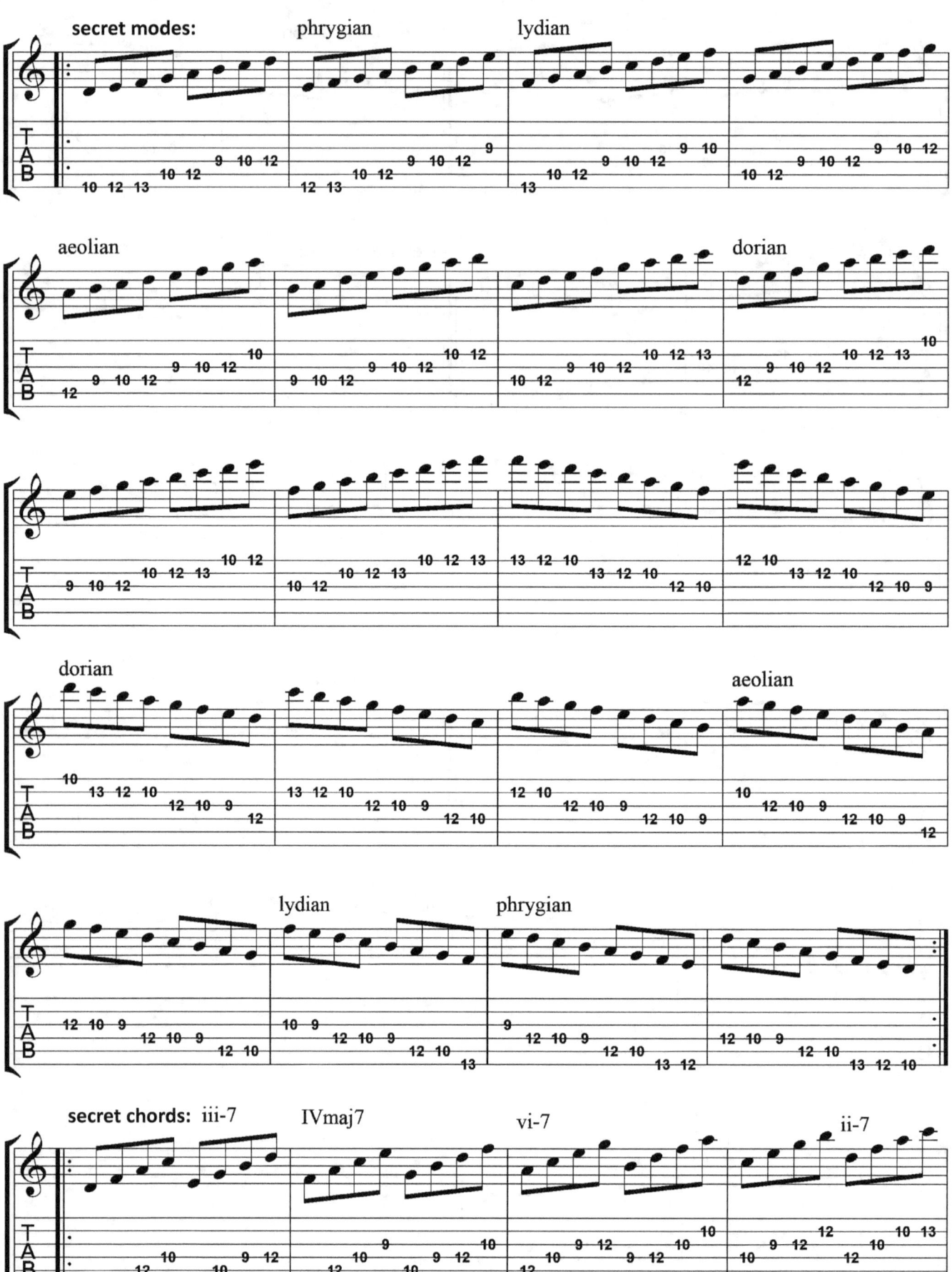

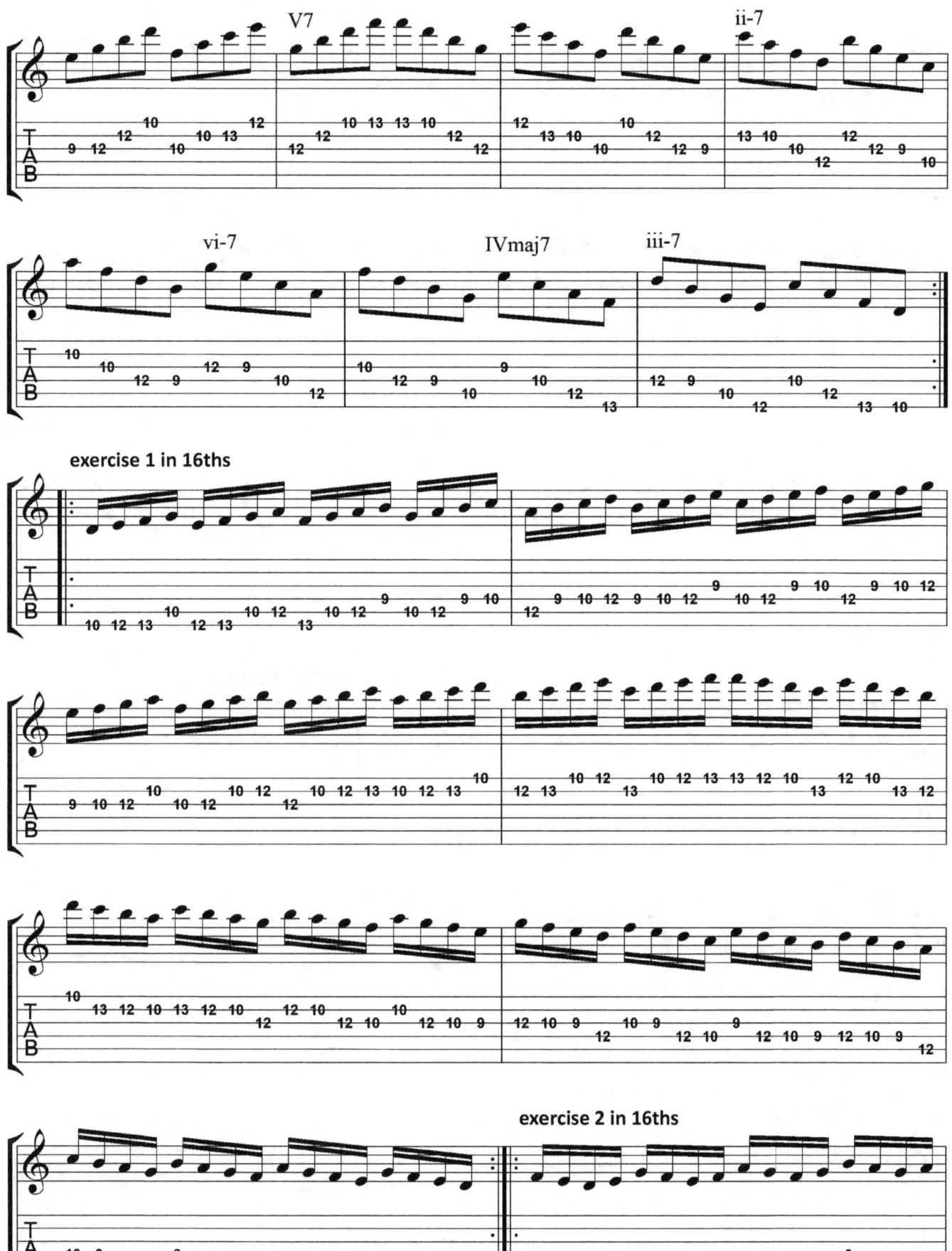

Chapter 6 the modes vertically

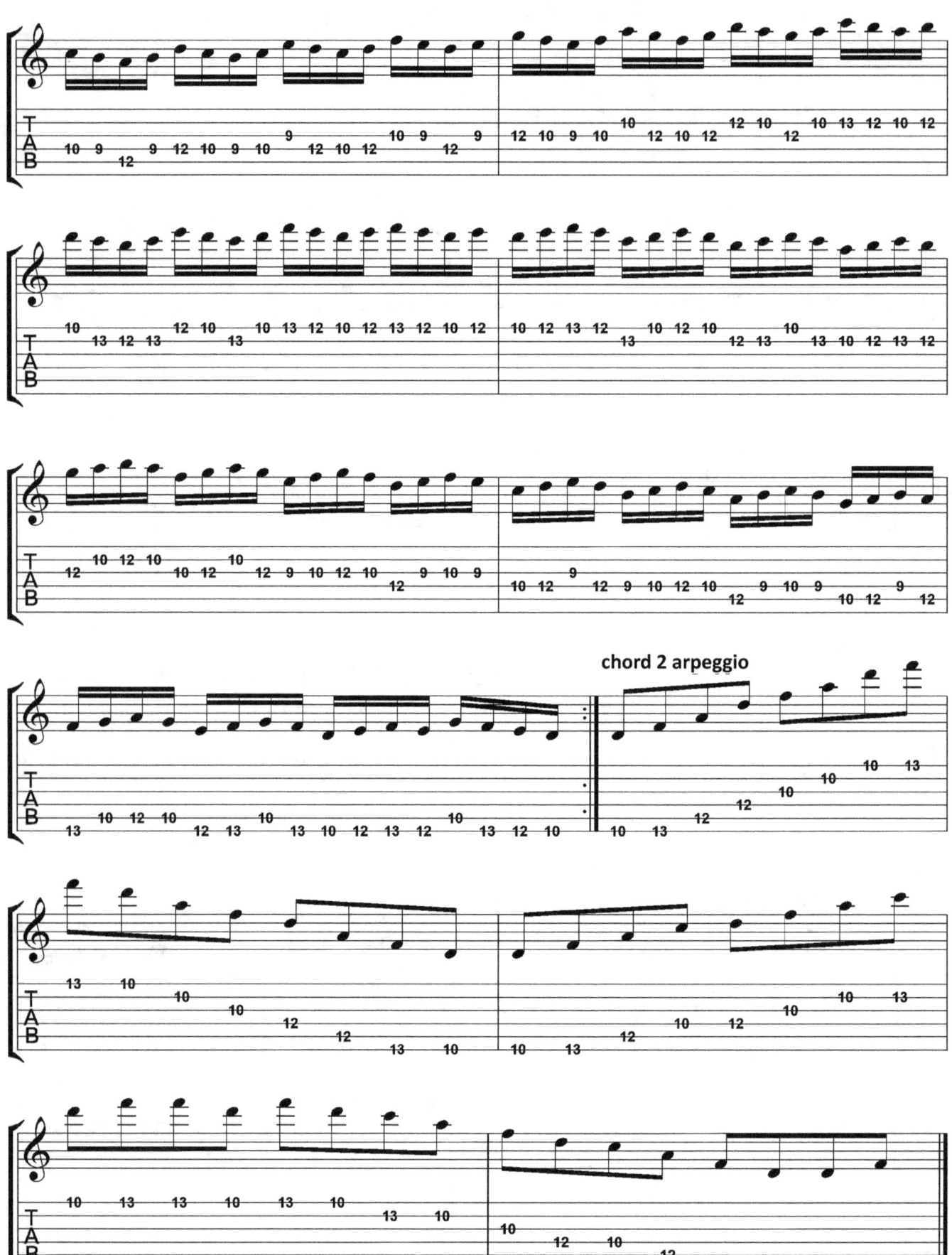

Position 3-4 studies in C major

III-IV shape 1
VI shape 1
II shape 2
V shape 3

main modes

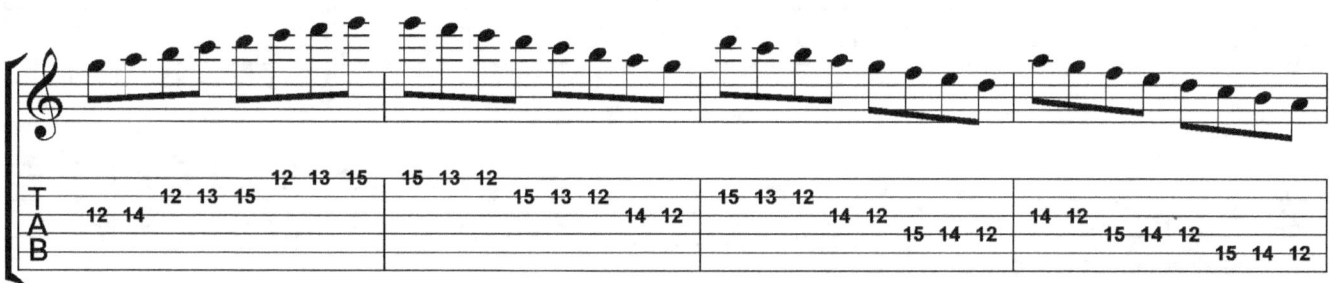

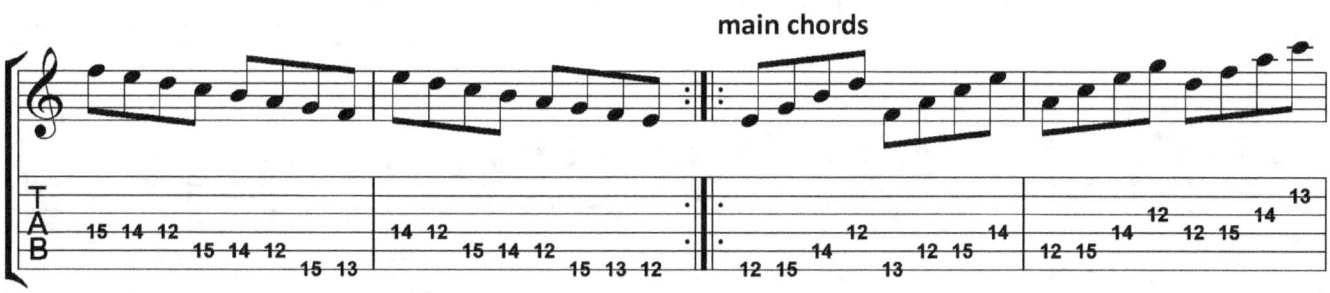

main chords

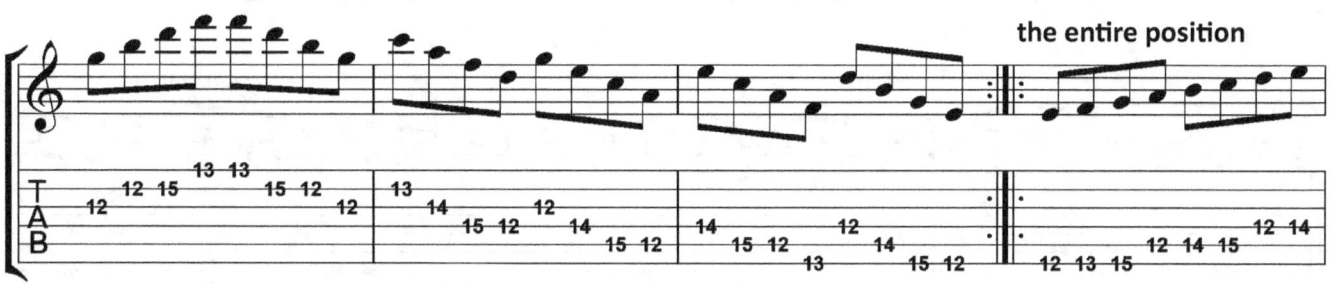

the entire position

Chapter 6   the modes vertically

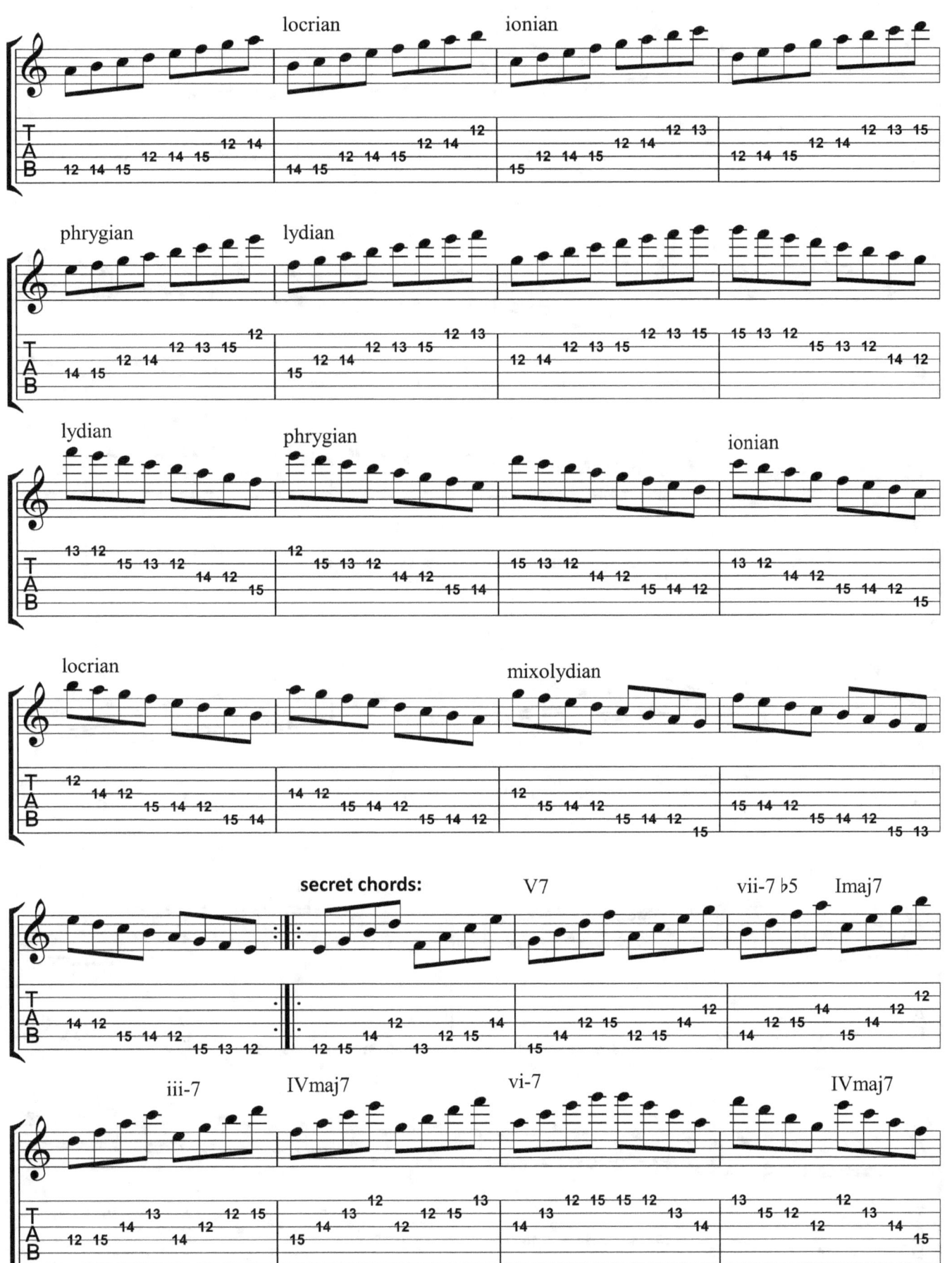

Chapter 6 the modes vertically

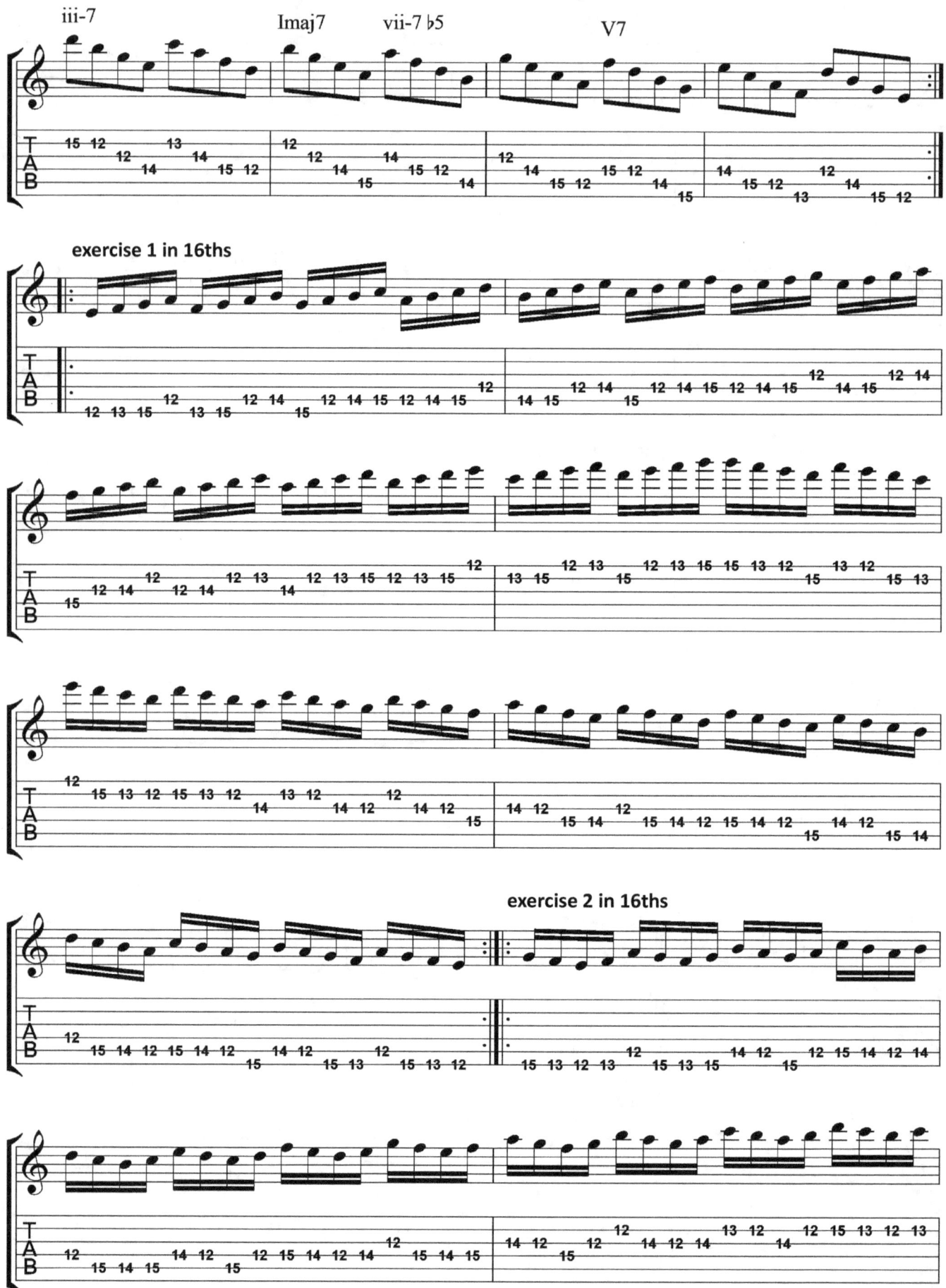

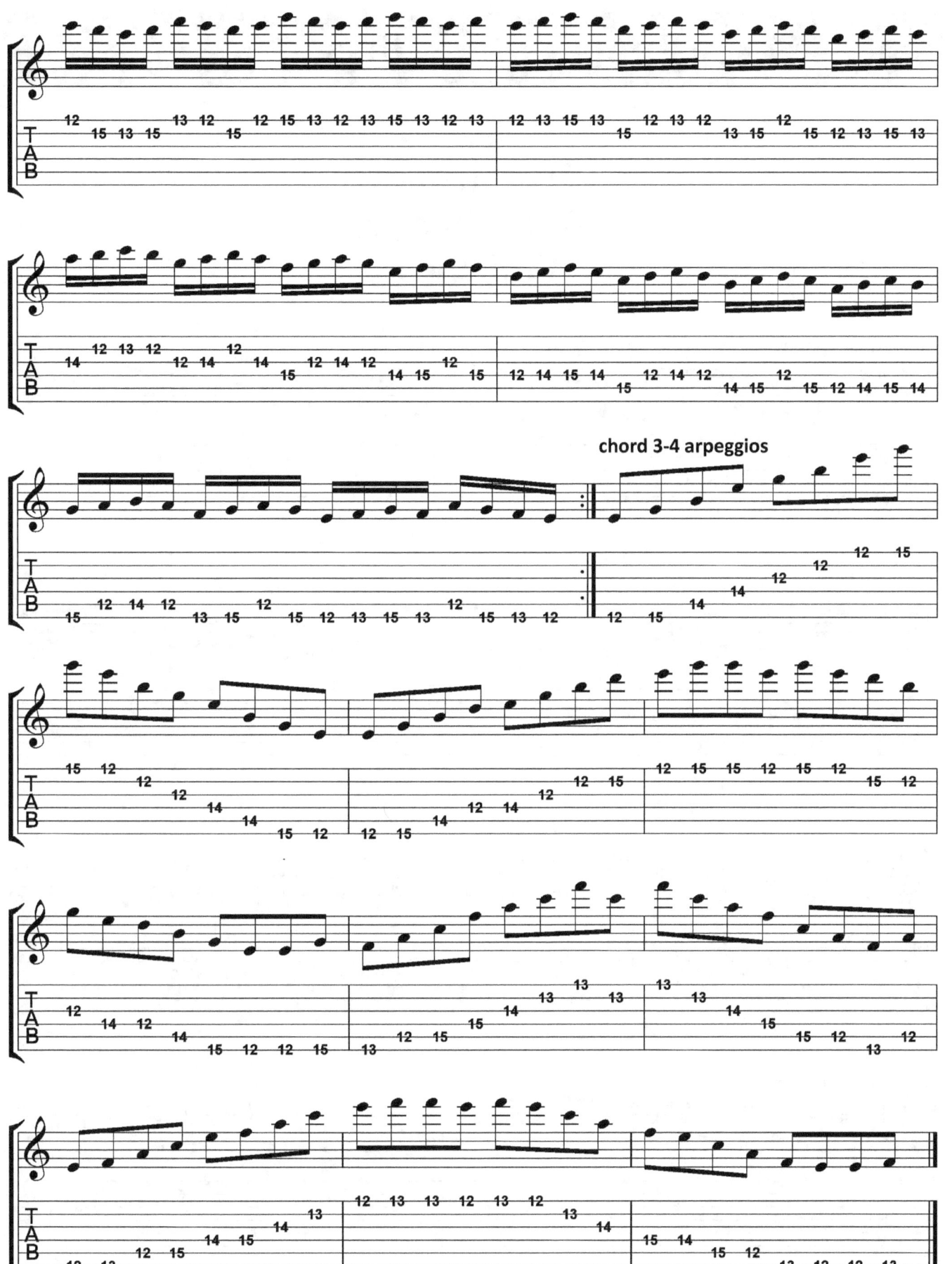

Chapter 6 the modes vertically

Position 5 studies in C major

V shape 1
VII-I shape 1
III-IV shape 2
VI shape 3

main modes

main chords

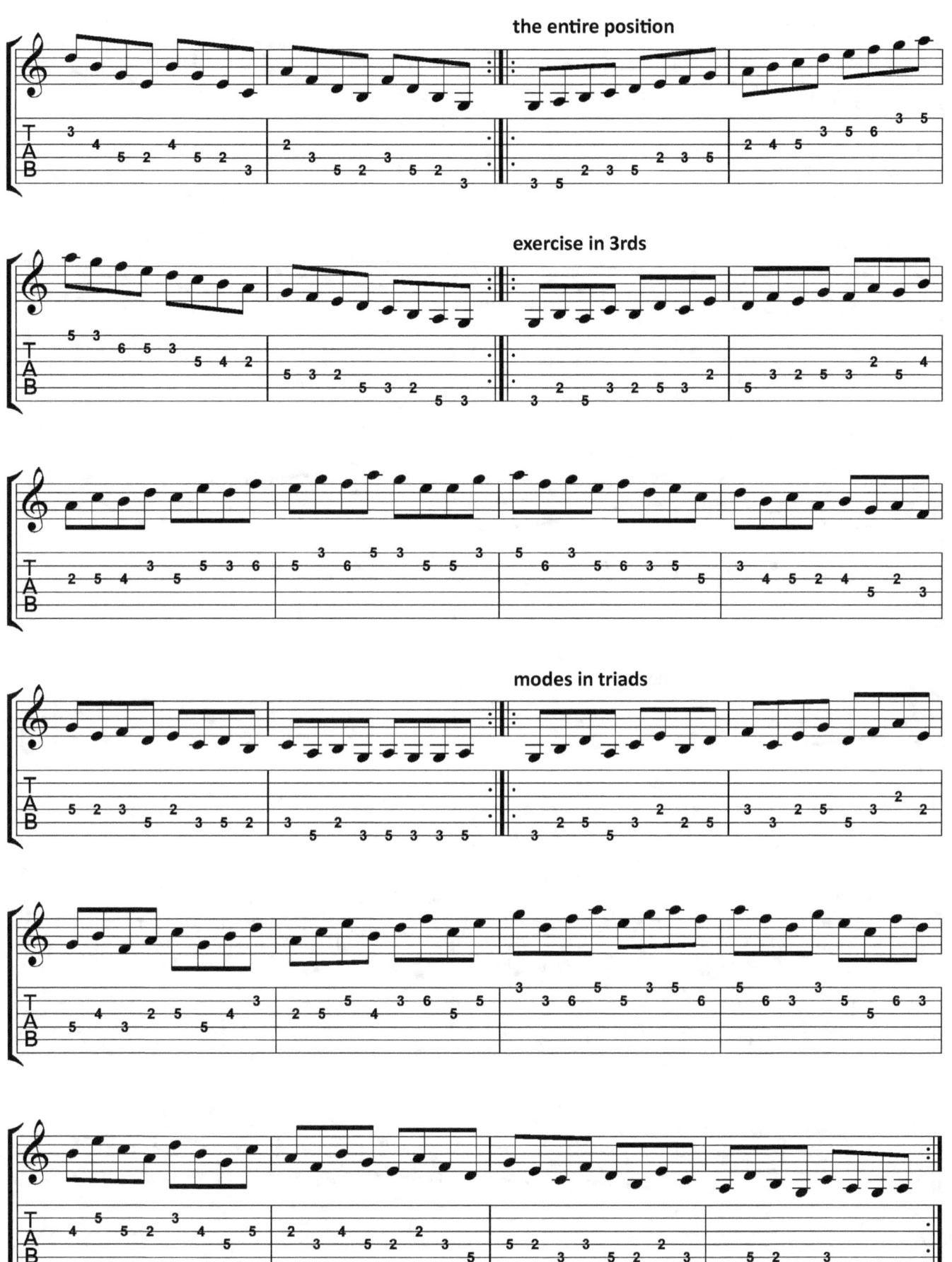

Chapter 6 the modes vertically

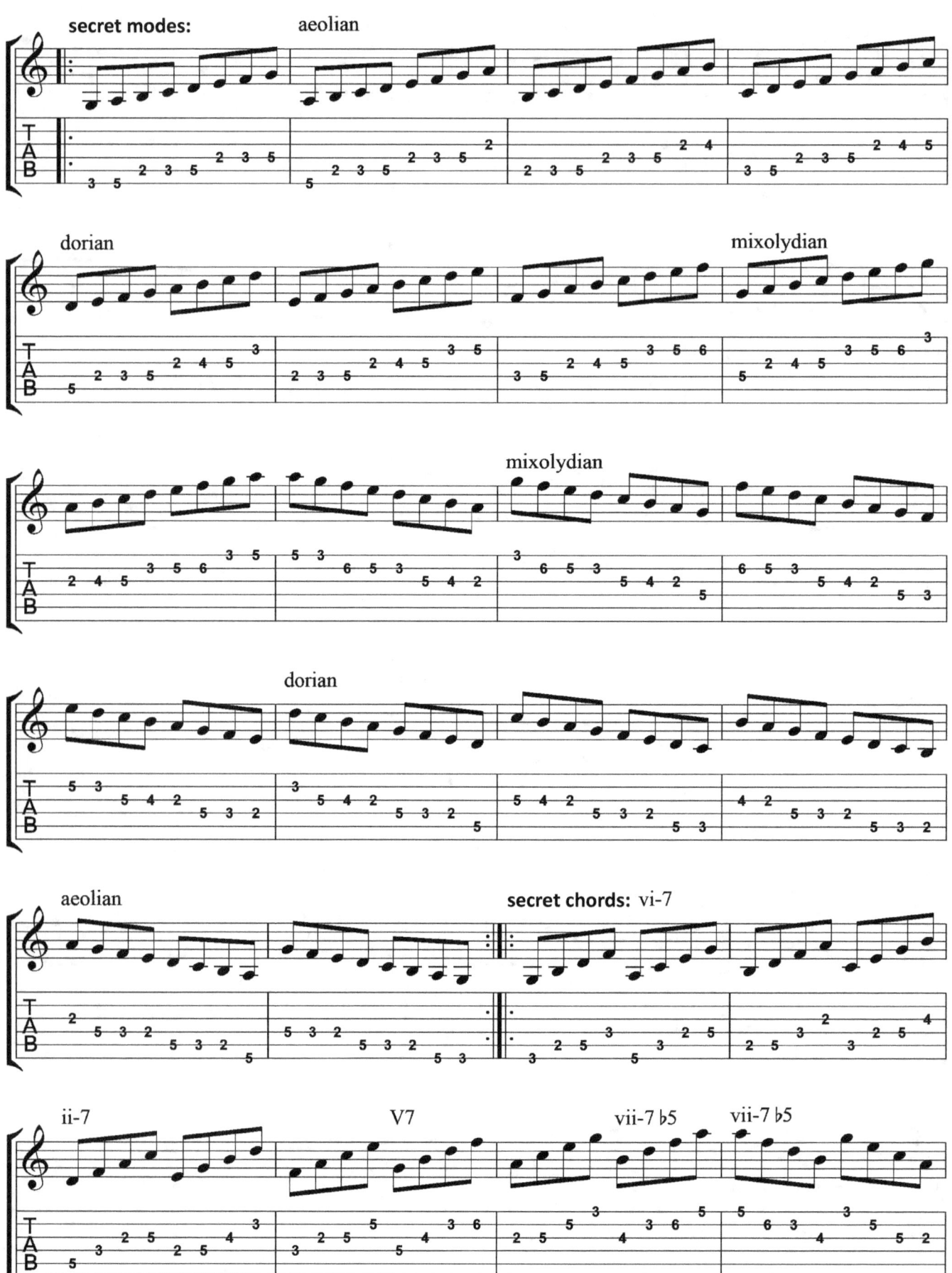

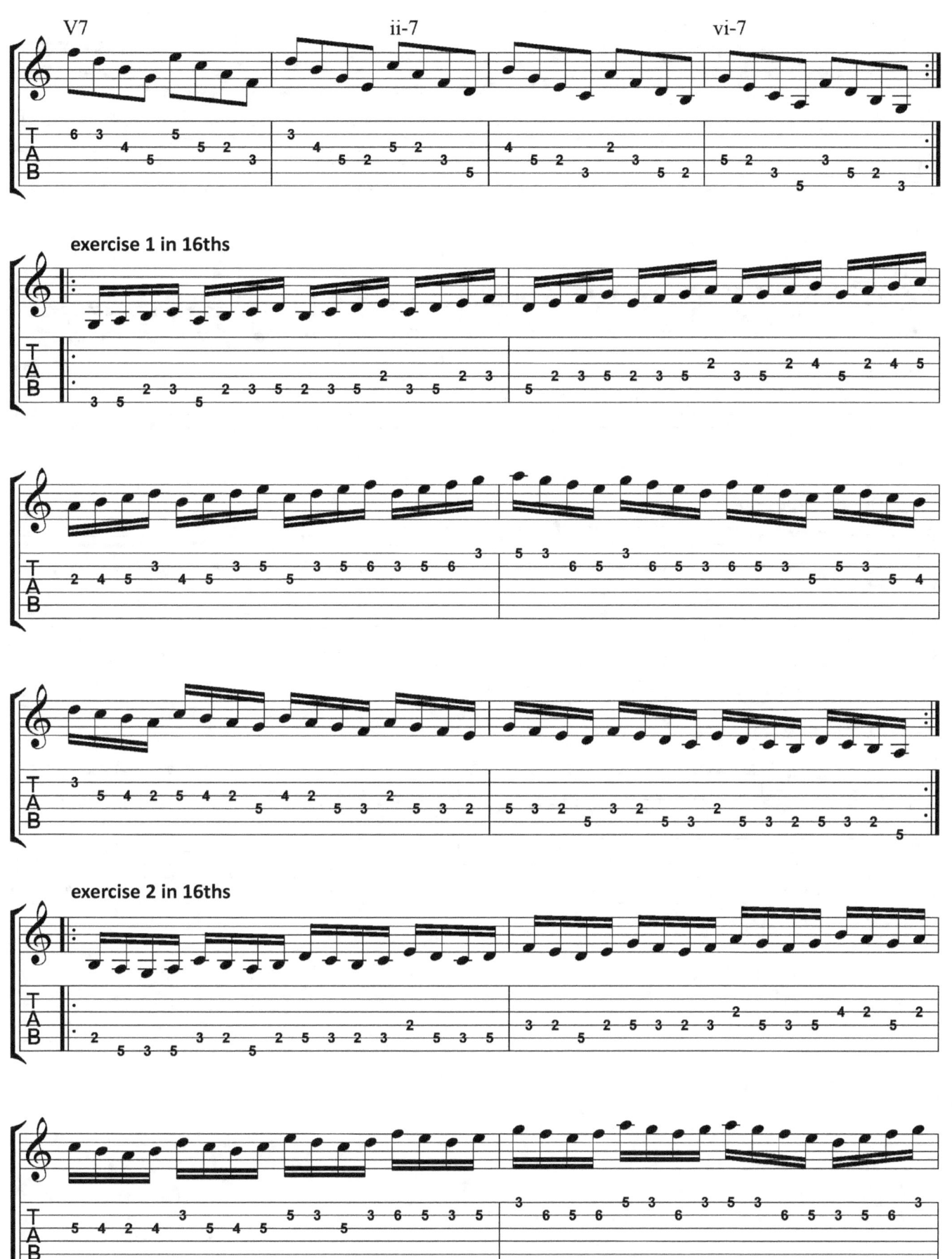

chord 5 arpeggio

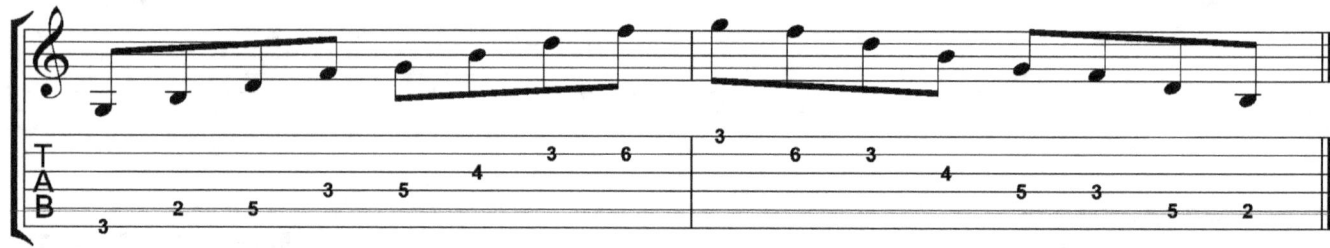

Position 6 studies in C major

**VI shape 1
II shape 1
V shape 2
VII-I shape 3**

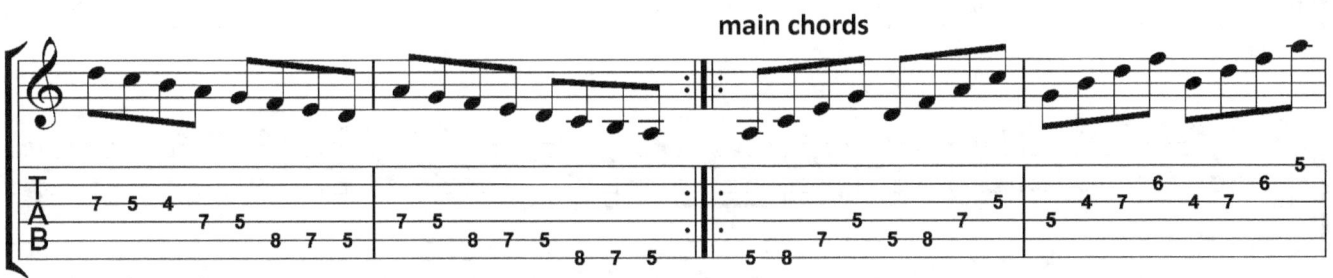

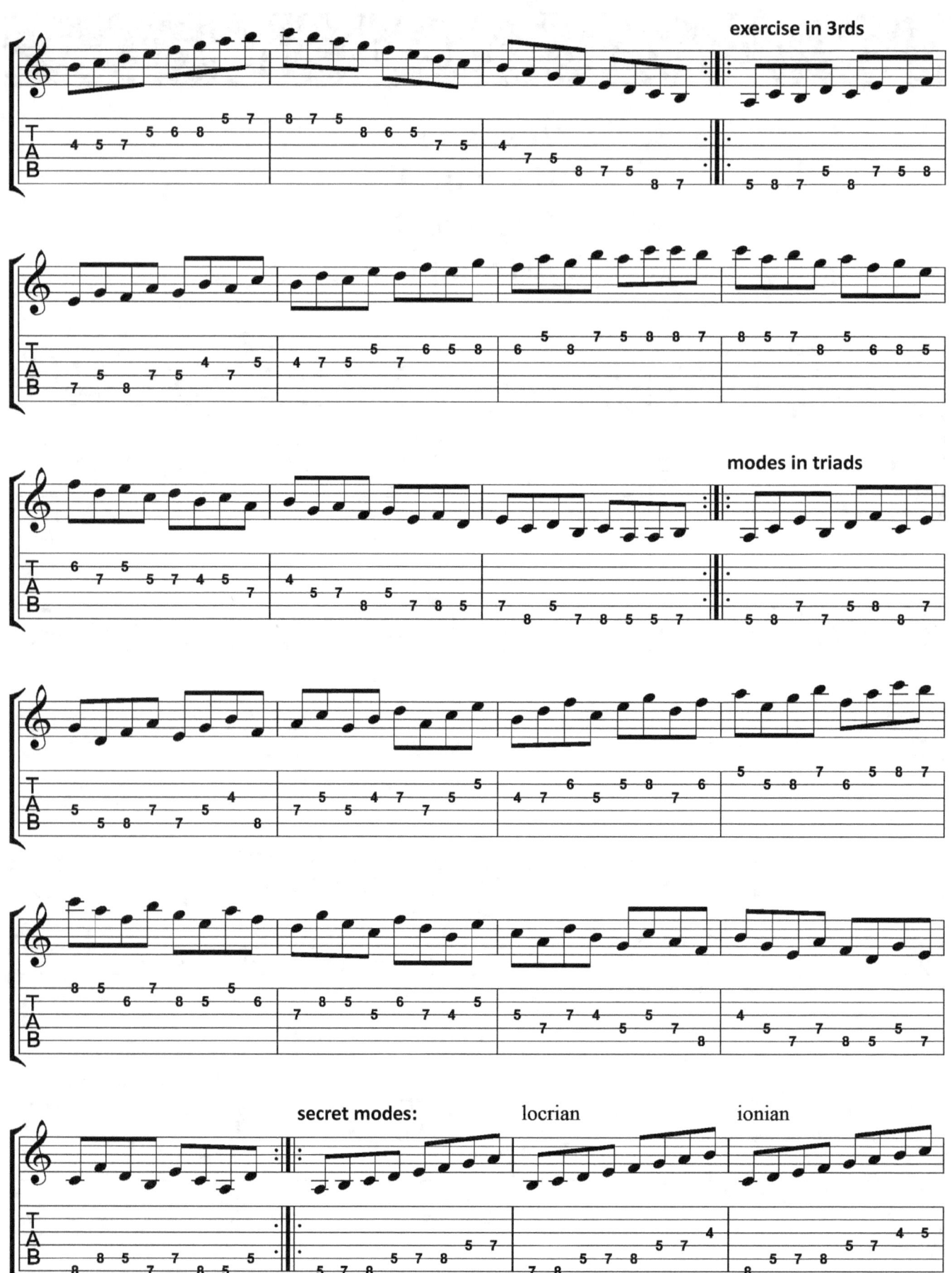

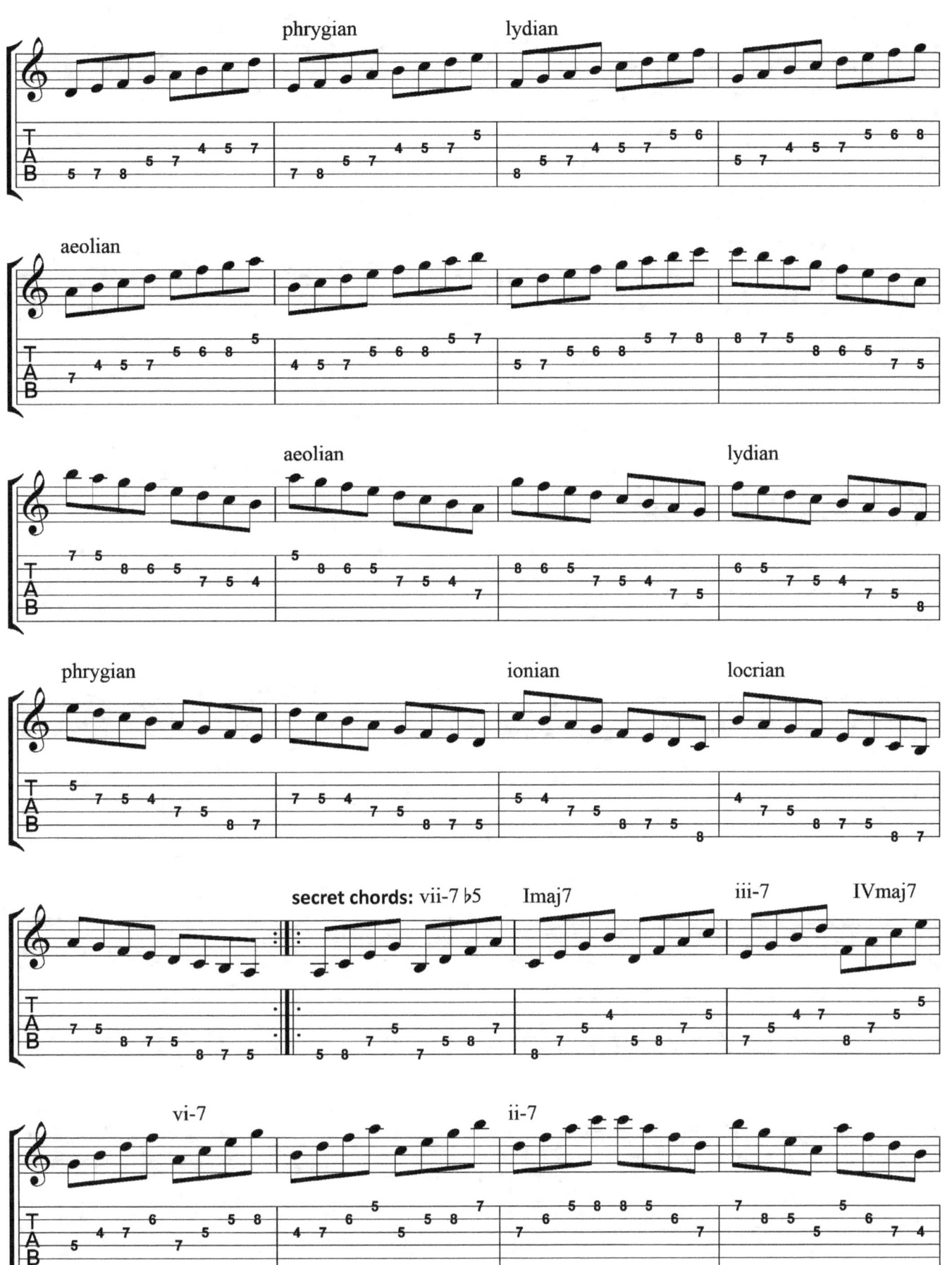

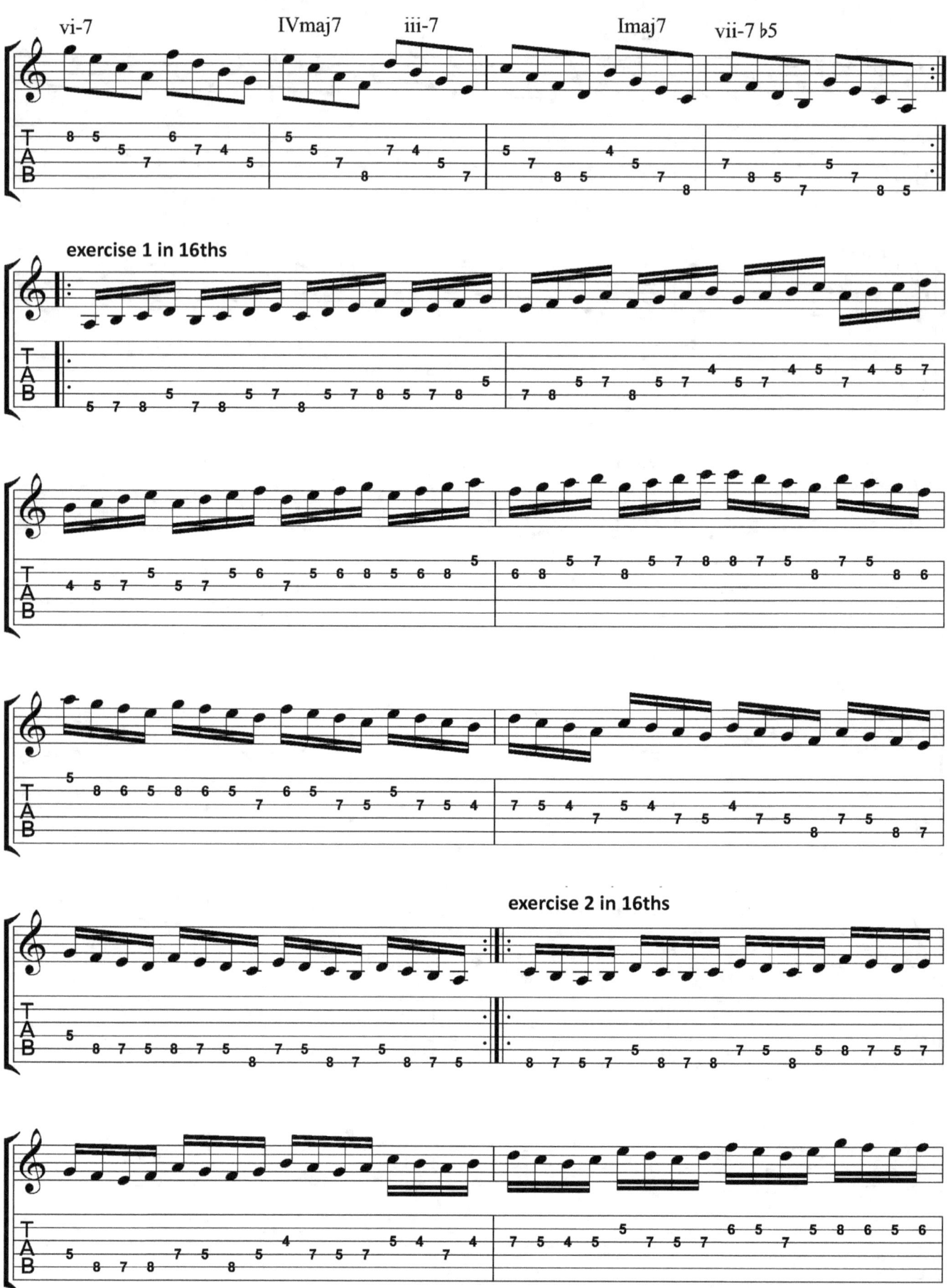

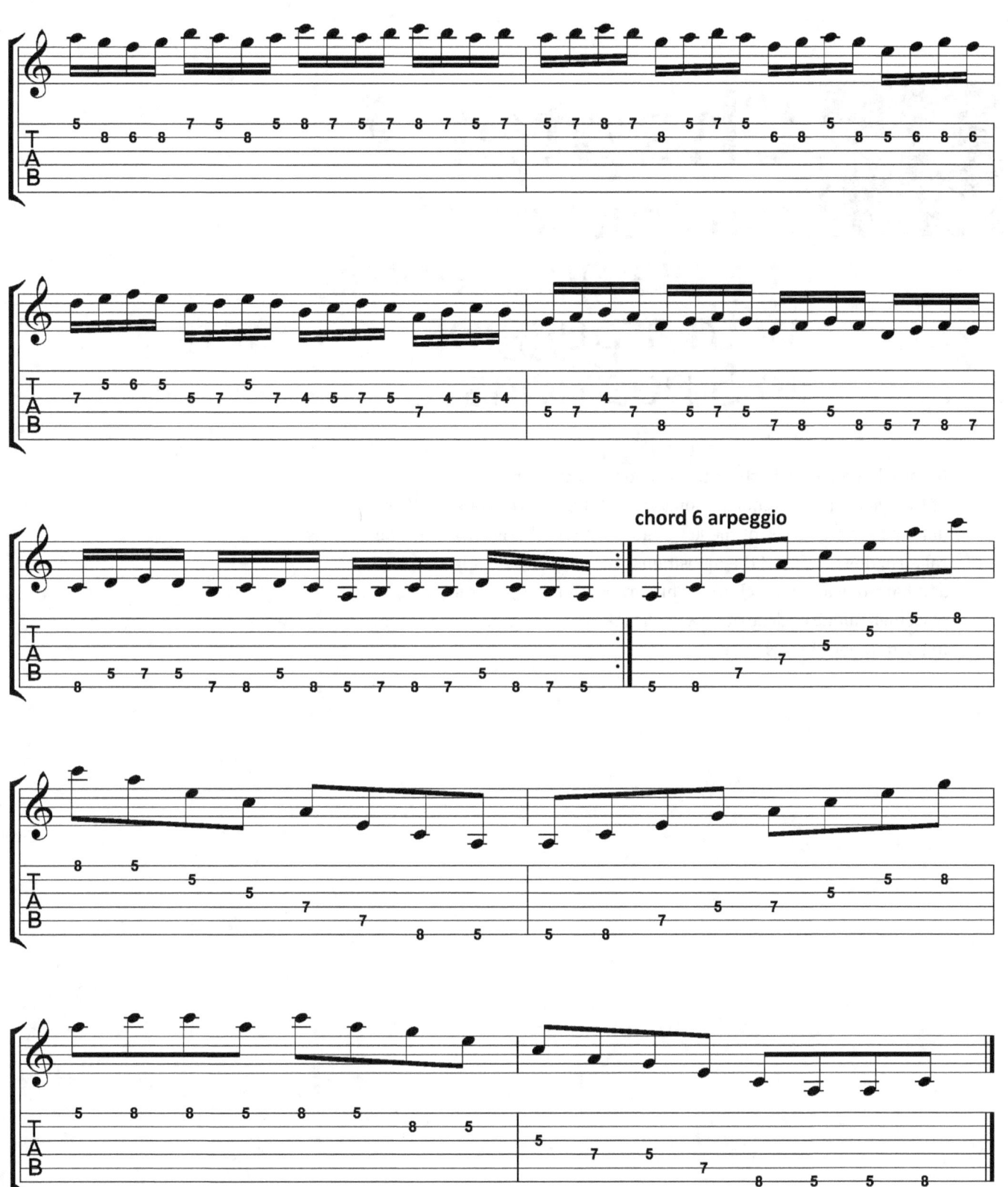

Chapter 6 the modes vertically

Chapter 7
construction of the diatonic chords with arpeggios in 5 positions

In this chapter we will study in each position the complete construction of the triads and 7th chords along with all their inversions in all seven diatonic scale degrees of the key center. We will do that with the vertical form of each one of the 5 positions both melodically, with arpeggios, and harmonically, with chords. This covers and analyzes their complete placement along each position, which makes this chapter one of the most important ones in this book.

Position 7-1 arpeggio & chord studies

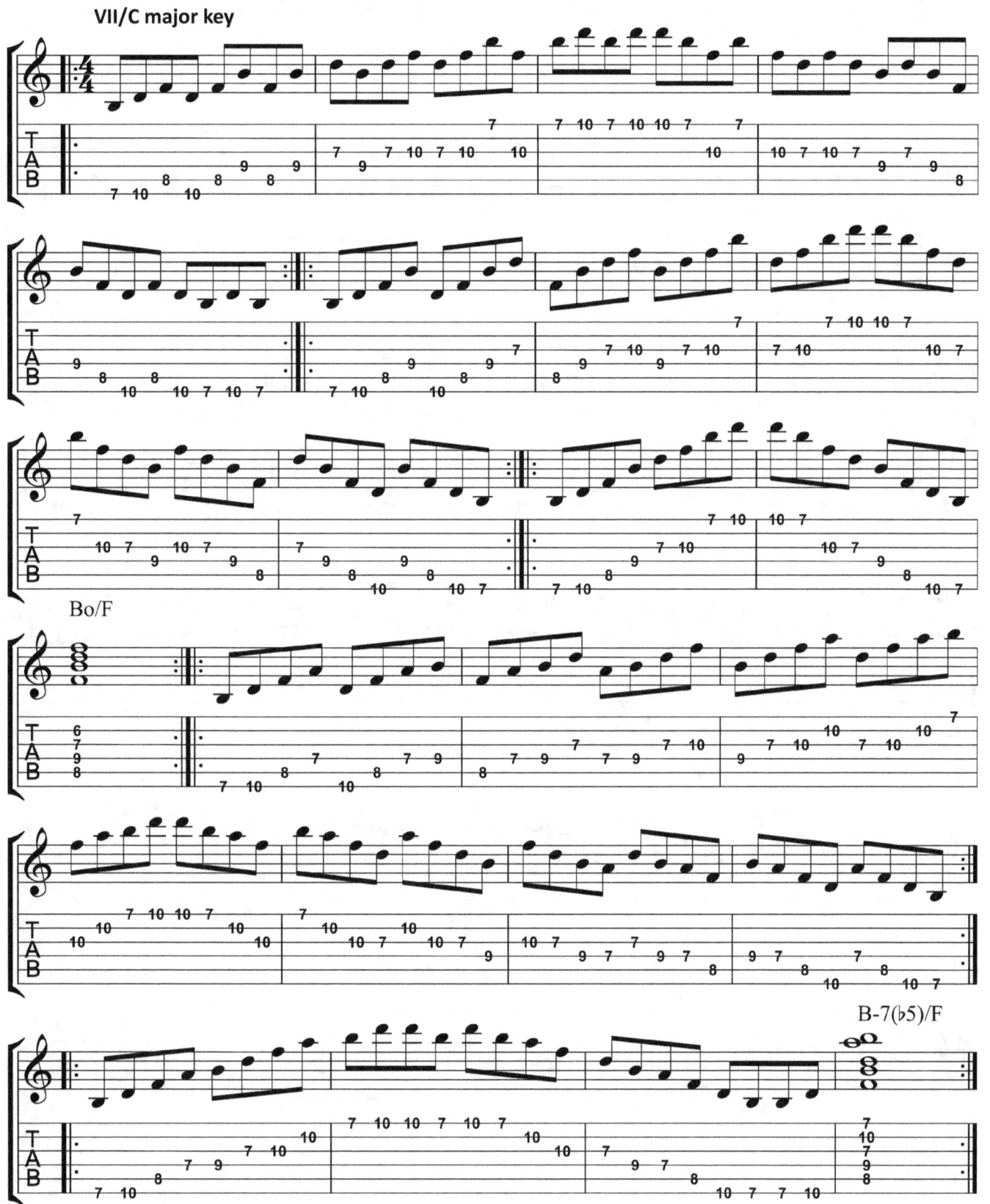

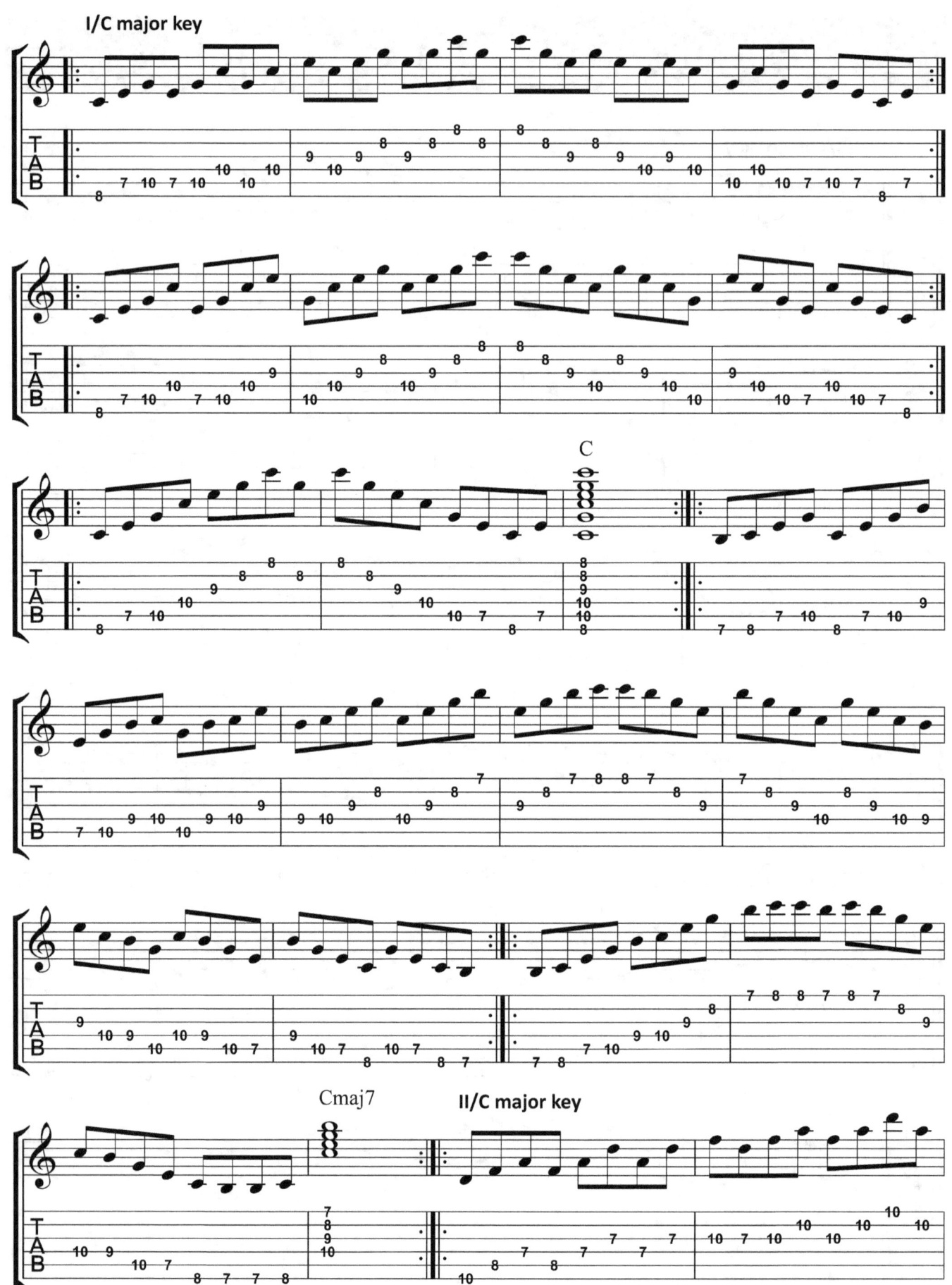

232   The complete guitar book 1

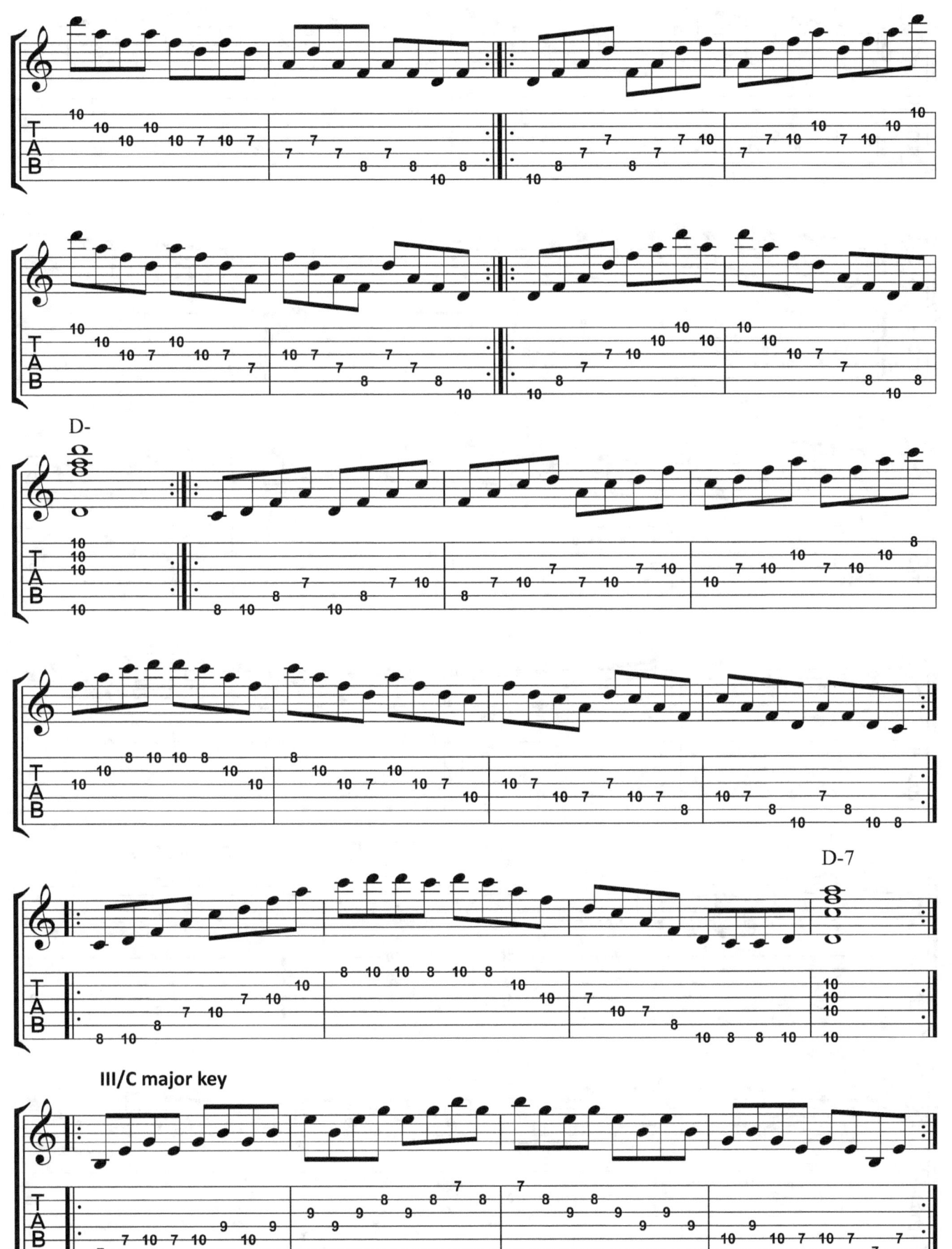

Chapter 7 construction of the diatonic chords with arpeggios in 5 positions

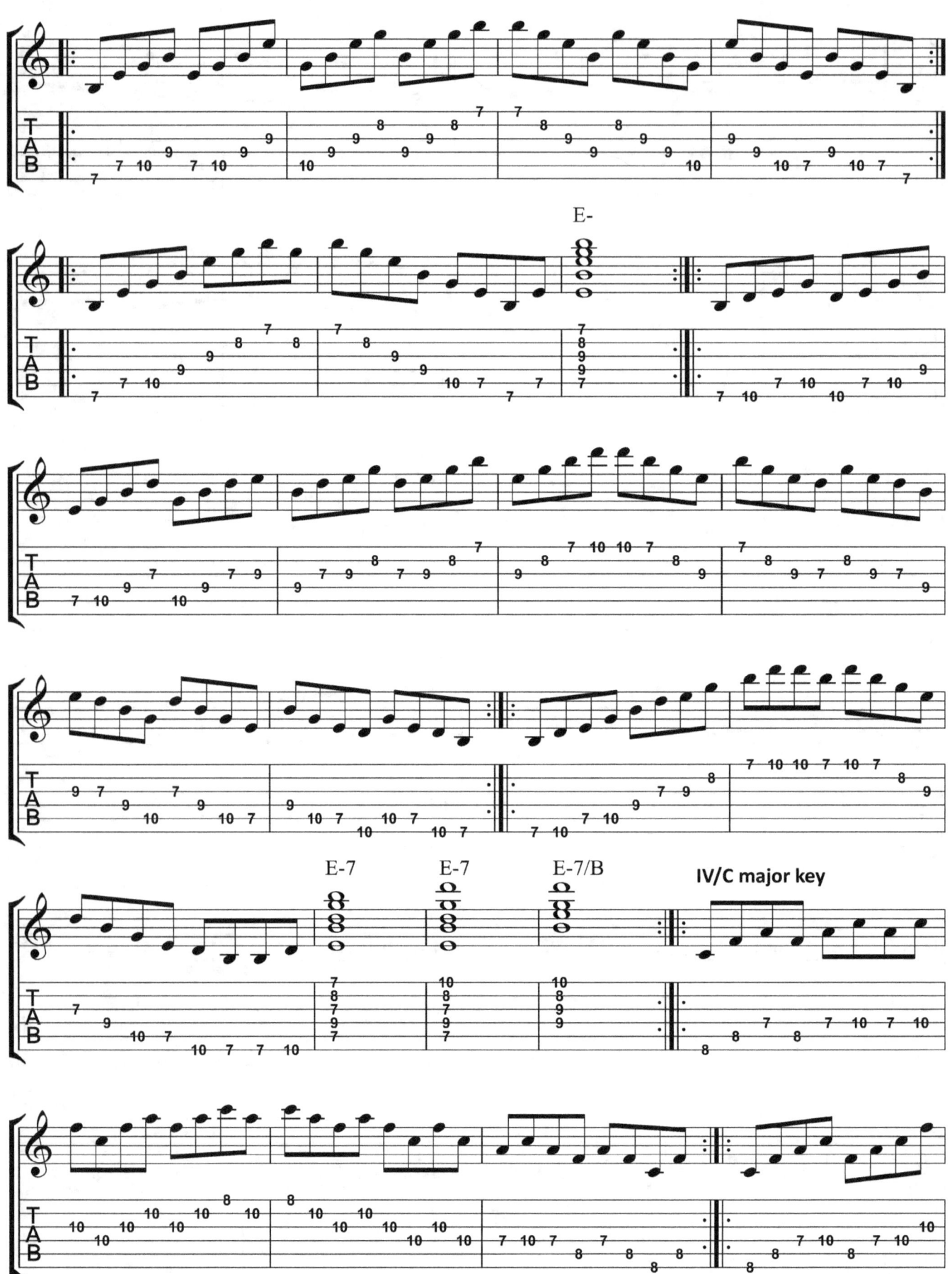

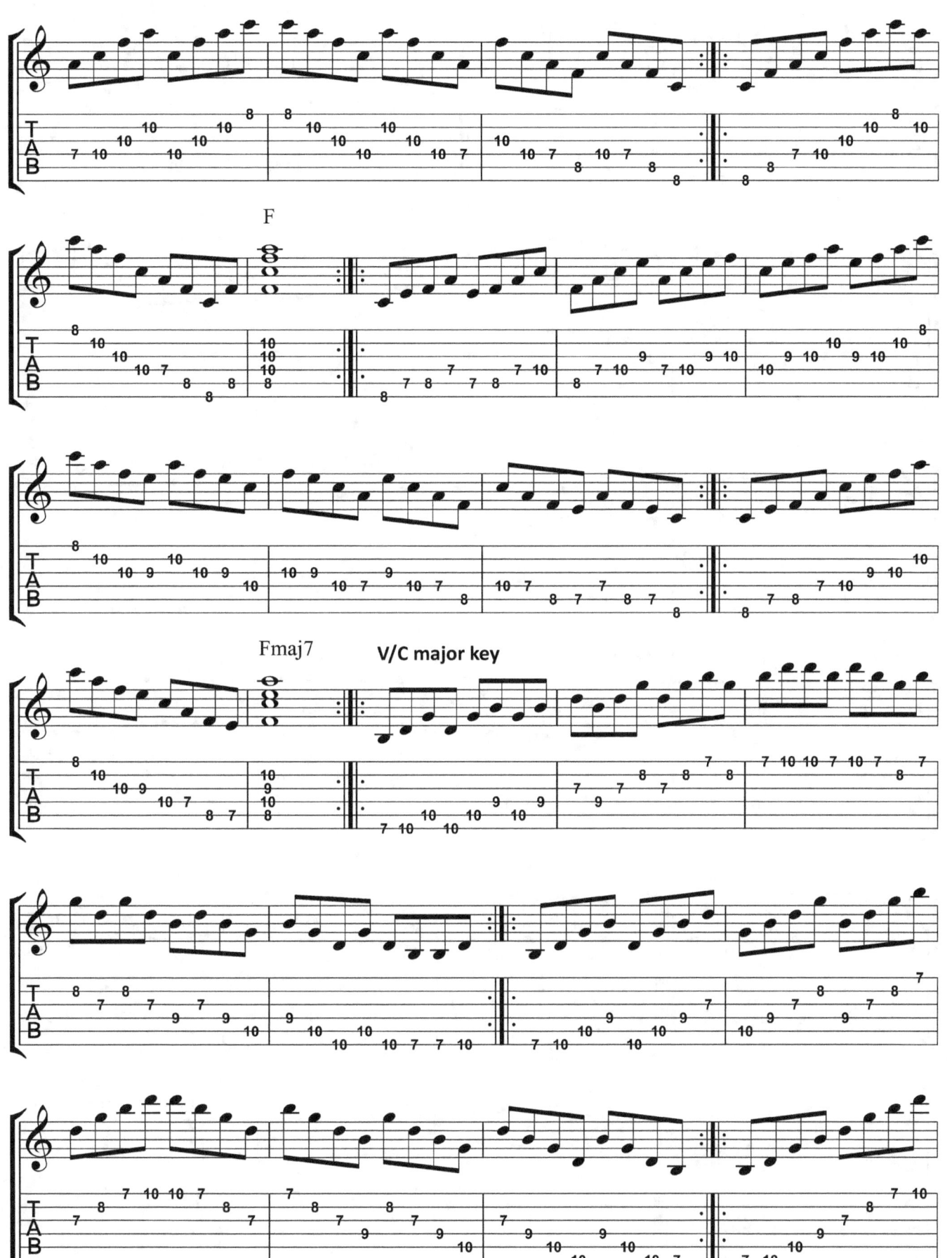

Chapter 7   construction of the diatonic chords with arpeggios in 5 positions

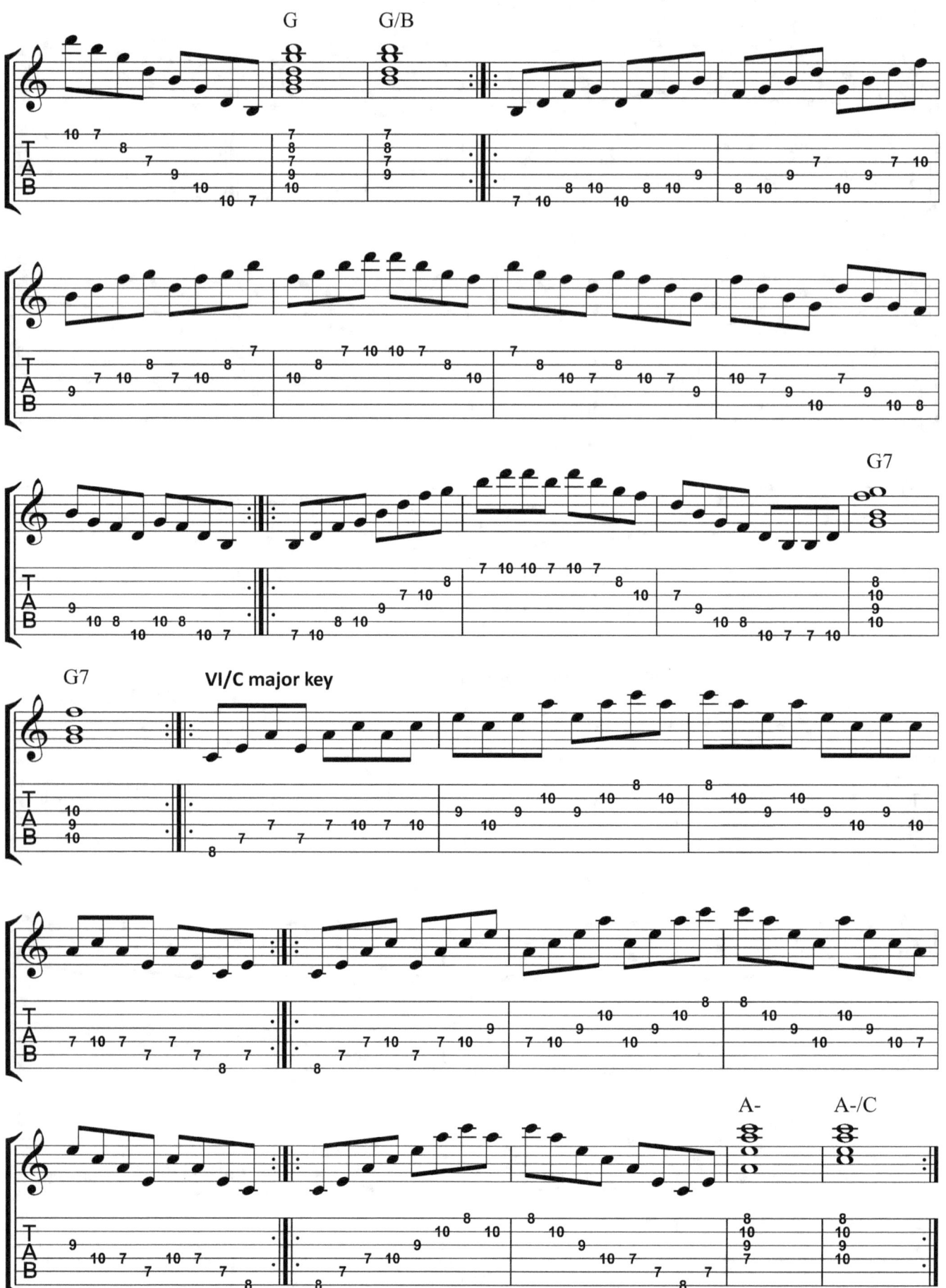

236   The complete guitar book 1

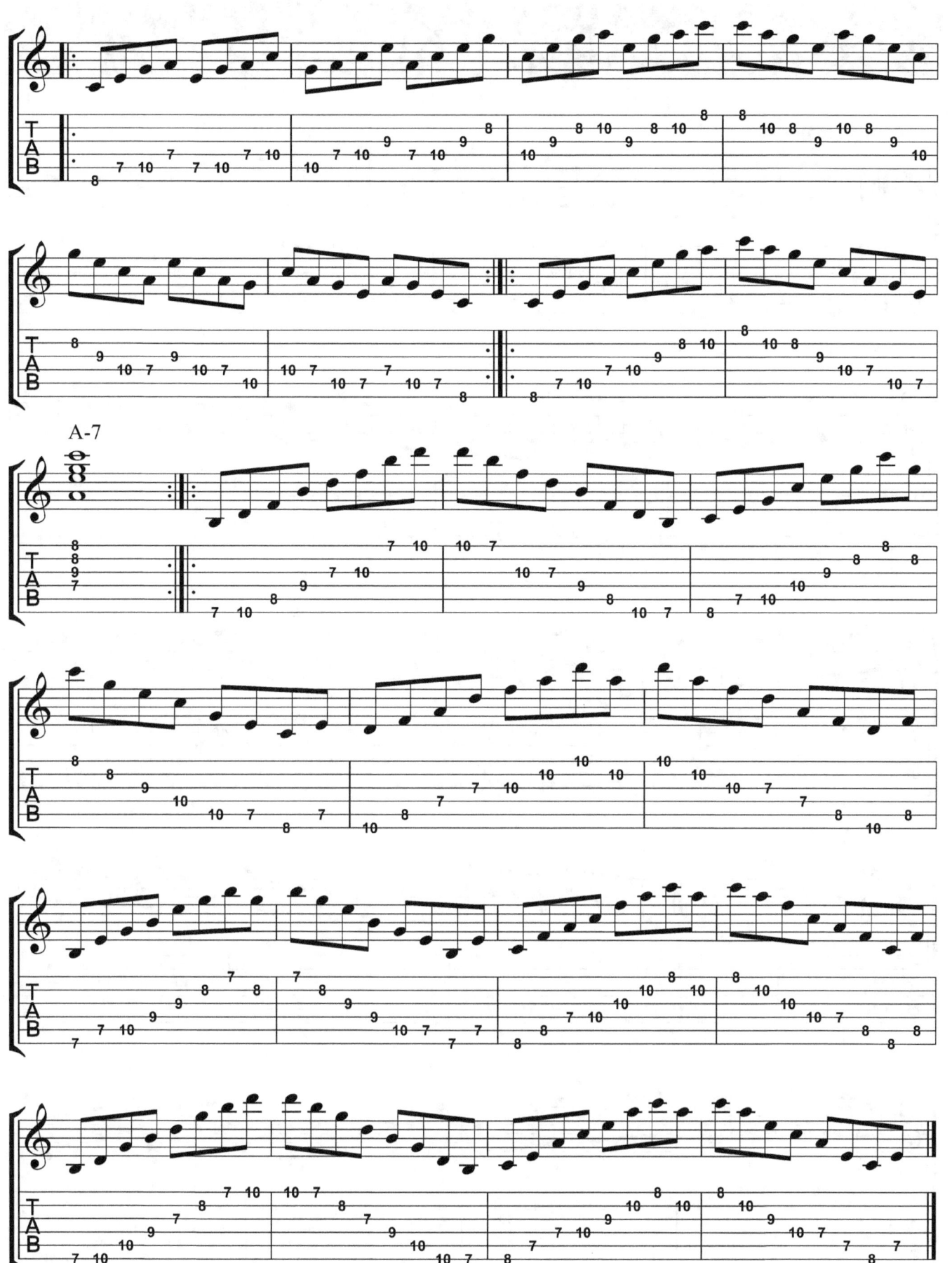

Chapter 7   construction of the diatonic chords with arpeggios in 5 positions

Position 2 arpeggio & chord studies

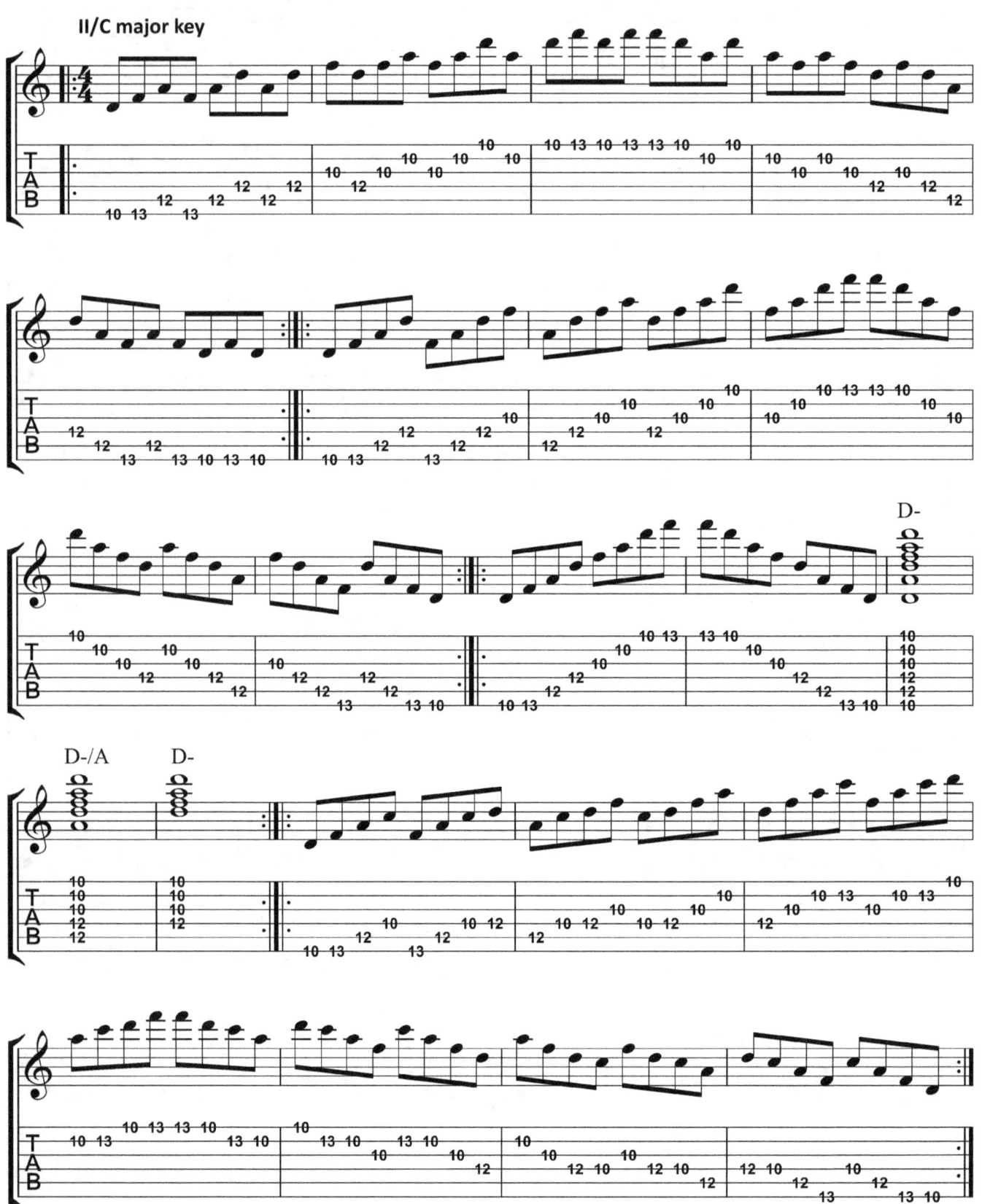

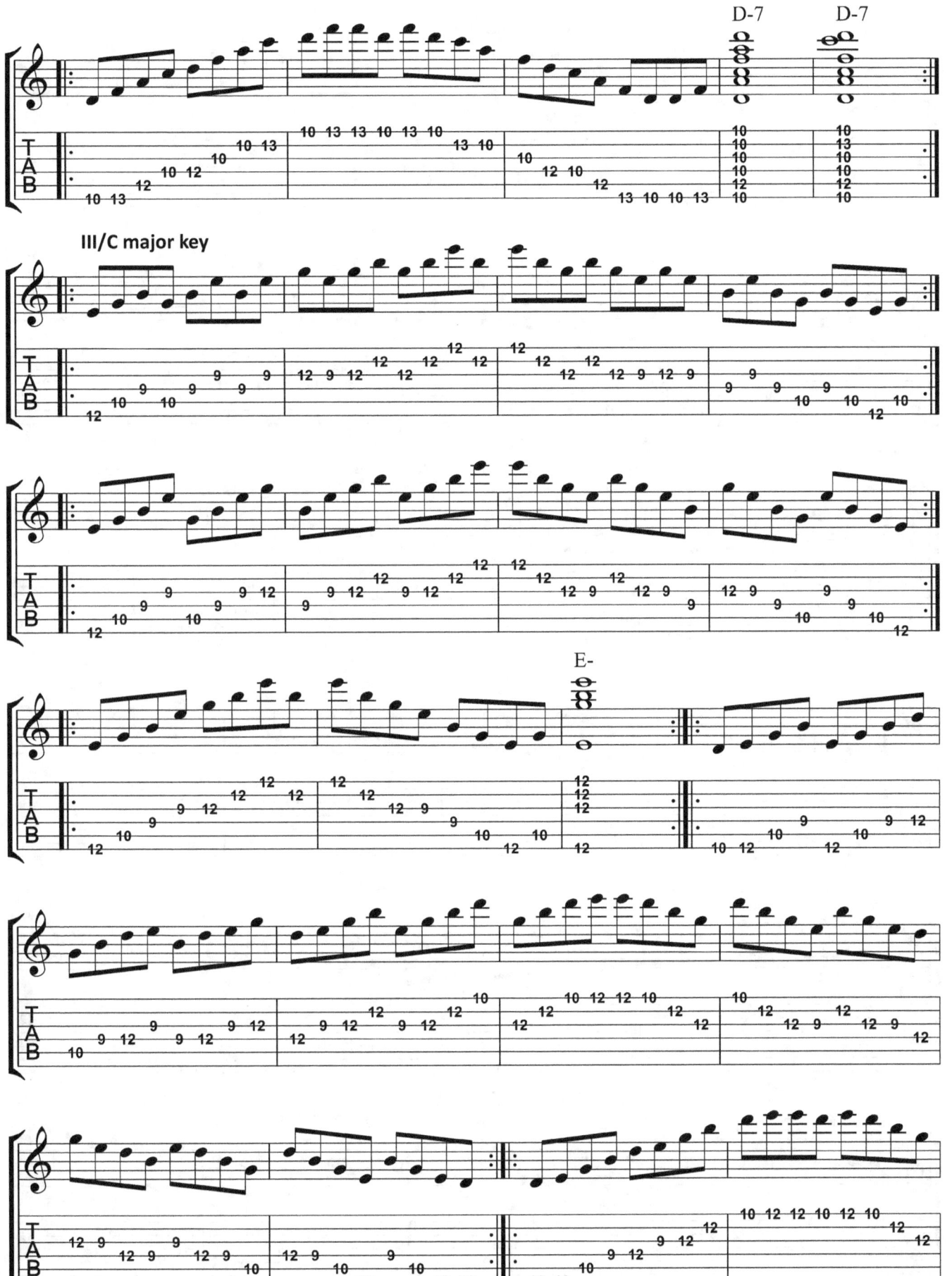

Chapter 7 construction of the diatonic chords with arpeggios in 5 positions

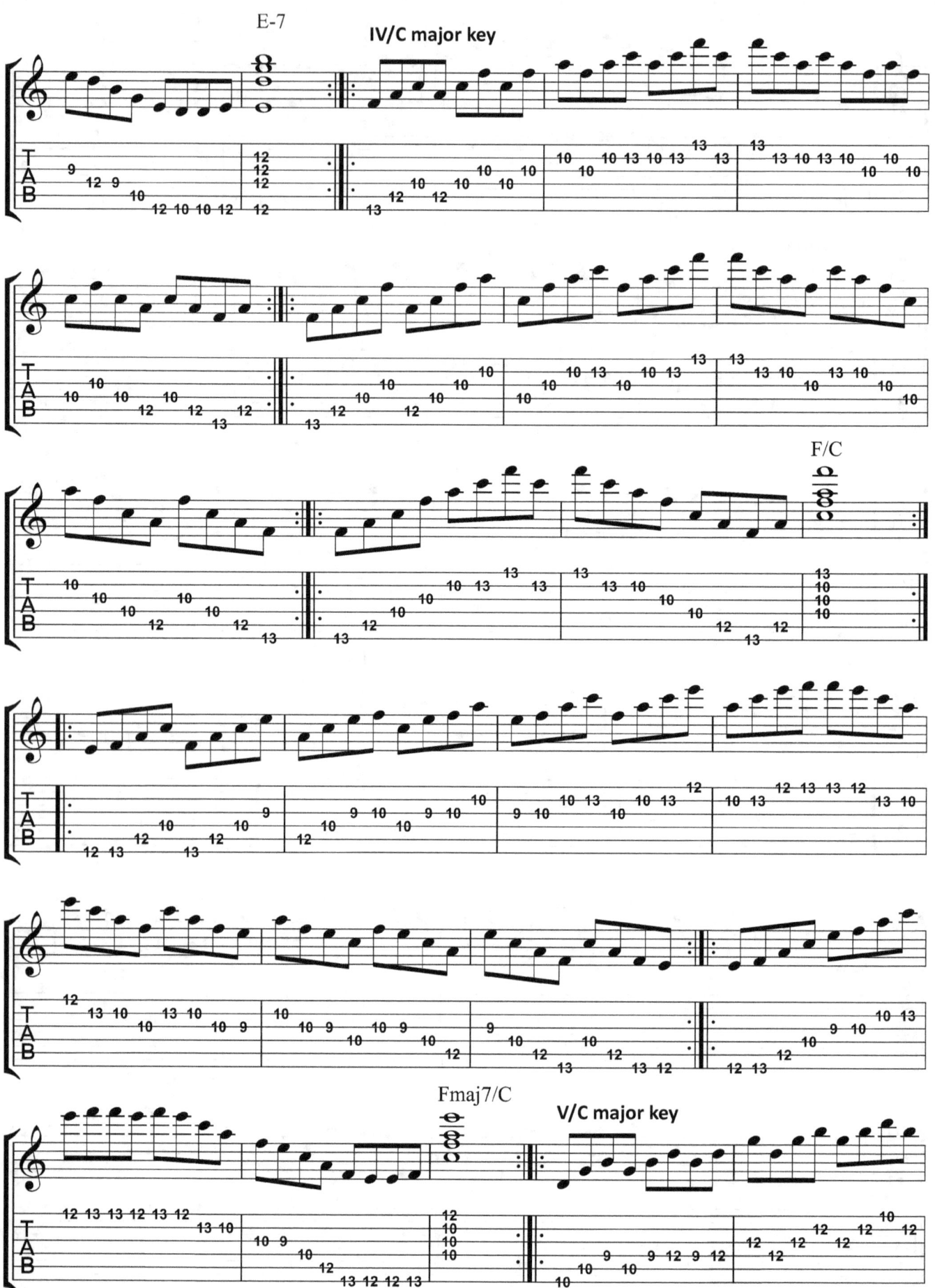

Chapter 7 construction of the diatonic chords with arpeggios in 5 positions

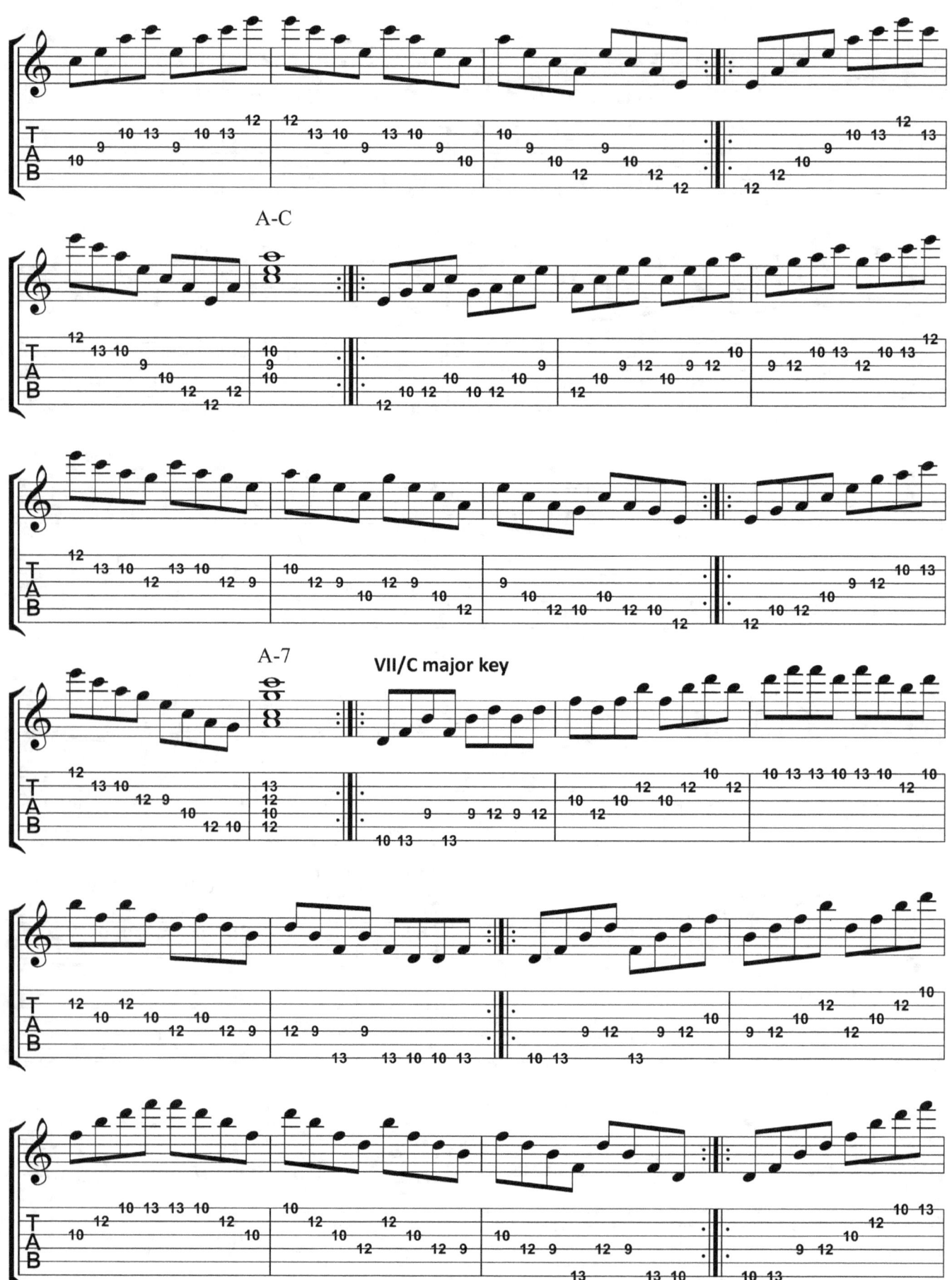

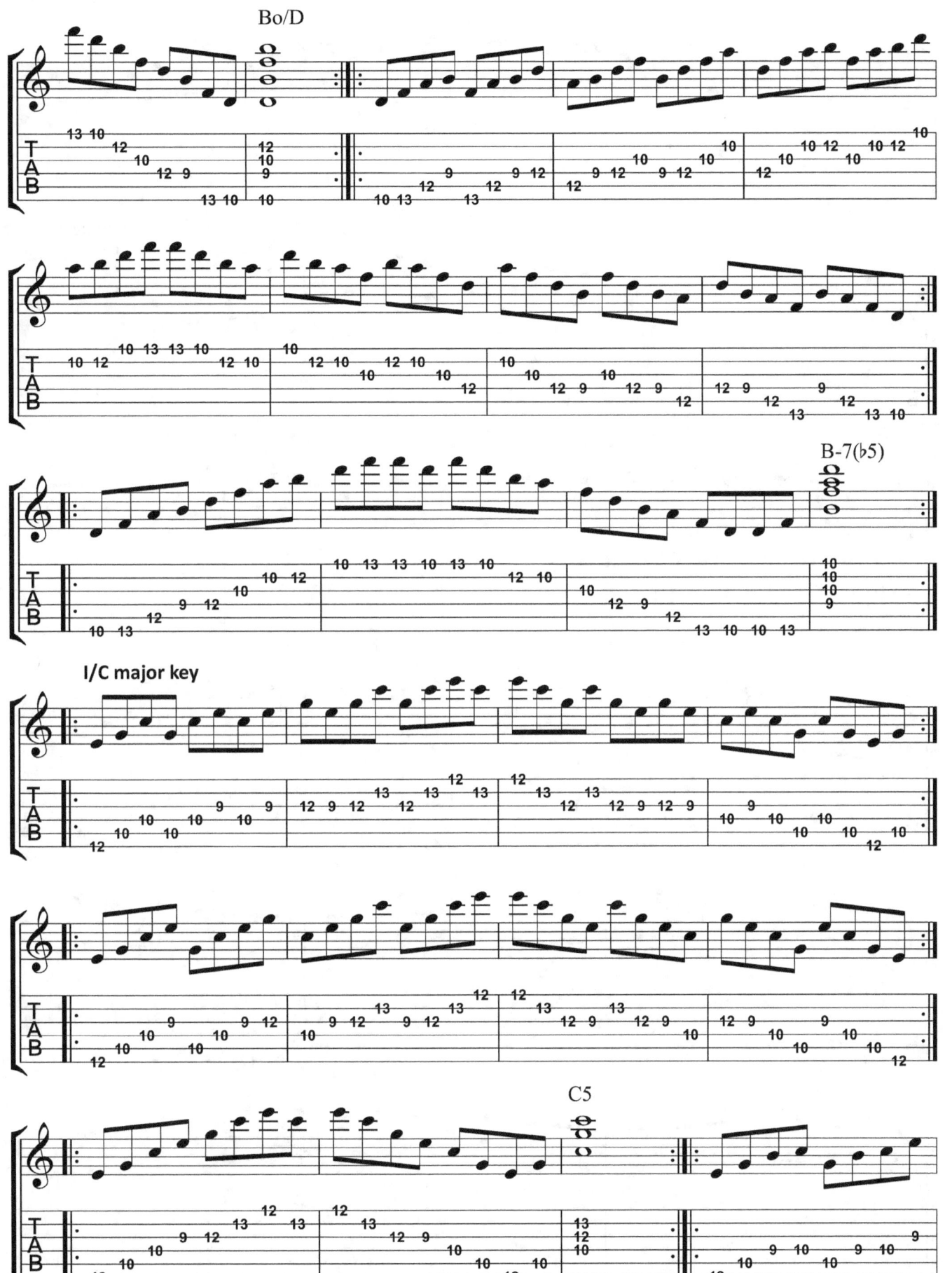

Chapter 7 construction of the diatonic chords with arpeggios in 5 positions

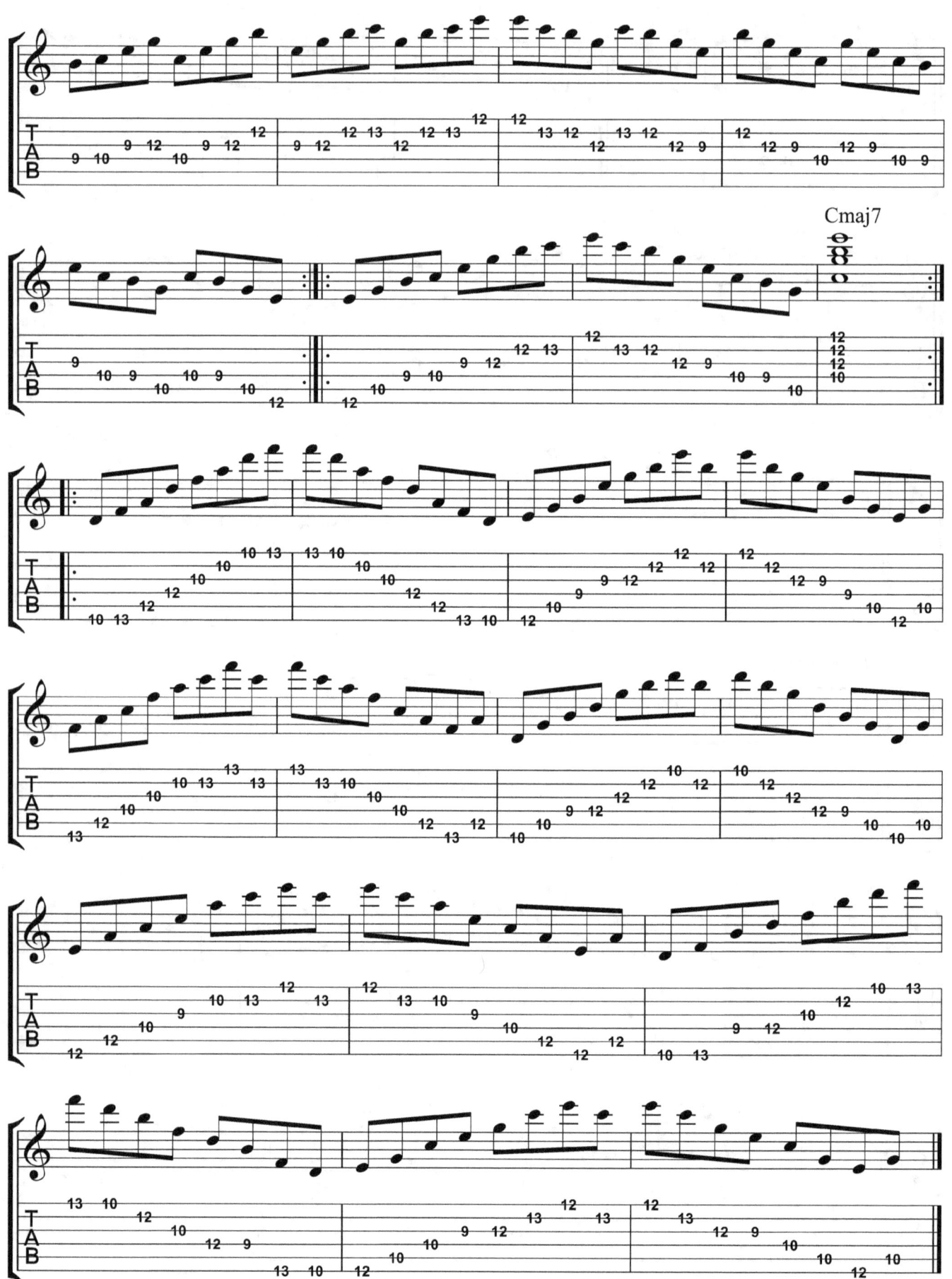

Position 3-4 arpeggio & chord studies

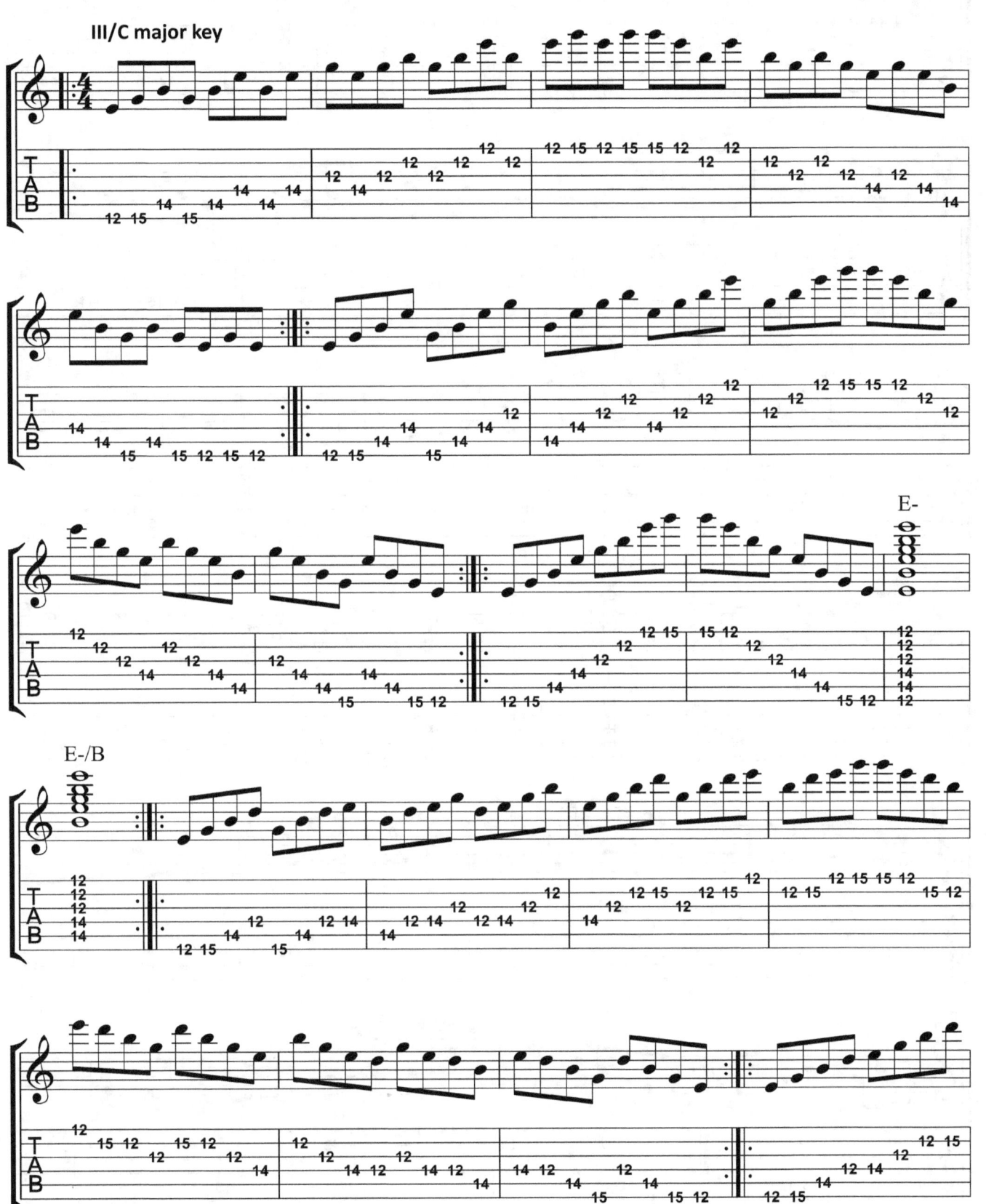

Chapter 7 construction of the diatonic chords with arpeggios in 5 positions

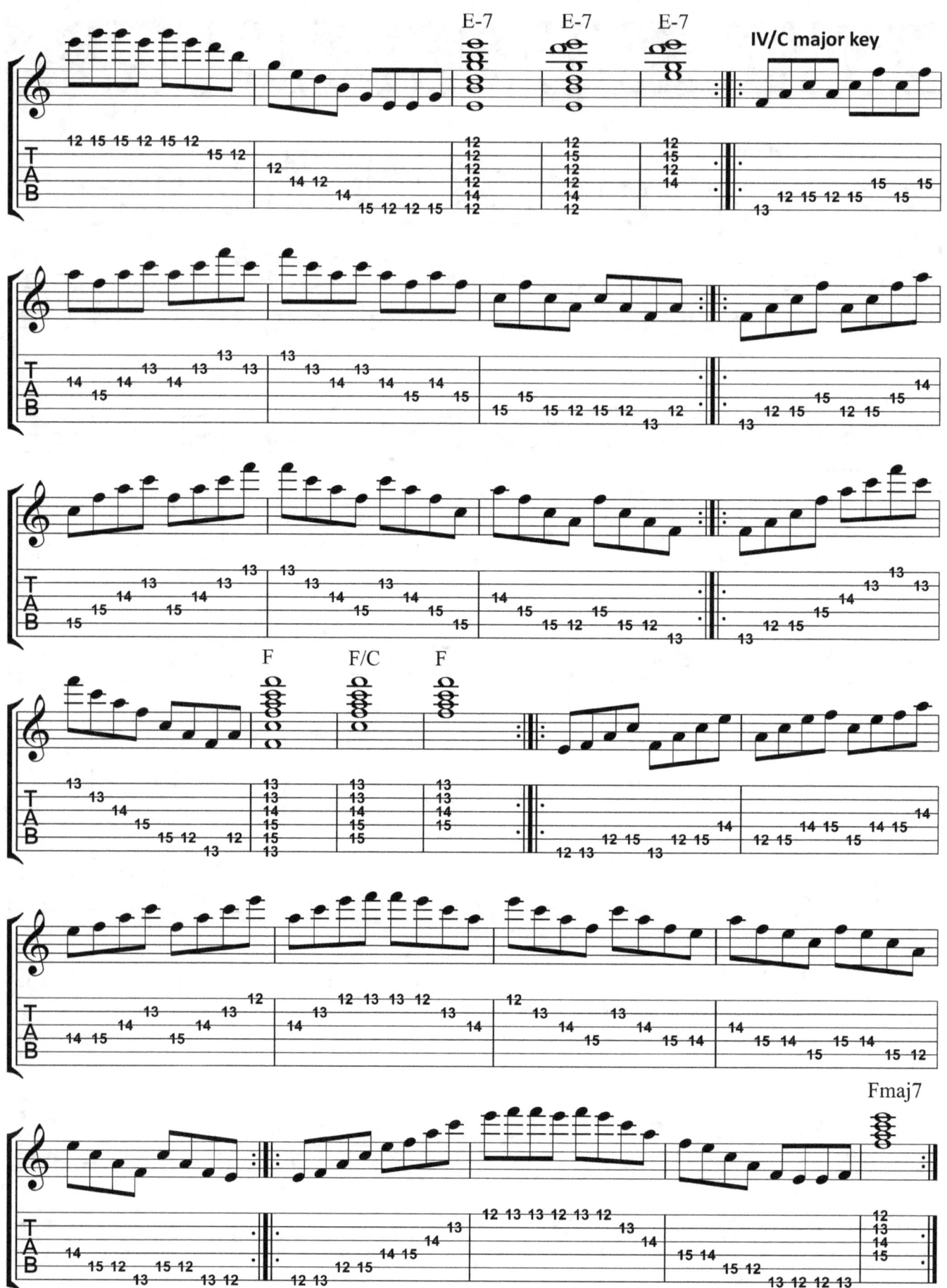

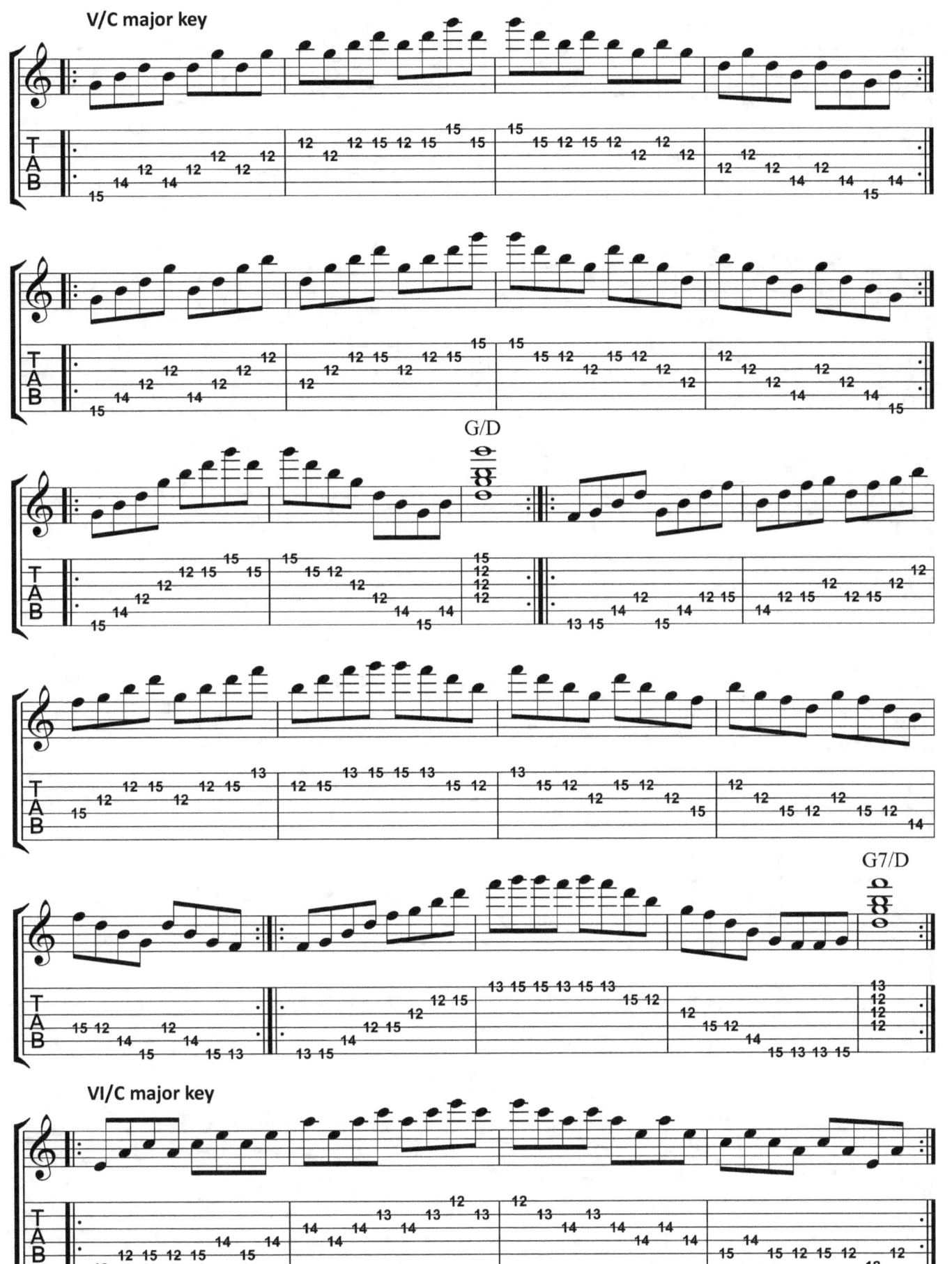

Chapter 7 construction of the diatonic chords with arpeggios in 5 positions

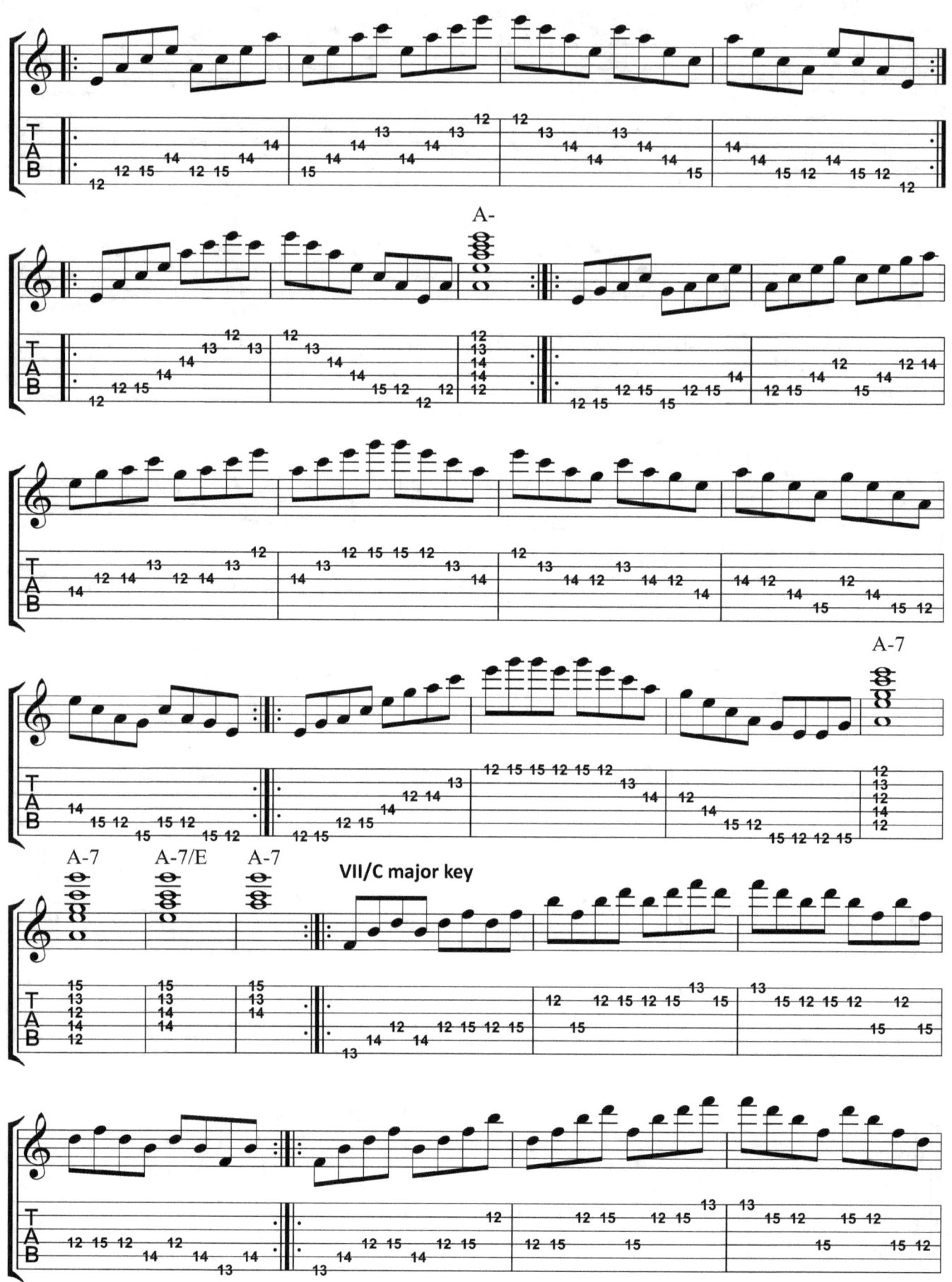

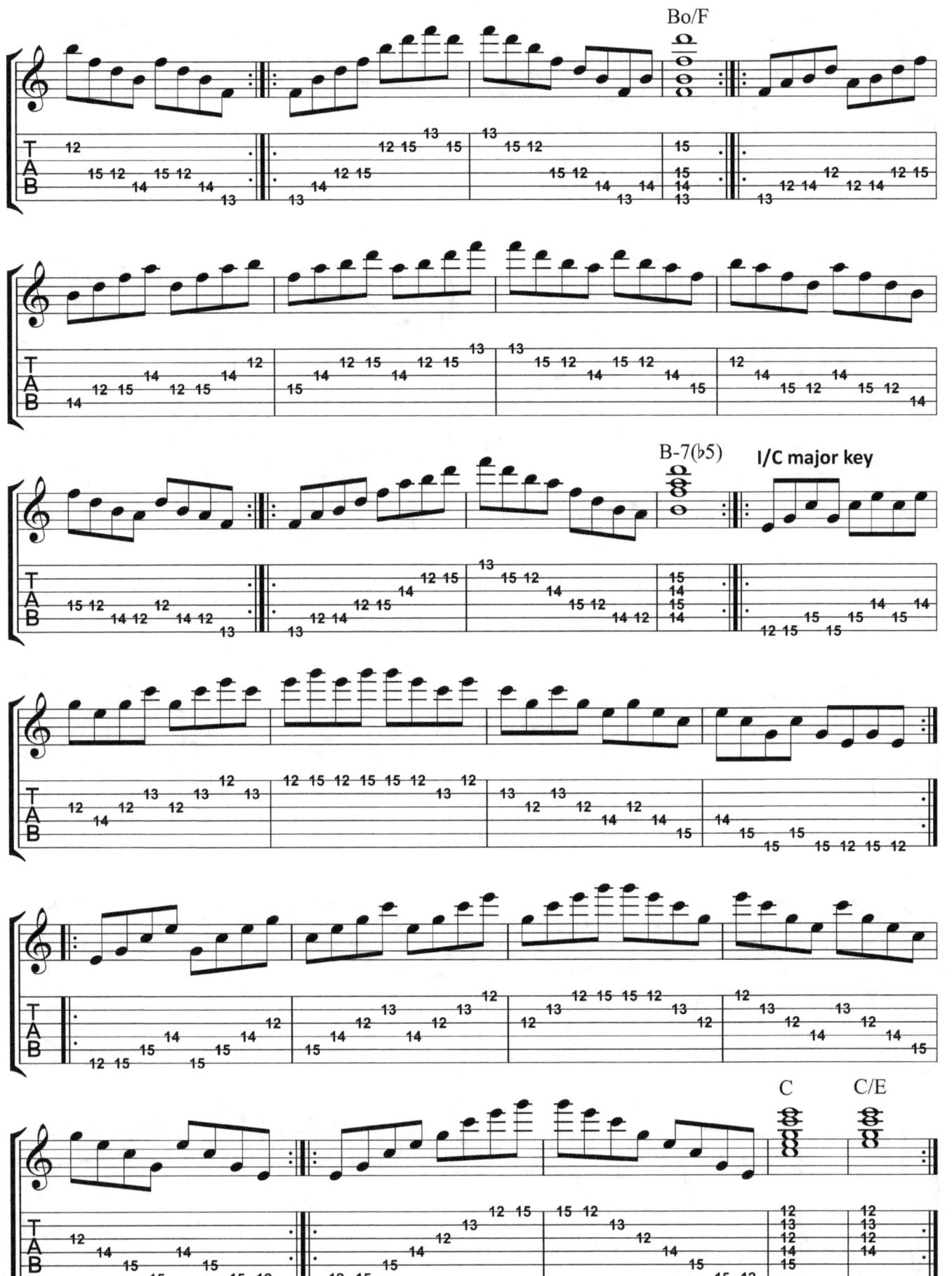

Chapter 7 construction of the diatonic chords with arpeggios in 5 positions

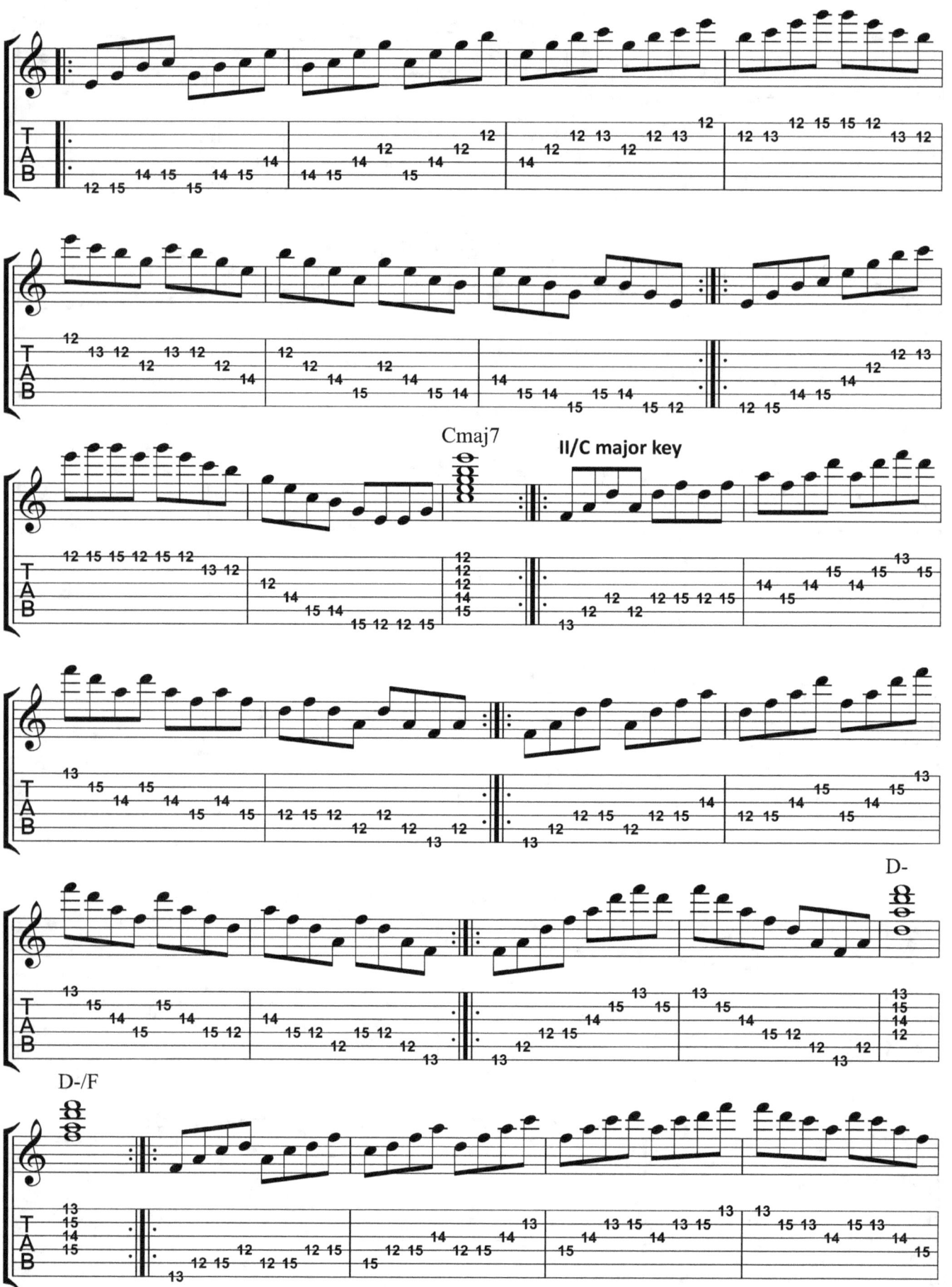

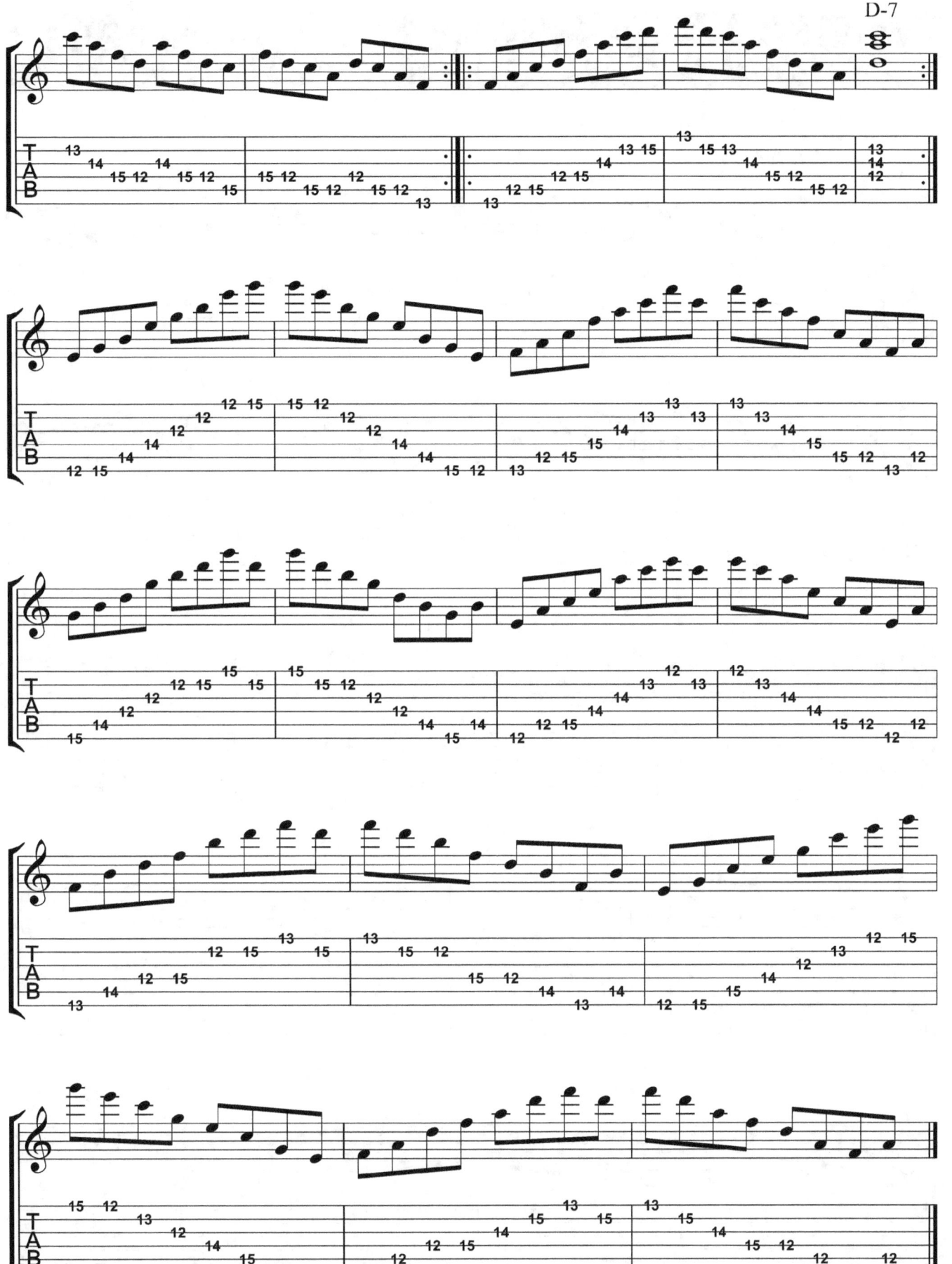

Chapter 7 construction of the diatonic chords with arpeggios in 5 positions

251

Position 5 arpeggio & chord studies

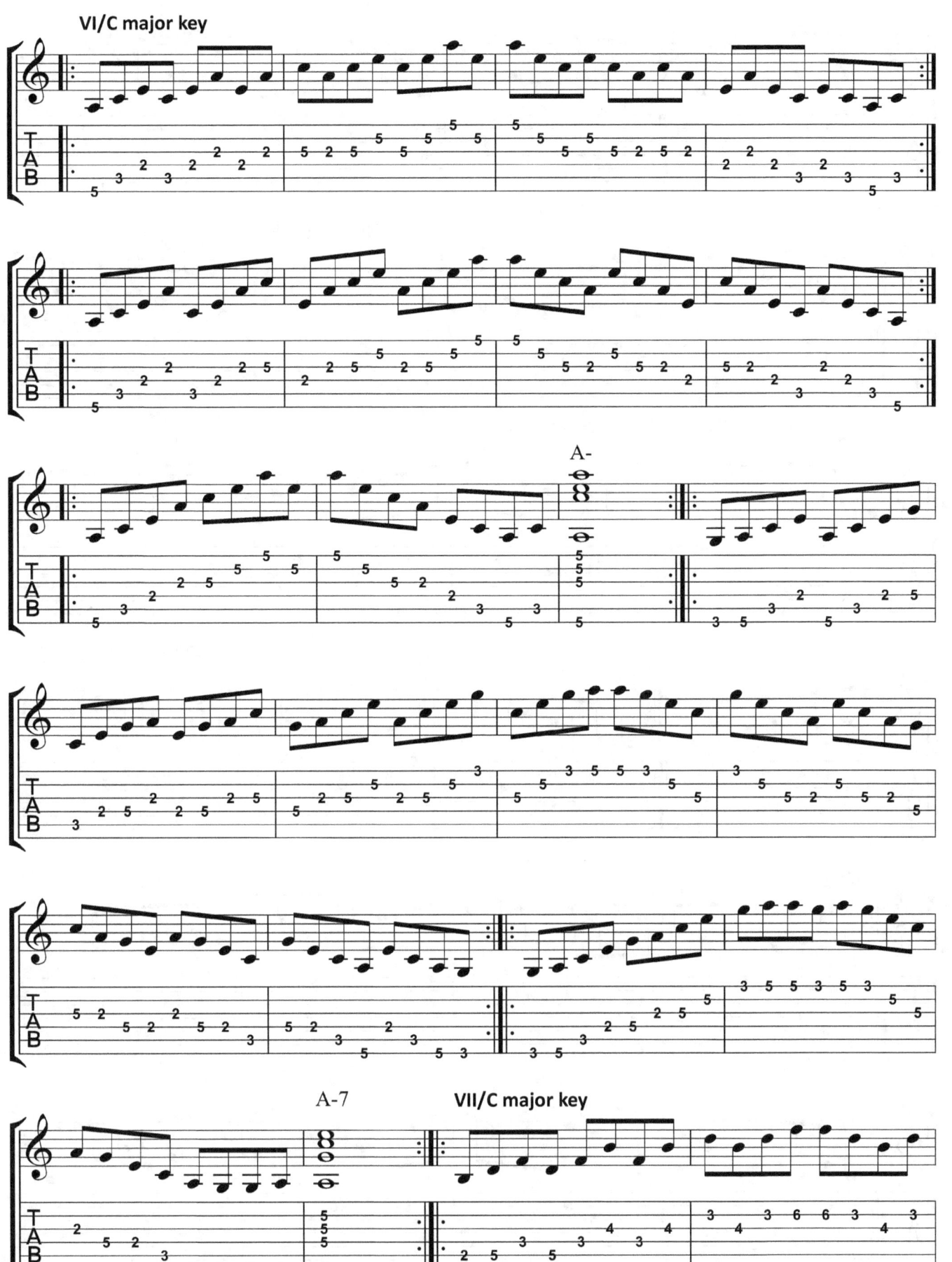

Chapter 7 construction of the diatonic chords with arpeggios in 5 positions

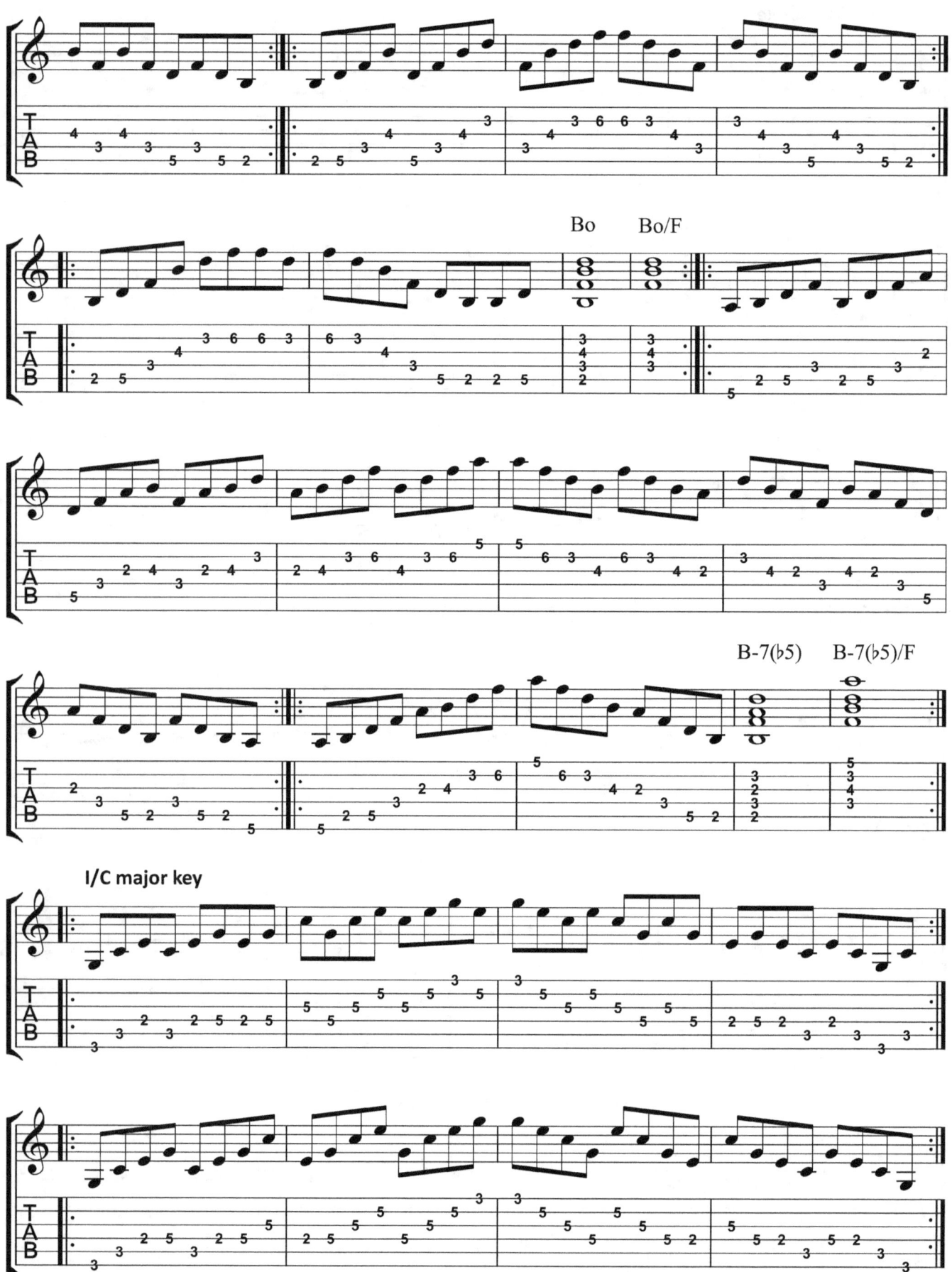

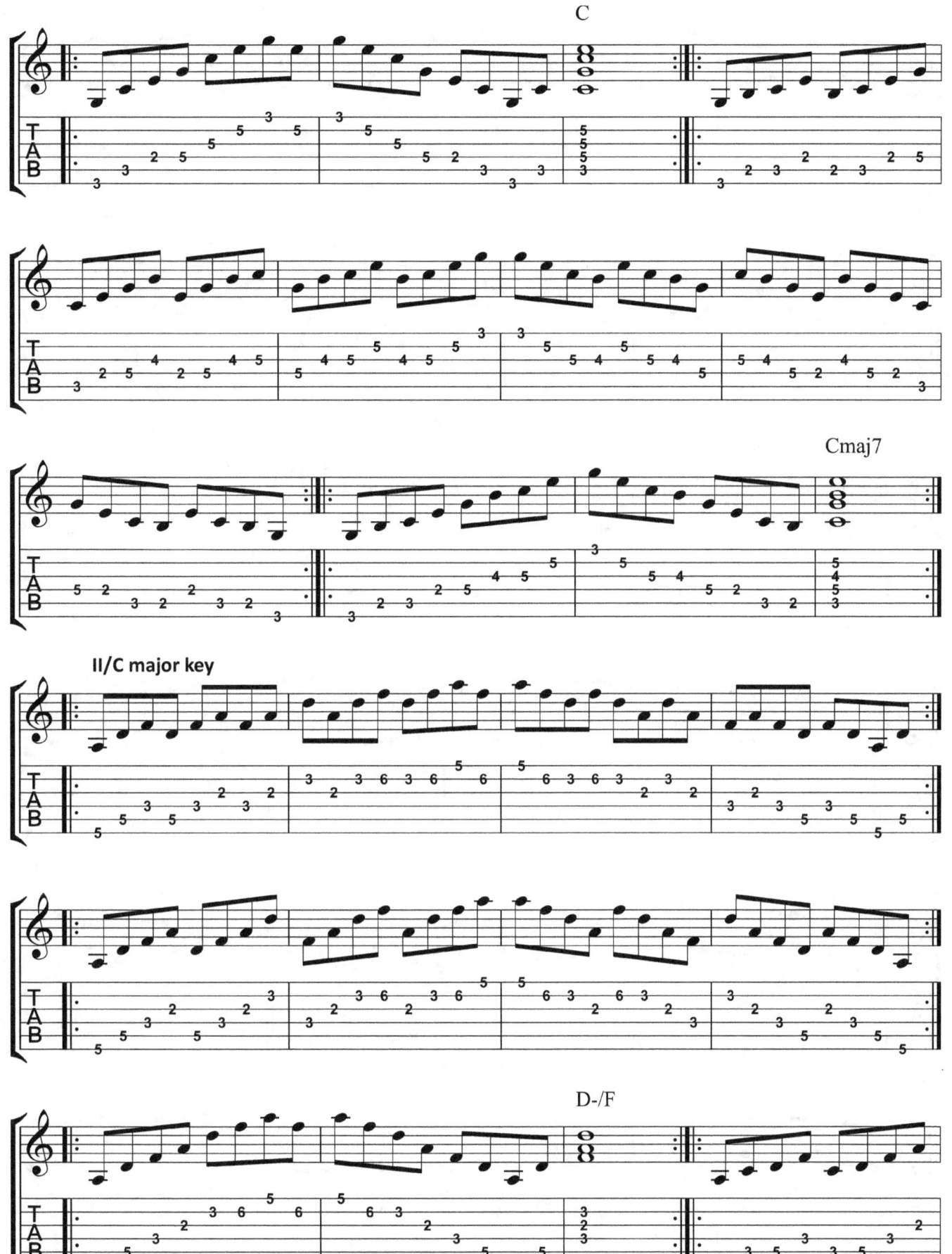

Chapter 7 construction of the diatonic chords with arpeggios in 5 positions

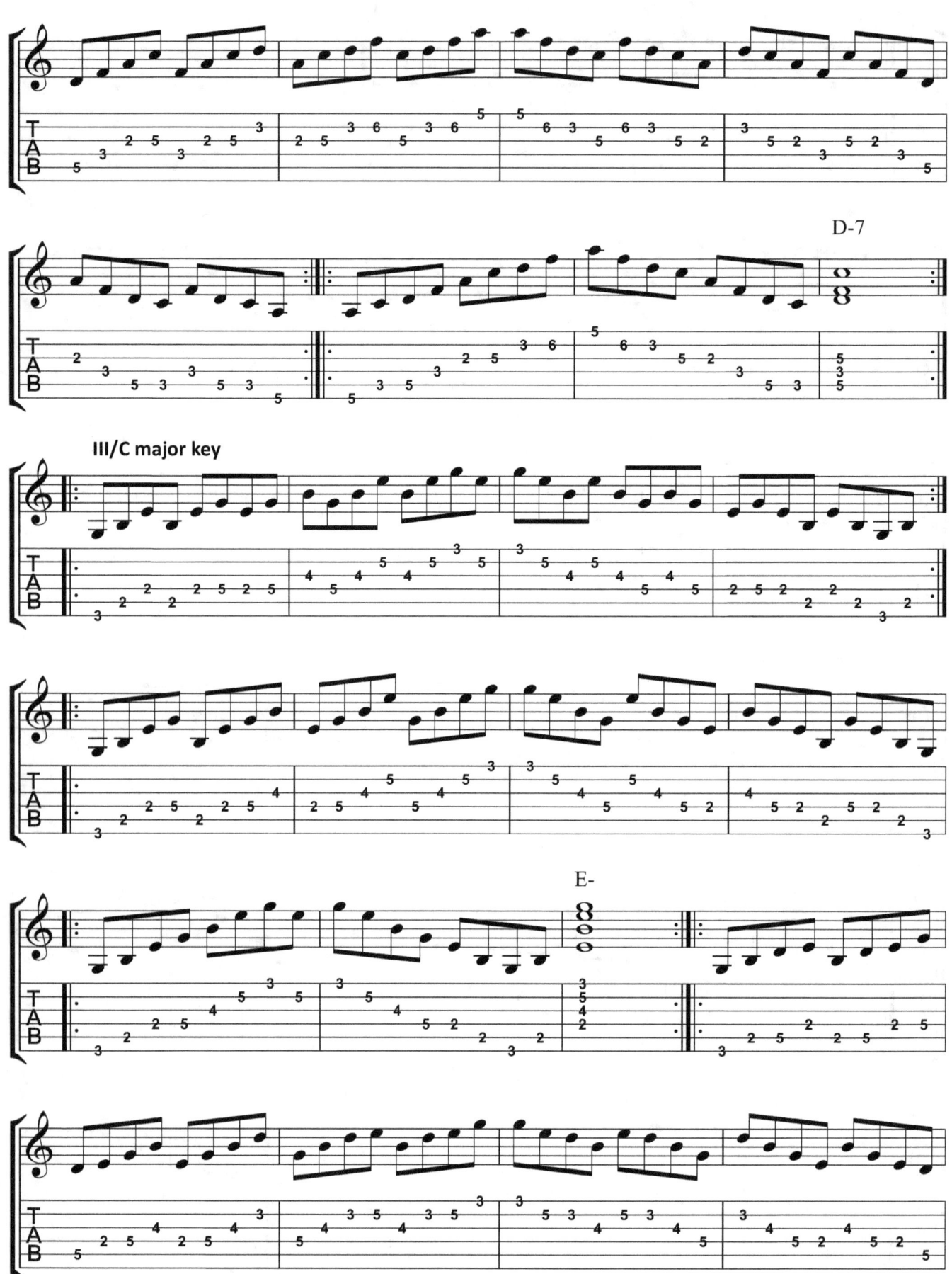

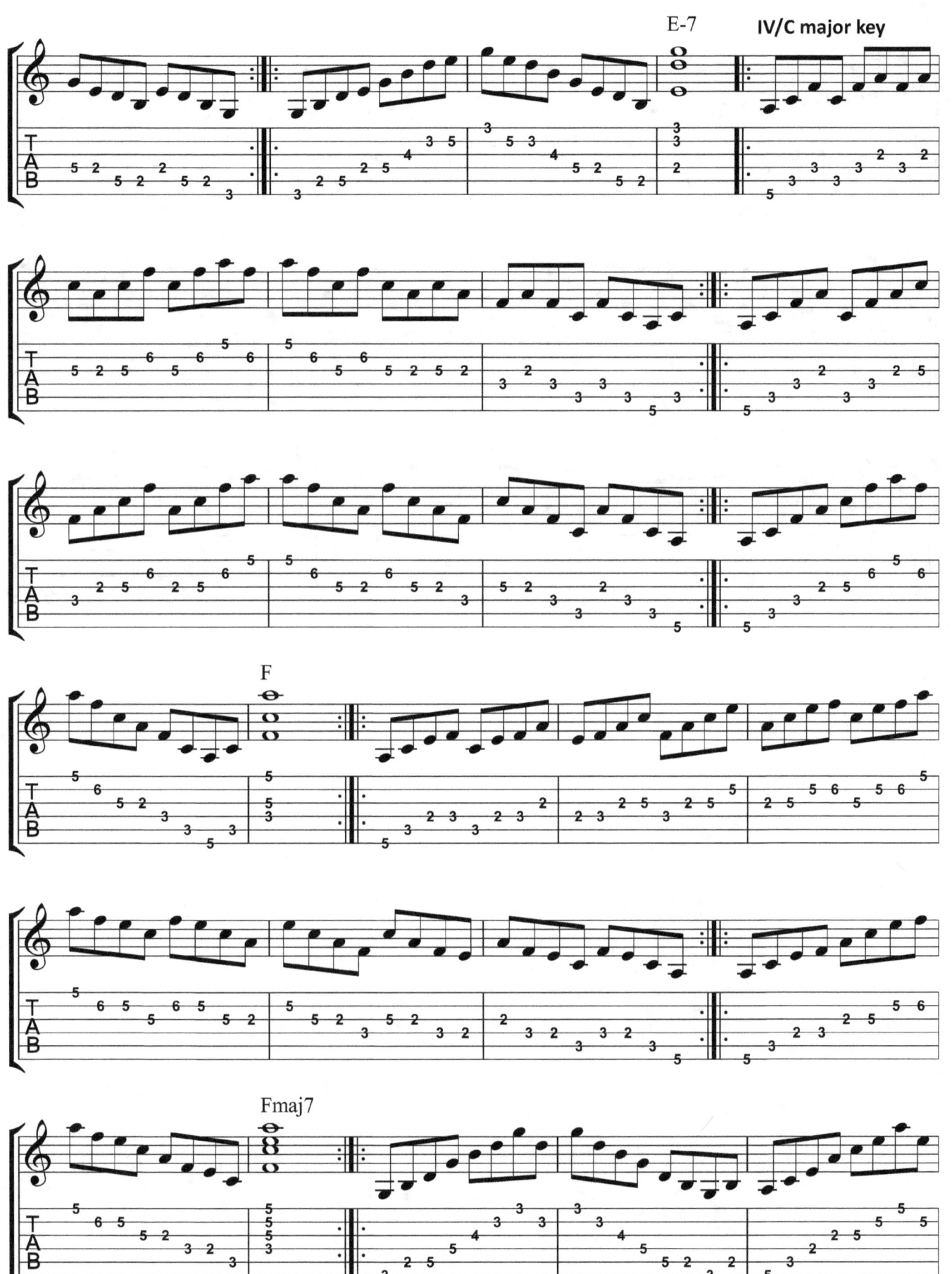

Chapter 7 construction of the diatonic chords with arpeggios in 5 positions

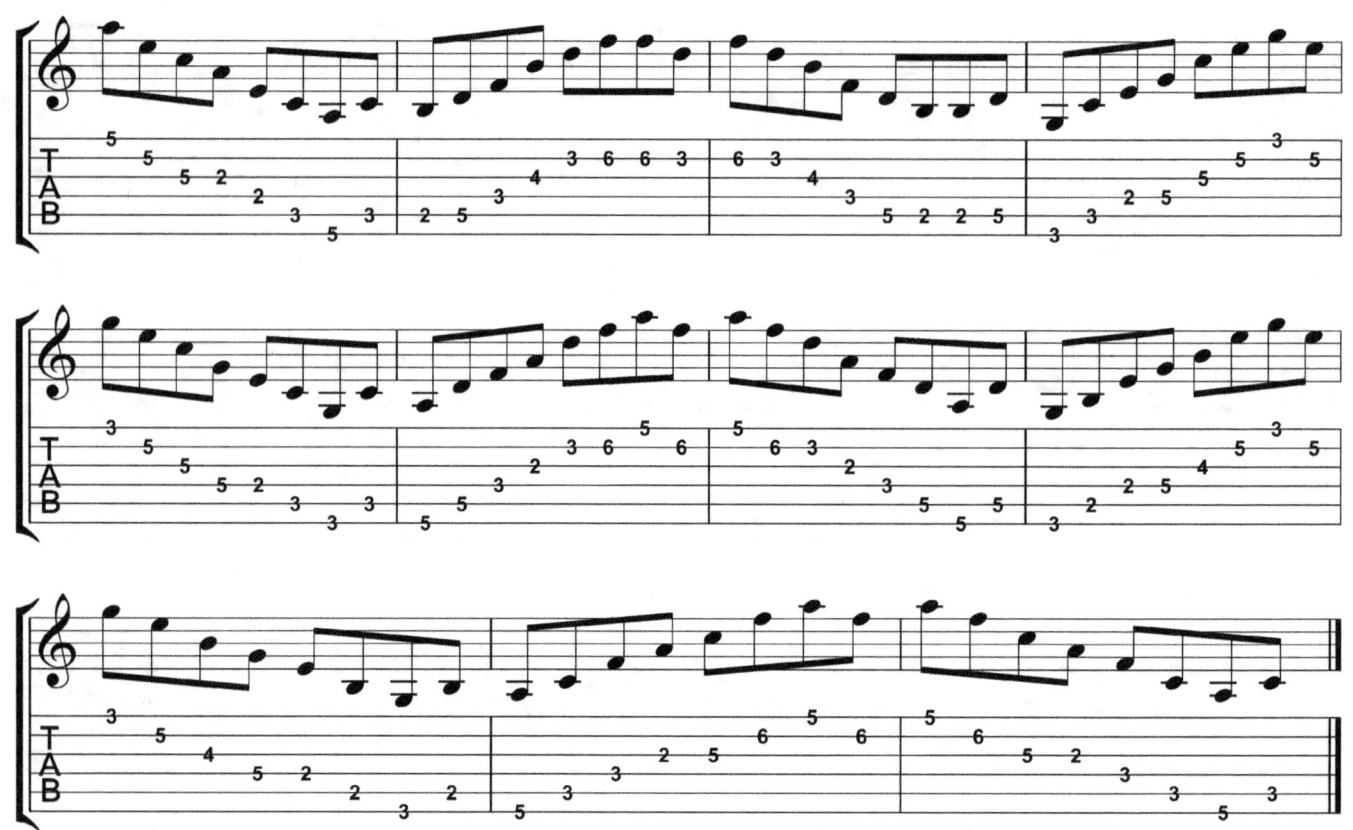

Position 6 arpeggio & chord studies

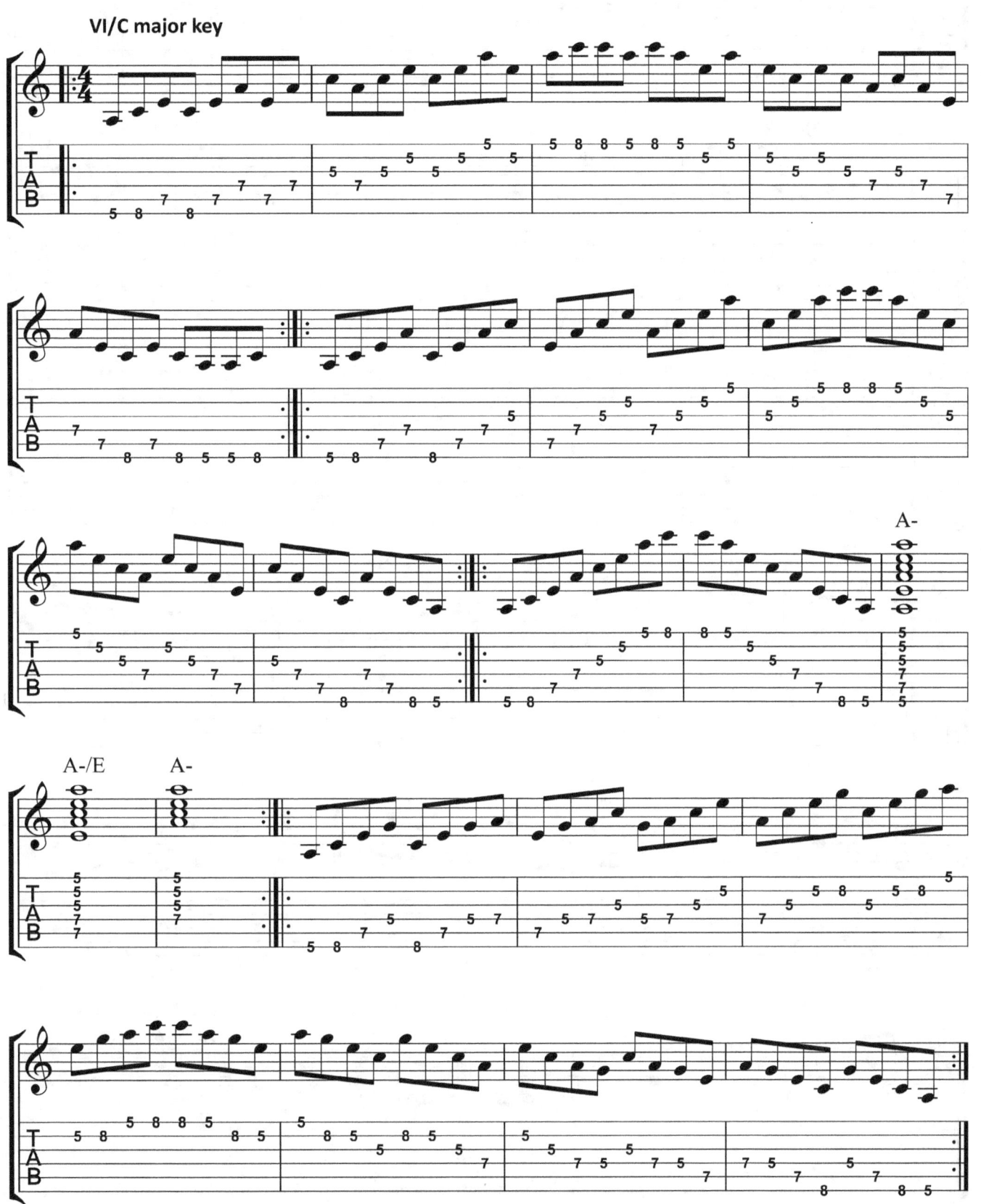

Chapter 7   construction of the diatonic chords with arpeggios in 5 positions

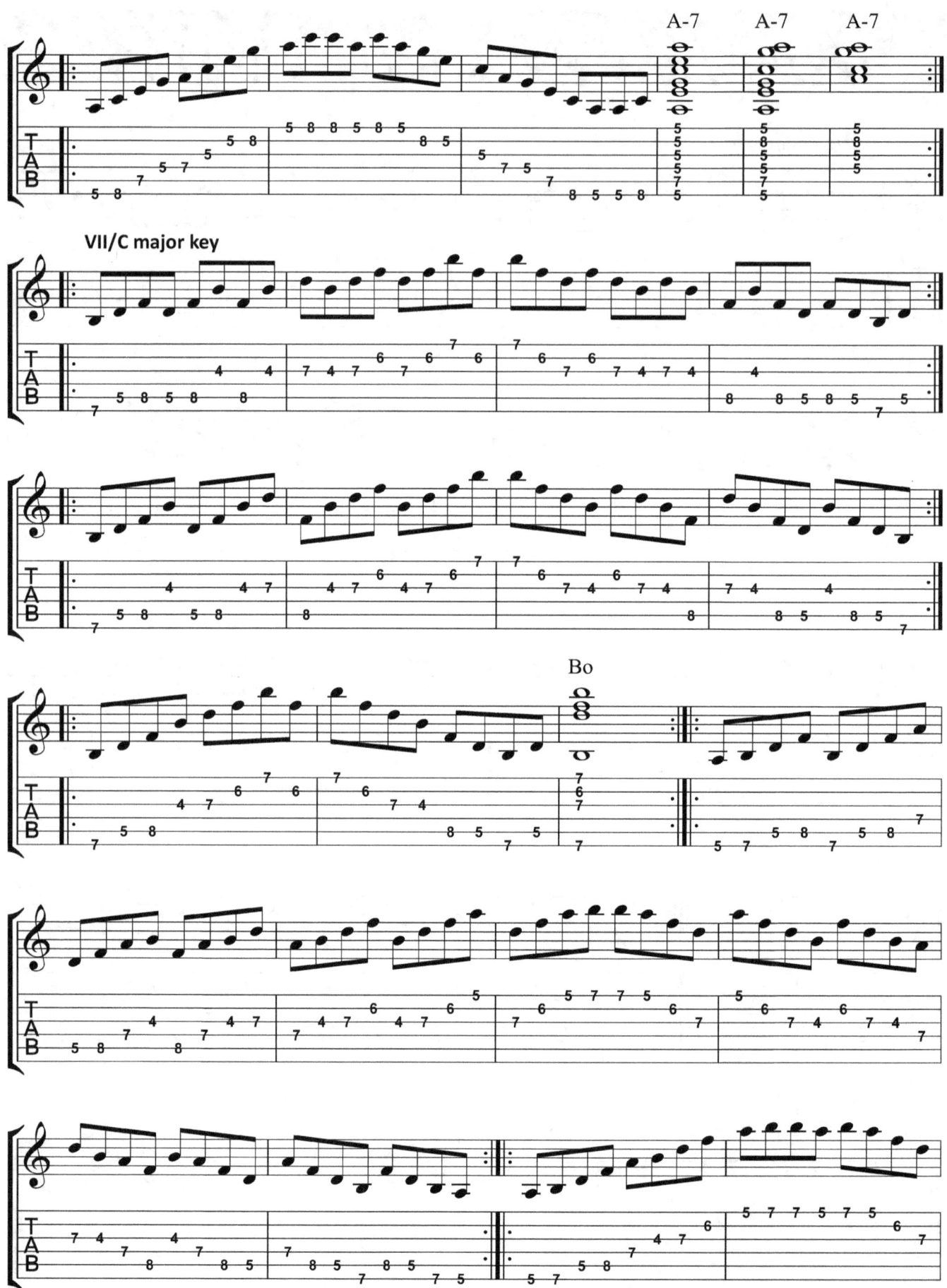

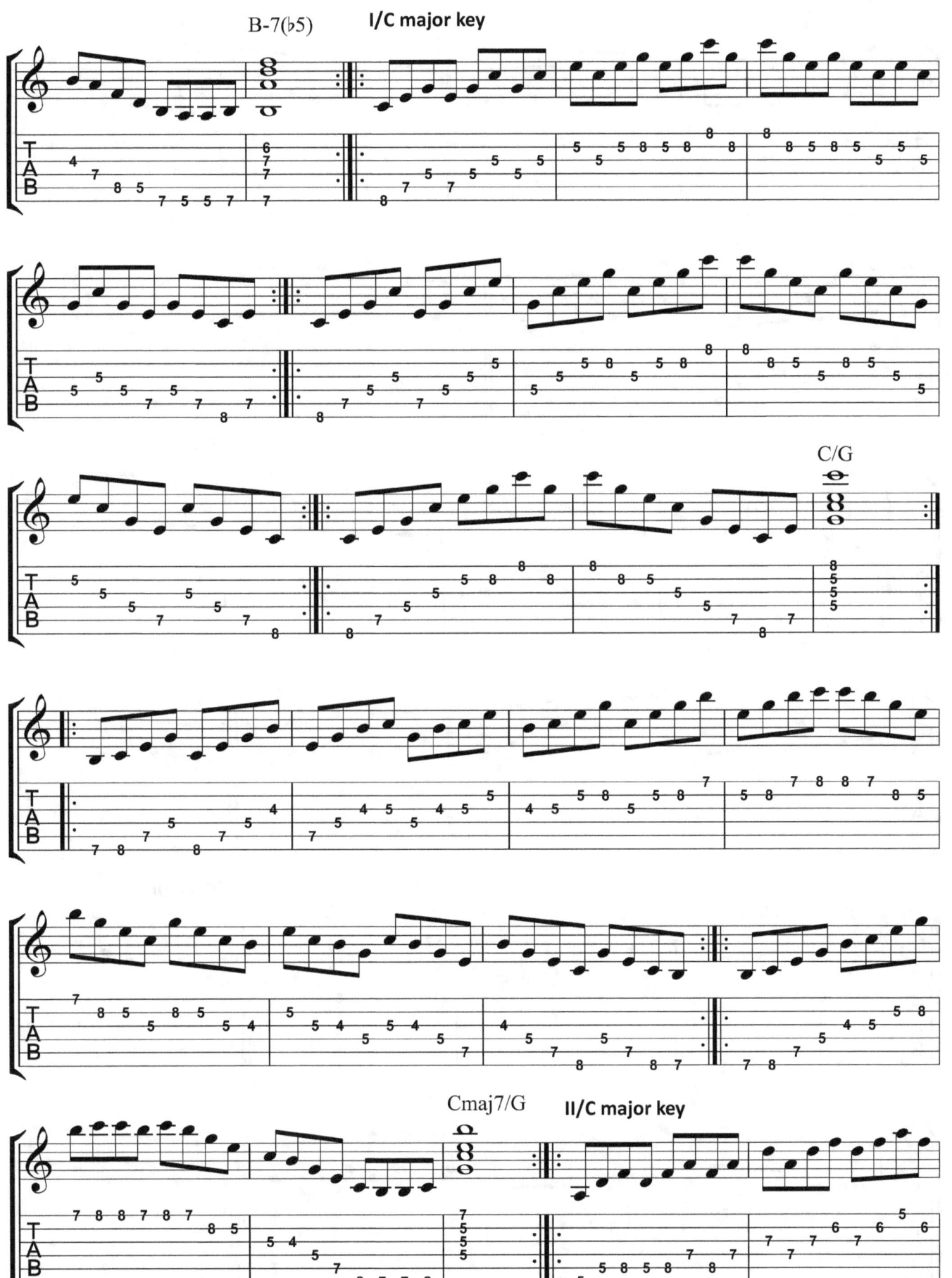

Chapter 7   construction of the diatonic chords with arpeggios in 5 positions

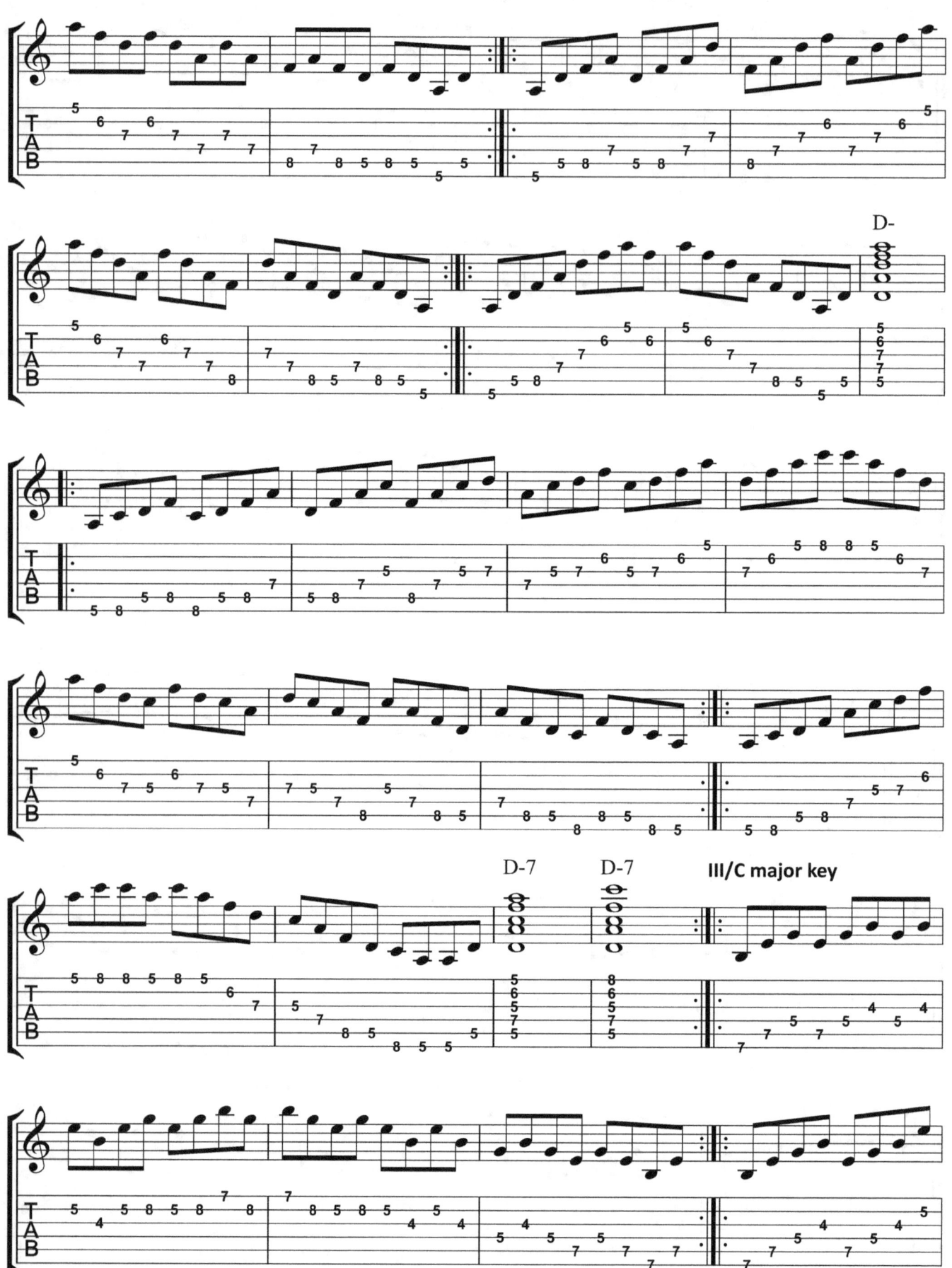

262

The complete guitar book 1

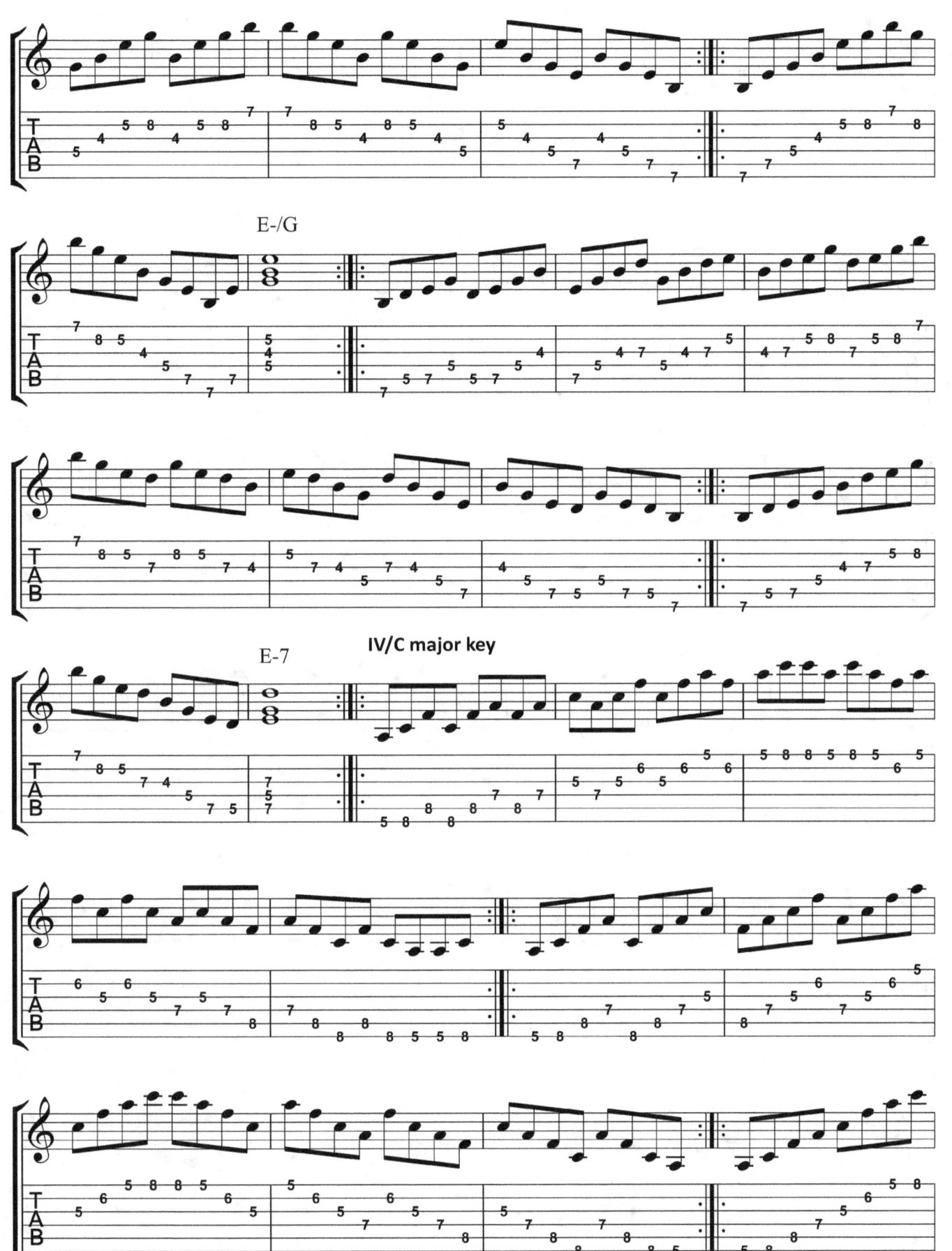

Chapter 7 construction of the diatonic chords with arpeggios in 5 positions

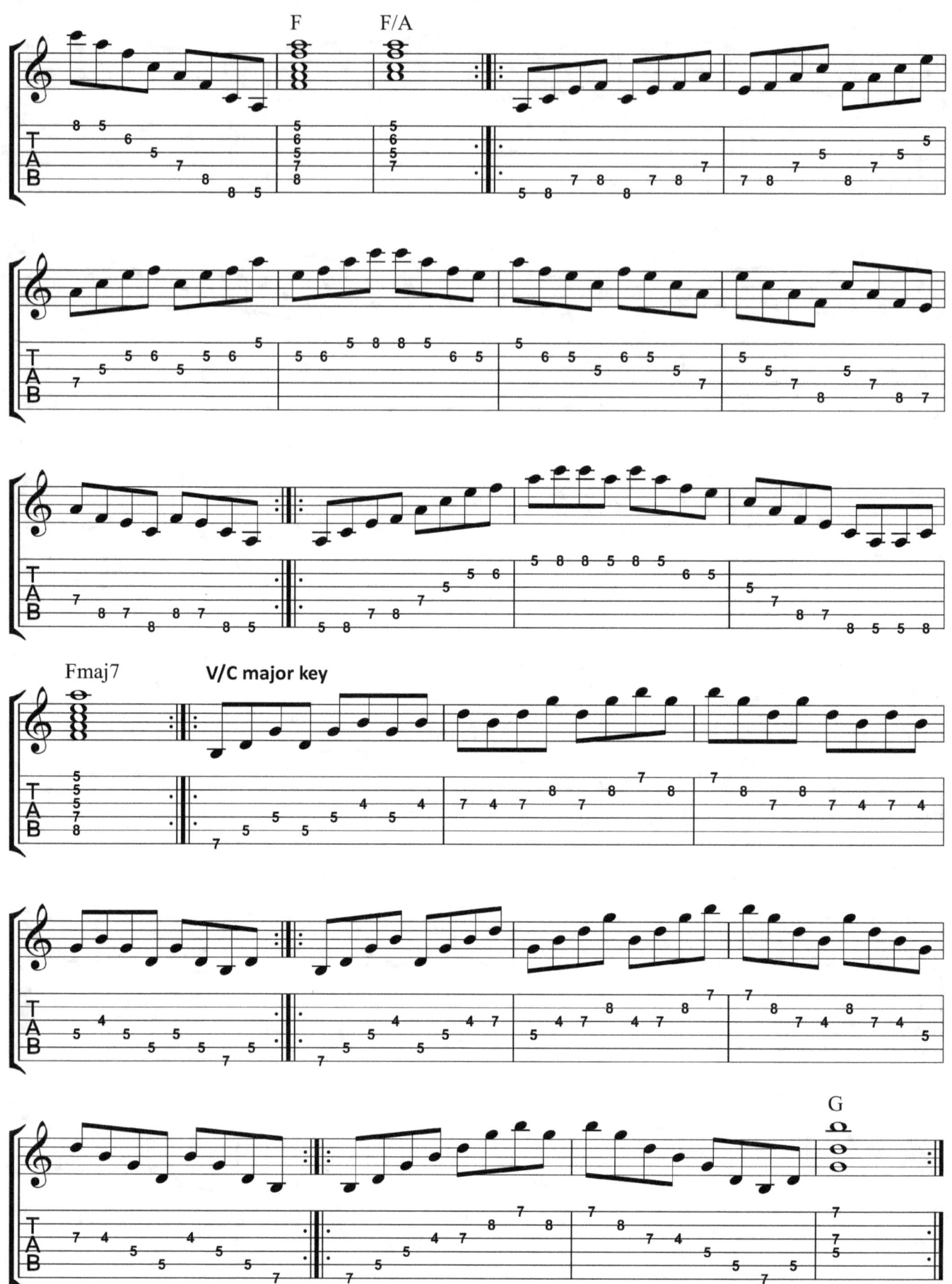

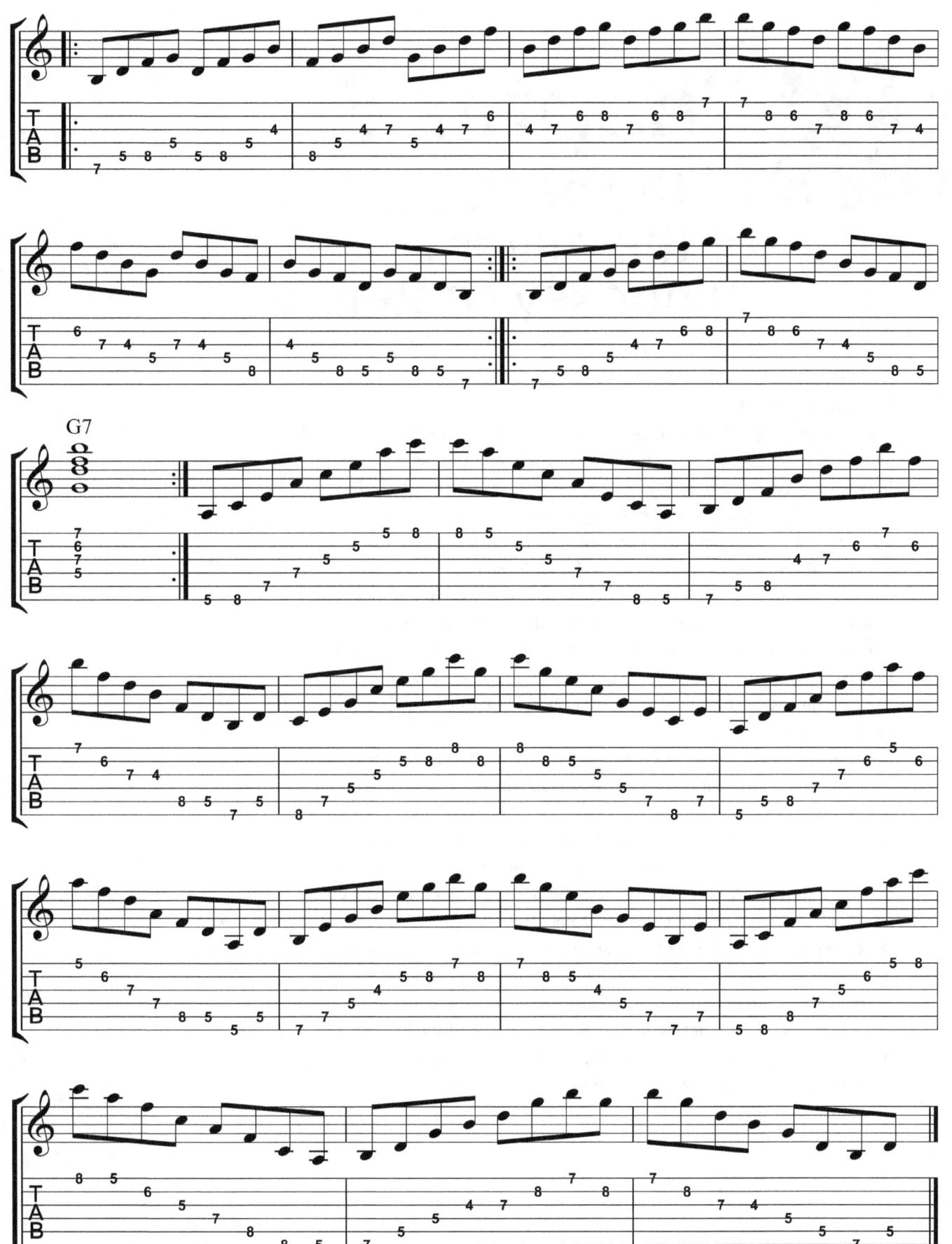

Chapter 7 construction of the diatonic chords with arpeggios in 5 positions

Chapter 8
all the positions of the major & minor key centers

The 12 key centers

In this chapter we will examine the position where each key center starts and ends on the fingerboard. This way we will have a complete picture for each key center, and as a result we will be able to use at any time, on any part of the fingerboard, vertically, horizontally, and with ease the notes we need for musical expression when playing a music tune, whether harmonically (accompaniment) or melodically (solo).

You will also notice that for each key center there are three different numbered positions which represent three different key centers that derive from the three most important modes of the mother major scale, the Ionian (major scale), the Aeolian (natural minor) and the Phrygian.

Let's examine each key center, one by one, in the order that they appear on the circle of fifths.

Depending on the number of frets that each fingerboard has, each key center ends in a different place. What ensures a safe result is finding the lowest note of each key center on the E string. In order to find that, we need to figure out what is the first scale degree of each key center (mode) that appears complete at the beginning of the fingerboard. Once we find that scale degree, we automatically find the position where it belongs, and therefore the place where the key center starts.

For example, if we want to find the key center of D major, we see that the lowest note we can find on the fingerboard is F♯, which is the 3rd scale degree of D. Therefore, we will play F♯ Phrygian, and the position that starts with the III scale degree is position 3-4. Since we have found the position where the key center starts, we find the remaining positions in their order, Position 5, Position 6, Position 7-1, Position 2, etc. until we cover the entire fingerboard.

All positions in C major

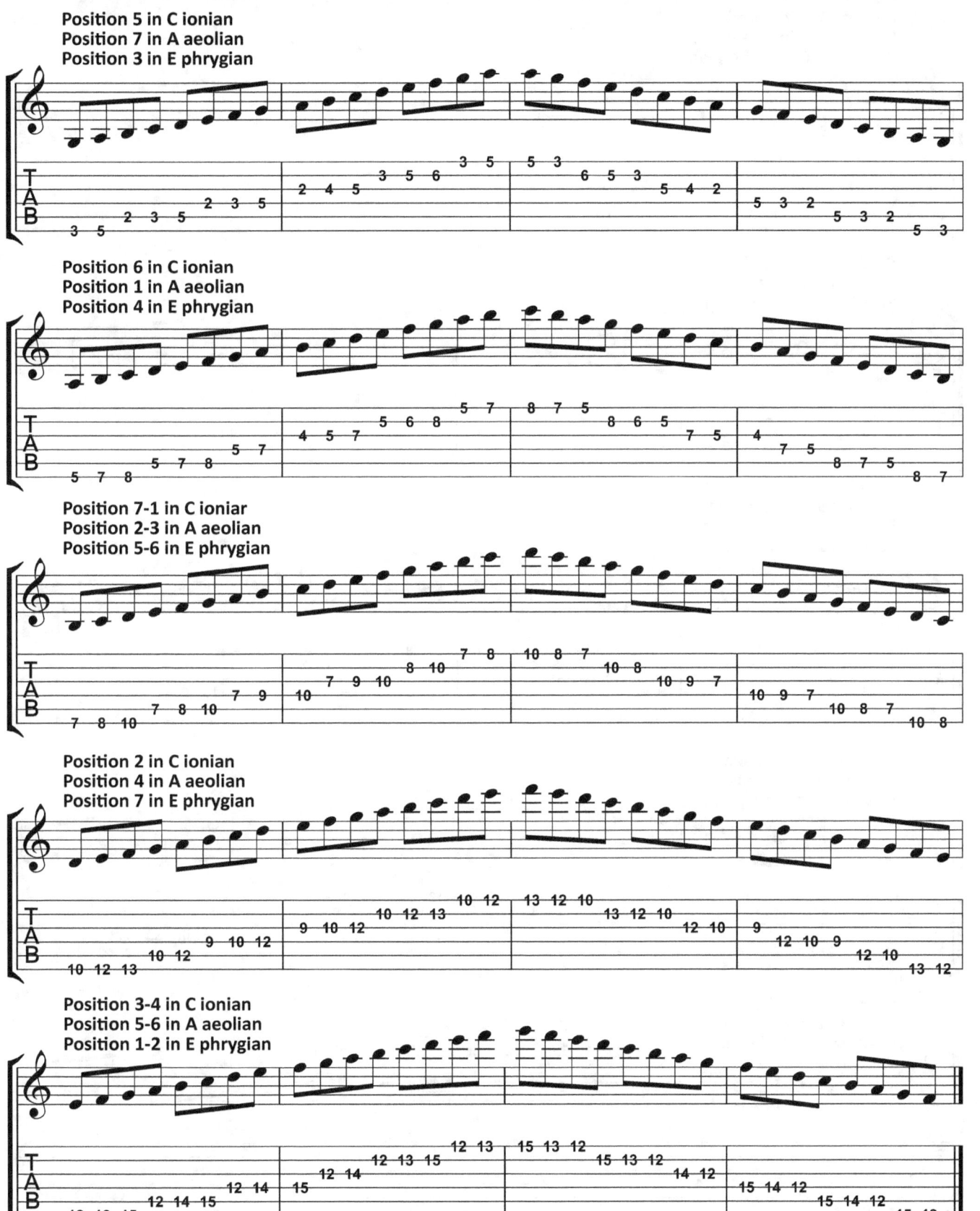

Chapter 8 all the positions of the major & minor key centers

All positions in G major

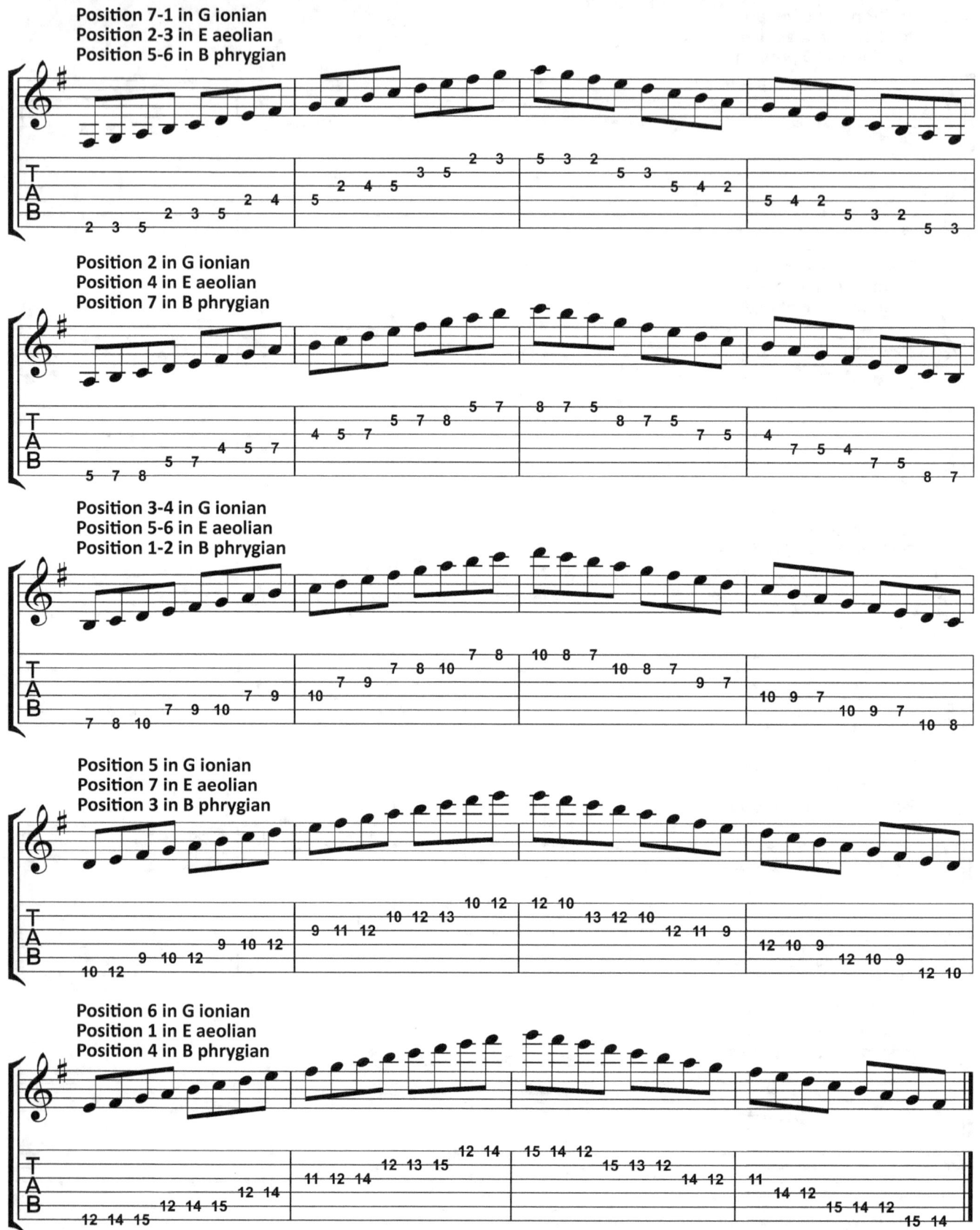

All positions in D major

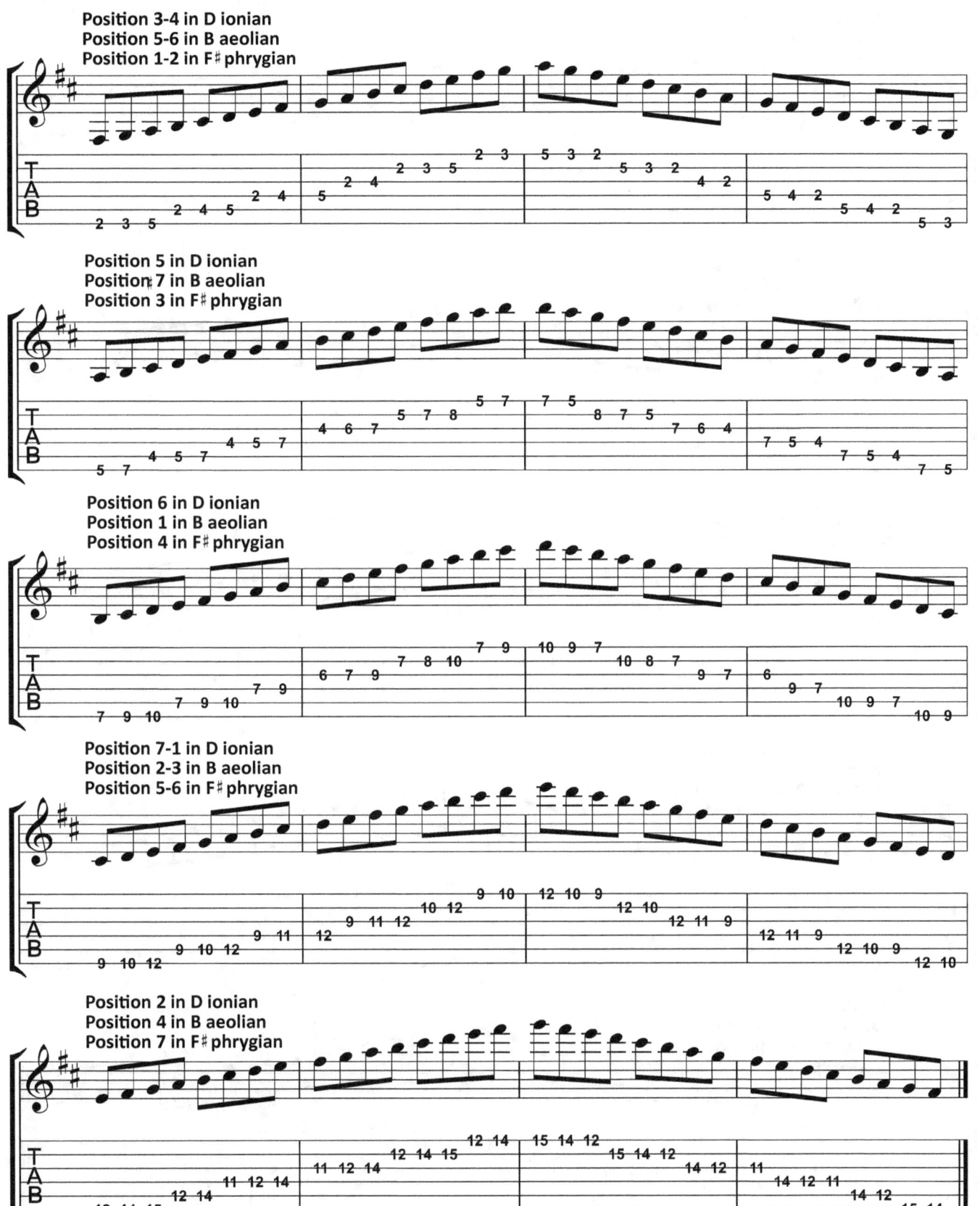

Chapter 8 all the positions of the major & minor key centers

All positions in A major

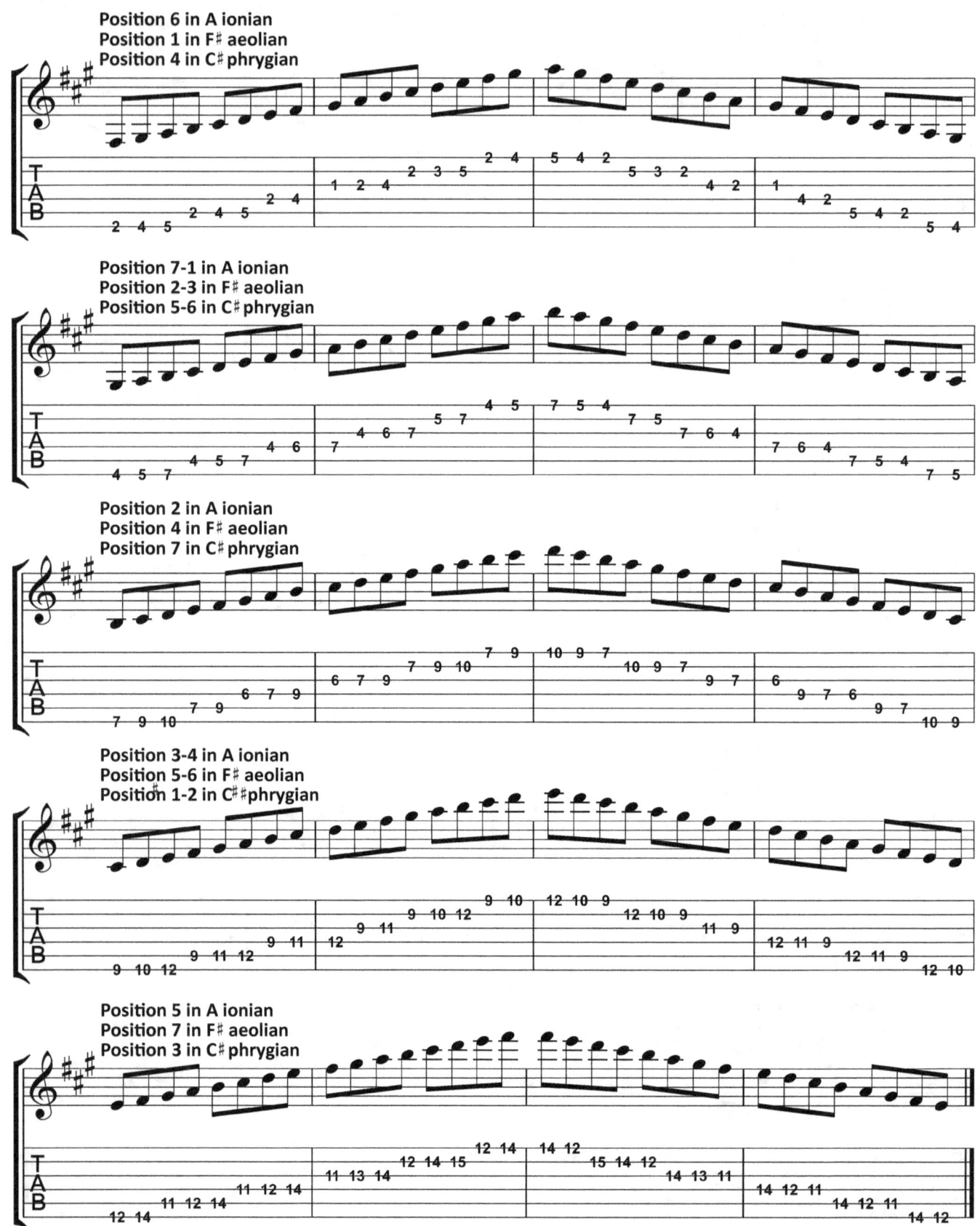

All positions in E major

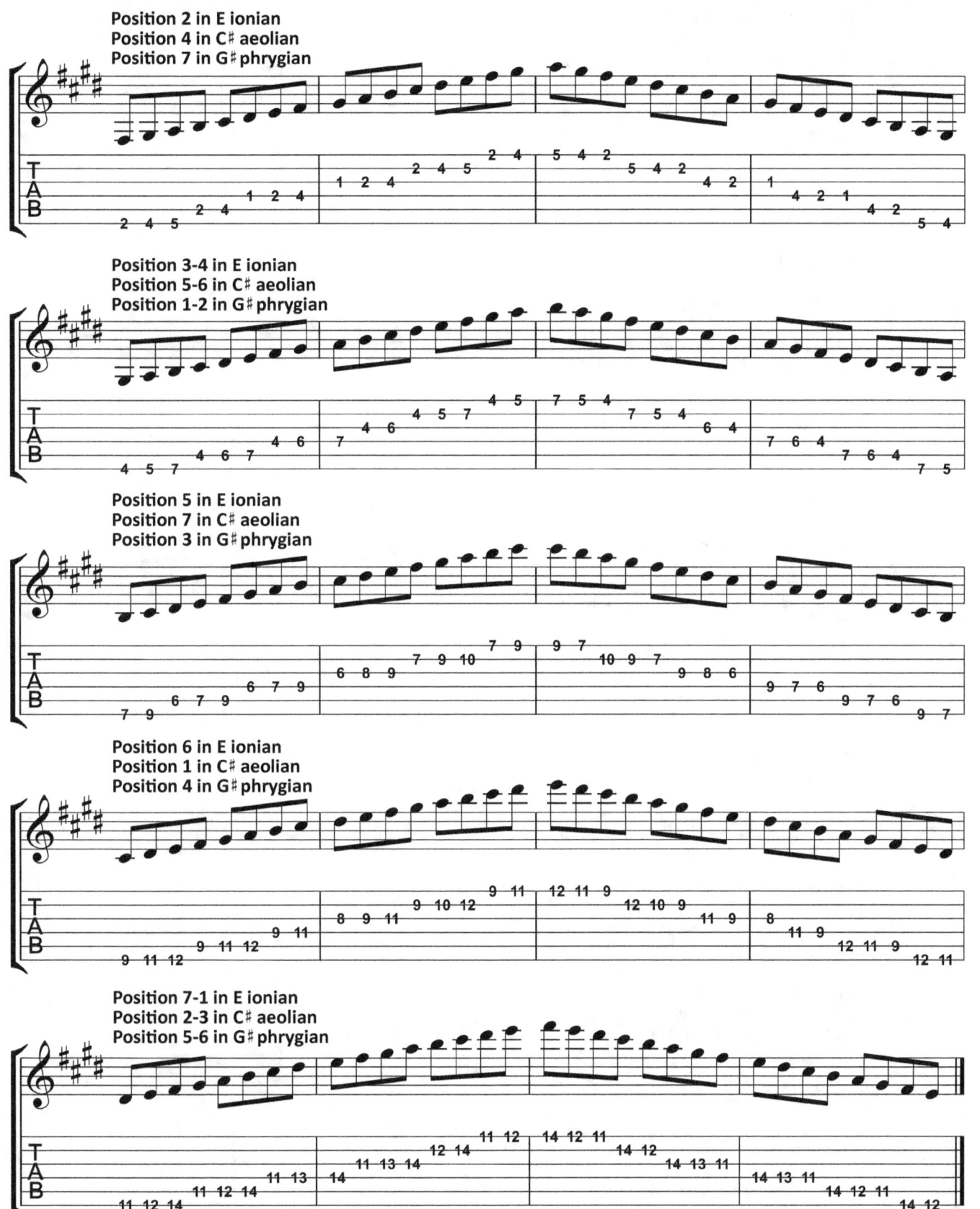

Chapter 8 all the positions of the major & minor key centers

All positions in B major

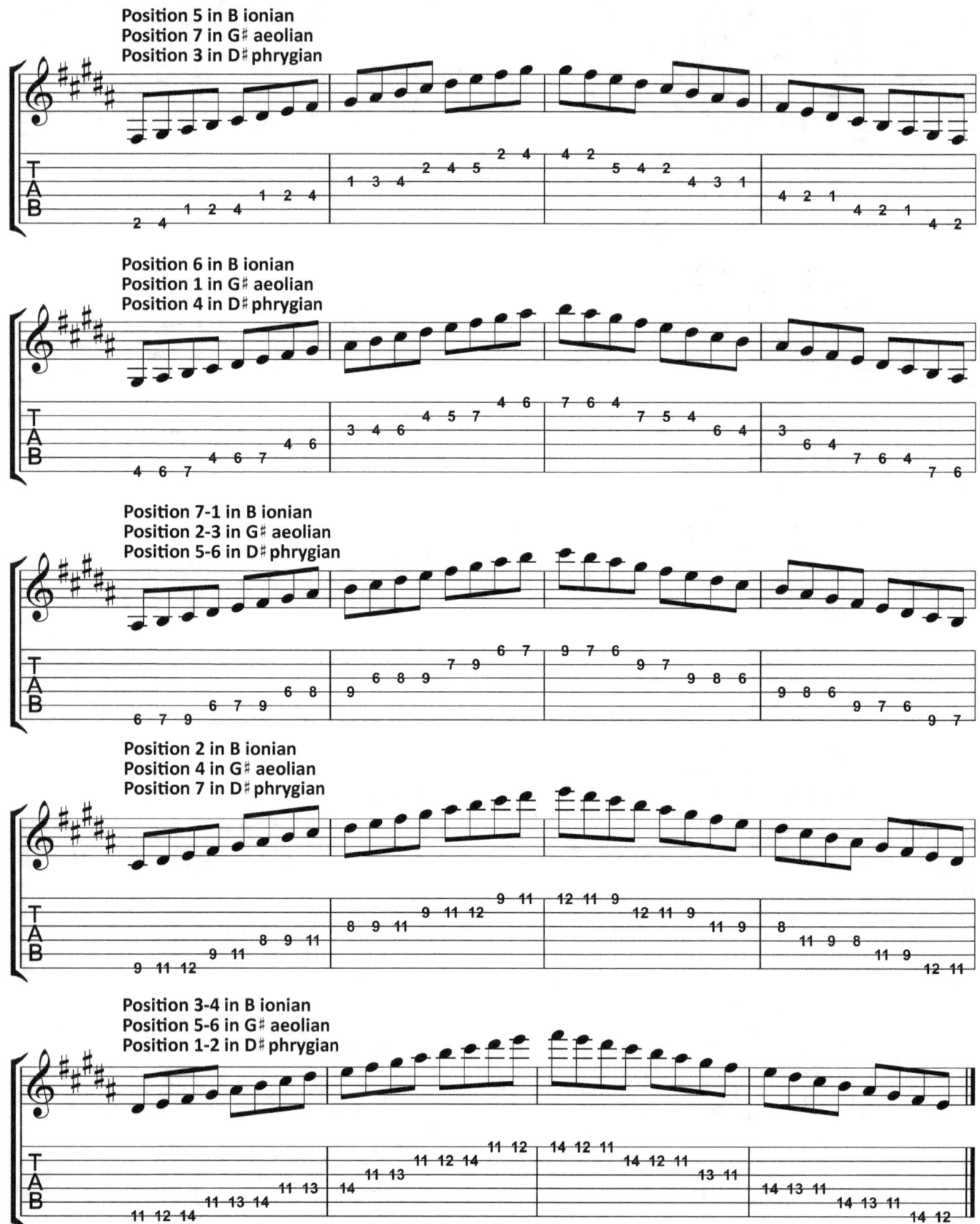

All positions in F♯ major

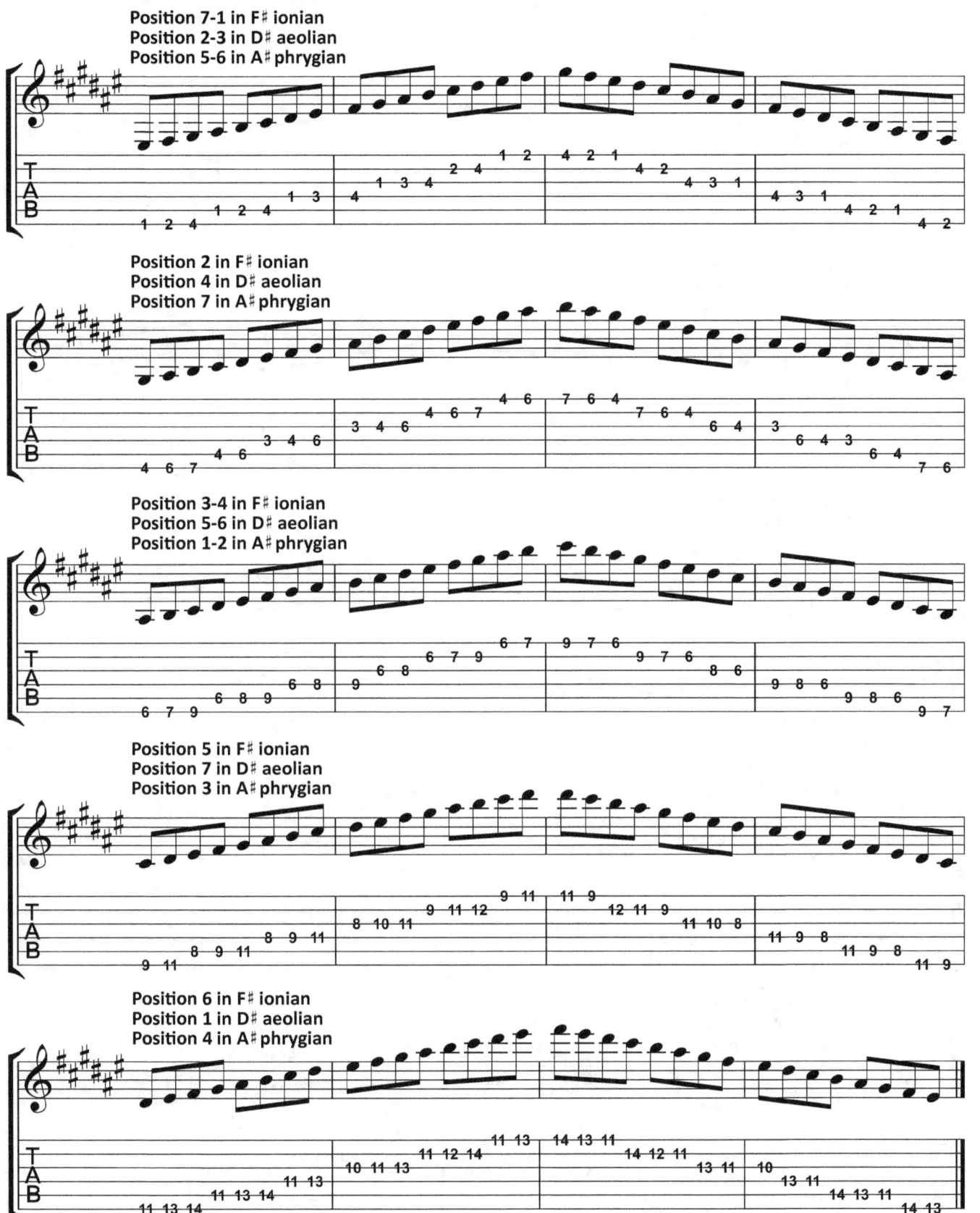

Chapter 8 all the positions of the major & minor key centers

All positions in D♭ major

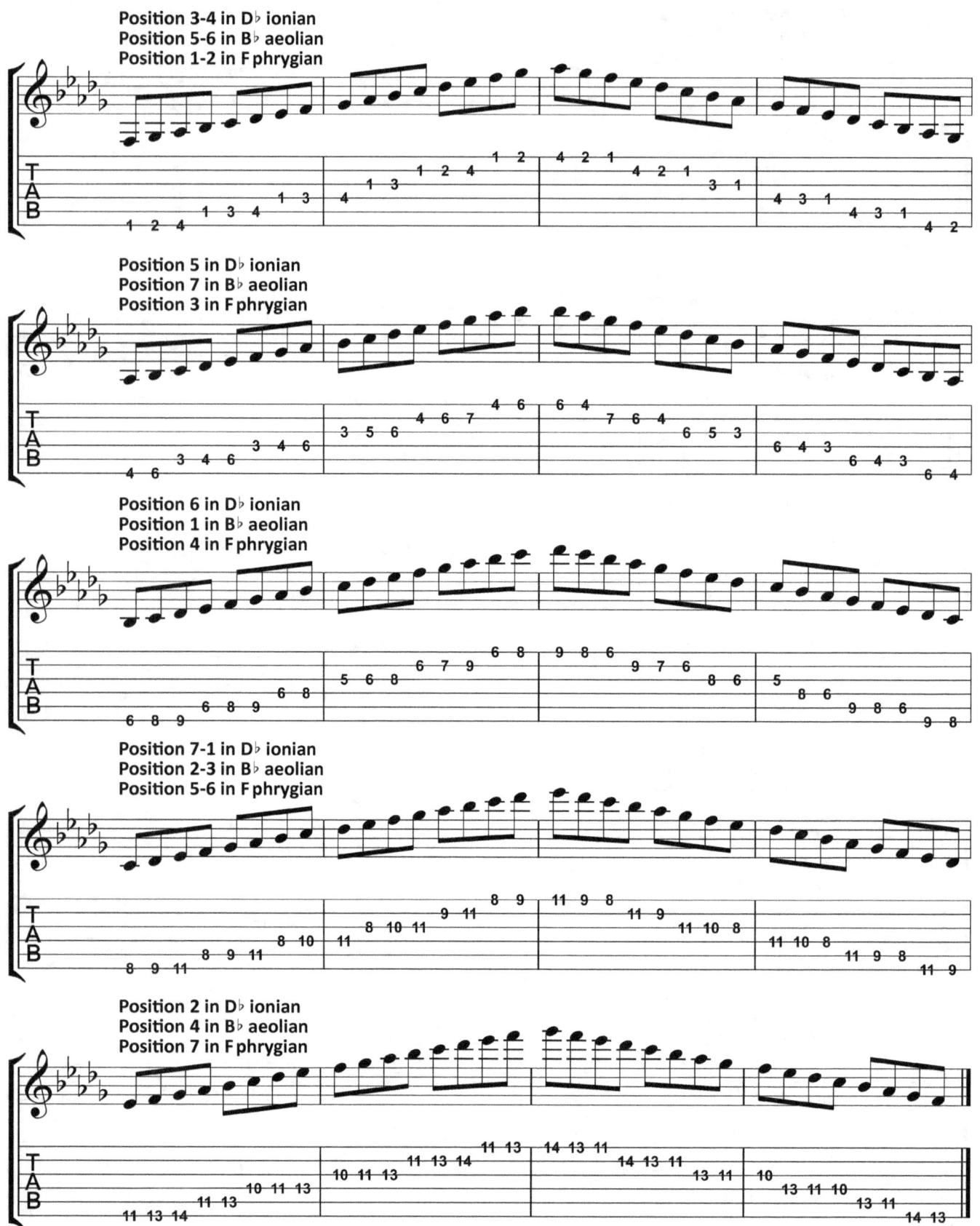

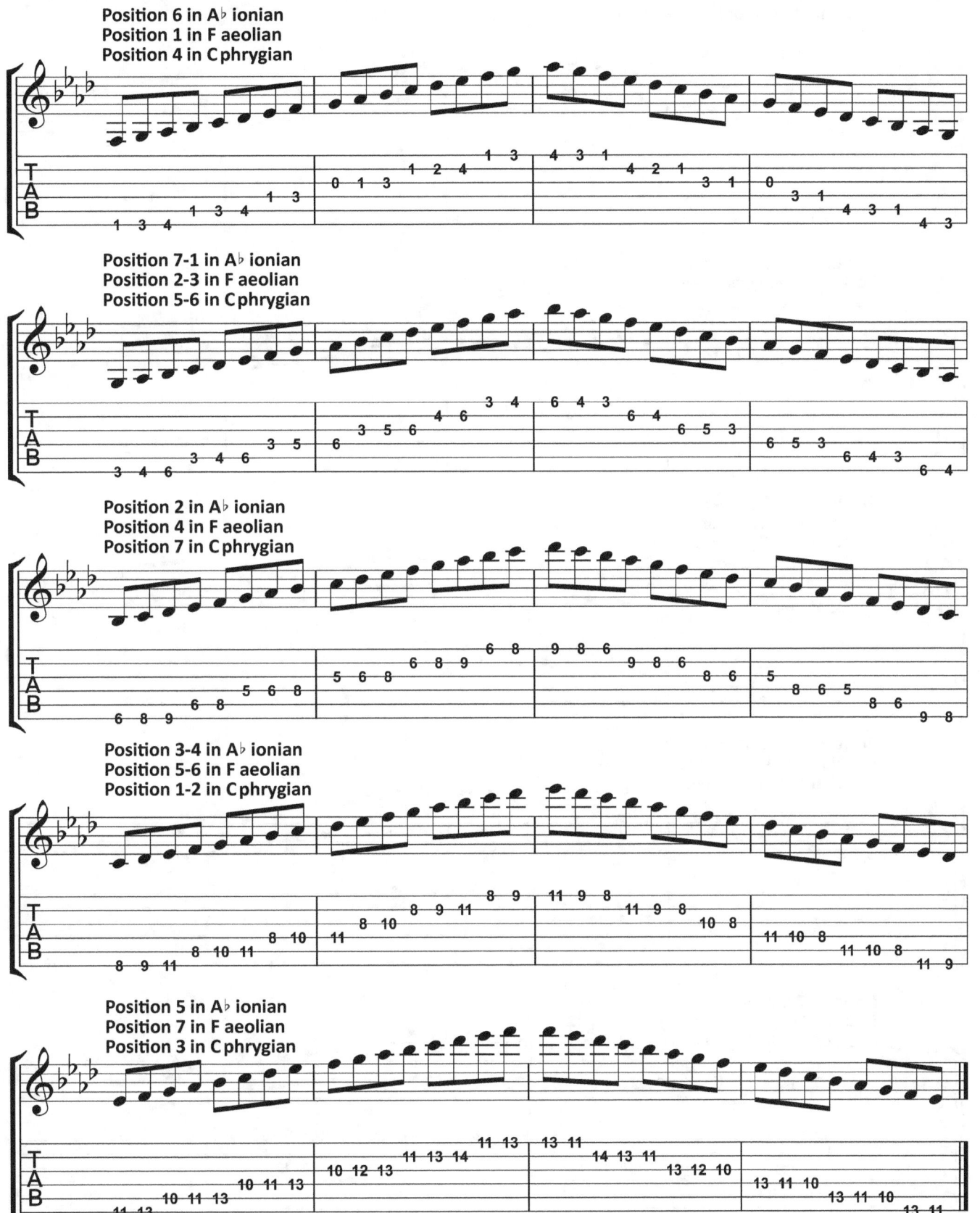

All positions in E♭ major

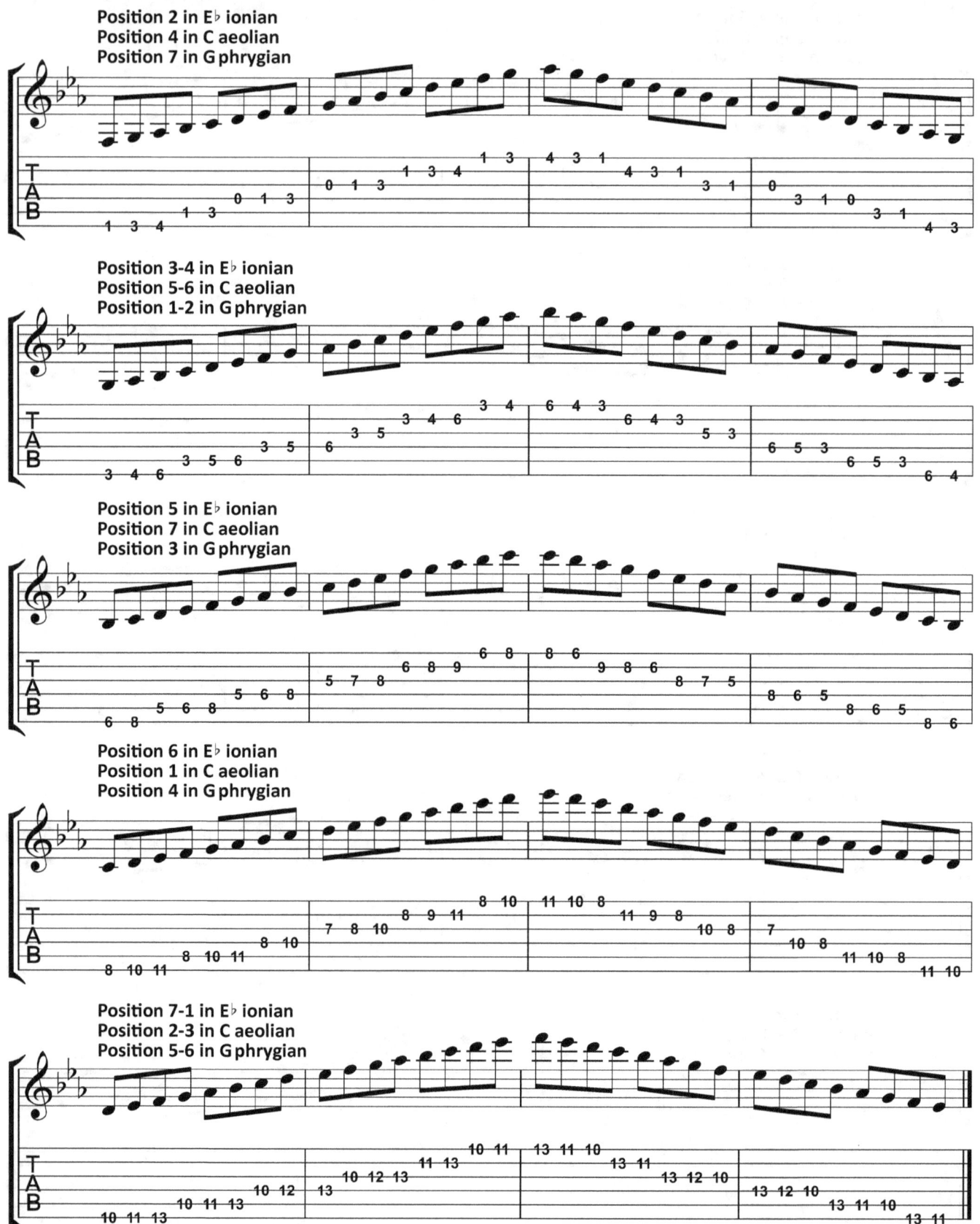

All positions in B♭ major

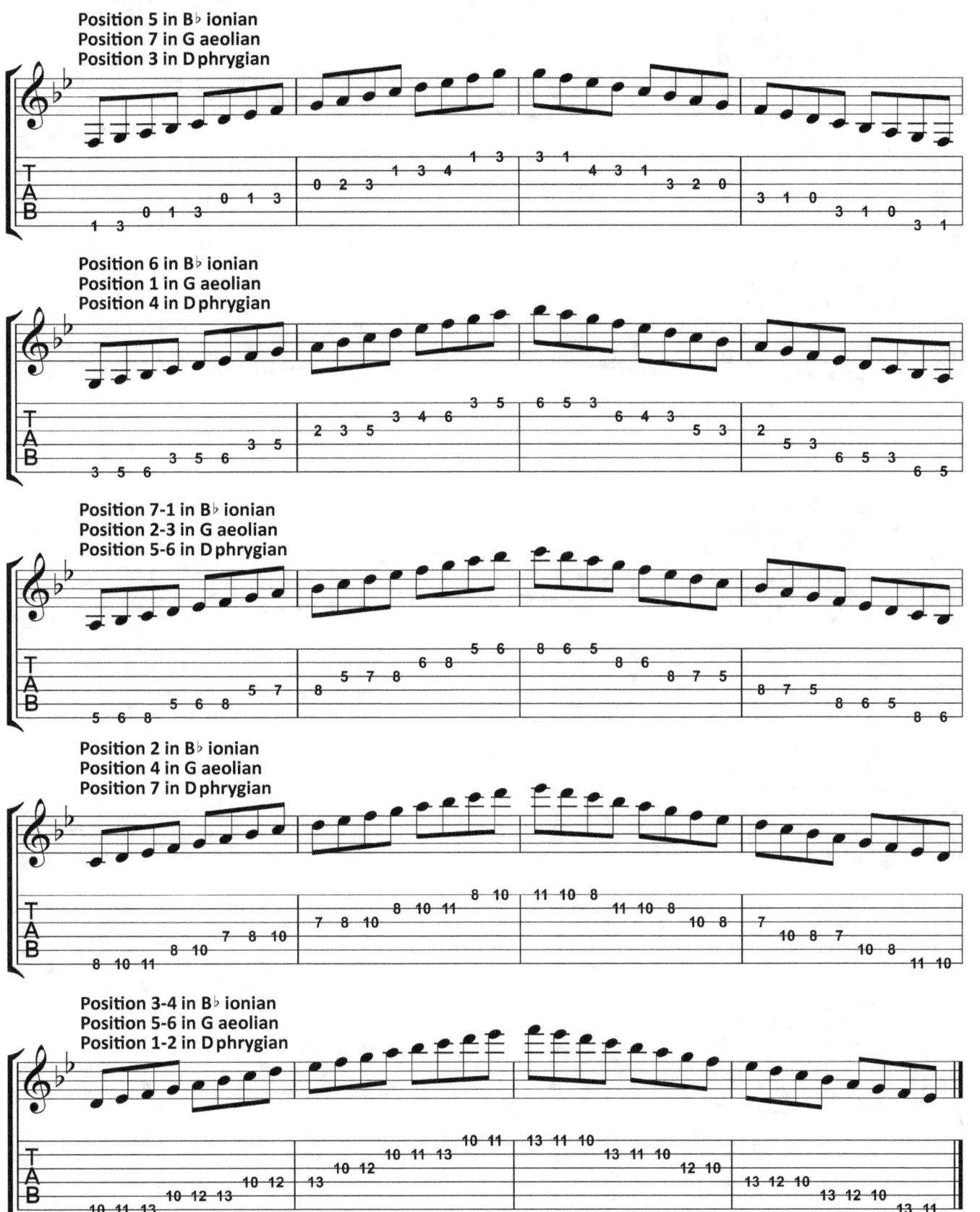

Chapter 8 all the positions of the major & minor key centers

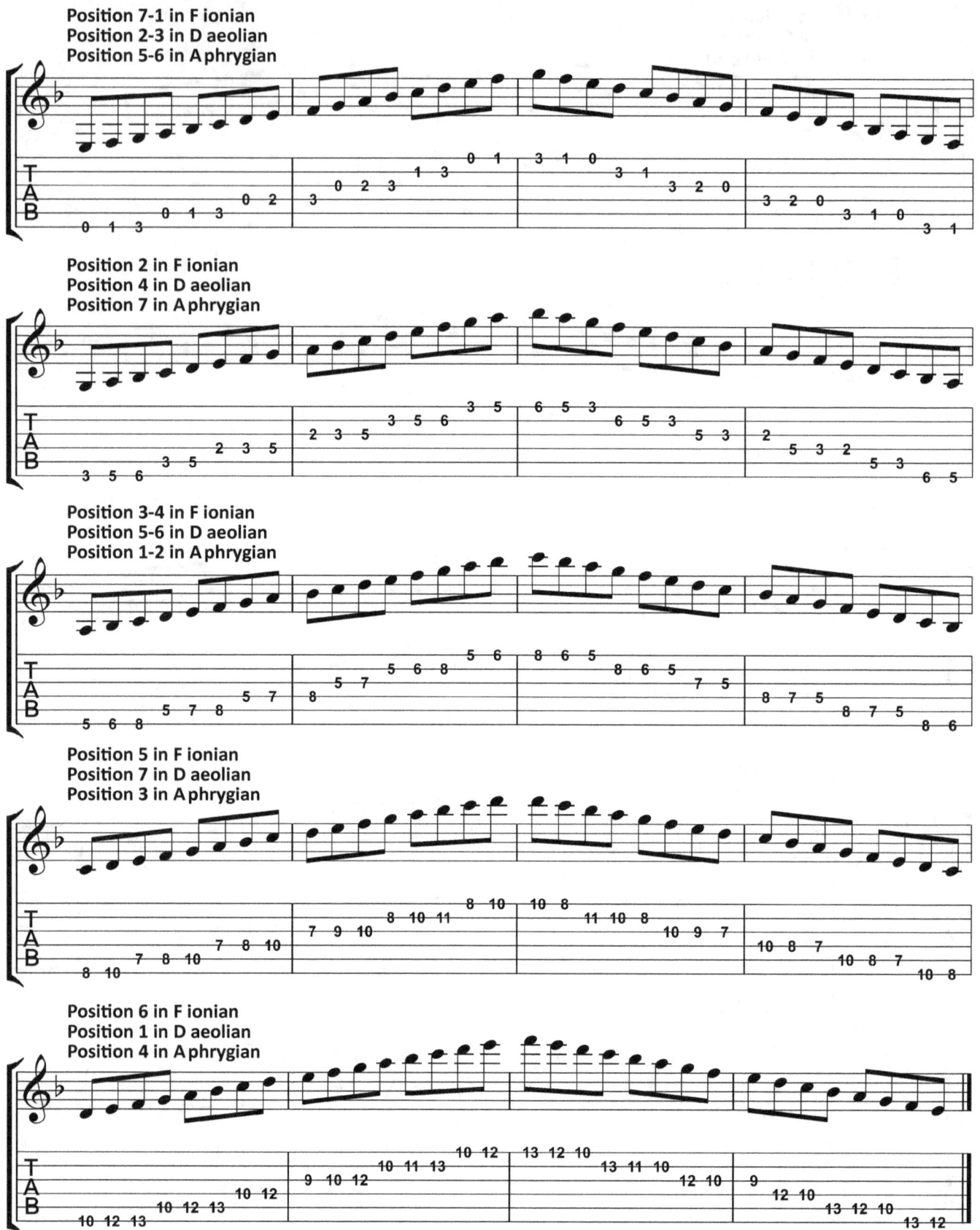

Chapter 9
diagonal construction of the modes with tetrachords

The system of the diagonal construction of the modes is based on the symmetrical alternating order of the tetrachords, which are always in a specific order, and it allows us to play every mode diagonally for up to 3 octaves.

This happens as follows:

If we start with the **G Ionian** mode on our lowest string and we play its first tetrachord, we will see that it is a major tetrachord. Then we move with an interval of a major 2nd and we play the second tetrachord of the Ionian mode which, at the same time, is the first tetrachord of the **D Mixolydian** mode and has a major quality.

We then move again with an interval of a major 2nd in order to play the second tetrachord of D Mixolydian which, at the same time, is the first tetrachord of the **A Dorian** mode and is a minor tetrachord.

Then we move again with an interval of a major 2nd in order to play the second tetrachord of the A Dorian mode which, at the same time, is the first tetrachord of the **E Aeolian** mode and is also a minor tetrachord.

At this point, and due to the change in the symmetry of the strings, we need to play the first tetrachord of the Aeolian mode with shape 2, and, in general, we will see that every tetrachord we find that starts on the G string will have to be played with shape 2 of the respective string.

We move again with an interval of a major 2nd and we play the second tetrachord of the E Aeolian mode which is also the first tetrachord of the **B Phrygian** mode and is a Phrygian tetrachord.

From there, we move again with an interval of a major 2nd and we play the second tetrachord of the B Phrygian mode which is also the first tetrachord of the **F♯ Locrian** mode and has a Phrygian quality.

Finally, we move again, but this time with an interval of a minor 2nd, and we play the second tetrachord of the F♯ Locrian mode which is also the first tetrachord of the **C Lydian** mode and is a Lydian tetrachord.

If we move again with an interval of a major 2nd and we play the second tetrachord of the C Lydian mode, we see that it is the first tetrachord of the **G Ionian** mode from which we begun our construction, and we continue in the same way we started.

We clearly see that the construction of the tetrachords follows a specific and repeated order which, starting with the Ionian mode, is: major - *major - minor - minor - phrygian - phrygian - lydian,* and then all over again with the same pattern.

A basic requirement in order for the system to work is to maintain with each mode the fingering that we have learned until now. This will happen if we play each beginning tetrachord following the fingering of the new mode it represents. The order of the modes that we find along with the tetrachords is: *Ionian - Mixolydian - Dorian - Aeolian - Phrygian - Locrian - Lydian*

Of course, we can start from any mode and simply follow the construction order of the tetrachords, and this way we can easily and without much thought play each mode in as many octaves as we desire.

Ionian diagonal tetrachords

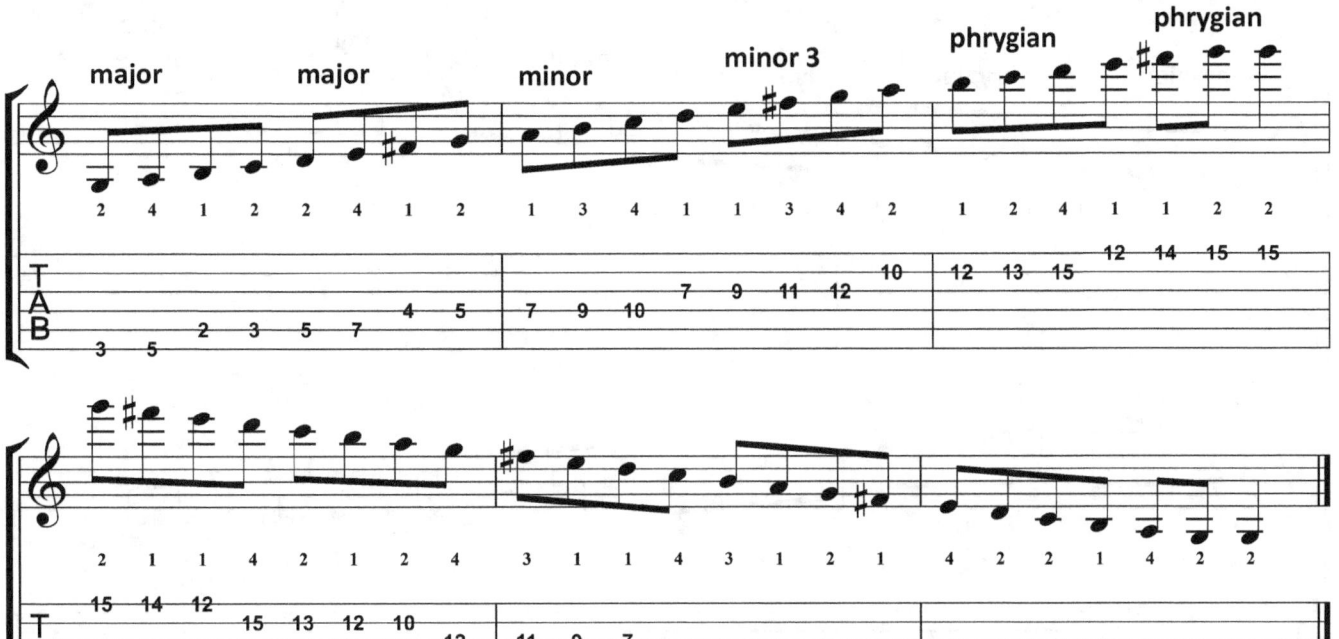

Dorian diagonal tetrachords

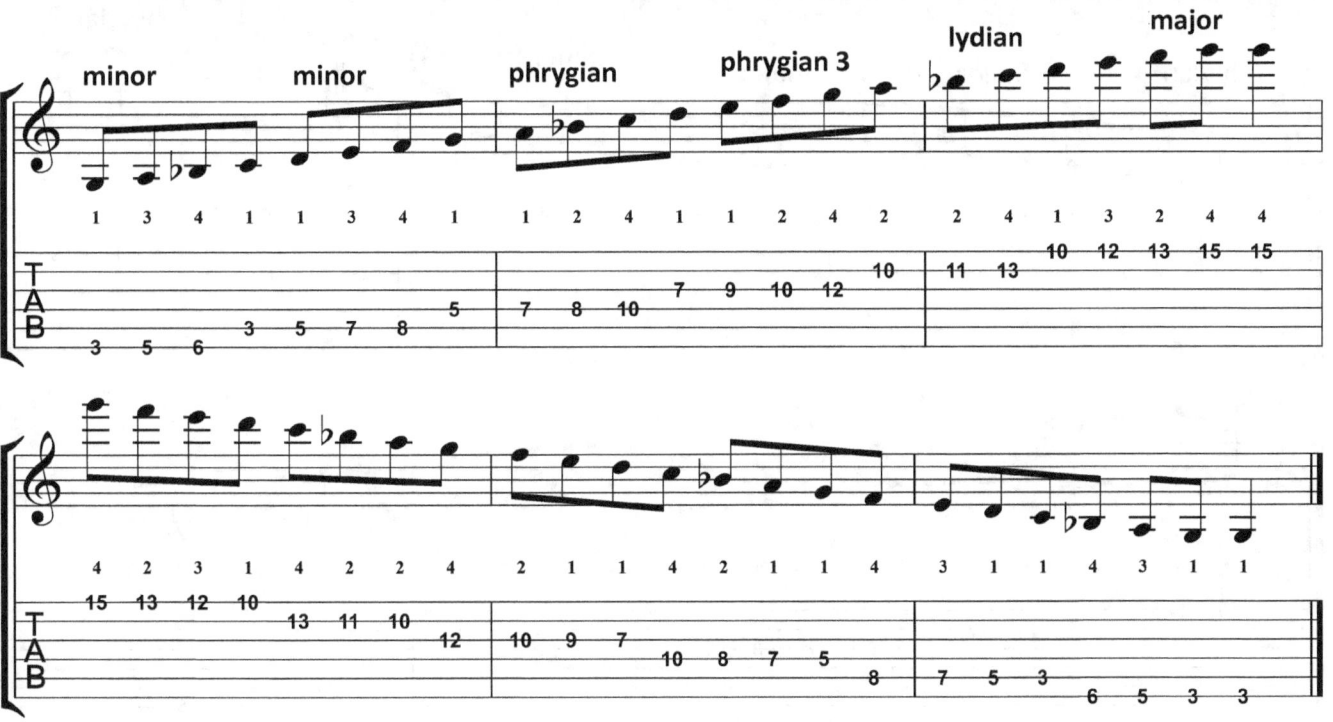

Phrygian diagonal tetrachords

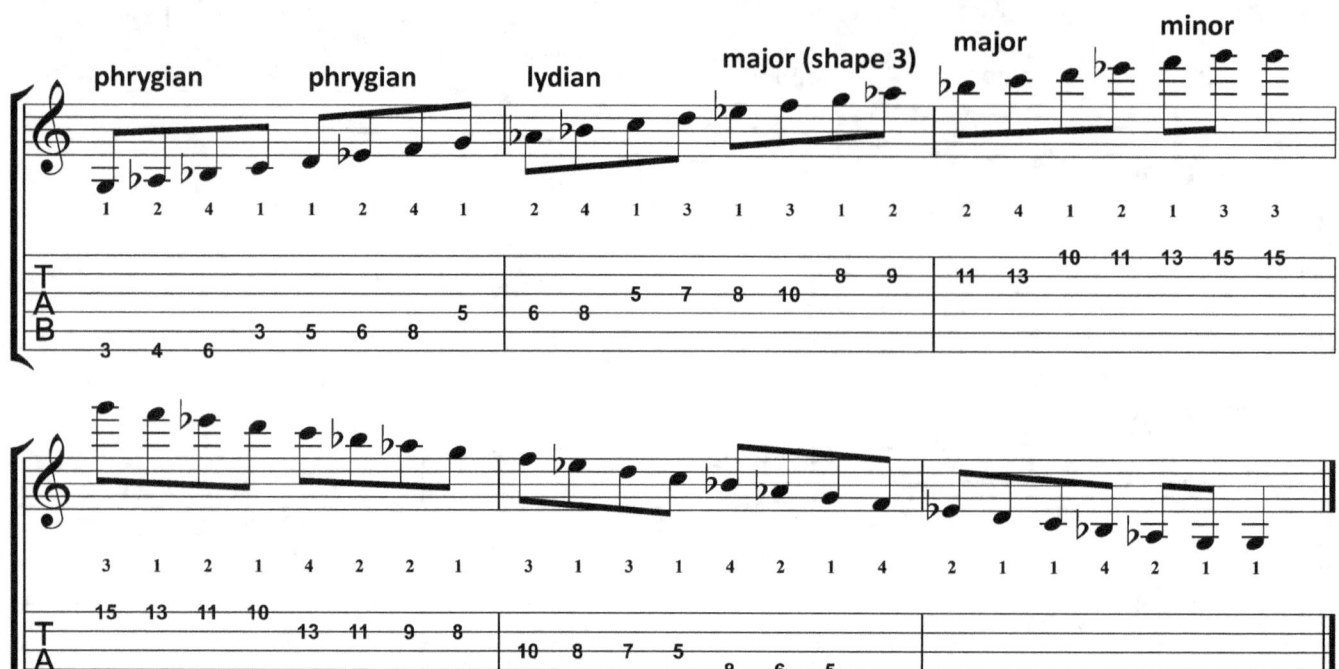

Lydian diagonal tetrachords

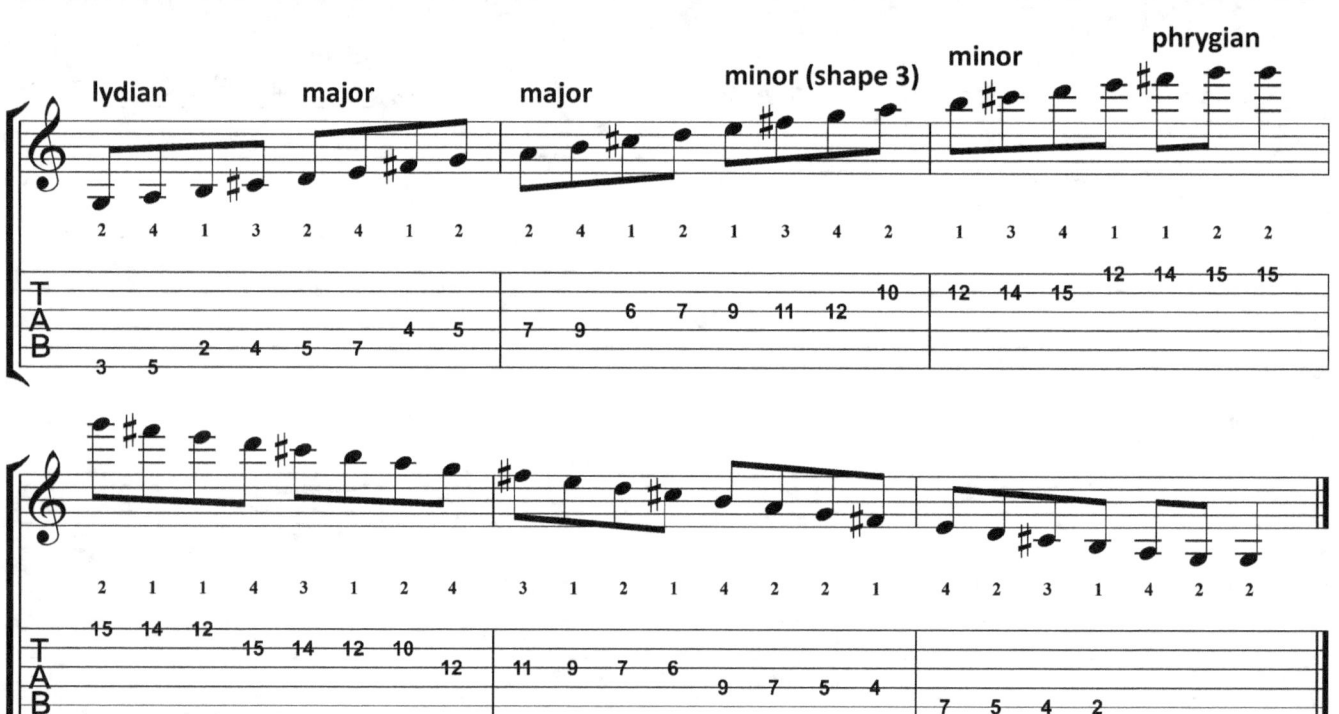

Mixolydian diagonal tetrachords

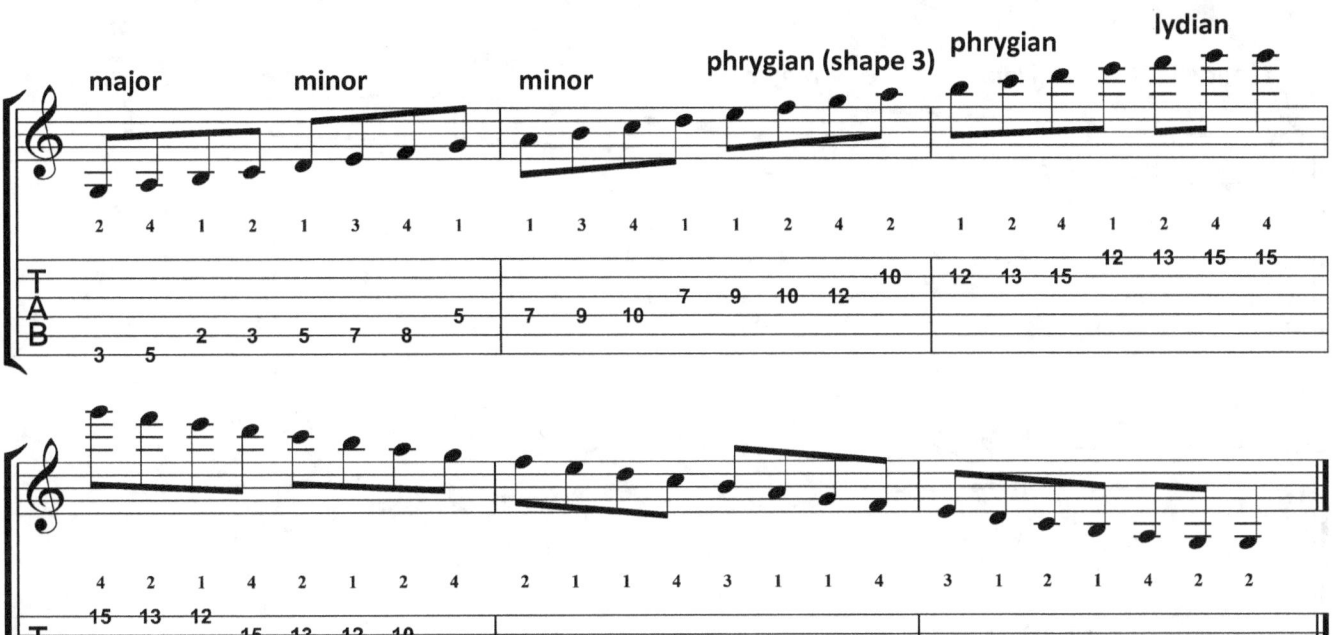

Aeolian diagonal tetrachords

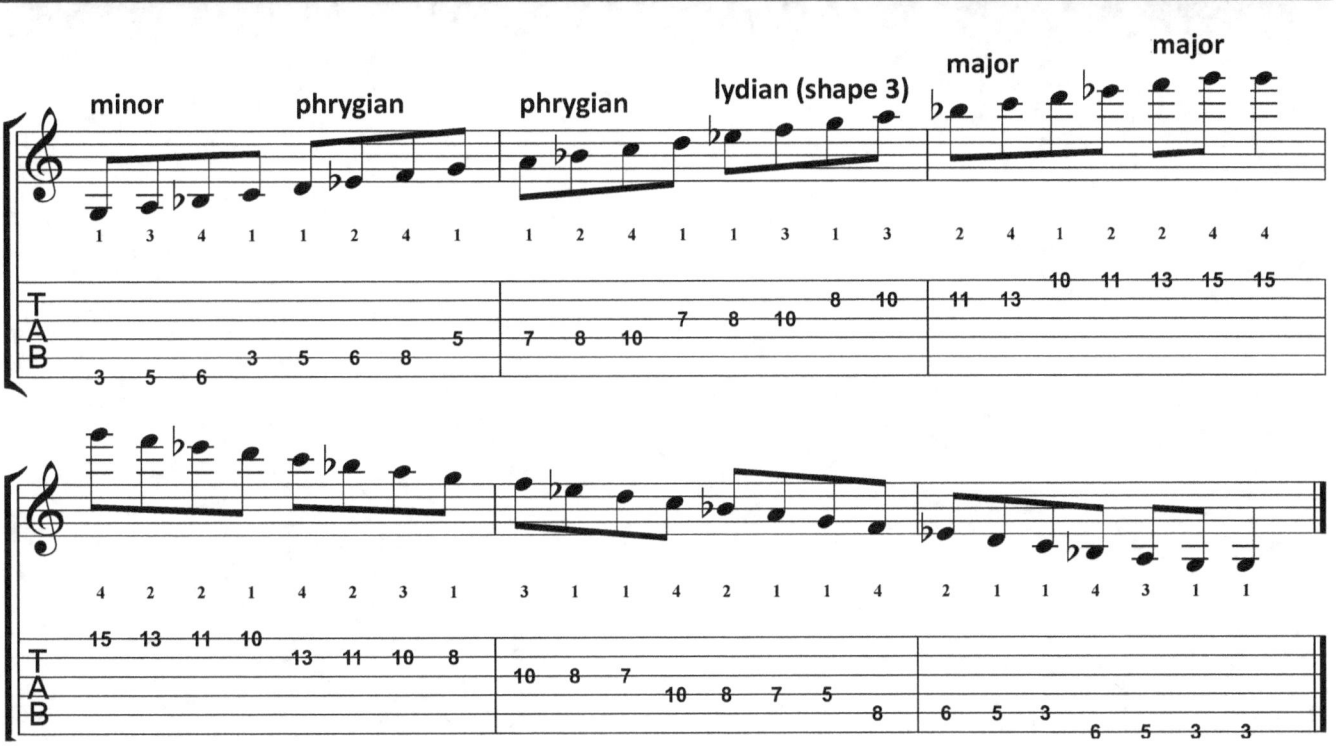

Chapter 9   diagonal construction of the modes with tetrachords

Locrian diagonal tetrachords

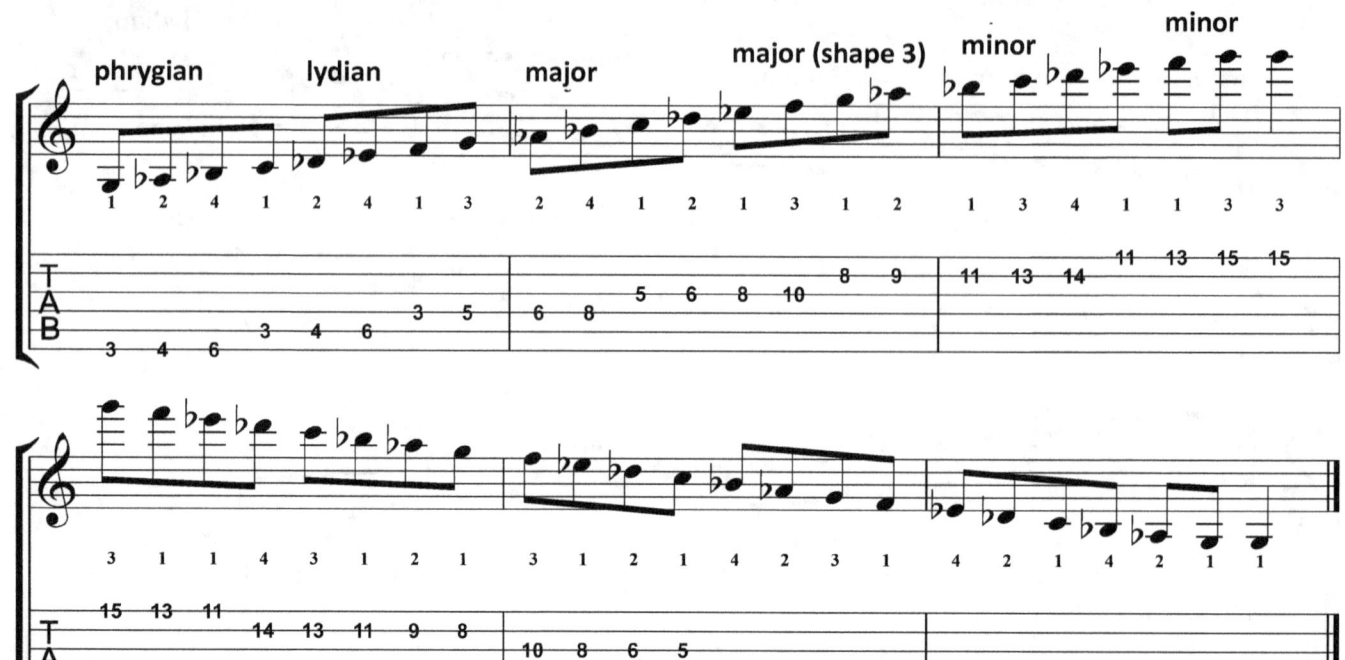

www.ingramcontent.com/pod-product-compliance
Lightning Source LLC
Chambersburg PA
CBHW081718100526
44591CB00016B/2420